The Waite Group's
New
C Primer Plus

The Waite Group's
New
C Primer Plus

Mitchell Waite and Stephen Prata

SAMS

A Division of Macmillan Computer Publishing

11711 North College, Carmel, Indiana 46032 USA

With love to Vicky and Bill Prata,
who, for more than fifty years,
have been showing how rewarding
marriage can be.

SP

FIRST EDITION
SECOND PRINTING—1990

International Standard Book Number: 0-672-22687-1
Library of Congress Catalog Card Number: 89-62990

From The Waite Group, Inc.
Development Editor: *Mitchell Waite*
Managing Editor: *Scott Calamar*
Technical Editor: *Bryan Costales*

From SAMS
Acquisitions Editor: *James S. Hill*
Development Editor: *James Rounds*
Manuscript Editor: *Diana Francoeur*
Indexer: *Ted Laux*
Compositor: *Shepard Poorman Communications Corp.*

Printed in the United States of America

Overview

Contents

6 C Control Statements: Looping   **177**

7   C Control Statements: Branching and Jumps   231

8   Character Input/Output and Redirection   283

9 Functions   315

10   Arrays and Pointers   365

11   Character Strings and String Functions   *411*

13   Storage Classes and Program Development   497

16   The C Preprocessor and the C Library   613

Preface

C was a relatively little-known language when we wrote *C Primer Plus* in 1984. Since then, the language has boomed. Although we don't claim that our book caused the boom, it is true that the book has helped many people learn C. Now that C is getting a new standard (ANSI C), we felt it was time for a new *C Primer Plus*. So here it is, now titled *The Waite Group's New C Primer Plus*.

What's new with this edition? Here are the main changes:

► Completely revamped text to bring the book into accord with the ANSI C Standard. This Standard was developed by a committee of the American National Standards Institute (ANSI) in response to a need created by C's success and its spread to a variety of computer platforms. The Standard is scheduled for final adoption soon.

► Revised examples, figures, and explanations.

► New order of presentation, based on reader feedback.

► Expanded coverage of C topics, including bitwise operators, enumerated types, and the C preprocessor.

► More complete discussion of functions from the C library.

We've also retained much from the earlier editions. In particular, we've kept the philosophy that the book should be a friendly, easy-to-use, self-study guide, as is reflected in the following points:

► We don't assume that you are a professional programmer. We explain programming ideas along with the C language.

► We emphasize an interactive approach. Because you learn by doing, we often use short, easily typed examples that illustrate just one or two concepts at a time.

► We clarify ideas with figures and illustrations.

- We summarize the main C features in highlighted boxes.
- We provide review questions and programming exercises so that you can test and improve your understanding of C.

Our goal in writing this introduction to C has been to make it instructive, clear, and helpful. To gain the greatest benefit, you should take as active a role as possible. Don't just read the examples. Enter them into your system and try them. C is a very portable language, but you may find differences between how a program works on your system and how it works on ours. Experiment—change part of a program to see what the effect is. Modify a program to do something slightly different. Ignore our occasional warnings and see what happens when you do the wrong thing. Try the questions and exercises. The more you do yourself, the more you will learn and remember.

We wish you good fortune in learning C. We've tried to make this book meet your needs, and we hope it helps you reach your goals.

Acknowledgments

The authors wish to thank Scott Calamar of The Waite Group for guiding this book through the writing, editing, and production stages. We particularly wish to thank Bryan Costales for his useful and knowledgeable editing of the first draft.

Trademarks

Turbo C is a registered trademark of Borland International Inc.

UNIX is a trademark of American Telephone and Telegraph Corporation.

VAX is a registered trademark, and VMS is a trademark, of Digital Equipment Corporation.

WordPerfect is a registered trademark of WordPerfect Corporation.

WordStar is a registered trademark of MicroPro International Corporation.

About the Authors

 Mitchell Waite is president of The Waite Group, a developer of computer books. He is an experienced programmer fluent in a variety of computer languages, including C, Pascal, BASIC, Assembly, and HyperTalk. He wrote his first computer book in 1976, and is coauthor of *C: Step-by-Step, Microsoft QuickC Programming, UNIX Primer Plus,* and many other titles.

 Stephen Prata is a professor of physics and astronomy at The College of Marin in Kentfield, California, where he teaches UNIX and the C language. He received his B.S. from the California Institute of Technology and his Ph.D. from the University of California, Berkeley. His association with computers began with the computer modeling of star clusters. Dr. Prata is coauthor of *C: Step-by-Step, UNIX Primer Plus,* and *Microsoft QuickC Programming,* and author of *Advanced C Primer++.*

1

Getting Ready

In this chapter you learn about C's history and features, examine the steps needed to write programs, learn a bit about compilers and linkers, and look at C standards.

Welcome to the world of C. C is a vigorous, professional programming language popular with amateur and commercial programmers alike. This chapter prepares you for learning and using this powerful and popular language, and it introduces you to the kinds of environments in which you most likely will develop your C-legs.

First, we look at C's origin and examine some of its features, both strengths and drawbacks. Then we examine some general principles for programming. Finally, we discuss how to run C programs on some common systems.

Whence C?

Dennis Ritchie of Bell Labs created C in 1972 as he and Ken Thompson worked on designing the UNIX operating system. C didn't spring full-grown from Ritchie's head, however. It came from Thompson's B language, which came from. . . . But that's another story. The important point is that C was created as a tool for working programmers. Thus, its chief goal is to be a *useful* language.

Most languages aim to be useful, but often they have other concerns. The main goal for Pascal, for instance, was to provide a sound basis for teaching programming principles. BASIC, on the other hand, was developed to resemble English so that it could be easily learned by students unfamiliar with computers. These are important goals, but they are not always compatible with pragmatic, workaday usefulness. C's development as a language designed for programmers, however, has made it the modern-day language of choice.

Why C?

During the last decade, C has become one of the most important and popular programming languages. It has grown because people try it and like it. As you learn C, you will recognize its many virtues (see Figure 1.1). Let's preview a few of them now.

Figure 1.1 *The virtues of C*

Flexible control structures Structured format

Compact code—small programs Portable to other computers

Design Features

C is a modern language incorporating the control features that computer science theory and practice find desirable. The design of C makes it natural for users to use top-down planning, structured programming, and modular design. The result is a more reliable, understandable program.

Efficiency

C is an efficient language. Its design takes advantage of the abilities of current computers. C programs tend to be compact and to run quickly. In fact, C exhibits some of the fine control usually associated with assembly language. If you choose, you can fine-tune your programs for maximum speed or most efficient use of memory.

Portability

C is a portable language. This means that C programs written on one system can be run with little or no modification on other systems. If modifications are necessary, they can often be made just by changing a few entries in a "header" file accompanying the main program. Of course, most languages are meant to be portable, but anyone who has converted an IBM PC BASIC program to Apple BASIC (and they are close cousins) or tried to run an IBM mainframe FORTRAN program on a UNIX system will know that *porting* is troublesome at best. C is a leader in portability. C compilers are available for about 40 systems, running from 8-bit microprocessors to Cray supercomputers.

You Can Take C Home

Because C is portable, you can, say, take your UNIX C programs home to use on a personal computer. Several C compilers are available now to let you do that.

Power and Flexibility

C is powerful and flexible (two favorite words in computer literature). For example, most of the powerful, flexible UNIX operating system is written in C. Many compilers and interpreters for other languages, such as FORTRAN, APL, Pascal, LISP, Logo, and BASIC have been written in C. So when you use FORTRAN on a UNIX machine, ultimately a C program has done the work of producing the final executable program. C programs have been used for solving physics and engineering problems and even for animating special effects for movies such as *The Return of the Jedi*.

Programmer Oriented

C is oriented towards the needs of programmers. It gives you access to hardware and it lets you manipulate individual bits in memory. It has a rich selection of operators that let you express yourself succinctly. C is less strict than, say, Pascal, in limiting what you can do. This is both an advantage and a danger. The advantage is that many tasks, such as converting forms of data, are much simpler in C. The danger is that C will allow you to make mistakes that are impossible in some languages. C gives you more freedom, but it also puts more responsibility on you.

Also, most C implementations have a large library of useful C functions. These functions deal with many needs commonly facing the programmer.

Shortcomings

C does have some faults. Often, as with people, faults and virtues are opposite sides of the same feature. For example, we've mentioned that C's freedom of expression also requires added responsibility. C's use of pointers, in particular, enables you to make programming errors that are very difficult to trace. As one computer preliterate once commented, the price of liberty is eternal vigilance.

C's conciseness combined with its wealth of operators makes it possible to prepare code that is extremely difficult to follow. You aren't compelled to write obscure code, but the opportunity is there. After all, what other language has a yearly Obfuscated Code contest?

There are more virtues and, undoubtedly, a few more faults. Rather than delve further into the matter, let's move on to a new topic.

Whither C?

By the early 1980s, C already was a dominant language in the minicomputer world of UNIX systems. Since then, it has spread to personal computers (microcomputers) and to mainframes (the big guys). See Figure 1.2. Many software houses use C as the preferred language for producing word processing programs, spreadsheets, compilers, and other products. These companies know that C produces compact and efficient programs. More important, they know that these programs will be easy to modify and easy to adapt to new models of computers.

What's good for the companies and the C veterans is good for other users, too. More and more computer users are turning to C to secure its advantages for themselves. You don't have to be a computer professional to use C.

Figure 1.2 *Where C is used*

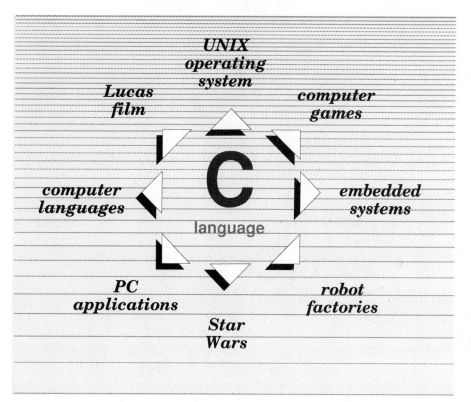

In short, C is one of the most important programming languages and will continue to be during the next decade. It is used on mainframes, minicomputers, and personal computers. It is used by software companies, computer science students, and enthusiasts of all sorts. And if you want a job writing software, one of the first questions you should be able to answer "yes" to is: "O say can you C?"

Using C: Seven Steps

C is a *compiled language*. If you are accustomed to using a compiled language, such as Pascal or FORTRAN, you will be familiar with the basic steps in putting together a C program. But if your background is in an *interpreted* language, such as BASIC or Logo, or if you have no background at all, you will need to learn how to compile. We'll soon guide you through that process, and you'll see that it is straightforward and sensible.

Chapter 1

But first, to give you an overview of programming, we'll break down the act of writing a C program into seven steps.

Step 1: Define the Program Objectives

Naturally enough, you should start with a clear idea of what you want the program to do. Think in terms of the information your program needs, the feats of calculation and manipulation the program needs to do, and the information the program should report back to you. At this level of planning, you should be thinking in general terms, not in terms of some specific computer language.

Step 2: Design the Program

Once you have a conceptual picture of what your program ought to do, you should decide how the program will go about it. What should the user interface be like? How should the program be organized? Who will the target user be? How much time do you have to complete the program?

You also need to decide how to represent the data in the program and, possibly, in auxiliary files, and which methods to use to process the data. As you first learn programming in C, the choices will be simple. But as you deal with more complex situations, you will find that these decisions require more thought. Choosing a good way to represent the information often can make designing the program and processing the data much easier.

Again, you should be thinking in general terms, not about specific code. But some of your decisions may be based on general characteristics of the language. For example, a C programmer has more options in data representation than, say, a BASIC programmer.

Step 3: Write the Code

Now that you have a clear design for your program, you can begin to implement it by writing the code. That is, you translate your program design into the C language. Here is where you really have to put your knowledge of C to work. You can sketch your ideas on paper, but eventually you have to get your code into the computer. The mechanics of this process depend on your programming environment. We'll present the details for some common environments soon. In general, you use a text editor to create what is called a *source code* file. This file contains the C rendition of your program design. Listing 1.1 shows an example of C source code.

8

Listing 1.1 *An Example of C Source Code*

```
#include <stdio.h>
main()
{
  int dogs;

  printf("How may dogs do you have?\n");
  scanf("%d", &dogs);
  printf("So, you have %d dog(s)!\n", dogs);
}
```

As part of this step, you should document your work. The simplest way is to use C's comment facility to incorporate explanations into your source code. We'll explain more about using comments in Chapter 2.

Step 4: Compile

The next step is to *compile* the source code. Again, the details depend on your programming environment, and we'll look at some common environments shortly. Here, we'll take a more conceptual view of what happens.

The compiler is a program whose job is to convert *source code* into *executable code*. Executable code is code in the native, or *machine*, language of your computer. Different computers have different machine languages, and a C compiler translates C to a particular machine language. C compilers also incorporate code from C *libraries* into the final program; the libraries contain a fund of standard routines, such as `printf()` and `scanf()`, for your use. (More accurately, a program called a *linker* brings in the library routines, but on most systems the compiler runs the linker for you.) The end result is an *executable file* containing code that the computer understands and that you can run.

The compiler also checks that your program is valid C. If the compiler finds errors, it reports them to you and doesn't produce an executable file. Understanding a particular compiler's complaints is another skill that you will pick up.

Step 5: Run the Program

Traditionally, the executable file is a runnable program. To run the program in many common environments, including UNIX and MS-DOS, just type the name of the executable file. Other environments, such as VMS on a VAX, may require a *run* command or some other mechanism. More recently, integrated environments such as Turbo C and QuickC let you run your executable C program from within the integrated environment by selecting names from a list or by pressing special keys.

Step 6: Test and Debug the Program

The fact that your program runs is a good sign, but it's possible that it may run incorrectly. Therefore, you should check to see that your program does what it is supposed to do. You'll find that some of your programs will have mistakes—*bugs* in computer jargon. *Debugging* is the finding and fixing of program errors. Making mistakes is a natural part of learning. It also seems inherent to programming. So when you combine learning and programming, you had best prepare yourself to be reminded often of your fallibility. And as you become a more powerful and subtle programmer, your errors, too, will become more powerful and subtle.

You have many opportunities to err. You can make a basic design error. You can implement good ideas incorrectly. You can overlook unexpected input that will mess up your program. You can use C incorrectly. You can make typing errors. You can put parentheses in the wrong place. And so on—you'll find your own items to add to this list.

Fortunately, the situation isn't hopeless, although there may be times when you feel it is. The compiler catches many kinds of errors, and there are things you can do to help yourself track down the ones that the compiler doesn't catch. Throughout this book we'll give you debugging advice.

Step 7: Maintain and Modify the Program

When you create a program for yourself or for someone else, that program may see extensive use. If it does, you'll probably find reasons to make changes in it. Perhaps there is a minor bug that shows up only when someone enters a name beginning with "Zz." Or, you may think of a better way to do something in the program. You may add a clever new feature. You may adapt the program so that it runs on a different computer system. All these tasks are greatly simplified if you document the program clearly and if you follow sound design practices.

Commentary

Programming is not always as linear a process as we've just described. Sometimes you'll have to go back and forth between steps. For instance,

Figure 1.3 *The seven steps of programming*

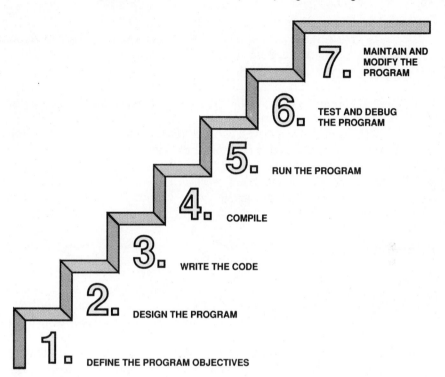

when you are writing code, you may find that your plan was impractical, or you may see a better way of doing things. Or, after you see how a program runs, you may feel motivated to change the design. Documenting your work will help you move back and forth between levels.

Most learners tend to neglect steps 1 and 2 (defining program objectives and designing the program) and go directly to step 3 (writing the program). The first programs you write are simple enough that you can visualize the whole process in your head. If you make a mistake, it's easy to find. But as your programs grow longer and more complex, mental visualizations begin to fail, and errors get harder to find. Eventually, those who neglect the planning steps are condemned to hours of lost time, confusion, and frustration as they produce ugly, dysfunctional, and abstruse programs.

The moral here is that you should develop the habit of planning before coding. Use the ancient but honorable pen-and-pencil technology to jot down the objectives of your program and to outline the design. If you do so, you eventually will reap substantial dividends in time saved and satisfaction gained.

Programming Mechanics

The exact steps you must follow to produce a program depend on your computer environment. Currently, the most widespread environments are UNIX C on a UNIX system, Borland's Turbo C on IBM PCs and clones, and Microsoft C and QuickC on IBM PCs and clones. We'll discuss all four, filling in some of the details we glossed over when summarizing the programming process.

First, however, let's look at some aspects shared by many C environments, including the four we just mentioned. You don't really need to know what follows to run a C program, but it is good background. And it may help you understand why you have to go through some particular steps to get a C program.

Source Code Files

When you write a program in the C language, you store what you write in a text file called a *source code file*. Most C systems, including the ones we mentioned, require that the name of the file end in .c: for example, wordcount.c and budget.c. The part of the name before the period is called the *basename* and the part after the period is called the *extension*. So budget is a basename and c is an extension. The combination budget.c is the *filename*. The name also should satisfy the requirements of the particular computer operating system. For example, PC DOS and MS-DOS (hereafter just DOS) are operating systems for IBM PCs and clones. They require that the basename be no more than 8 characters long. Some UNIX systems place a 14-character limit on the whole name, including the extension; other UNIX systems allow longer names, up to 255 characters.

So that we'll have something concrete to refer to, let's assume we have a source file called concrete.c containing the C source code of Listing 1.2.

Listing 1.2 *concrete.c*

```
#include <stdio.h>
main()
{
    printf("Concrete contains gravel and cement.\n");
}
```

Don't worry about the details of the source code file shown in Listing 1.2; you'll learn about them in Chapter 2.

Object Code Files, Executable Files, and Libraries

The basic strategy in C programming is to use programs that convert your source code file to an *executable file*, which is a file containing ready-to-run machine language code. C implementations do this in two steps: compiling and linking. The *compiler* converts your source code to an intermediate code, and the *linker* combines this with other code to produce the executable file. C uses this two-part approach to facilitate the modularization of programs. You can compile individual modules separately and then combine the compiled modules later. That way, if you need to change one module, you don't have to recompile the other ones.

There are several choices for the form of the intermediate files. The most prevalent choice, and the one taken by the implementations we describe, is to convert the source code to machine language code, placing the result in an *object code file*, or *object file* for short. (We are assuming that your source code consists of a single file.) Although the object file contains machine language code, it is not ready to run. The object file contains the translation of *your* source code, but it is not yet a complete program.

The first element missing from the object code file is something called *start-up* code. This is code that acts as an interface between your program and the operating system. For example, you can run, say, an IBM AT clone under DOS or under XENIX, a UNIX variety. The hardware is the same in either case, so the same object code would work with both. But you would need different start-up code for DOS than you would for XENIX, since these systems handle programs differently from one another.

The second missing element is the code for library routines. Nearly all C programs make use of *routines* (called "functions") that are part of the standard C library. For example, `concrete.c` uses the function `printf()`. The object code file does not contain the code for this function; it merely contains instructions saying to *use* the `printf()` function. The actual code is stored in another file, called a *library*. A library file contains object code for many functions.

The role of the linker is to bring together these three elements—your object code, the standard start-up code for your system, and the library code—and put them together into a single file, the executable file. For library code the linker extracts only the code needed for the functions you use from the library. See Figure 1.4.

In short, an object file and an executable file both consist of machine language instructions. The object file, however, contains the machine language translation only for the code you used, while the executable file also has machine code for the library routines you use and for the start-up code.

Figure 1.4 *Compiler and linker*

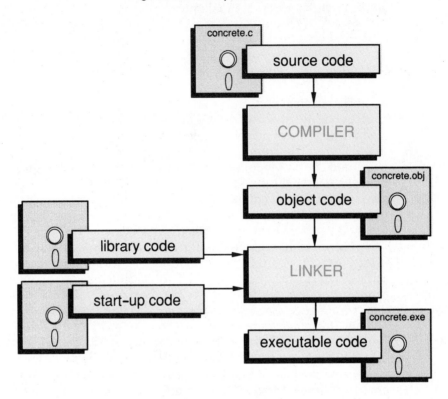

On some systems you must run the compile and link programs separately. On other systems the compiler starts the linker automatically, so that you have to give only the compile command.

Now let's look at some specific systems.

Preparing a C Program on a UNIX System

Because C's popularity began on UNIX systems, we will start there.

Editing on a UNIX System

Unlike BASIC, UNIX C does not have its own editor. Instead, you use one of the general-purpose UNIX editors, such as ed, ex, edit, emacs, jove or vi.

Your two main responsibilities are typing the program correctly and choosing a name for the file that will store the program. As we discussed, the name should end with .c. Note that UNIX distinguishes between upper- and lowercase. Thus, budget.c, BUDGET.c, and Budget.c are three distinct and valid names for C source files. But BUDGET.C is not a valid name because it uses an uppercase C instead of a lowercase c.

Here is an example. Using the vi editor we prepared the following program and stored it in a file called inform.c.

```
#include <stdio.h>
main()
{
    printf("A .c is used to end a C program filename.\n");
}
```

The text we just typed is the *source code*, and inform.c is the *source file*. The important point here is that the source file is the beginning of a process, not the end.

Compiling on a UNIX System

Our program, although undeniably brilliant, is still gibberish to a computer. A computer doesn't understand things like #include or printf. (At this point, you probably don't either. But you will soon learn, whereas the computer won't.) As we discussed earlier, we need the help of a compiler to translate *our* code (source code) to the *computer's* code (machine code). The result of our efforts will be the executable file, which contains all the machine code that the computer needs to get the job done.

The UNIX C compiler is called cc. To compile the inform.c program, you need type only

```
cc inform.c
```

After a few seconds, the UNIX prompt will return, telling you that the deed is done. (You may get warnings and error messages if you failed to write the program properly, but let's assume you did everything right.) If you use ls to list your files, you will find that there is a new file called a.out (see Figure 1.5). This is the executable file containing the translation (or compilation) of the program. To run it, just type

```
a.out
```

and wisdom pours forth:

```
.c is used to end a C program filename.
```

If you want to keep the executable file (a.out), you should rename it. Otherwise, the file is replaced by a new a.out the next time you compile a program.

What about the object code? The cc compiler creates an object code

Figure 1.5 *Preparing a C program using UNIX*

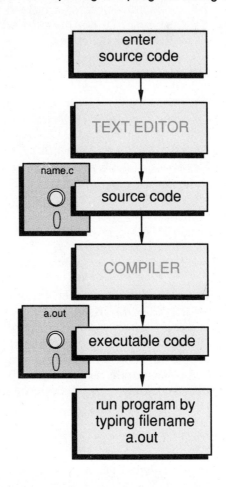

file having the same basename as the source code but with an o extension. So, in our example, the object code file is called inform.o. But you won't find it, for the linker removes it once the executable program has been completed. However, if the original program used more than one source code file, the object code files would be saved. When we discuss multiple-file programs later in the text, you will see that this is a fine idea.

Preparing a C Program on an IBM PC (Microsoft C)

Here we'll describe using Microsoft 4.0, 5.0, and 5.1; QuickC merits a separate discussion. Also, we assume that you are using PC DOS 3.1 or later or MS-DOS 3.1 or later.

Editing on an IBM PC

First, you need to select an editor. PC DOS and MS-DOS come with a rather primitive, but adequate, editor called EDLIN. However, you probably have access to a word processor such as WordStar, WordPerfect, or Microsoft Word. You can use these word processors to write C programs. However, you *cannot* use the normal file formats that these word processors use. These files contain a lot of text formatting information in addition to the text you see when writing. This additional information will foil the compiler. So you must take care to create simple *ASCII* files, that is, files containing nothing but the text you type. If you have WordStar, for example, use the N (for non-document) mode for program files. For WordPerfect, use the Text In/Out key to save the file as a "DOS file."

A better choice is to use an editor specifically designed for programming. Microsoft, for example, includes a programming editor called the Microsoft Editor with release 5.1 of the Microsoft C compiler. Similarly, WordPerfect includes a Program Editor in its WordPerfect Library package. There are several commercial program editors available, including Kedit and Brief, as well as ports of the vi and emacs editors to the DOS environment.

Whichever editor you use, you should, as with UNIX, use a filename ending with the c extension. Also, with DOS, the part of the name before the period is limited to 8 characters. Thus, budget.c and wordcnt.c are valid names, but countwords.c is not. DOS won't reject countwords.c; it simply trims the basename to 8 characters and saves the file as countword.c. DOS does not distinguish between uppercase and lowercase, so both budget.c and BUDGET.C are valid names for the same file.

As an example, use the editor of your choice to create a file called inform.c having these contents:

```
#include <stdio.h>
main()
{
    printf("A .c is used to end a C program filename.\n");
}
```

Compiling

Once you have a source code file whose name ends in .c, you can invoke the Microsoft C compiler with this command:

```
cl inform.c
```

Like the UNIX cc compiler, the Microsoft cl compiler first produces an object code file. For DOS systems, the name of the original file is used, but with the c extension replaced by obj. Thus, for our example, the object code file would be called `inform.obj`. Next, the compiler requests the system linker to finish the job. On DOS systems, this is a program called `link`. The `link` program pulls in code from the C library (which comes with the compiler) and adds the start-up code to produce an executable file called `inform.exe`. In general, the name of the executable file is the name of the source file with the `c` extension replaced with `exe`. Unlike the UNIX compiler, `cl` does not erase the object file when done. Figure 1.6 shows the steps for preparing a C program using Microsoft C.

To run the program, type the following command at the DOS prompt:

```
inform
```

Under DOS, this is equivalent to typing `inform.exe`. The program runs, producing the following output:

```
.c is used to end a C program filename.
```

Turbo C and QuickC

Borland and Microsoft probably will shudder at having their products lumped together, but Turbo C and QuickC both provide fast, integrated environments for putting together C programs. The key points are that each of these two programs has a built-in editor that you can use to write a C program. Each provides menus that let you name and save your source code file, as well as menus that let you compile and run your program without leaving the Turbo C or QuickC program. Each dumps you back into the editor if the compiler finds any errors, and each identifies the offending lines and matches them to the appropriate error messages. Both allow you to create object and executable files so that you can create stand-alone programs that can be run directly from the DOS level.

Turbo C and QuickC follow the standard DOS naming conventions, so source code files should have a `.c` extension. Object files are given the `obj` extension, and executable files are given the `exe` extension.

Why Compile?

Those of you used to BASIC may wonder about going through these steps to run a program. It may seem time-consuming. It may even *be* time-consuming. But once a program is compiled, it will run much faster than a standard BASIC program. You trade some inconvenience in getting a program running for a swifter final product. And if you use an integrated package, the inconvenience is much reduced.

Figure 1.6 *Preparing a C program in Microsoft C*

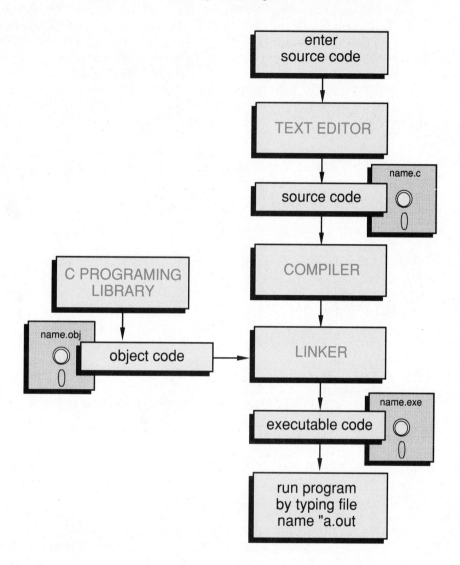

Language Standards

Currently, many C implementations are available. Ideally, once you write a C program, it should work the same on any implementation, providing it doesn't use machine-specific programming. For this to be true in practice, different implementations need to conform to a recognized standard.

At first, there was no official standard for C. Instead, the first edition of *The C Programming Language* by Brian Kernighan and Dennis Ritchie (1978) became the accepted standard, usually referred to as *K&R C*. In particular, "C Reference Manual" in the book's appendix acted as the guide to C implementors. Compilers, for example, would claim to offer a full K&R implementation. However, although this appendix defined the C language, it did not define the C library. More than most languages, C depends on its library, so there is need for a library standard, too. In the absence of any official standard, the library supplied with the UNIX implementation became a de facto standard.

As C evolved and as it become more widely used on a greater variety of systems, the C community realized that it needed a more comprehensive, up-to-date, and rigorous standard. To meet this need, the American National Standards Institute (ANSI) established a committee (X3J11) in 1983 to develop a new standard. At the time of this writing, the committee has nearly completed its work. This new standard (ANSI C) defines both the language and a standard C library.

For the most part, we will follow the ANSI C Standard. Often, ANSI C and K&R C are much the same. However, ANSI C does support some extensions and changes. We'll mention many of these where appropriate. Because you may find yourself using implementations that lack some ANSI C features, we'll point out where there are conflicts.

Some Conventions

We are almost ready to begin our study of the C language itself. Here are some of the conventions that we will use in presenting material.

Typeface

For text representing programs and computer input and output, we will use a type font that resembles what you might see on a screen or on printed output. We already have used it a few times. In case it slipped by you, the font looks like this:

```
#include <stdio.h>
main()
{
    printf("Concrete contains gravel and cement.\n");
}
```

Screen Output

Output from the computer is printed in color. Where lines of output are interspersed with user input, only the screen output is in color. For instance, here is program output from a Chapter 14 example:

```
Please enter the book title.
Press [enter] at the start of a line to stop.
My Life as a Budgie
Now enter the author.
Mack Zackles
```

The lines printed in color are program output, and the other lines are user input.

Input and Output Devices

There are many ways that you and a computer can communicate with each other. However, we will assume that you type in commands by using a keyboard and that you read the response on a screen.

Special Keystrokes

Usually, you send a line of instructions onward by pressing a key labeled "Enter," "c/r," "Return," or some variation of these. We will refer to this key in the text as the Enter key. When showing it as part of input in a program example, we use [enter]. The brackets mean that you press a single key rather than type the word "enter."

We also will refer to control characters such as Control-D. This notation means to type the *D* key while you are depressing the key labeled "Control" (or, perhaps, "Ctrl").

Our System

Some aspects of C, such as the amount of space used to store a number, depend on the system. When we give examples and refer to "our system," we speak of a Zenith Z-200 (an IBM AT compatible) running under MS-DOS 3.30 and using a Microsoft C compiler.

We also occasionally refer to running programs on a UNIX system. The one we use is Berkeley's BSD 4.3 version of UNIX running on a VAX 11/750 computer.

Chapter Summary

C is a powerful, concise programming language. It is popular because it provides useful programming tools and good control over hardware and because C programs are easier than most to transport from one system to another.

C is a *compiled* language. C *compilers* and *linkers* are programs that convert C language source code into executable code.

Programming in C can be taxing, difficult, and frustrating. But it also can be intriguing, exciting, and satisfying. We hope that you will find it as enjoyable and fascinating as we do.

Review Questions

1. What does *portability* mean in the context of programming?
2. Explain the difference between source code file, object code file, and executable file.
3. What are the seven major steps in programming?
4. What does a compiler do?
5. What does a linker do?

Programming Exercise

We don't expect you to write C code yet, so this exercise concentrates on the earlier stages of the programming process.

1. You have just been employed by MacroMuscle, Inc. (Software for Hard Bodies). They are entering the European market and want a program that converts inches to centimeters ($1'' = 2.54$ cm). They want the program set up so that it prompts the user to enter an inch value. Your assignment is to define the program objectives and to design the program (steps 1 and 2 of the programming process).

2

Introducing C

Operator
► =

Functions
► main( ), printf( )

In this chapter you learn how to put together a simple C program, how to create integer-valued variables and assign them values, and how to display those values on screen. Also, you find out what the newline character is, how to include comments in your programs, how to create programs containing more than one function, how to find program errors, and what keywords are.

W hat does a C program look like? If you skim through this book, you'll see many examples. Quite likely, you'll find that C is peculiar-looking, sprinkled with symbols like {, cp-> tort, and *ptr++. As you read through this book, you will find that the appearance of these and of other characteristic C symbols grows less strange, more familiar, perhaps even welcome! In this chapter we begin by presenting a simple example program and explaining what it does. At the same time we highlight some of the basic features of C.

A Simple Sample of C

Let's take a look at a simple C program. (Figure 2.1 outlines a more extensive example.) This program, shown in Listing 2.1, serves to point out some of the basic features of programming in C. Before you read the upcoming line-by-line explanation of the program, read through Listing 2.1 to see if you can figure out for yourself what it will do.

Listing 2.1 *A Simple C Program*

```
#include <stdio.h>
main()                      /* a simple program            */
{
    int num;                /* define a variable called num */
    num = 1;                /* assign a value to num       */

    printf("I am a simple "); /* use the printf() function   */
    printf("computer.\n");
    printf("My favorite number is %d because it is first.\n",num);
}
```

If you think this program will print some things on your screen, you are right! But exactly what will be printed may not be apparent, so run the program and see the results. First, use your favorite editor to create a file containing the text from Listing 2.1. Give the file a name that ends in `.c` and that satisfies your local system's name requirements. You can use `first.c`, for instance. Now compile and run the program. If all went well, the output should look like this:

```
I am a simple computer.
My favorite number is 1 because it is first.
```

All in all, this result is not too surprising. But what happened to the \n's and the %d in the program? And some of the lines in the program do look strange. It is time for an explanation.

The Explanation

We'll take two passes through the program's source code. The first pass will highlight the meaning of each line, and the second will explore specific implications and details. Figure 2.1 summarizes the parts of a C program.

Pass 1: Quick Synopsis

```
#include <stdio.h>    ←include another file
```

This line tells the computer to include information found in the file `stdio.h`. The `stdio.h` file is a standard part of all C compiler packages.

```
main()    ←a function name
```

C programs consist of one or more functions, the basic modules of a C program. This program consists of one function called `main`. The parentheses identify `main()` as a function name.

```
/* a simple program */    ←a comment
```

The symbols `/*` and `*/` enclose comments. *Comments* are remarks that help to clarify a program. They are intended only for the reader and are ignored by the compiler.

```
{    ←beginning of the body of the function
```

This opening brace marks the start of the statements that make up the function. The function definition is ended with a closing brace, `}`.

Figure 2.1 *Anatomy of a C program*

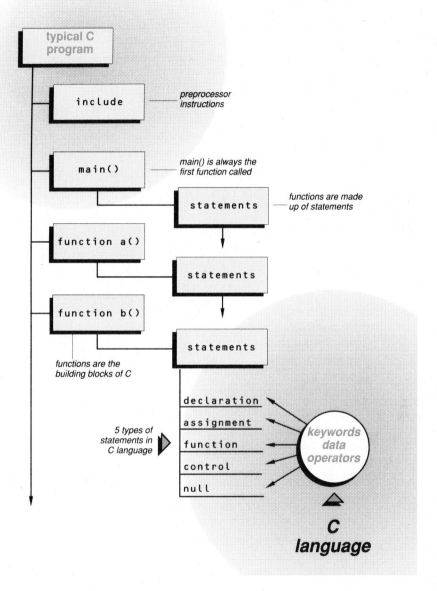

```
int num;   ←a declaration statement
```

This statement announces that we will be using a variable called num and that num will be an int (integer) type.

```
num = 1;    ←an assignment statement
```

The statement num = 1; assigns the value 1 to the variable called num.

```
printf("I am a simple ");    ←a print statement
```

The first printf statement displays the phrase I am a simple on your screen, leaving the cursor on the same line.

```
printf("computer.\n");    ←another print statement
```

The next printf statement tacks on computer to the end of the last phrase printed. The \n is code telling the computer to start a new line, that is, to move the cursor to the beginning of the next line.

```
printf("My favorite number is %d because it is first.\n", num);
```

The last printf statement prints the value of num (which is 1) embedded in the phrase in quotes. The %d instructs the computer where and in what form to print the value of num.

```
}    ←the end
```

As promised, the program ends with a closing brace.

Pass 2: Details

Now let's take a closer look at the program.

#include Directives and Header Files

```
#include <stdio.h>
```

The effect of #include <stdio.h> is the same as if we had typed the entire contents of the stdio.h file into our file at the point where the #include line appears. *Include* files provide a convenient way to share information that is common to many programs.

The stdio.h file is supplied as part of all C compiler packages. It contains information about input and output functions, such as printf(), for the compiler to use. The name stands for *st*andard *i*nput/*o*utput *h*eader. C people call a collection of information that goes at the top of a file a *header*, and C implementations typically come with several header files. One goal of ANSI C is to standardize which header files must be provided.

Some programs need to include stdio.h; some don't. The documentation for a particular C implementation should include a description of the functions in the C library. These function descriptions identify which header files are needed. For example, the description for printf() says to use stdio.h. Omitting the proper header file may not affect a particular program, but it is best not to rely on that. Each time we use library functions, we'll use the include files specified by the ANSI Standard for those functions. Because the compiler uses the information in the stdio.h to build a program, any information that the compiler does not use does not become part of the program. Therefore, including an unnecessary file does not make the final program any longer.

The #include statement is an example of a C *preprocessor directive*. In general, C compilers perform some preparatory work on source code before compiling; this is termed *preprocessing*.

Why Input and Output Are Not Built-in

Perhaps you are wondering why something as basic as input and output information isn't included automatically. One answer is that not all programs use this I/O (input/output) package, and part of the C philosophy is to avoid carrying unnecessary weight. Incidentally, the #include line is not even a C language statement! The # symbol in column 1 identifies it as a line to be handled by the C preprocessor. As you know, the preprocessor handles some tasks before the compiler takes over. We will encounter more examples of preprocessor instructions later.

The *main( )* Function

```
main()
```

True, main is a rather plain name, but it is the only choice available. A C program always begins execution with the function called main(). You are free to choose names for other functions you may use, but main() must be there to start things off. What about the parentheses? They identify main() as a function. You will learn more about functions soon. For now, just remember that functions are the basic modules of a C program.

The parentheses following a function name generally enclose information being passed along to the function. For our simple example, nothing is being passed along, so the parentheses remain empty. Don't leave them out, but don't worry about them yet.

Comments

```
/* a simple program */
```

Using comments makes it easier for someone (including yourself) to understand your program. One nice feature of C comments is that they can be placed anywhere, even on the same line as the material they explain. A longer comment can be placed on its own line or even spread over more than one line. Everything between the opening /* and the closing */ is ignored by the compiler. Here are some valid and invalid comment forms:

```
/* This is a C comment. */
/* This comment is spread over
   two lines. */
/*
  You can do this, too.
*/
/* But this is invalid
```

Braces, Bodies, and Blocks

```
{
   .
   .
   .
}
```

Braces mark the beginning as well as the end of the body of a function. Only braces { } work for this purpose, not parentheses ( ) and not brackets [ ].

Braces also can be used to gather statements inside a program into a unit or *block*. If you are familiar with Pascal, ADA, Modula-2, or Algol, you will recognize the braces as being similar to begin and end in those languages.

Declarations

```
int num;
```

The *declaration statement* is one of the most important features of C. This particular example declares two things. First, somewhere in the function, we have a *variable* called num. Second, the int proclaims num as an *integer*, that is, a whole number without a decimal point. The compiler uses this information to arrange for suitable storage space in memory for the num variable. The semicolon at the end of the line identifies the line as a C *statement* or instruction. The semicolon is part of the statement, not just a separator between statements as it is in Pascal.

The word int is a C *keyword* identifying one of the basic C data types. Keywords are the words used to express a language, and you can't usurp them for other purposes. For instance, you can't use int as the name of a function or a variable.

In C *all* variables should be declared before they are used. This means that you have to provide lists of all the variables you use in a program, and that you have to show which *type* each variable is. Declaring variables is considered to be a good programming technique.

At this point, you probably have three questions. First, what are data types? Second, what choices do you have in selecting a name? Third, why do you have to declare variables at all? Let's look at some answers.

Data Types

C deals with several kinds (or types) of data: integers, characters, and "floating point," for example. Declaring a variable to be an integer or a character type makes it possible for the computer to store, fetch, and interpret the data properly. We'll investigate the variety of available types in the next chapter.

Name Choice

We suggest that you use meaningful names for variables. The number of characters you can use will vary among implementations, but the lower limit will be at least 8 characters. The ANSI C Standard calls for up to 31 characters, except for external identifiers (see Chapter 13), for which only 8 characters need be recognized. Actually, you can use more than the maximum number of characters, but the compiler won't pay attention to the extra characters. Thus, on a system with an 8-character limit, shakespeare and shakespencil would be considered the same name because they have the same first 8 characters. The characters at your disposal are the lowercase letters, the uppercase letters, the digits, and the underscore _. The first character must be a letter or an underscore. Here are some examples:

Valid Names	Invalid Names
wiggles	$Z]**
cat1	1cat
Hot_Tub	Hot-Tub
_kcab	don't

Four Good Reasons to Declare Variables

1. Putting all the variables in one place makes it easier for a reader to grasp what the program is about. This is particularly true if you give your variables meaningful names (such as taxrate instead of

r). If the name doesn't suffice, use the comment facility to explain what the variables represent. Documenting a program in this manner is one of the basic techniques of good programming.

2. Thinking about what to put into the variable declaration section encourages you to do some planning before plunging into writing a program. What information will the program need to get started? What exactly do I want the program to produce as output? What is the best way to represent the data?

3. Declaring variables helps prevent one of programming's more subtle and hard-to-find bugs, that of the misspelled variable name. For example, suppose that in some language, which lacks declarations, you made the statement

```
RADIUS1 = 20.4;
```

and that elsewhere in the program you mistyped

```
CIRCUM = 6.28 * RADIUSl;
```

You unwittingly replaced the numeral 1 with the letter l. That other language would create a new variable called `RADIUSl` and use whatever value it had (perhaps zero, perhaps garbage). `CIRCUM` would be given the wrong value, and you might have a heck of a time trying to find out why. This can't happen in C (unless you were silly enough to declare two such similar variable names) because the compiler will complain when the undeclared `RADIUSl` shows up.

4. Your C program will not compile if you don't declare your variables. If the preceding reasons fail to move you, you should give this one serious thought.

Assignment

```
num = 1;
```

The *assignment statement* is one of the basic operations in C. This particular example means "assign the value 1 to the variable num." The earlier `int num;` line allotted computer space for the variable num, and the assignment line gives it its value. You can assign num a different value later on if you wish; that is why num is a variable. Note that the assignment statement assigns a value from the right side to the left side. Also, the statement is completed with a semicolon, as shown in Figure 2.2.

The *printf( )* Function

```
printf("I am a simple ");
printf("computer.\n");
printf("My favorite number is %d because it is first.\n",num);
```

Figure 2.2 *The assignment statement is one of the basic C operations*

num = 1;

assignment operator

These lines all use a standard C function called `printf()`. The parentheses signify a function. The material enclosed in the parentheses is information passed from the `main()` function to the `printf()` function. For example, the first line passes the phrase "I am a simple" to the `printf()` function. Such information is called the *argument* of a function (see Figure 2.3). And what does the function `printf()` do with this argument? It looks at whatever lies between the double quotation marks and prints that text on the screen.

Figure 2.3 *The function* printf( ) *with an argument*

printf()

argument

printf("That's mere contrariness!\n");

This first `printf()` line provides an example of how you *call* or *invoke* a function in C. You need type only the name of the function, placing the desired argument(s) within the parentheses. When the program reaches this line, control is turned over to the named function (`printf()` in this case). When the function is finished with whatever it does, control is returned to the original (the *calling*) program—main() in our example.

But what about this next printf() line? It has the characters \n included in the quotes, and they didn't get printed! What's going on? The \n actually is an instruction to start a new line. The \n combination (typed as two characters) represents a single character called the *newline* character. Its meaning is "start a new line at the far left margin." In other words, the newline character performs the same function as the Enter key of a typical keyboard. Why not just use the Enter key? Because that would be interpreted as an immediate command to your editor, not as an instruction to be stored in your source code. In other words, when you press the Enter key, the editor quits the current line on which you are working and starts a new one.

The newline character is an example of an *escape sequence*. An escape sequence is used to represent difficult- or impossible-to-type characters. Other examples are \t for tab and \b for backspace. In each case the escape sequence begins with the backslash character, \. We'll return to this subject in Chapter 3.

Well, that explains why our three printf() statements produced only two lines: the first print instruction didn't have a newline character in it, but the second and third did.

The final printf() line brings up another oddity: what happened to the %d when the line was printed? As you will recall, the output for this line was

```
My favorite number is 1 because it is first.
```

Aha! The digit 1 was substituted for the symbol group %d when the line was printed, and 1 was the value of the variable num. The %d is a placeholder to show where the value of num is to be printed. This line is similar to the BASIC statement:

```
PRINT "My favorite number is "; num; " because it is first."
```

The C version does a little more than this, actually. The % alerts the program that a variable is to be printed at that location, and the d tells it to print the variable as a digit. The printf() function allows several choices for the format of printed variables. Indeed, the f in printf() is a reminder that this is a *f*ormatting print function.

The Structure of a Simple Program

Now that you've seen a specific example, you are ready for a few general rules about C programs. A *program* consists of a collection of one or more functions, one of which must be called `main()`. The description of a *function* consists of a header and a body. The *header* contains preprocessor statements, such as `#include`, and the function name. You can recognize a function name by the parentheses, which may be empty. The *body* is enclosed by braces ( ) and consists of a series of statements, each terminated by a semicolon (see Figure 2.4). Our example had a *declaration statement*, announcing the name and type of variable being used. Then it had an *assignment statement* giving the variable a value. Finally, there were three *print statements*, each calling the `printf()` function. The print statements are examples of *function call statements*.

Figure 2.4 *A function has a header and a body*

Header

preprocessor instructions ———

function name with arguments ——

```
#include <stdio.h>
main()
```

Body

declaration statement ———

assignment statement ———

function statement ———

```
{
int num;
num=1;
printf("%d is neat.\n");
}
```

Tips on Making Your Programs Readable

Making your programs readable is good programming practice. A readable program is much easier to understand, and that makes it easier to correct or modify your program. The act of making a program readable also helps clarify your own concept of what the program does.

We've already mentioned two techniques for improving readability: choose meaningful variable names and use comments. Note that these two techniques complement each other. If you give a variable the name `width`, you don't need a comment saying that this variable represents a width. But a variable called `video_routine_4` begs for an explanation of what video routine 4 does.

Another technique is using blank lines to separate one conceptual section of a function from another. For example, in our simple program, we had a blank line separating the declaration section from the action section. The blank line is not required by C, but it enhances readability.

A fourth technique we followed was to use one line per statement. Again, this is a readability convention, not a C requirement. C has a "free-form format." You can place several statements on one line or spread one statement over several. The following is legitimate, but ugly, code:

```
main() { int four; four
=
4
;
printf(
    "%d\n",
four); }
```

The semicolons tell the compiler where one statement ends and the next begins, but the program logic is much clearer if you follow the conventions we used in our example. See Figure 2.5.

Figure 2.5 *Making your program readable*

```
main() /* converts 2 fathoms to feet */ ——————— use comments
{
int feet, fathoms; ——————————————————————— pick names
                    ——————————————————————— use space

fathoms=2;
feet=6*fathoms; ————————————————————— one statement per line
print("There are %d feet in %d fathoms!\n", feet, fathoms);
}
```

Taking Another Step

Our first example program was pretty easy, and our next example, shown in Listing 2.2, isn't much harder.

```
Listing 2.2   fathm_ft.c

/* fathm_ft.c -- converts 2 fathoms to feet */
#include <stdio.h>
main()
{
    int feet, fathoms;

    fathoms = 2;
    feet = 6 * fathoms;
    printf("There are %d feet in %d fathoms!\n", feet, fathoms);
}
```

What's new? We provided a program description, declared multiple variables, did some multiplication, and printed the values of two variables. Let's examine these points in more detail.

Documentation

First, we began the program with a comment identifying the filename and the purpose of the program. This kind of program documentation takes but a moment to do and is helpful later on when you browse through several files or print them.

Multiple Declarations

Next, we declared two variables instead of just one in a single declaration statement. To do this, we separated the two variables (`feet` and `fathoms`) by a comma in the declaration statement. That is,

```
    int feet, fathoms;
```

and

```
    int feet;
    int fathoms;
```

are equivalent.

Multiplication

Third, we made a calculation. We harnessed the tremendous computational power of our computer system to multiply 2 by 6. In C, as in many languages, the * is the symbol for multiplication. Thus, the statement

```
feet = 6 * fathoms;
```

means "look up the value of the variable fathoms, multiply it by 6, and assign the result of this calculation to the variable feet."

Printing Multiple Values

Finally, we made fancier use of printf(). If you compile and run the example, the output should look like this:

```
There are 12 feet in 2 fathoms!
```

This time we made *two* substitutions. The first %d in the quotes was replaced by the value of the first variable (feet) in the list following the quoted segment, and the second %d was replaced by the value of the second variable (fathoms) in the list. Note that the list of variables to be printed comes at the tail end of the statement after the quoted part. Also note that each item is separated from the others by a comma.

This program is limited in scope, but it could form the nucleus of a program for converting fathoms to feet. All that is needed is a way to assign other values to feet; we will explain how to do that in later chapters.

And While We're at It . . .
Multiple Functions

So far our programs have used the standard printf() function. Listing 2.3 shows you how to incorporate a function of your own—besides main()—into a program.

Listing 2.3 *two_func.c*

```
/* two_func.c -- a program using two functions in one file */
#include <stdio.h>
```

```
void butler(void);                 /* ANSI C function prototyping */
                 /* pre-ANSI C uses void butler(); instead */
main()
{
   printf("I will summon the butler function.\n");
   butler();
   printf("Yes. Bring me some tea and floppy disks.\n");
}

void butler(void)              /* start of function definition */
{
   printf("You rang, sir?\n");
}
```

The output looks like this:

```
I will summon the butler function.
You rang, sir?
Yes. Bring me some tea and floppy disks.
```

The butler() function appears three times in this program. The first appearance is in the *prototype*, which informs the compiler about the functions to be used. The second appearance is in main() in the form of a function call. Finally, the program presents the *function definition*, which is the source code for the function itself. We'll look at each of these three appearances in turn.

Prototypes are an ANSI C addition, and pre-ANSI compilers may not recognize them. (We'll tell you in a moment what to do with pre-ANSI compilers.) A prototype is a form of declaration that tells the compiler that we will be using a particular function. It also specifies properties of the function. For example, the first void in the prototype for the butler() function indicates that butler() does not have a return value. (In general, a function can return a value to the calling function for its use, but butler() doesn't.) The second void, the one in butler(void) means that the butler() function has no arguments. Thus, when the compiler reaches the point in main() where butler() is used, it can check to see if butler() is used correctly. Note that void is used to mean empty, not invalid.

Pre-ANSI C supports a more limited form of function declaration in which you just specify the return type but omit describing the arguments:

```
void butler();
```

Most C code currently in existence uses function declarations like this instead of function prototypes. ANSI C recognizes this older form but indicates it will be phased out in time. Later chapters will return to prototyping, function declarations, and return values.

Next, we invoke `butler()` in `main()` simply by giving its name, including parentheses. When `butler()` finishes its work, the program moves to the next statement in `main()`.

Finally, the function `butler()` is defined in the same manner as `main()`, with a function header and the body enclosed in braces. The header repeats the information given in the prototype: `butler()` takes no arguments and has no return value. For pre-ANSI C, omit the second `void`.

One point to note is that it is the location of the `butler()` call in `main()`—not the location of the `butler()` definition in the file—that determines when the `butler()` function is executed. You could, for instance, put the `butler()` definition above the `main()` definition in this program, and the program would still run the same, with the `butler()` function executed between the two calls to `printf()` in `main()`. Remember, all C programs begin with `main()`, no matter where `main()` is located in the program files. However, C practice is to list `main()` first, since it normally provides the basic framework for a program.

The ANSI C Standard recommends that you provide function prototypes for all functions that you use. The standard `include` files take care of this task for the standard library functions. For example, under ANSI C, the `stdio.h` file has a function prototype for `printf()`. When we introduce defining functions with return values in Chapter 6, we'll show you how to extend prototyping to non-`void` functions, including `main()`. (ANSI C mandates that `main()` be type `int`.)

Debugging

Now that you can write a simple C program, you are in a position to make simple errors. Listing 2.4 presents a program with some errors. See how many you can spot.

Listing 2.4 *nogood.c*

```
/*  nogood.c -- a program with errors */
#include <stdio.h>
main()
```

```
(
    int n, int n2, int n3;
        /* this program has several errors

    n = 5;
    n2 = n * n;
    n3 = n2 * n2;
    printf("n = %d, n squared = %d, n cubed = %d\n", n, n2, n3)
)
```

Syntax Errors

Listing 2.4 contains several *syntax* errors. You commit a syntax error when you don't follow C's rules. It's analogous to a grammatical error in English. For instance, consider the following sentence: *Bugs frustrate be can.* This sentence uses valid English words but doesn't follow the rules for word order, and it doesn't have quite the right words, anyway. C syntax errors use valid C symbols in the wrong places.

So what syntax errors did we make? First, we used parentheses instead of braces to mark the body of the function—we used a valid C symbol in the wrong place. Second, the declaration should have been this:

```
int n, n2, n3;
```

or perhaps this:

```
int n;
int n2;
int n3;
```

Next, we omitted the */ symbol pair necessary to complete a comment. Finally, we omitted the mandatory semicolon that should terminate the printf() statement.

How do you detect syntax errors? First, before compiling, you can look through the source code and see if you spot anything obvious. Second, you can examine errors found by the compiler, since part of the compiler's job is to detect syntax errors. When you compile this program, the compiler will report back any errors that it finds, identifying the nature and location of each error.

However, the compiler can get confused. A true syntax error in one location may cause the compiler to mistakenly think it has found other errors. For instance, because our example does not declare n2 and n3 correctly, the compiler may think it has found further errors whenever those variables are used. If some of the supposed errors don't make sense to you, first correct the errors before them, recompile, and see if the compiler still complains. Continue in this way until the program works.

Semantic Errors

Semantic errors are errors in meaning. For instance, consider the following sentence: *Furry inflation thinks greenly.* The syntax is fine because adjectives, nouns, verbs, and adverbs are in the right places. But the sentence doesn't mean anything. In C, you commit a semantic error when you follow the rules of C correctly but to an incorrect end. Our example has one such error:

```
n3 = n2 * n2;
```

Here, n3 is supposed to represent the cube of n, but we've set it up to be the fourth power of n.

The compiler does not detect semantic errors, for they don't violate C rules. The compiler has no way of divining your true intentions. That leaves it to you to find these kinds of errors. One way is to compare what a program does to what you expected it to do. For instance, suppose you fix the syntax errors in our example so that it now reads as shown in Listing 2.5.

Listing 2.5 *stillbad.c*

```
/* stillbad.c -- a program with its syntax errors fixed */
#include <stdio.h>
main()
{
   int n, n2, n3;
      /* this program has a semantic error */

   n = 5;
   n2 = n * n;
   n3 = n2 * n2;
   printf("n = %d, n squared = %d, n cubed = %d\n", n, n2, n3);
}
```

Its output is

```
n is 5, n squared is 25, n cubed is 625
```

If you are cube-wise, you'll see that 625 is the wrong value. The next stage is to track down how we wound up with this answer. For this example, you probably can spot the error by inspection. But, in general, you need to take a more systematic approach. One method is to pretend you are the computer and to follow the program steps one by one. Let's try that method now.

The body of our program starts by declaring three variables: n, n2, and n3. We can simulate this situation by drawing three boxes and labeling them with the variable names (see Figure 2.6). Next, the program assigns 5 to n. Simulate that by writing 5 into the n box. Next, the program multiplies n by n and assigns the result to n2. So we look in the n box, see that the value is 5, multiply 5 by 5 to get 25, and place 25 in box n2. To duplicate the next C statement (n3 = n2 * n2;), we look in n2 and find 25. We multiply 25 by 25, get 625, and place it in n3. Aha! We are squaring n2 instead of multiplying it by n.

Figure 2.6 *Tracing a program*

Well, perhaps this procedure is overkill for this example, but going through a program step-by-step in this fashion is often the best way to see what's going on.

Program State

By tracing the program step-by-step, keeping track of each variable, we monitor the *program state*. The program state is simply the set of values of all the variables at a given point in program execution. It is a snapshot of the current state of computation.

We just discussed one method of tracing the state: executing the program step-by-step yourself. In a program that makes, say, 10,000 iterations, you may not feel up to that task. Still, you can go through a few iterations to see if your program does what you intend. However, there is always the possibility that you will execute the steps as you intended them to be executed rather than as you actually wrote them, so try to be faithful to the actual code.

Another approach to locating semantic problems is to sprinkle extra printf() statements throughout to monitor the values of selected variables at key points in the program. Seeing how the values change can illuminate what's happening. Once you have the program working to your satisfaction, you can remove the extra statements and recompile.

A third method for examining the program states is to use a *debugger*. A debugger is a program that lets you run another program step-by-step and to examine the value of that program's variables. Debuggers come in various levels of ease of use and sophistication. The more advanced debuggers show which line of source code is being executed. This is particularly handy for programs with alternative paths of execution, since it is easy to see which particular paths are being followed. If your compiler comes with a debugger, take time now to learn how to use it. Try it with Listing 2.4, for example.

Keywords

Keywords are the vocabulary of C. Because they are special to C, you can't use them for variable names. Many of these keywords specify various types, such as int. Others, such as if, are used to control the order in which program statements are executed. In the following list, asterisks indicate new keywords added by the ANSI C Standard.

ANSI C Keywords

auto	double	int	static
break	else	long	struct
case	enum	register	switch
char	extern	return	typedef
*const	float	short	union
continue	for	while	unsigned
default	goto	signed	void
do	if	sizeof	*volatile

Chapter Summary

A C program consists of one or more C *functions*. Every C program must contain a function called `main()` because it is the function called when the program starts up. A simple function consists of a *header* followed by an opening brace, followed by the statements constituting the function *body*, followed by a terminating, or closing, brace.

Each C statement is an instruction to the computer and is marked by a terminating semicolon. A *declaration statement* creates a name for a variable and identifies the type of data to be stored in the variable. An *assignment statement* assigns a value to a variable or, more generally, to a storage area. A *function call statement* causes the named function to be executed. When the called function is done, the program returns to the next statement after the function call.

The `printf()` function can be used to print phrases and the values of variables.

The *syntax* of a language is the set of rules that governs the way in which valid statements in that language are put together. The *semantics* of a statement is its meaning. The compiler will help you detect syntax errors, but semantic errors show up in a program's behavior only after it is compiled. Detecting semantic errors may involve tracing the *program state*, that is, the values of all variables, after each program step.

Keywords are the vocabulary of the C language.

Review Questions

1. What are the basic modules of a C program called?

2. What is a syntax error? Give an example of one in English and of one in C.

3. What is a semantic error? Give an example of one in English and of one in C.

4. Ichabod Bodie Marfoote has prepared the following program and brought it to you for approval. Please help him out.

```
include studio.h
main{} /* this program prints the number of weeks in a year /*
(
int s

s := 56;
print(There are s weeks in a year.);
```

5. Assuming that each of the following examples is part of a complete program, what will each one print?

    a. `printf("Baa Baa Black Sheep.");`
       `printf("Have you any wool?\n");`

    b. `printf("Begone!\nO creature of lard!");`

    c. `printf("What?\nNo/nBonzo?\n");`

    d. `int num;`

       `num = 2;`
       `printf("%d + %d = %d", num, num, num + num);`

6. Which of the following are C keywords? `main, int, function, char, =`

7. How would you print the values of `words` and `lines` in the form `There were 3020 words and 350 lines.`? Here, 3020 and 350 represent values for the two variables.

8. Consider the following program:

```
#include <stdio.h>
main()
{
  int a, b;

    a = 5;
    b = 2;    /* line 5 */
    b = a;    /* line 6 */
    a = b;    /* line 7 */
    printf("%d %d\n", b, a);
}
```

What is the program state after line 5? line 6? line 7?

Programming Exercises

Reading about C isn't enough. You should try writing one or two simple programs to see if writing a program goes as smoothly as it looks in this chapter. Here are a few suggestions, but you should also try to think up some problems yourself.

1. Write a program that uses one `printf()` call to print your first name and last name on one line, uses a second `printf()` call to print your first and last name on two separate lines, and uses a pair of `printf()` calls to print your first and last name on one line. The output should look like this:

```
Mae West    ←first print statement
Mae         ←second print statement
West        ←still the second print statement
Mae West    ←third and fourth print statements
```

2. Write a program to print your name and address.

3. Write a program that converts your age in years to days. At this point, don't worry about fractional years and leap years.

4. Write a program that produces this output:

```
For he's a jolly good fellow!
For he's a jolly good fellow!
For he's a jolly good fellow!
Which nobody can deny!
```

Have the program use two user-defined functions: one that prints the jolly good message once, and one that prints the final line once.

5. Write a program that creates an integer variable called `toes`. Have the program set `toes` to 10. Also have the program calculate what twice `toes` is and what `toes` squared is. The program should print all three values, identifying them.

3

Data and C

Keywords
- ▷ int, short, long
- ▷ unsigned, char float, double

Operators
- ▷ sizeof

Function
- ▷ scanf( )

In this chapter you learn about the basic data types that C uses and about the distinctions between integer types and floating-point types. You practice writing constants and declaring variables of those types. You begin studying how to use the `printf()` and `scanf()` functions to read and write values of different types.

P rograms work with data. You feed numbers, letters, and words to the computer, and you expect it to do something with the data. For example, you may want the computer to calculate an interest payment or display a sorted list of vintners. In this chapter you will do more than just read about data; you will practice manipulating data, which is much more fun.

This chapter explores the two great families of data types: integer and floating point. C offers several varieties of these types. You'll learn what the types are, how to declare them, how to use them, and when to use them. Also, you'll discover the differences between constants and variables. And, as a bonus, your first interactive program will be coming up shortly.

A Sample Program

Once again we begin with a sample program. As before, you'll find some unfamiliar wrinkles that we'll soon iron out for you. The program's general intent should be clear, so try compiling and running the source code shown in Listing 3.1. To save time, you can omit typing the comments. (For reference, we've included a program name as a comment. We will continue this practice with future programs.)

Listing 3.1 *goldyou.c*

```
/* goldyou.c  -- the worth of your weight in gold */
#include <stdio.h>
main()
{
```

(continued)

Listing 3.1 *(continued)*

```
      float weight, value;      /* 2 floating-point variables */
      char beep;                /* a character variable       */

      beep = '\007';
            /* assigning a special character to beep       */
      printf("Are you worth your weight in gold?\n");
      printf("Please enter your weight in pounds, ");
      printf("and we'll see.\n");
      scanf("%f", &weight);
            /* getting input from the user                 */
      value = 400.0 * weight * 14.5833;
            /* assumes gold is $400 per ounce              */
            /* 14.5833 converts pounds avd. to ounces troy */
      printf("%cYour weight in gold is worth $%.2f%c.\n",
            beep,value,beep);
      printf("You are easily worth that! If gold prices drop, ");
      printf("eat more\nto maintain your value.\n");
}
```

When you type this program, you may wish to change the 400.0 to the current price of gold. We suggest, however, that you don't fiddle with the 14.5833, which represents the number of ounces in a pound. (That's ounces *troy*, used for precious metals, and pounds *avoirdupois*, used for people, precious and otherwise.) Note that "entering" your weight means to type your weight and then press the Enter or Return key. (Don't just type your weight and wait.) Pressing Enter informs the computer that you have finished typing your response. When we ran the program, the results looked like this:

```
Are you worth your weight in gold?
Please enter your weight in pounds, and we'll see.
175
Your weight in gold is worth $1020831.00.
You are easily worth that! If gold prices drop, eat more
to maintain your value.
```

This program also has a nonvisual aspect. You will have to run the program yourself to find out what that is, but the name of one of the variables should provide a clue.

What's New in This Program?

There are several new elements of C in this program.

► Notice that we use two new kinds of variable declarations. Previously, we used only an integer variable type (int), but now we've added a floating-point variable type (float) and a character variable type (char) so that we can handle a wider variety of data. The float type can hold numbers with decimal points, and the char type can hold characters.

► We've included some new ways of writing constants. We now have numbers with decimal points, and we have a rather peculiar-looking notation to represent the character named beep.

► To print these new kinds of variables, we use the %f and the %c codes of printf() to handle floating-point and character variables, respectively. We use the .2 modifier to the %f code to fine-tune the appearance of the output so that it displays two places to the right of the decimal.

► To provide keyboard input to the program, we use the scanf() function. The %f instructs scanf() to read a floating-point number from the keyboard, and the &weight tells scanf() to assign the input value to the variable named weight. The scanf() function uses the & notation to indicate where it can find the weight variable. We'll discuss & further in the next chapter; meanwhile, trust us that you need it here.

► Perhaps the most outstanding new feature is that this program is *interactive*. The computer asks you for information and then uses the number you type in. An interactive program is more interesting to use than the noninteractive types. More important, the interactive approach makes programs more flexible. For instance, our example program can be used for any reasonable weight, not just for 175 pounds. We don't have to rewrite the program every time we want to try it on a new person. The scanf() and printf() functions make this possible. The scanf() function reads data from the keyboard and delivers that data to the program, and printf() reads data from a program and delivers that data to your screen. Together, these two functions let you establish a two-way communication with your computer (see Figure 3.1), and that makes using a computer much more fun.

This chapter will explain the first two items in this list of new features: variables and constants of various data types. Chapter 4 will cover the last three items, but we will continue to make limited use of scanf() and printf() in this chapter.

Figure 3.1 *The functions* scanf( ) *and* printf( ) *at work*

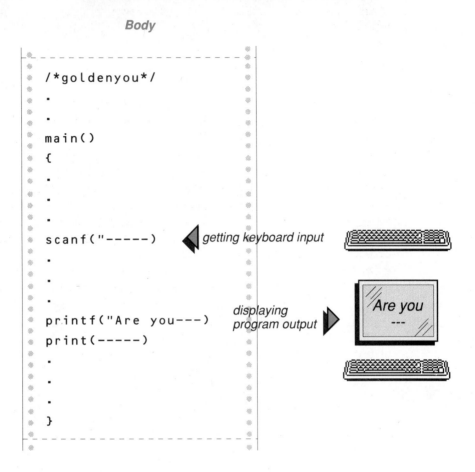

Data: Variables and Constants

A computer, under the guidance of a program, can do many things. It can add numbers, sort names, command the obedience of a speaker or video screen, calculate cometary orbits, prepare a mailing list, dial phone numbers, draw stick figures, draw conclusions, or anything else your imagination can create. To do these tasks, the program needs to work with *data*, the numbers and characters that bear the information you use. Some data are preset before a program is used and keep their values unchanged throughout the life of the program. These are *constants*. Other data may change or be assigned values as the program runs; these are *variables*. In our sample program, weight is a variable and 14.5833 is a constant. What about the 400.0? True, the price of gold isn't a constant in real life, but our program treats it as a constant. The difference between a variable and a constant is that a variable can have its value assigned or changed while the program is running, and a constant can't.

Data: Data-Type Keywords

Beyond the distinction between variable and constant is the distinction between different *types* of data. Some data are numbers. Some are letters or, more generally, characters. The computer needs a way to identify and use these different kinds. C does this by recognizing several fundamental *data types*. If a datum is a constant, the compiler usually can tell its type just by the way it looks: 46 is an integer, and 46.100 is floating point. A variable, however, needs to have its type announced in a declaration statement. You'll learn the details of declaring variables as we move along. First, though, let's look at the fundamental types recognized by C. K&R C recognized seven keywords. ANSI C added four to the list. Two of these—void (see Chapter 2) and signed—had come into general use previously. Here are the keywords:

Original K&R Keywords	Keywords from ANSI C
int	signed
long	void
short	const
unsigned	volatile
char	
float	
double	

We'll discuss the K&R keywords and the signed keyword here. The const and volatile keywords are covered in Chapter 13.

The int keyword provides the basic class of integers used in C. The next three keywords (long, short, and unsigned) and the ANSI addition signed are used to provide variations of the basic type. Next, the char keyword designates the type used for letters of the alphabet and for other characters, such as #, $, %, and &. Finally, float, double, and the ANSI C combination long double are used to represent numbers with decimal points.

The types created with these keywords can be divided into two families on the basis of how they are stored in the computer. The first five keywords from the pre-ANSI C list create *integer* types, while the last two create *floating-point* types.

Bits, Bytes, and Words

The terms "bit," "byte," and "word" can be used to describe units of computer data or to describe units of computer memory. We'll concentrate on the second usage here.

The smallest unit of memory is called a *bit*. It can hold one of two values: 0 or 1. (Or we can say that the bit is set to "off" or "on"; this is another way of saying the same thing.) You can't store much information in 1 bit, but a computer has a tremendous stock of them. The bit is the basic building block of computer memory.

The *byte* is the usual unit of computer memory. For nearly all machines a byte is 8 bits, and that is the standard definition. Since each bit can be either 0 or 1, there are 256 (that's 2 times itself 8 times) possible bit patterns of *0*s and *1*s that can fit in a byte. These patterns can be used, for example, to represent the integers from 0 to 255 or to represent a set of characters. Representation can be accomplished using *binary code*, which uses (conveniently enough) just *0*s and *1*s to represent numbers. (We discuss binary code in Chapter 15, but you can read through the introductory material of that chapter now if you like.)

A *word* is the natural unit of memory for a given computer design. For 8-bit microcomputers, such as the original Apples, a word is just 1 byte. The IBM AT and its clones are 16-bit machines. This means that they have a word size of 16 bits, which is 2 bytes. Machines like the 80386-based PCs and the Macintosh II have 32-bit words. More powerful computers can have 64-bit words or even larger. Our examples have a word size of 16 bits unless noted otherwise.

Integer versus Floating-Point Types

Integer types? Floating-point types? If you find these terms disturbingly unfamiliar, relax. We are about to give you a brief rundown of their meanings. If you are unfamiliar with "bits," "bytes," and "words," you may wish to read the next box first. Do you *have* to learn all the details? Not really, not any more than you have to learn the principles of internal combustion engines to drive a car. But knowing a little about what goes on inside a computer or engine can occasionally help you out.

For a human, the difference between integers and floating-point numbers is reflected in the way they can be written. For a computer, the difference is reflected in the way they are stored. Let's look at each of the two classes in turn.

The Integer

An *integer* is a whole number. It never has a fractional part, and in C it never is written with a decimal point. Examples are 2, −23, and 2456. Numbers like 3.14, 0.22, and 2.000 are not integers. Integers are stored as binary numbers. The integer 7, for example, is written 111 in binary. Thus, to store this number in a byte, just set the first 5 bits to 0 and the last 3 bits to 1. See Figure 3.2.

Figure 3.2 *Storing the integer 7 using a binary code*

The Floating-Point Number

A *floating-point* number more or less corresponds to what mathematicians call a "real number." *Real numbers* include the numbers between the integers. Here are some floating-point numbers: 2.75, 3.16E7, 7.00, and 2e−8. Obviously, there is more than one way to write a floating-point number. We will discuss the "E"-notation more fully later. In brief, the notation "3.16E7" means to multiply 3.16 by 10 to the 7th power; that is, by 1 followed by 7 zeros. The 7 would be termed the *exponent* of 10.

The key point here is that the scheme used to store a floating-point number is different from the one used to store an integer. Floating-point representation involves breaking up a number into a fractional part and an exponent part and storing the parts separately. Thus, the 7.00 in this list would not be stored in the same manner as the integer 7, even though both have the same value. The decimal analogy would be to write 7.0 as 0.7E1. Here, 0.7 is the fractional part, and the 1 is the exponent part. Figure 3.3 shows another example of floating-point storage. A computer, of course, would use binary numbers and powers of two instead of powers of ten for internal storage. You'll find more on this topic in Chapter 15. Now, let's concentrate on the practical differences, which are these:

▶ Integers are whole numbers; floating-point numbers can represent both whole and fractional numbers.

► Floating-point numbers can represent a much larger range of values than integers can. See Table 3.2 near the end of this chapter.

► For some arithmetic operations, such as subtracting one large number from another, floating-point numbers are subject to greater loss of precision.

► Floating-point operations normally are slower than integer operations. However, microprocessors specifically developed to handle floating-point operations are now available, and they are quite swift.

Figure 3.3 *Storing the number pi in floating-point format (decimal version)*

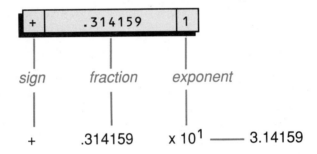

C Data Types

Now let's look at the specifics of the basic data types used by C. For each type, we describe how to declare a variable, how to represent a constant, and what a typical use would be. Some C compilers do not support all these types, so check your manual to see which ones you have available.

The *int* Type

C offers a variety of integer types. They vary in the range of values offered and in whether negative numbers can be used. The int type is the basic choice, but should you need other choices to meet the requirements of a particular task or machine, they are available.

The int type is a *signed integer*. That means it must be a whole number and it can be positive, negative, or zero. The range in possible values depends on the computer system. Typically, an int uses one machine word for storage. Thus, an IBM PC, which has a 2-byte word, uses 2 bytes (16 bits) to store an int. This allows a range in values from −32768 to +32767.

Other machines may have different ranges. See Table 3.2 near the end of this chapter for examples. ANSI C specifies that the minimum range for type int should be from −32767 to +32767. Typically, systems represent signed integers by reserving 1 bit for indicating the sign.

Declaring an *int* Variable

As you saw in Chapter 2, the keyword int is used to declare the basic integer variable. First comes int, then the chosen name of the variable, and then a semicolon. To declare more than one variable, you can declare each variable separately, or you can follow the int with a list of names in which each name is separated from the next by a comma. The following are valid declarations:

```
int erns;
int hogs, cows, goats;
```

We could have used a separate declaration for each variable, or we could have declared all four variables in the same statement. The effect is the same: associate names and arrange storage space for four int-sized variables.

These declarations create variables but don't provide values for them. How do variables get values? You've seen two ways that they can pick up values in the program. First, there is assignment:

```
cows = 112;
```

Second, a variable can pick up a value from a function, from scanf(), for example. Now let's look at a third way.

Initializing a Variable

To *initialize* a variable means to assign it an initial, or starting, value. In C, this can be done as part of the declaration. Just follow the variable name with the assignment operator (=) and the value you want the variable to have. Here are some examples:

```
int hogs = 21;
int cows = 32, goats = 14;
int dogs, cats = 94;          /* valid, but poor, form */
```

In the last line, only cats is initialized. A quick reading might lead you to think that dogs is also initialized to 94, so it is best to avoid putting initialized and noninitialized variables in the same declaration statement.

In short, these declarations create and label the storage for the variables and assign starting values to each. See Figure 3.4.

Figure 3.4 *Defining and initializing a variable*

Type *int* Constants

The various integers (21, 32, 14, and 94) in the last example are integer constants. When you write a number without a decimal point and without an exponent, C recognizes it as an integer. Thus, 22 and −44 are integer constants, while 22.0 and 2.2E1 are not. C treats most integer constants as type int. Very large integers may be treated differently; see the later discussion of the long int type.

Printing *int* Values

You can use the printf() function to print int types. As you saw in Chapter 2, the %d notation is used to indicate just where in a line the integer is to be printed. The %d is an example of a format specifier, for it indicates the form that printf() uses to display a value. Each %d in the format string must be matched by a corresponding int value in the list of items to be printed. That value can be an int variable, an int constant, or any other expression having an int value. Listing 3.2 presents a simple program that initializes a variable and prints the value of the variable, the value of a constant, and the value of a simple expression.

Listing 3.2 *print1.c*

```
/* print1.c -- displays some properties of printf() */
#include <stdio.h>
main()
{
```

```
    int ten = 10;

    printf("%d minus %d is %d\n", ten, 2, ten - 2 );
}
```

Compiling and running the program produces this output:

```
10 minus 2 is 8
```

Thus, the first %d represents the int variable ten, the second %d represents the int constant 2, and the third %d represents the value of the int expression ten - 2.

Octal and Hexadecimal

Normally, C assumes that integer constants are decimal, or base 10, numbers. However, octal (base 8) and hexadecimal (base 16) numbers are popular with many programmers. Because 8 and 16 are powers of 2, and 10 is not, these number systems occasionally provide a more convenient way for expressing computer-related values. For example, the number 65536, which often pops up in 16-bit machines, is just 10000 in hexadecimal. But how can the computer tell whether 10000 is meant to be a decimal, hexadecimal, or octal value? In C, special prefixes indicate which number base you are using. A prefix of 0x or 0X (zero-exe) means that you are specifying a hexadecimal value, so 16 is written as 0x10, or 0X10, in hexadecimal. Similarly, a 0 (zero) prefix means that you are writing in octal. For example, in C the decimal value 16 is written as 020 in octal. Chapter 15 discusses these alternative number bases more fully.

Be aware that this option of using different number systems is provided as a service for your convenience. It doesn't affect how the number is stored. That is, you can write 16 or 020 or 0x10, and the number will be stored exactly the same way in each case—in the binary code used internally by computers.

Printing Octal and Hexadecimal

Just as C lets you write a number in any one of three number systems, it also lets you print a number in any of these three systems. To print an integer in octal notation instead of decimal, use %o instead of %d. To print an integer in hexadecimal, use %x. Listing 3.3 shows a short example:

Listing 3.3 *bases.c*

```
/* bases.c -- prints 100 in decimal, octal, and hex */
#include <stdio.h>
main()
{
    int x = 100;

    printf("dec = %d; octal = %o; hex = %x\n", x, x, x);
}
```

Compiling and running this program produces this output:

```
dec = 100; octal = 144; hex = 64
```

We see the same value displayed in three different number systems. The printf() function makes the conversions. Note that the 0 and the 0x prefixes are not displayed in the output. ANSI C provides that the specifiers %#o, %#x, and %#X generate the 0, 0x, and 0X prefixes, respectively.

Other Integer Types

When you are just learning the language, the int type probably will meet most of your integer needs. But, to be complete, we'll look at the other forms now. If you like, you can skim this section and jump to the discussion of the char type, returning here when you have a need.

C offers three *adjective keywords* to modify the basic integer type: short, long, and unsigned.

▶ The type short int or, more briefly, short may use less storage than int, thus saving space when only small numbers are needed. Like int, short is a signed type.

▶ The type long int, or long, may use more storage than int, thus allowing you to express larger integer values. Like int, long is a signed type.

▶ The type unsigned int, or unsigned, is used for variables that will have only nonnegative values. This type shifts the range of numbers that can be stored. For example, a 2-byte unsigned int allows a range from 0 to 65535 in value instead of from −32768 to +32767. The bit used to indicate the sign of signed numbers now becomes another binary digit, allowing the larger number.

▶ ANSI C and many pre-ANSI C compilers also recognize as valid types unsigned long int, or unsigned long, and unsigned short int, or unsigned short.

Declaring Other Integer Types

Other integer types are declared in the same manner as the int type. The following list shows several examples. Not all pre-ANSI C compilers will recognize the last two:

```
long int estine;
long johns;
short int erns;
short ribs;
unsigned int s_count;
unsigned players;
unsigned long headcount;
unsigned short yesvotes;
```

Why Three Sizes?

Why do we say that long and short types "may" use more or less storage than int? Because C guarantees only that short is no longer than int and that long is no shorter than int. The idea is to fit the types to the machine. On an IBM PC, for example, an int and a short are both 16 bits, while a long is 32 bits. On a VAX 750, however, a short is 16 bits, while both int and long are 32 bits. The natural word size on a VAX is 32 bits. Since this allows integers in excess of 2 billion (see Table 3.2), the implementors of C on the VAX did not see a necessity for anything larger; thus, long is the same as int. But for many uses, integers of that size are not needed, so a space-saving short was created. The IBM PC, on the other hand, has only a 16-bit word, which means that a larger long was needed.

The most common practice today is to set up long as 32 bits, short as 16 bits, and int to either 16 bits or 32 bits, depending on the machine's natural word size. In principle, however, these three types could represent three distinct sizes.

ANSI C provides guidelines specifying the minimum allowable size for each basic data type. The minimum range for both short and int is −32767 to +32767, corresponding to a 2-byte unit, and the minimum range for long is −2147483647 to +2147483647, corresponding to a 4-byte unit. For unsigned short and unsigned int, the minimum range is 0 to 65535, and for unsigned long the minimum range is 0 to 4294967295.

When do you use the various int types? First, consider unsigned types. It is natural to use them for counting, since you don't need negative numbers and the unsigned types let you reach higher positive numbers than the signed types.

Use the `long` type if you need to use numbers that `long` can handle and that `int` cannot. However, on systems for which `long` is bigger than `int`, using `long` may slow down calculations, so don't use `long` if it is not essential. One further point: If you are writing code on a machine for which `int` and `long` are the same size, and if you do need 32-bit integers, you should use `long` instead of `int` so that the program will function correctly if transferred to a 16-bit machine.

Use `short` to save storage space or if, say, you need a 16-bit value on a system where `int` is 32-bit. Saving storage space usually is important only if your program uses arrays of integers that are large relative to a system's available memory.

Integer Overflow

What happens if an integer tries to get too big for its type? Let's set an integer to its largest possible value, add to it, and see what happens:

```
/* toobig.c -- exceeds maximum int size on our system */
#include <stdio.h>
main()
{
    short i = 32767;

    printf("%d %d %d\n", i, i+1, i+2);
}
```

Here's the result for our system:

```
32767 -32768 -32767
```

The integer i is acting like a car's odometer. When it reaches its maximum value, it starts over at the beginning. The main difference is that an odometer begins at 0, while our `short int` begins at −32768. Notice that you are not informed that i has exceeded ("overflowed") its maximum value. You would have to include your own programming to keep tabs on that.

The behavior described here is not mandated by the rules of C, but it is the typical implementation.

Type *long* Constants

Normally, when you use a number like 2345 in your program code, it is stored as an `int` type. But what if you use a number like 1000000 on a system in which `int` will not hold such a large number? Then the compiler treats it as a `long int`, assuming that type is large enough. If the number is larger than the `long` maximum, C will treat it as `unsigned long`.

Sometimes you may want the compiler to store a small number as a `long` integer. Programming that involves explicit use of memory addresses on an IBM PC, for instance, can create such a need. Also, some standard C functions require type `long` values. To cause a small constant to be treated as type `long`, you can append an *l* (lowercase "ell") or *L* as a suffix. We recommend the second form, since it looks less like the digit 1. Thus, a system with a 16-bit `int` and a 32-bit `long` treats the integer 7 as 2 bytes and the integer 7L as 4 bytes. The *l* and *L* suffixes also can be used with octal and hex integers, as in 020L and 0x10L.

Printing *long*, *short*, and *unsigned* Types

To print an `unsigned int` number, use the `%u` notation. To print a `long` value, use the `%ld` format specifier. If `int` and `long` are the same size on your system, just `%d` will suffice, but your program will not work properly when transferred to a system on which the two types are different. You can use the *l* prefix for x and o, too. Thus, you would use `%lx` to print a long integer in hexadecimal format and `%lo` to print in octal format.

ANSI C provides several additional `printf()` forms. First, you can use an *h* prefix for `short` types. Thus, `%hd` displays a `short` integer in decimal form, and `%ho` displays a `short` integer in octal form. Both the h and l prefixes can be used with *u* for unsigned types. For instance, you would use the `%lu` notation for printing `unsigned long` types. Listing 3.4 provides a sample.

Listing 3.4 *print2.c*

```
/* print2.c -- more printf() properties */
#include <stdio.h>
main()
{
  unsigned un = 40000;
```

(continued)

Listing 3.4 *(continued)*

```
long ln = 2000000000;
unsigned long uln = 2 * 2000000000; /* or 4000000000 */
short sn = 200;

printf("un = %u and not %d\n", un, un);
printf("ln = %ld and not %d\n", ln, ln);
printf("uln = %lu and not %u\n", uln, uln);
printf("sn = %hd and, on this system, %d\n", sn, sn);
}
```

And here is the output:

```
un = 40000 and not -25536
ln = 2000000000 and not -27648
uln = 4000000000 and not 10240
sn = 200 and, on this system, 200
```

This example points out that using the wrong specification can produce unexpected results. It also points out that you should be wary of implementation differences. For instance, we used 2 * 2000000000 instead of 4000000000 because one of our compilers does not recognize written decimal integers beyond the long limit; in this respect, it falls short of the ANSI C Standard. (The * symbol is used in C to indicate multiplication.) Also, because we ran this program on a system in which int and short are the same size, both the %hd and the %d produced the same result.

Using Characters: Type *char*

The char type is used for storing characters such as letters and punctuation marks, but technically it is an integer type. Why? Because the char type actually stores integers, not characters. To handle characters, the computer uses a numerical code in which certain integers represent certain characters. The most commonly used code is the ASCII code given in Appendix E. It is the code we will assume for this book. In it, for example, the integer value 65 represents an uppercase *A*. So to store the letter *A*, we actually need to store the integer 65. (Many IBM mainframes use a different code, called EBCDIC, but the principle is the same.)

The standard ASCII code runs numerically from 0 to 127. This range is small enough that 7 bits can hold it. The char type typically is defined as a 1-byte (or 8-bit) unit of memory, so it is more than large enough to encompass the standard ASCII code. Many systems, such as the IBM PC and the Apple Macintosh, offer extended ASCII codes (different for the two systems) that still stay within an 8-bit limit. More generally, C guarantees that the `char` type is large enough to store the basic character set for the system on which C is implemented.

Declaring Type *char* Variables

As you might expect, `char` variables are declared in the same manner as other variables. Here are some examples:

```
char response;
char itable, latan;
```

This program would create three `char` variables: `response`, `itable`, and `latan`.

Character Constants and Initialization

Suppose you want to initialize a character constant to the letter *A*. Computer languages are supposed to make things easy; we shouldn't have to memorize the ASCII code. And we don't. We can assign the character A to `grade` with the following initialization:

```
char grade = 'A';
```

A single letter contained between single quotes is a C character constant. When the compiler sees `'A'`, it converts the `'A'` to the proper code value. The single quotes are essential:

```
char broiled;        /* declare a char variable      */
broiled = 'T';       /* OK                           */
broiled = T;         /* NO! Thinks T is a variable   */
broiled = "T";       /* NO! Thinks "T" is a string   */
```

If you leave off the quotes, the compiler will think that T is the name of a variable. If you use double quotes, it will think you are using a "string." We'll discuss strings in Chapter 4.

Because characters really are stored as numeric values, you also can use the numerical code to assign values:

```
char grade = 65;
```

In this example, 65 is type `int`, but, since the value is smaller than the maximum `char` size, it can be assigned to `grade` without any problems.

Because 65 is the ASCII code for the letter *A*, this example assigns the value A to grade. Note, however, that this examples assumes that the system is using ASCII code. Using 'A' instead of 65 produces code that works on any system. Therefore, it's better to use character constants than numeric code values.

Nonprinting Characters

The single quote technique is fine for characters, digits, and punctuation marks, but if you look through Appendix E, you will see that some of the ASCII characters are *nonprinting*. For example, some represent actions such as backspacing or going to the next line or making the terminal bell ring (or speaker beep). How can these be represented? C offers three ways.

The first way we have already mentioned: just use the ASCII code. For example, the ASCII value for the beep character is 7, so we can do this:

```
char beep = 7;
```

The second way to represent certain awkward characters in C is to use special symbol sequences. These are called *escape sequences*. Table 3.1 shows the escape sequences and their meanings.

Table 3.1 Escape Sequences

Sequence	Meaning
\a	Alert (ANSI C)
\b	Backspace
\f	Form feed
\n	Newline
\r	Carriage return
\t	Horizontal tab
\v	Vertical tab (ANSI C)
\\	Backslash (\)
\'	Single quote (')
\"	Double quote (") (ANSI C)
\0oo	Octal value (o represents an octal digit)
\xhh	Hexadecimal value (h represents a hexadecimal digit)

Escape sequences must be enclosed in single quotes when assigned to a character variable. For example, we could make the statement:

```
nerf = '\n';
```

and then print the variable `nerf` to advance the printer or screen one line.

Let's take a closer look at what each escape sequence does. The alert character (`\a`), added by ANSI C, produces an audible or visible alert. The nature of the alert depends on the hardware, with the beep being the most common. The ANSI Standard states that the alert character shall not change the "active position." By *active position*, the Standard means the location on the display device (screen, teletype, printer, etc.) at which the next character would otherwise appear. In short, the active position is a generalization of the screen cursor you probably are accustomed to. Using the alert character in a program displayed on a screen should produce a beep without moving the screen cursor. If you have a compiler that supports this new escape sequence, you can use it instead of `'\007'` in the `goldyou.c` program:

```
char beep = '\a';
```

Next, the `\b`, `\f`, `\n`, `\r`, `\t`, and `\v` escape sequences are common output device control characters. They are best described in terms of how they affect the active position. A backspace (`\b`) moves the active position back one space on the current line. A form feed (`\f`) advances the active position to the start of the next page. A newline (`\n`) sets the active position to the beginning of the next. A carriage return (`\r`) moves the active position to the beginning of the current line. A horizontal tab (`\t`) moves the active position to the next horizontal tab stop; typically, these are found at character positions 1, 9, 17, 25, and so on. A vertical tab (`\v`) moves the active position to the next vertical tab position.

These escape characters do not necessarily work with all display devices. For instance, the form feed and vertical tab characters produce odd symbols on a PC screen rather than any cursor movement. But they work as described if sent to a printer instead of to the screen.

The next three escape sequences (`\\`, `\'`, and `\"`) let you use `\`, `'`, and `"` as character constants. (Because these symbols are used to define character constants as part of a `printf()` command, the situation could get confusing if you use them literally.) If you want to print the line

```
Gramps sez, "a \ is a backslash."
```

use

```
printf("Gramps sez, \"a \\ is a backslash.\"\n");
```

The final two forms (`\0oo` and `\xhh`) are special representations of the ASCII code. To represent a character by its octal ASCII code, precede it with a backslash (`\`), and enclose the whole thing in single quotes. We did this in our program `goldyou.c` (Listing 3.1) at the beginning of this chapter:

```
beep = '\007';
```

You can omit the leading zeros, so '\07' or even '\7' will do. This notation causes numbers to be interpreted as octal even if there is no initial 0.

ANSI C and many new implementations accept a hexadecimal form for character constants. In this case, the backslash is followed by an x or X and one to three hexadecimal digits. For example, the Control-P character has an ASCII hex code of 10 (16, in decimal), so it can be expressed as '\x10' or '\X010'. Figure 3.5 shows some representative integer types.

Figure 3.5 *Writing constants with the* int *family*

Int Family Constants			
member	hex	octal	decimal
char	'\X1A'	'\034'	N.A.
short	±0X23	±078	±92
unsigned short	0X23	078	92
long	±0X23L	±078L	±92L

When you use ASCII code, note the difference between numbers and number characters. For example, the *character* "4" is represented by ASCII code value 52. This represents the symbol "4," not the numerical value 4.

At this point you may have two questions. One, why aren't the escape sequences enclosed in single quotes in the last example (printf("Gramps sez, \"a is a backslash.\"\n");)? Two, when should you use the ASCII code, and when should you use the escape sequences? Here are the answers:

1. When a character, be it an escape sequence or not, is part of a string of characters enclosed in double quotes, don't enclose it in single quotes. Notice that none of the other characters in this example (G,r,a,m,p,s, etc.) are marked off by single quotes. A string of characters enclosed in double quotes is called a *character string*. We will explore strings in Chapter 4. Similarly, printf("Hello! \007\n"); will print Hello! and beep. But printf("Hello!7\n"); will print Hello!7. Digits not part of an escape sequence are treated as ordinary characters to be printed.

2. If you have a choice between using one of the special escape sequences, say '\f', or an equivalent ASCII code, say '\014', use the '\f'. First, the representation is more mnemonic. Second, it is

more portable. If you have a system that doesn't use ASCII code, the '\f' will still work.

Printing Characters

The printf() function uses %c to indicate that a character should be printed. Recall that a character is stored as a 1-byte integer value. Thus, if you print the value of a char variable with the usual %d specifier, you get an integer. The %c format specifier tells printf() to convert the integer to the corresponding character. Listing 3.5 shows a char variable both ways.

Listing 3.5 *charcode.c*

```
/* charcode.c -- displays code number for a character */
#include <stdio.h>
main()
{
    char ch;

    printf("Please enter a character.\n");
    scanf("%c", &ch);    /* user inputs character */
    printf("The code for %c is %d.\n", ch, ch);
}
```

Here is a sample run:

```
Please enter a character.
C
The code for C is 67.
```

When you use the program, remember to press the Enter or Return key after typing the character. The scanf() function then fetches the character you typed, and the ampersand (&) causes the character to be assigned to the variable ch. The printf() function then prints the value of ch twice, first as a character (prompted by the %c code) and then as a decimal integer (prompted by the %d code). Note that the printf() specifiers determine how data is *displayed*, not how it is *stored*. See Figure 3.6.

Signed or Unsigned?

Some C implementations make char a signed type. This means a char can hold values typically in the range −128 through +127. Other implementations make char an unsigned type. This provides a range of 0 through 255. Your compiler manual should tell you which type your char is.

Figure 3.6 Data display versus data storage

ANSI C and many newer implementations allow you to use the keywords signed and unsigned with char. Then, regardless of what your default char is, signed char would be signed, and unsigned char would be unsigned.

Types *float* and *double*

The various integer types serve well for most software development projects. However, mathematically oriented programs often make use of *floating-point* numbers. In C, such numbers are called type float. They correspond to the real types of FORTRAN and Pascal. The floating-point approach, as we have already mentioned, allows you to represent a much greater range of numbers, including decimal fractions. Floating-point number representation is similar to *scientific notation*, a system used by scientists to express very large and very small numbers. Let's take a look.

In scientific notation, numbers are represented as decimal numbers times powers of ten. Here are some examples.

Number	Scientific Notation	Exponential Notation
1,000,000,000	$= 1.0 \times 10^9$	$= 1.0e9$
123,000	$= 1.23 \times 10^5$	$= 1.23e5$
322.56	$= 3.2256 \times 10^2$	$= 3.2256e2$
0.000056	$= 5.6 \times 10^{-5}$	$= 5.6e-5$

The first column shows the usual notation, the second column scientific notation, and the third column exponential notation, which is the way scientific notation is usually written for and by computers, with the "e" followed by the power of ten.

Often, systems use 32 bits to store a floating-point number. Eight bits are used to give the exponent its value and sign, and 24 bits are used to represent the nonexponent part. The important points are that this produces a digit precision of six or seven decimals and a range of 10^{-37} to 10^{+38}. This is handy if you like to use numbers such as the mass of the sun (2.0e30 kilograms) or the charge of a proton (1.6e$-$19 coulombs) or the national debt.

Figure 3.7 *Some floating-point numbers*

C also has a `double` (for double precision) floating-point type. Although `double` is not required to be any more precise than `float` (just as `long` is not required to be bigger than `int`), it usually uses twice as many bits, typically 64. Some systems use all 32 additional bits for the nonexponent part. This increases the number of significant figures and reduces roundoff errors. Other systems use some of the bits to accommodate a larger exponent; this increases the range of numbers that can be accommodated.

ANSI C allows for a third floating-point type: `long double`. The intent is to provide for even more precision than `double`. However, ANSI C guarantees only that `long double` is at least as precise as `double`.

Declaring Floating-Point Variables

Floating-point variables are declared and initialized in the same manner as their integer cousins. Here are some examples:

```
float noah, jonah;
double trouble;
float planck = 6.63e-34;
long double gnp;
```

Floating-Point Constants

There are many choices open to you when you write a floating-point constant. The basic form of a floating-point constant is a signed series of digits including a decimal point, followed by an e or E, followed by a signed exponent indicating the power of 10 used. Here are two examples of valid floating-point constants:

$-1.56E+12$

$2.87e-3$

You can leave out positive signs. You can do without a decimal point (2E5) or an exponential part (19.28), but not both simultaneously. You can omit a fractional part (3.E16) or an integer part (.45E−6), but not both (that wouldn't leave much!). Here are some more valid floating-point constants:

3.14159

.2

4e16

.8E−5

100E

Don't use spaces in a floating-point constant:

WRONG   1.56 E+12

By default, the compiler assumes floating-point constants are double precision. Suppose, for example, that some is a float variable, and that you have the statement

```
some = 4.0 * 2.0;
```

Then the 4.0 and 2.0 are stored as double, using (typically) 64 bits for each. The product is calculated using double precision arithmetic, and only then is the answer trimmed to regular float size. This ensures greater precision for your calculations but can slow down a program.

ANSI C lets you override this default by using an f or F suffix to make the compiler treat a floating-point constant as type `float`: examples are 2.3f and 9.11E9F. An `l` or `L` suffix makes it type `long double`; examples are 54.3l and 4.32e4L. Note that `L` is less likely to be mistaken for a 1 than is `l`. If the floating-point number has no suffix, it is type `double`.

Printing Floating-Point Values

The `printf()` function uses the `%f` format specifier to print type `float` and `double` numbers using decimal notation, and it uses `%e` to print them in exponential notation. Listing 3.6 illustrates this.

Listing 3.6 showf_pt.c

```
/* showf_pt.c -- displays float value in two ways */
#include <stdio.h>
main()
{
    float value = 32000.0;

    printf("%f can be written %e\n", value, value);
}
```

This is the output:

```
32000.000000 can be written 3.200000e+004
```

The preceding example illustrates the default output. The next chapter discusses how to control the appearance of this output by setting field widths and the number of places to the right of the decimal.

Those implementations that support the new ANSI C `long double` type use the `%Lf` and `%Le` specifiers to print that type.

Other Types

That finishes our list of fundamental data types (see Figure 3.8). For some of you, the list must seem long. Others of you might be thinking that more types are needed. What about a Boolean type or a string type? C doesn't have them, but it still can deal quite well with logical manipulations and with strings. We will take a first look at strings in Chapter 4.

Floating-Point Overflow and Underflow

What happens if you try to make a `float` variable exceed its limits? For example, suppose you multiply 1.0e38 by 100 (overflow) or divide 1.0e−37 by 1.0e8 (underflow)? The result depends on the system. With Microsoft C on an IBM PC, any number that overflows will cause the program to abort and to print a "runtime error" message; any number that underflows will be replaced by 0. Turbo C, on the other hand, aborts a program for both overflow and underflow. Other systems may not issue warnings or may offer you a choice of responses. If this matter concerns you, check the rules for your system. If you can't find the information, don't be afraid of a little trial and error.

Figure 3.8 *C data types for a typical system*

Derived Types
- *arrays*
- *pointers*
- *strings*
- *structures*
- *unions*

C does have other types derived from the basic types. These types include arrays, pointers, structures, and unions. Although these are subject matter for later chapters, we already have smuggled some pointers into this chapter's examples. (A *pointer* "points to" the location of a variable or other data object. The & prefix we used with the scanf() function creates a pointer telling scanf() where to place information.)

Floating-Point Roundoff Errors

Take a number. Add 1 to it, and subtract the original number. What do you get? You get 1. But a floating-point calculation, such as the following, may give another answer:

```
/* floaterr.c -- demonstrates round-off error */
#include <stdio.h>
main()
{
    float a,b;

    b = 2.0e20 + 1.0;
    a = b - 2.0e20;
    printf("%f \n", a);
}
```

The output is:

```
0.000000              ←VAX 750, UNIX
-13584010575872.000000   ←Turbo C
4008175468544.000000     ←QuickC
```

The reason for these odd results is that the computer doesn't keep track of enough decimal places to do the operation correctly. The number 2.0e20 is 2 followed by 20 zeros, and by adding 1, we are trying to change the 21st digit. To do this correctly, the program would need to be able to store a 21-digit number. But a float number typically is just 6 or 7 digits scaled to bigger or smaller numbers with an exponent. The attempt is doomed. On the other hand, if we used, say, 2.0e4 instead of 2.0e20, we would get the correct answer because we are trying to change the 5th digit, and float numbers are precise enough for that.

Summary: The Basic Data Types

Keywords

The basic data types are set up using eight *keywords*—int, long, short, un-signed, char, float, double, and signed (ANSI C).

Signed Integers

These can have positive or negative values.

> int: the basic integer type for a given system.
>
> long or long int: can hold an integer at least as large as the largest int and possibly larger.
>
> short or short int: the largest short integer is no larger than the largest int and may be smaller. Typically, long will be bigger than short, and int will be the same as one of the two. For example, Turbo C and Microsoft C for the PC provide 16-bit short and int and 32-bit long. It all depends on the system.

Unsigned Integers

These have zero or positive values only. This extends the range of the largest possible positive number. Use the keyword unsigned before the desired type: unsigned int, unsigned long, unsigned short. A lone unsigned is the same as unsigned int.

Characters

These are typographic symbols such as A, &, and +. Typically, only 1 byte of memory is used.

> char: the keyword for this type. Some implementations use a signed char, while others use an unsigned char. ANSI C allows you to use the keywords signed and unsigned to specify which form you want.

Floating Point

These can have positive or negative values.

> float: the basic floating-point type for the system.

double: a (possibly) larger unit for holding floating-point numbers. It may allow more significant figures and perhaps larger exponents than float.

long double: a (possibly) even larger unit for holding floating-point numbers. It may allow more significant figures and perhaps larger exponents than double.

Summary: How to Declare a Simple Variable

1. Choose the type you need.

2. Choose a name for the variable.

3. Use the following format for a declaration statement: *type-specifier variable-name;*. The *type-specifier* is formed from one or more of the type keywords; examples are: int erest; and unsigned short cash;.

4. You may declare more than one variable of the same type by separating the variable names with commas, for example, char ch, init, ans;.

5. You can initialize a variable in a declaration statement: float mass = 6.0E24;.

Type Sizes

Table 3.2 shows type sizes, in bytes, for some common C environments. What is your system like? Try running the program in Listing 3.7 to find out.

Table 3.2 *Type Facts for Representative Systems*

Type	Macintosh (Lightspeed C)	DEC VAX	IBM PC (Microsoft and Turbo C)	ANSI C Minimum
char	1	1	1	1
int	2	4	2	2
short	2	2	2	2
long	4	4	4	4
float	4	4	4	6 digits*
double	10	8	8	10 digits*
Exponent range (double)	−4930 to 4932	−38 to 38	−307 to 308	−37 to 37

*These are decimal digits of precision.

Listing 3.7 *typesize.c*

```
/* typesize.c -- prints out type sizes */
#include <stdio.h>
main()
{
   printf("Type int has a size of %d bytes.\n", sizeof(int));
   printf("Type char has a size of %d bytes.\n", sizeof(char));
   printf("Type long has a size of %d bytes.\n", sizeof(long));
   printf("Type double has a size of %d bytes.\n",
          sizeof(double));
}
```

C has a built-in operator called sizeof that gives sizes in bytes. Our output from this program was:

```
Type int has a size of 2 bytes.
Type char has a size of 1 bytes.
Type long has a size of 4 bytes.
Type double has a size of 8 bytes.
```

This program found the size of only four types, but you can easily modify it to find the size of any other type that interests you.

Incidentally, notice in the last line how the printf() statement is spread over two lines. You can do this as long as the break does not occur in the quoted section or in the middle of a word.

Using Data Types

When you develop a program, note the variables you need and which type they should be. Most likely you can use `int` or possibly `float` for the numbers and `char` for the characters. Declare them at the beginning of the function that uses them. Choose a name for the variable that suggests its meaning. When you initialize a variable, match the constant type to the variable type.

```
int apples = 3;       /* RIGHT */
int oranges = 3.0;    /* WRONG */
```

C is more forgiving about type mismatches than, say, Pascal. Most C compilers will pass the second initialization, but they may complain, particularly if you have activated a higher warning level. It is best not to develop sloppy habits.

Arguments and Pitfalls

The items of information passed to a function, as you may recall, are termed *arguments*. For instance, the function call `printf("Hello, pal.")` has one argument: `"Hello, pal."`. A series of characters in quotes, such as `"Hello, pal."`, is called a *string*. We'll discuss strings in Chapter 4. For now the important point is that one string, even one containing several words and punctuation marks, counts as one argument.

Similarly, the function call `scanf("%d", &weight)` has two arguments: `"%d"` and `&weight`. C uses commas to separate arguments to a function. The `printf()` and `scanf()` functions are unusual in that they aren't limited to a particular number of arguments. For example, we've used calls to `printf()` with one, two, and even three arguments. For a program to work properly, it needs to know how many arguments there are. The `printf()` and `scanf()` functions use the first argument to indicate how many additional arguments are coming. The trick is that each format specification in the initial string indicates an additional argument. For instance, the statement

```
printf("%d cats ate %d cans of tuna\n", cats, cans);
```

has two format specifiers: `%d` and `%d`. This tells the program to expect two more arguments. And, indeed, there are two more: `cats` and `cans`.

Your responsibility as a programmer is to make sure that the number of format specifications matches the number of additional arguments. The new ANSI C function prototyping mechanism checks to see if a function call has the correct number of arguments, but it doesn't work with `printf()` and `scanf()` because they take a variable number of arguments.

What happens if you don't live up to the programmer's burden? Suppose, for example, you write a program like that of Listing 3.8.

Listing 3.8 *badcount.c*

```
/* badcount.c -- incorrect argument counts */
#include <stdio.h>
main()
{
    int f = 4;
    int g = 5;

    printf("%d\n", f, g);  /* too many arguments */
    printf("%d %d\n",f);   /* too few arguments  */
}
```

None of the four compilers we tried raised any objections to this code. Nor were there any complaints when we ran the program. All four versions printed 4 for the first line. For the second line we got 4 5 (twice), 4 130, and 4 936. As you can see, the computer doesn't catch this kind of error during run time. And, because the program may otherwise run correctly, you may not notice the errors, either. But if a program doesn't print the expected number of values or if it prints unexpected values, check to see if you've used the correct number of printf() arguments.

One More Example

Let's run one more printing example, one that makes use of some of C's special escape characters. In particular, the program in Listing 3.9 shows how backspace (\b), tab (\t), and carriage return (\r) work.

Listing 3.9 *escape.c*

```
/* escape.c -- uses escape characters */
#include <stdio.h>
main()
```

```
{
        float salary;

        printf("Enter your desired monthly salary:");   /* 1 */
        printf(" $_____\b\b\b\b\b\b\b");               /* 2 */
        scanf("%f", &salary);
        printf("\n\t$%.2f a month is $%.2f a year.", salary,
                salary * 12.0);                          /* 3 */
        printf("\rGee!\n");                              /* 4 */
}
```

What Happens

Let's walk through this program step by step as it would work under an ANSI C implementation. The first printf() statement (the one we've numbered 1) prints the following:

```
Enter your desired monthly salary:
```

Because there is no \n at the end of the string, the cursor is left positioned after the colon.

The second printf() statement picks up where the first one stops, so after it is finished, the screen looks like this:

```
Enter your desired monthly salary: $_____
```

The space between the colon and the dollar sign is there because the string in the second printf() statement starts with a space. The effect of the seven backspace characters is to move the cursor seven positions to the left. This backs the cursor over the seven underline characters, placing the cursor directly after the dollar sign. Note that backspacing does not erase the characters that are backed over.

At this point, you type your response, say 2000.00. Now the line looks like this:

```
Enter your desired monthly salary: $2000.00
```

The characters you type replace the underline characters. And when you press Enter (or Return) to enter your response, the cursor moves to the beginning of the next line.

The third printf() statement output begins with \n\t. The newline

character moves the cursor to the beginning of the next line. The tab character moves the cursor to the next tab stop on that line, typically to column 9.
Then the rest of the string is printed. So after this statement, the screen
looks like this:

```
Enter your desired monthly salary: $2000.00


        $2000.00 a month is $24000.00 a year.
```

Because the `printf()` statement doesn't use the newline character, the cursor remains just after the final period.

The fourth `printf()` statement begins with \r. This positions the cursor at the beginning of the current line. Then `Gee!` is displayed there, and
the \n moves the cursor to the next line. So the final appearance of the
screen is this:

```
Enter your desired monthly salary: $2000.00

Gee!    $2000.00 a month is $24000.00 a year.
```

A Possible Problem

Some older C implementations do not work as we've just described. The
problem lies in when `printf()` actually sends output to the screen. In general, `printf()` statements send output to an intermediate storage area
called a buffer. Every now and then, the material in the buffer is sent to the
screen. Under ANSI C, the rules for when output is sent from the buffer to
the screen are clear. It is sent when the buffer gets full or when a newline
character is encountered or when there is impending input. (This is called
flushing the buffer.) For instance, the first two `printf()` statements don't fill
the buffer and don't contain a newline, but they are immediately followed by
a `scanf()` statement asking for input. That forces the `printf()` output to
be sent to the screen.

Some older C implementations, however, do not invoke the third
condition (impending input) for flushing the buffer. If you run Listing 3.9
with one of these compilers, the output of the first two `printf()` statements remains in the buffer. If you type a response anyway and then press
Enter, the newline generated by the Enter key flushes the buffer. You have to
type your answer before you see the question! One solution to this awkward
situation is to use a newline at the end of the `printf()` statement preceding
the input. That newline will flush the buffer. The code can be changed to
look like this:

```
printf("Enter your desired monthly salary:\n");
scanf("%f", &salary);
```

This code works whether or not impending input flushes the buffer. However, it also puts the cursor on the next line, preventing you from entering data on the same line as the prompting string. A sample run would look like this:

```
Enter your desired monthly salary:
2000.00
```

To maintain greater portability, we'll follow this model (with the response on the line following the prompt) for the rest of this book. Another solution is to use the fflush() function described in Chapter 12.

Chapter Summary

C has a variety of data types. The basic types fall into two categories: *integer* types and *floating-point* types. The two distinguishing features for integer types are the amount of storage allotted to a type and whether it is signed or unsigned. The smallest integer type is char, which may be either signed or unsigned, depending on the implementation. ANSI C allows you to use signed char and unsigned char to explicitly specify which you want. The other integer types include short, int, and long. C guarantees that each of these types is at least as large as the preceding type. Each of these is a signed type, but with ANSI C you can use the unsigned keyword to create the corresponding unsigned types: unsigned short, unsigned int, and unsigned long. K&R C recognizes only unsigned int from this trio.

The three floating-point types are float, double, and, new with ANSI C, long double. Each is at least as large as the preceding type.

Integers can be expressed in decimal, octal, or hexadecimal form. A leading 0 indicates an octal number, and a leading 0x or 0X indicates a hexadecimal number. For example, 32, 040, and 0x20 are decimal, octal, and hexadecimal representations of the same value, respectively. An l or L suffix indicates a long value.

Character constants are represented by placing the character in single quotes: 'Q', '8', and '$', for example. C escape sequences, such as '\n' represent certain nonprinting characters. You can use the form '\007' to represent a character by its ASCII code.

Floating-point numbers can be written with a fixed decimal point, as in 9393.912, or in exponential notation, as in 7.38E10.

The printf() function lets you print various types of values by using conversion specifiers, which, in their simplest form, consist of a percent sign and a letter indicating the type, as in %d or %f.

Review Questions

1. Which data type would you use for each of the following kinds of data?
   a. The population of Rio Frito.
   b. The average weight of a Rembrandt painting.
   c. The most common letter in this chapter.
   d. The number of times that the letter occurs.

2. Virgila Ann Xenopod has concocted an error-laden program. Help her find the mistakes.

```
#
include <stdio.h>
main
(
  float g; h;
  float tax, rate;

  g = e21;
  tax = rate*g;
)
```

3. Identify the data type (as used in declaration statements) and the `printf()` format specifier for each of the following constants:

Constant	Type	Specifier
a. 012		
b. 2.9e05L		
c. 's'		
d. 100000		
e. '\n'		
f. 20.0f		
g. 0x44		

4. Correct this silly program. (The / in C means division.)

```
main() / this program is perfect /
{
cows, legs integer;

printf("How many cow legs did you count?\n);
scanf("%c", legs);
cows = legs / 4;
printf("That implies there are %f cows.\n", cows)
}
```

Programming Exercises

1. Find out what your system does with integer overflow, floating-point overflow, and floating-point underflow by using the experimental approach; i.e., write programs having these problems.

2. Write a program that asks you to enter an ASCII code value, such as 66, and then prints the character having that ASCII code.

3. Write a program that sounds the alert and then prints the following text:

```
Startled by the sudden sound, Sally shouted, "By the Great
Pumpkin, what was that!"
```

4. Write a program that reads in a floating-point number and prints it first in decimal-point notation and then in exponential notation. Have the output use the following format:

```
The input is 21.290000 or 2.129000e+001.
```

5. There are approximately 3.156×10^7 seconds in a year. Write a program that requests your age in years and then displays the equivalent number of seconds.

6. The mass of a single molecule of water is about 3.0×10^{-23} grams. A quart of water is about 950 grams. Write a program that requests an amount of water, in quarts, and displays the number of water molecules in that amount.

4

Character Strings and Formatted Input/Output

Function
▶ strlen( )

This chapter introduces you to character strings. You see how they are created and stored, and how you can use scanf() and printf() to read and display them. Also, you learn how to use the strlen() function to measure string lengths, and you examine the C preprocessor's #define directive for creating symbolic constants.

In this chapter we'll concentrate on input and output. We'll add personality to our programs by making them interactive and using character strings. We will also take a more detailed look at those two handy C input/output functions, printf() and scanf(). With these two functions, you will have the program tools you need to communicate with users and to format output to meet your needs and tastes. Finally, we'll take a quick look at an important C facility, the C preprocessor, and show you how to define and use symbolic constants.

Introductory Program

By now you probably expect a sample program at the beginning of each chapter, and we won't disappoint you. Listing 4.1 presents a program that engages in a dialogue with the user.

Listing 4.1 *talkback.c*

```
/* talkback.c -- nosy, informative program */
#include <stdio.h>
#define DENSITY 62.4 /* human density in lbs per cu ft */
main()
{
   float weight, volume;
   int size, letters;
   char name[40];

   printf("Hi! What's your first name?\n");
   scanf("%s", name);
```

(continued)

Listing 4.1 *(continued)*

```
    printf("%s, what's your weight in pounds?\n", name);
    scanf("%f", &weight);
    size = sizeof name;
    letters = strlen(name);
    volume = weight/DENSITY;
    printf("Well, %s, your volume is %2.2f cubic feet.\n",
        name, volume);
    printf("Also, your first name has %d letters,\n",
        letters);
    printf("and we have %d bytes to store it in.\n", size);
}
```

Running `talkback` produces results such as the following:

```
Hi! What's your first name?
Angelica
Angelica, what's your weight in pounds?
102.5
Well, Angelica, your volume is 1.64 cubic feet.
Also, your first name has 8 letters,
and we have 40 bytes to store it in.
```

Here are the main new features of this program:

▶ We used an *array* to hold a *character string*. Here, someone's name is read into the array.

▶ We used the `%s` *conversion specification* to handle the input and output of the string. Note that `name`, unlike `weight`, does not use the & prefix when used with `scanf()`. (As you'll see later, both `&weight` and `name` are addresses.)

▶ We used the C preprocessor to define the symbolic constant `DENSITY`.

▶ We used the C function `strlen()` to find the length of a string.

The C approach may seem a little complex compared with the input/output of, say, BASIC. However, this complexity buys a finer control of I/O and a greater program efficiency. And it is surprisingly easy once you get used to it.

Let's investigate these new ideas.

Character Strings—An Introduction

A *character string* is a series of one or more characters. An example of a string is

```
"Zing went the strings of my heart!"
```

The double quotation marks are not part of the string. They inform the compiler that they enclose a string, just as single quotation marks identify a character.

Type *char* Arrays and the Null Character

C has no special variable type for strings. Instead, strings are stored in an array of `char` type. For simplicity, you can think of the characters in a string as being stored in adjacent memory cells, one character per cell (see Figure 4.1).

Figure 4.1 *A string in an array*

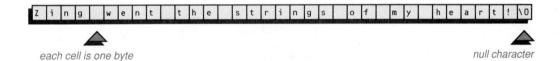

each cell is one byte   null character

Note that Figure 4.1 shows the character \0 in the last array position. This is the *null character*, and C uses it to mark the end of a string. The null character is not the digit zero; it is the nonprinting character whose ASCII code value is 0. Strings in C always are stored with this terminating null character. The presence of the null character means that the array must have at least one more cell than the number of characters to be stored.

Now just what is an array? You can think of an array as several memory cells in a row. Or, if you prefer more formal and exact language, an *array* is an ordered sequence of data elements of one type. In our example, we created an array of 40 memory cells, or elements, each of which can store one `char`-type value. We accomplished this with the declaration

```
char name [40];
```

The brackets after `name` identify it as an array. The 40 within the brackets indicates the number of elements in the array. The `char` identifies the type of each element (see Figure 4.2).

Figure 4.2 *Declaring an array name of type* char

symbolic links

char name [3] "links" together
three char-type data objects

Using a character string is beginning to sound complicated! You have to create an array, place the characters of a string into an array one by one, and remember to add a \0 at the end. Fortunately for us, the computer can take care of most of the details itself.

Using Strings

Try the program in Listing 4.2 to see how easy it really is to use strings.

Listing 4.2 *praise1.c*

```
/* praise1.c -- uses an assortment of strings */
#include <stdio.h>
#define PRAISE "My sakes, that's a grand name!"
main()
{
    char name[40];

    printf("What's your name?\n");
    scanf("%s", name);
    printf("Hello, %s. %s\n", name, PRAISE);
}
```

The %s tells printf() to print a string. The %s appears twice because the program prints two strings: the one stored in the name array and the one represented by PRAISE. Running praise1.c should produce an output similar to this:

```
What's your name?
```

```
Porcilla Tusker
Hello, Porcilla. My sakes, that's a grand name!
```

We did not have to put the null character into the array `name` ourselves. That task was done for us by `scanf()` when it read the input. Nor did we include a null character in the *character string constant* `PRAISE`. We'll explain the `#define` statement soon; for now, simply note that the double quotation marks that enclose the text following `PRAISE` identify the text as a string. The compiler takes care of putting in the null character.

Note (and this is important) that `scanf()` just reads Porcilla Tusker's first name. After `scanf()` starts to read input, it stops reading at the first *whitespace* (blank, tab, or newline) it encounters. Thus, it stops scanning for `name` when it reaches the blank between `Porcilla` and `Tusker`. In general, `scanf()` is used with `%s` to read only a single word, not a whole phrase as a string. C has other input-reading functions, such as `gets()`, for handling general strings. Later chapters will explore string functions more fully.

Strings versus Characters

The string constant `"x"` is not the same as the character constant `'x'`. One difference is that `'x'` is a basic type (`char`), while `"x"` is a derived type, an array of `char`. A second difference is that `"x"` really consists of two characters, `'x'` and `'\0'`, the null character (see Figure 4.3).

Figure 4.3 *The character 'x' and the string "x"*

'x' the character

"x" the string

null character ends string

String Length—*strlen()*

In the last chapter we unleashed the `sizeof` operator, which gives the size of things in bytes. The `strlen()` function gives the length of a string in characters. Since it takes 1 byte to hold 1 character, you might suppose that both would give the same result when applied to a string, but they don't. In Listing 4.3 let's add a few lines to our example and see why.

```
Listing 4.3  praise2.c

/* praise2.c */
#include <stdio.h>
#define PRAISE "My sakes, that's a grand name!"
main()
{
  char name[40];

  printf("What's your name?\n");
  scanf("%s", name);
  printf("Hello, %s. %s\n", name, PRAISE);
  printf("Your name of %d letters occupies %d memory cells.\n",
          strlen(name), sizeof name);
  printf("The phrase of praise has %d letters ",
          strlen(PRAISE));
  printf("and occupies %d memory cells.\n", sizeof PRAISE);
}
```

If you are using an ANSI C compiler, you should add the line

```
#include <string.h>
```

after the other #include line. The `string.h` file contains function prototypes for several string-related functions. Although not necessary for this
particular example, this addition will make the program more harmonious
with the ANSI spirit. We'll discuss this file in Chapter 12. (By the way,
some pre-ANSI UNIX systems use `strings.h` instead of `string.h` to contain declarations for string functions.)

Notice that Listing 4.3 uses two methods to handle long `printf()`
statements. The first method spreads one print statement over two lines.
(You can break a line between arguments but not in the middle of a string,
i.e., between the quotation marks.) The second method uses two `printf()`
statements to print just one line. The newline character (\n) appears only
in the second statement. Running the program could produce this interchange:

```
What's your name?
Tuffy
Hello, Tuffy. My sakes, that's a grand name!
Your name of 5 letters occupies 40 memory cells.
The phrase of praise has 30 letters and occupies 31 memory cells.
```

See what happens. The array `name` has 40 memory cells, and that is what the `sizeof` operator reports to us. But only the first 5 cells are needed to hold `Tuffy`, and that is what `strlen()` reports. The sixth cell in the array `name` contains the null character, and its presence tells `strlen()` when to stop counting. Figure 4.4 illustrates this concept.

Figure 4.4 *The* strlen( ) *function knows when to stop*

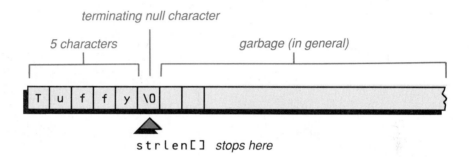

When we get to `PRAISE`, we find that `strlen()` again gives us the exact number of characters (including spaces and punctuation) in the string. The `sizeof` operator gives us a number one larger, for it also counts the invisible null character used to end the string. We didn't tell the computer how much memory to set aside to store the phrase. It had to count the number of characters between the double quotes itself.

One other point: in the preceding chapter we used `sizeof` with parentheses, and in this chapter we don't. Whether or not you use parentheses depends on whether you want the size of a type or the size of a particular quantity. Parentheses are required for types but are optional for particular quantities. That is, you would use `sizeof(char)` or `sizeof(float)`, but `sizeof name` or `sizeof 6.28`.

In the last example, our use of `strlen()` and `sizeof` was not a very important one. We merely wanted to satisfy our curiosity. Actually, however, `strlen()` and `sizeof` are important programming tools. For example, `strlen()` is useful in all sorts of character-string programs, as you'll see in Chapter 11.

Let's move on to the `#define` statement.

Constants and the C Preprocessor

Sometimes you need to use a constant in a program. For example, you could give the circumference of a circle as

```
circ = 3.14 * diameter;
```

Here, the constant 3.14 represents the world-famous constant pi. To use a constant, just type in the actual value, as in the example. However, there are good reasons to use a *symbolic constant* instead. That is, you could use a statement like the following and have the computer substitute in the actual value later:

```
circ = pi * diameter;
```

Why is it better to use a symbolic constant? First, a name tells you more than a number does. Compare these two statements:

```
owed = 0.015 * housevl;
owed = taxrate * housevl;
```

If you read through a long program, the meaning of the second version is plainer.

Second, suppose you have used a constant in several places, and it becomes necessary to change its value. After all, tax rates do change. Then you need merely alter the definition of the symbolic constant, rather than find and change every occurrence of the constant in the program.

Okay, how do you set up a symbolic constant? One way is to declare a variable and set it equal to the desired constant. You could write:

```
float taxrate;
taxrate = 0.015;
```

This way is all right for a small program, but it is somewhat wasteful because the computer has to peek into the `taxrate` memory location every time `taxrate` is used. This is an example of *execution time* substitution because the substitutions take place while the program is running. Fortunately, C has a better idea.

The better idea is the C preprocessor. In Chapter 2 you saw how the preprocessor uses `#include` to include information from another file. The preprocessor also lets you define constants. Just add a line like this at the top of the file containing your program:

```
#define TAXRATE 0.015
```

When your program is compiled, the value 0.015 will be substituted everywhere you have used `TAXRATE`. This is called a *compile time* substitution. By the time you run the program, all the substitutions have already been made (see Figure 4.5). Such defined constants often are termed *manifest constants*.

Figure 4.5 *What you type versus what is compiled*

Note the format. First comes #define. In older implementations, the # sign should be in the left-most column; ANSI C removes this restriction. Next comes the symbolic name (TAXRATE) for the constant and then the value (0.015) for the constant:

```
#define NAME value
```

No semicolon is used, since this is a substitution mechanism, not a C statement. Why is TAXRATE capitalized? It is a sensible C tradition to type constants in uppercase. Then, when you encounter one in the depths of a program, you will know immediately that it is a constant, not a variable. Capitalizing constants is just another technique to make programs more readable. Your programs will still work if you don't capitalize the constants, but capitalizing them is a good habit to cultivate.

The names you use for symbolic constants must satisfy the same rules that the names of variables do. You can use uppercase and lowercase letters, digits, and the underscore character. The first character cannot be a digit. Listing 4.4 provides a simple example.

Listing 4.4 pizza.c

```
/* pizza.c -- uses defined constants in a pizza context */
#include <stdio.h>
#define PI 3.14159
main()
{
   float area, circum, radius;

   printf("What is the radius of your pizza?\n");
   scanf("%f", &radius);
   area = PI * radius * radius;
   circum = 2.0 * PI *radius;
   printf("Your basic pizza parameters are as follows:\n");
   printf("circumference = %1.2f, area = %1.2f\n", circum,
          area);
}
```

The %1.2f in the printf() statement causes the printout to be rounded to two decimal places. Of course, this program may not reflect your major pizza concerns, but it does fill a small niche in the world of pizza programs. Here is a sample run:

```
What is the radius of your pizza?
6.0
Your basic pizza parameters are as follows:
circumference = 37.70, area = 113.10
```

The `#define` statement can be used for character and string constants, too. Just use single quotes for the former and double quotes for the latter. Thus, the following examples are valid:

```
#define BEEP '\007'
#define TEE 'T'
#define ESC '\033'
#define OOPS "Now you have done it!"
```

Remember that everything following the symbolic name is substituted for it. Don't make this common error:

```
/* the following is wrong */
#define TOES = 20
```

If you do this, `TOES` is replaced by `= 20`, not just `20`. In that case, a statement like

```
digits = fingers + TOES;
```

is converted to the following misrepresentation:

```
digits = fingers + = 20;
```

Using *#define* and *#include* Together

Here is a special treat for the lazy. Suppose you develop a whole packet of programs that use the same set of constants. You can do the following:

▶ Collect all your `#define` statements in one file; call it, say, `const.h`.
▶ At the head of each source code file of your program, insert the statement `#include "const.h"`.

Then, when you run the program, the preprocessor will read the file `const.h` and use all the `#define` statements there for your program. Incidentally, the `.h` at the end of the filename is a reminder to you that the file is a *header*, i.e., full of information to be placed at the head of your program. The preprocessor itself doesn't care whether you use a `.h` in the name.

Note that we used `"const.h"`, not `<const.h>`. The difference lies in where the compiler first looks for the `include` file, and it is implementation dependent. On UNIX systems, placing the filename in angle brackets causes the preprocessor to look in specific system directories for the files. Placing the filename in quotes causes the preprocessor to look in the current directory first and then in the system directories. Or you can specify a full pathname, as in `"/usr/tiger/myincludes/bar.h"`, in which case just the indicated directory (`/usr/tiger/myincludes`) is searched. Microsoft C and Turbo C follow similar conventions in the DOS environment. In Microsoft C you set an environmental variable called INCLUDE to the system directory that you use for the standard include files. In Turbo C an environment menu identifies the standard include directory. For both, angle brackets mean to search the standard include directory, and quotes mean to search the current directory first. Incidentally, while UNIX uses the slash (/) in pathnames, the DOS environment uses the backslash (\) for the same purpose.

C—A Master of Disguise: Creating Aliases

The capabilities of #define go beyond the symbolic representation of constants. Consider, for instance, the program in Listing 4.5.

Listing 4.5 alias.c

```
/* alias.c -- users preprocessor */
#include <stdio.h>
#include "alias.h"    /* see text for more on this file */
program
  begin
    whole yours, mine then
    spitout("Give me an integer, please.\n ") then
    takein("%d", &yours) then
    mine = yours times TWO then
    spitout("%d is twice your number!\n ", mine) then
  end
```

Hmm, Listing 4.5 looks vaguely familiar, a little like Pascal, but it doesn't seem to be C. The secret, of course, is in the file alias.h. What's in it? Read on.

```
/* alias.h -- a silly abuse of preprocessing power */
#define program
main()
#define begin    {
#define end      }
#define then     ;
#define takein   scanf
#define spitout  printf
```

```
#define TWO     2
#define times   *
#define whole int
```

This example illustrates how the preprocessor works. Your program is searched for items defined by #define statements, and all finds are then replaced. In our example, all thens are rendered into semicolons at compilation. The resulting program is identical to what you would have received by typing in the usual C terms at the start. (By the way, this example is meant to be an entertaining illustration of how the preprocessor works; it is not intended to be a model to emulate.)

This powerful defining facility also can be used to define a *macro*, which is sort of a poor man's function. We will return to this topic in Chapter 16.

The define feature has limitations. For example, parts of a program within double quotes are immune to substitution. The following combination wouldn't work:

```
#define MN "minimifidianism"
printf("He was a strong believer in MN.\n");
```

The printout would read simply:

```
He was a strong believer in MN.
```

This is because MN is enclosed in double quotes in the printf() statement. However, the statement

```
printf("He was a strong believer in %s.\n", MN);
```

would produce:

```
He was a strong believer in minimifidianism.
```

In this case, the MN was outside the double quotes, so it was replaced by its definition.

The C preprocessor is a useful, helpful tool, so take advantage of it when you can. We'll show you more applications as we move along.

Exploring and Exploiting *printf()* and *scanf()*

The functions printf() and scanf() let you communicate with a program. They are called *input/output* functions, or *I/O* functions for short.

They are not the only I/O functions you can use with C, but they are the most versatile. Historically, these functions, like all other functions in the C library, were *not* part of the definition of C. C originally left the implementation of I/O up to the compiler writers; this made it possible to better match I/O to specific machines. In the interests of compatibility, various implementations all came with versions of scanf() and printf(). However, there were occasional discrepancies between implementations. The ANSI C Standard describes standard versions of these functions, and we'll follow that Standard. The discrepancies should disappear as the Standard is implemented.

Generally, printf() and scanf() work much the same, each using a control string and a list of arguments. We will show how these work, first with printf() and then with scanf().

The *printf( )* Function

The instructions you give printf() when you ask it to print a variable depend on the variable type. For instance, we have used the %d notation when printing an integer and the %c notation when printing a character. These notations are called *conversion specifications* because they specify how the data is to be converted into displayable form. We'll list the conversion specifications that the ANSI C Standard provides for printf(), and then we'll show how to use the more common ones. Table 4.1 presents the conversion specifiers and the type of output they cause to be printed.

Table 4.1 Conversion Specifiers and Resulting Printed Output

Conversion Specification	Output
%c	Single character
%d	Signed decimal integer
%e	Floating-point number, e-notation
%E	Floating-point number, E-notation
%f	Floating-point number, decimal notation
%g	Use %f or %e, whichever is shorter
%G	Use %f or %E, whichever is shorter
%i	Signed decimal integer
%o	Unsigned octal integer
%p	A pointer
%s	Character string

(continued)

Table 4.1 *(continued)*

Conversion Specification	Output
%u	Unsigned decimal integer
%x	Unsigned hexadecimal integer, using hex digits 0–f
%X	Unsigned hexadecimal integer, using hex digits 0–F
%%	Print a percent sign

Note: The conversion specifiers in italic typeface (%E, %G, %i, %p, %X) did not appear in the first edition of Kernighan and Ritchie, and they are not yet commonly found in all implementations.

Using *printf( )*

Listing 4.6 contains a program that uses some of the examples we will discuss.

Listing 4.6 *printout.c*

```
/* printout.c -- uses conversion specifiers */
#include <stdio.h>
#define PI 3.141593
main()
{
   int number = 5;
   float ouzo = 13.5;
   int cost = 3100;

   printf("The %d women drank %f glasses of ouzo.\n",number,
          ouzo);
   printf("The value of pi is %f.\n", PI);
   printf("Farewell! thou art too dear for my possessing,\n");
   printf("%c%d\n", '$', 2 * cost);
}
```

The output, of course, is

```
The 5 women drank 13.500000 glasses of ouzo.
The value of pi is 3.141593.
Farewell! thou art too dear for my possessing,
$6200
```

The format for using printf() is

```
printf(Control-string, item1, item2,...);
```

Item1, *item2*, and so on, are the items to be printed. They can be variables or constants, or even expressions that are evaluated first before the value is printed. *Control-string* is a character string describing how the items are to be printed. As we mentioned in Chapter 3, the control string should contain a conversion specifier for each item to be printed. For example, consider this statement:

```
printf("The %d women drank %f glasses of ouzo.\n", number, ouzo);
```

The *control-string* is the phrase in double quotes. It contains two conversion specifiers corresponding to number and ouzo—the two items to be displayed. Figure 4.6 shows another example of a printf() statement.

Figure 4.6 *Arguments for* printf( )

Here is another line from our example:

```
printf("The value of pi is %f.\n", PI);
```

This time, the list of items has just one member—the symbolic constant PI.

As you can see from Figure 4.7, *control-string* contains two distinct forms of information:

1. Characters that are actually printed.
2. Conversion specifications.

Don't forget to use one conversion specification for each item in the list following *control-string*. Woe unto you should you forget this basic requirement! Don't do this:

```
printf("The score was Squids %d, Slugs %d.\n", score1);
```

Here, there is no value for the second %d. The result of this faux pas will depend on your system, but at best you will get nonsense.

Figure 4.7 *Anatomy of a control string*

literal
characters

literal
characters

conversion specification

If you want to print only a phrase, you don't need any conversion specifications. And if you just want to print data, you can dispense with the running commentary. Thus, each of the following statements from Listing 4.6 is quite acceptable:

```
printf("Farewell! thou art too dear for my possessing,\n");
printf("%c%d\n", '$', 2 * cost);
```

In the second statement, note that the first item on the print list was a character constant rather than a variable and that the second item is a multiplication. This illustrates that printf() uses values, be they variables, constants, or expressions.

Since the printf() function uses the % symbol to identify the conversion specifications, there is a slight problem if you wish to print the % sign itself. If you simply use a lone % sign, the compiler will think you have bungled a conversion specification. The way out is simple. Just use two % symbols:

```
pc = 2*6;
printf("Only %d%% of Sally's gribbles were edible.\n", pc);
```

The following output would result:

```
Only 12% of Sally's gribbles were edible.
```

Conversion Specification Modifiers for *printf()*

You can modify a basic conversion specification by inserting modifiers between the % and the defining conversion character. Tables 4.2 and 4.3 list the characters you can place there legally. If you use more than one modifier, they should be in the same order as they appear in Table 4.2. Not all combinations are possible. The tables reflect the ANSI C Standard; your implementation may not yet support all the options shown here.

Table 4.2 printf( ) *Modifiers*

Modifier	Meaning
flag	The five flags (-, +, *space*, #, and 0) are described in Table 4.3. Zero or more flags may be present. Example: "%-10d"
digit(s)	The minimum field width. A wider field will be used if the printed number or string won't fit in the field. Example: "%4d"
.digit(s)	Precision. For %e, %E, and %f conversions, the number of digits to be printed to the right of the decimal. For %g and %G conversions, the maximum number of significant digits. For %s conversions, the maximum number of characters to be printed. For integer conversions, the minimum number of digits to appear; leading zeros are used if necessary to meet this minimum. Using only . implies a following zero, so %.f is the same as %.0f. Example: "%5.2f" prints a float in a field 5 characters wide with 2 digits after the decimal point.
h	Used with an integer conversion to indicate a short int or unsigned short int value. Examples: "%hu" "%hx" "%6.4hd"
l	Used with an integer conversion to indicate a long int or unsigned long int. Examples: "%ld" "%8lu"
L	Used with a floating-point conversion to indicate a long double value. Examples: "%Lf" "%10.4Le"

Conversion of *float* Arguments

There are conversion specifiers to print floating types double and long double. However, there is no specifier for float. The reason is that, under K&R C, float values were automatically converted to type double before being used in an expression or as an argument. ANSI C, in general, does not automatically convert float to double. But to protect the enormous number of existing programs that assume float arguments are converted to double, all float arguments to printf()—as well as to any other C function—still are automatically converted to double. Thus, under either K&R C or ANSI C, no conversion specifier is needed for type float.

Table 4.3 printf( ) *Flags*

Flag	Meaning
-	The item is left-justified; that is, it is printed beginning at the left of the field. Example: "%-20s"
+	Signed values are displayed with a plus sign if positive and with a minus sign if negative. Example: "%+6.2f"
space	Signed values are displayed with a leading space (but no sign) if positive and with a minus sign if negative. A space overrides a + flag. Example: "% 6.2f"
#	Use an alternative form for the conversion specification. Produces an initial 0 for the %o form and an initial 0x or 0X for the %x and %X forms. For all floating-point forms, # guarantees that a decimal-point character is printed, even if no digits follow. For %g and %G forms, it prevents trailing zeros from being removed. Examples: "%#o" "%#8.0f" "%+#10.3E"
0	For numeric forms, pad the field width with leading zeros instead of with spaces. This flag is ignored if a - flag is present or if, for an integer form, a precision is specified. Examples: "%010d" "%08.3f"

Examples

Let's put these modifiers to work. We'll begin by looking at the effect of the field width modifier on printing an integer. Consider the program in Listing 4.7.

Listing 4.7 *width.c*

```
/* width.c -- field widths */
#include <stdio.h>
#define PAGES 336
main()
{
  printf("/%d/\n", PAGES);
  printf("/%2d/\n", PAGES);
  printf("/%10d/\n", PAGES);
  printf("/%-10d/\n", PAGES);
}
```

Listing 4.7 prints the same quantity four times—but using four different conversion specifications. We used a slash (/) to show you where each field begins and ends. The output looks like this:

```
/336/
/336/
/        336/
/336        /
```

The first conversion specification is %d with no modifiers. It produces a field with the same width as the integer being printed. This is the *default* option; i.e., what's printed if you don't give further instructions. The second conversion specification is %2d. This should produce a field width of 2, but since the integer is 3 digits long, the field is expanded automatically to fit the number. The next conversion specification is %10d. This produces a field 10 spaces wide, and, indeed, there are 7 blanks and 3 digits between the /'s, with the number tucked into the right end of the field. The final specification is %-10d. It also produces a field 10 spaces wide, and the - puts the number at the left end, just as advertised. Once you get used to it, this system is easy to use and gives you nice control over the appearance of your output. Try altering the value for PAGES to see how different numbers of digits are printed.

Now let's look at some floating-point formats. Enter, compile, and run the program in Listing 4.8.

Listing 4.8 *floats.c*

```
/* floats.c -- some floating-point combinations */
#include <stdio.h>
#define RENT 1234.56
main()
{
  printf("/%f/\n", RENT);
  printf("/%e/\n", RENT);
  printf("/%4.2f/\n", RENT);
  printf("/%3.1f/\n", RENT);
  printf("/%10.3f/\n", RENT);
  printf("/%10.3e/\n", RENT);
  printf("/%+4.2f/\n", RENT);
  printf("/%010.2f/\n", RENT);
}
```

This time we get the output:

```
/1234.560000/
/1.234560e+003/
/1234.56/
/1234.6/
/   1234.560/
/1.235e+003/
/+1234.56/
/0001234.56/
```

Again, we begin with the default version, %f. In this case there are two defaults: the field width and the digits to the right of the decimal. The second default is 6 digits, and the field width is whatever it takes to hold the number.

Next is the default for %e. It prints 1 digit to the left of the decimal point and 6 places to the right. We seem to be getting a lot of digits! The cure is to specify the number of decimal places to the right of the decimal, and the next four examples in this segment do that. Notice how the fourth and the sixth examples cause the output to be rounded off.

Finally, the + flag causes the result to be printed with its algebraic sign, which is a plus sign in this case, and the 0 flag produces leading zeros to pad the result to the full field width. Note that in the specifier %010 the first 0 is a flag, while the remaining digits (10) specify the field width.

You can modify the RENT value to see how variously sized values are printed. Listing 4.9 demonstrates a few more combinations.

Listing 4.9 *flags.c*

```
/* flags.c -- illustrates some formatting flags */
#include <stdio.h>
main()
{
  printf("%x %X %#x\n", 31, 31, 31);
  printf("**%d**% d**% d**\n", 42, 42, -42);
  printf("**%5d**%5.3d**%05d**%05.3d**\n", 6, 6, 6, 6);
}
```

On a system that conforms to the ANSI C Standard, the output looks like this:

```
**42** 42**-42**
**    6** 006**00006**  006*
```

First, 1f is the hex equivalent of 31. The x specifier yields a 1f, while the X specifier yields 1F. Using the # flag provides an initial 0x.

The second line illustrates how using a space in the specifier produces a leading space for positive values but not for negative values. This can produce pleasing output because positive and negative values with the same number of significant digits are printed with the same field widths.

The third line illustrates how using a precision specifier (%5.3d) with an integer form produces enough leading zeros to pad the number to the minimum value of digits. Using the 0 flag, however, pads the number with enough leading zeros to fill the whole field width. Finally, if you provide both the 0 flag and the precision specifier, the 0 flag is ignored.

Now let's examine some of the string options. Consider the example in Listing 4.10.

Listing 4.10 *strings.c*

```
/* strings.c -- string formatting */
#include <stdio.h>
#define BLURB "Outstanding acting!"
main()
{
    printf("/%2s/\n", BLURB);
    printf("/%22s/\n", BLURB);
    printf("/%22.5s/\n", BLURB);
    printf("/%-22.5s/\n", BLURB);
}
```

Here is the output:

```
/Outstanding acting!/
/   Outstanding acting!/
/                Outst/
/Outst                /
```

Notice how the field is expanded to contain all the specified characters. Also notice how the precision specification limits the number of characters printed. The `.5` in the format specifier tells `printf()` to print just 5 characters. Again, the `-` modifier left-justifies the text.

Applying Your Knowledge

Okay, you've seen some examples. Now how would you set up a statement to print something having the following form?

```
The NAME family just may be $XXX.XX dollars richer!
```

Here, `NAME` and `XXX.XX` represent values that will be supplied by variables in the program, say, `name[40]` and `cash`.

Here is one solution:

```
printf("The %s family just may be $%.2f richer!\n",name,cash);
```

The Meaning of Conversion

Let's take a closer look at what a conversion specification converts. It converts a value stored in the computer in some binary format to a series of characters (a string) to be displayed. For example, the number 76 may be stored internally as binary 01001100. The `%d` conversion specifier converts this to the characters 7 and 6, displaying 76. The `%x` conversion converts the same value (01001100) to the hexadecimal representation 4c. And the `%c` converts the same value to the character representation L.

The term *conversion* probably is somewhat misleading, since it wrongly suggests the original value is replaced with a converted value. Conversion specifications really are translation specifications; `%d` means translate the given value to a decimal integer text representation and print the representation.

Mismatched Conversions

Naturally, you should match the conversion specification to the type of value being printed. Often, you have choices. For instance, if you want to print a type `int` value, you can use `%d` or `%x` or `%o`. All these specifiers assume that you are printing a type `int` value; they merely provide different representations of the value. Similarly, you can use `%f`, `%e`, or `%g` to represent a type `double` value.

But what if you mismatch the conversion specification to the type? Listing 4.11 shows some examples of mismatches within the integer family.

```
Listing 4.11   intconv.c

/* intconv.c -- some mismatched integer conversions */
#include <stdio.h>
#define PAGES 336
#define WORDS 65616
main()
{
    int num = PAGES;
    int. mnum = -PAGES;

    printf("%d %u %d %u\n", num, num, mnum, mnum);
    printf("%d %c\n", num, num);
    printf("%ld %d\n", WORDS, WORDS);
}
```

Our system produces the following results:

```
336 336 -336 65200
336 P
65616 80
```

Looking at the first line, we see that both %d and %u produce 336 as output; no problem there. But the %u (unsigned) version came out as 65200, not as the 336 you might have expected. This results from the way that signed integers are represented on our reference system. First, they are 2 bytes in size. Second, the system uses a method called the *two's complement* to represent signed integers. In this method, the numbers 0 to 32767 represent themselves, and the numbers 32768 to 65535 represent negative numbers, with 65535 being −1, 65534 being −2, etc. Thus, −366 is represented by 65536 − 336, or 65200. So 65200 represents −336 when interpreted as a signed int and represents 65200 when interpreted as an unsigned int. Be wary! One number can be interpreted as two different values. Not all systems use this method to represent negative integers. Nonetheless, there is a moral: don't expect a %u conversion simply to strip the sign from a number.

The second line shows what happens if you try to convert a value greater than 255 to a character. On our system, an int is 2 bytes and a char is 1 byte. When printf() prints 336 using %c, it looks at only 1 byte out of the 2 used to hold 336. This truncation (see Figure 4.8) amounts to dividing the integer by 256 and keeping just the remainder. In this case, the remainder is 80, which is the ASCII value for the character P. More technically, we can say that the number is interpreted *modulo 256*, which means using the remainder when the number is divided by 256.

Figure 4.8. *Reading 336 as a character*

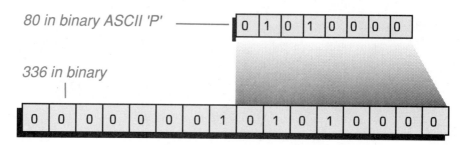

Finally, we tried printing an integer (65616) larger than the maximum int (32767) allowed on our system. Again, the computer does its modulo thing. The number 65616, because of its size, is stored as a 4-byte long value on our system. When we print it using the %d specification, printf() uses only the last 2 bytes. This corresponds to using the remainder after dividing by 65536. In this case, the remainder is 80. A remainder between 32767 and 65536 would be printed as a negative number because of the way negative numbers are stored. Systems with different integer sizes would have the same general behavior, but with different numerical values.

When you start mixing integer and floating types, the results are more bizarre. Consider, for example, Listing 4.12.

Listing 4.12 *floatcnv.c*

```
/* floatcnv.c -- mismatched floating-point conversions */
#include <stdio.h>
main()
{
    float n1 = 3.0;
    double n2 = 3.0;
    long n3 = 2000000000;
    long n4 = 1234567890;
```

(continued)

Listing 4.12   *(continued)*

```
    printf("%.1e %.1e %.1e %.1e\n", n1, n2, n3, n4);
    printf("%ld %ld\n", n3, n4);
    printf("%ld %ld %ld %ld\n", n1, n2, n3, n4);
}
```

On our system, Listing 4.12 produces the following output:

```
3.0e+000 3.0e+000 3.1e+046 3.1e+046
2000000000 1234567890
0 1074266112 0 1074266112
```

The first line of output shows that using a %e specifier does not convert an integer to a floating-point number. Consider, for example, what happens when we try to print n3 (type int) using the %e specifier. First, the %e specifier causes printf() to expect a type double value, which is an 8-byte value on our system. So when printf() looks at n3, which is a 4-byte value on our system, it also looks at the adjacent 4 bytes. Thus, it looks at an 8-byte unit in which the actual n3 is embedded. Second, it interprets the bits in this unit as a floating-point number. Some bits, for example, would be interpreted as an exponent. Thus, even if n3 had the correct number of bits, they would be interpreted differently under %e than under %ld. The net result is nonsense.

The first line also illustrates what we mentioned earlier: that float is converted to double when used as arguments to printf(). On our system, float is 4 bytes, but n1 was expanded to 8 bytes so that printf() would display it correctly.

The second line of output shows that printf() can print n3 and n4 correctly if the correct specifier is used.

The third line of output shows that even the correct specifier can produce phoney results if the printf() statement has mismatches elsewhere. As you might expect, trying to print a floating-point value with a %ld specifier fails. But here, trying to print a type long using %ld fails! The problem lies in how C passes information to a function. The exact details of this failure are implementation dependent, but the next box discusses a representative system.

The Return Value of *printf( )*

As we mentioned in Chapter 3, a C function generally has a *return value*. This is a value that the function computes and returns to the calling program. For example, the C library contains a sqrt() function that takes a

Passing Arguments

The mechanics of argument passing depend on the implementation. This is how argument passing works on our system. The function call looks like this:

```
printf("%ld %ld %ld %ld\n", n1, n2, n3, n4);
```

This call tells the computer to hand over the values of the variables n1, n2, n3, and n4 to the computer. It does so by placing them in an area of memory called the *stack*. When the computer puts these values on the stack, it is guided by the types of the variables, not by the conversion specifiers. So, for n1, it places 8 bytes on the stack (float is converted to double). Similarly, it places 8 more bytes for n2, followed by 4 bytes each for n3 and n4. Then control shifts to the printf() function. This function reads the values off the stack. But when it does so, it reads them according to the conversion specifiers. The %ld specifier indicates that printf() should read 4 bytes. So printf() reads the first 4 bytes in the stack as its first value; this is just the first half of n1, and it is interpreted as a long integer. The next %ld specifier reads 4 more bytes; this is just the second half of n1 and is interpreted as a second long integer (see Figure 4.9). Similarly, the third and fourth instances of %ld cause the first and second halves of n2 to be read and to be interpreted as two more long integers. So although we have the correct specifiers for n3 and n4, printf() is reading the wrong bytes.

number as an argument and returns its square root. The return value can be assigned to a variable, can be used in a computation, can be passed as an argument—in short, it can be used like any other value. The printf() function also has a return value: under ANSI C, it returns the number of characters it printed. If there is an output error, printf() returns a negative value. (Some pre-ANSI versions of printf() have different return values.)

The return value for printf() is incidental to its main purpose of printing output, and it usually isn't used. One reason you might use the return value is to check for output errors. This is more commonly done when writing to a file rather than to a screen. If a full floppy disk prevented writing from taking place, you could then have the program take some appropriate action, such as beeping the terminal for 30 seconds. But you have to know about the if statement before doing that sort of thing. So let's look at a simple example, shown in Listing 4.13, that shows how you can determine the return value.

Figure 4.9 *Passing arguments*

`printf("%ld %ld %ld %ld\n", n1, n2, n3, n4);`

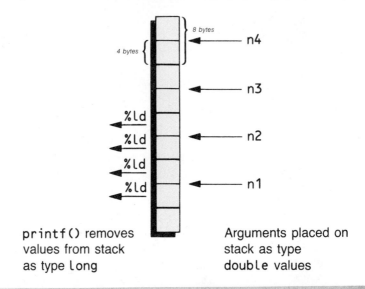

printf() removes values from stack as type long

Arguments placed on stack as type double values

Listing 4.13 *prntval.c*

```
/* prntval.c -- finding printf()'s return value */
#include <stdio.h>
main()
{
    int n = 212;
    int rv;

    rv = printf("%d F is water's boiling point.\n", n);
    printf("The printf() function printed %d characters.\n",
           rv);
}
```

The output is as follows:

```
212 F is water's boiling point.
The printf() function printed 32 characters.
```

First, we used the form `rv = printf(...);` to assign the return value to `rv`. This statement thus performs two tasks: printing information and assigning a value to a variable. Second, note that the count includes all the printed characters, including the spaces and the unseen newline character.

Printing Long Strings

Occasionally, `printf()` statements are too long to put on one line. Because C ignores whitespace (spaces, tabs, newlines) except when used to separate elements, you can spread a statement over several lines, as long as you put your line breaks between elements. For instance, in Listing 4.13, we used two lines for a statement:

```
printf("The printf() function printed %d characters.\n",
        rv);
```

We broke the line between the comma element and `rv`. To show that the line was being continued, we indented the `rv`. C ignores the extra spaces.

However, you cannot break a quoted *string* in the middle. Suppose you try something like this:

```
printf("The printf() function printed %d
        characters.\n", rv);
```

C will complain that you have an illegal character in a string constant. You can use \n in a string to symbolize the newline character, but you can't have the actual newline character generated by the Enter (or Return) key in a string.

If you do have to split a string, you have three choices, as shown in Listing 4.14.

Listing 4.14 *longstrg.c*

```
/* longstrg.c -- printing long strings */
#include <stdio.h>
main()
{
   printf("Here's one way to print a ");
   printf("long string.\n");
   printf("Here's another way to print a \
```

(continued)

Listing 4.14 *(continued)*

```
long string.\n");
    printf("Here's the newest way to print a "
            "long string.\n");        /* ANSI C */
}
```

Here is the output:

```
Here's one way to print a long string.
Here's another way to print a long string.
Here's the newest way to print a long string.
```

Method 1 is to use more than one printf() statement. Since the first string printed doesn't end with a \n character, the second string continues where the first ends.

Method 2 is to terminate the end of the first line with a backslash-return combination. This causes the text on the screen to start a new line but without including a newline character in the string. The effect is to continue the string over to the next line. However, the next line has to start at the far left, as shown. If we indent that line, say, five spaces, then those five spaces become part of the string.

Method 3, new with ANSI C, is *string concatenation*. If you follow one quoted string constant with another, separated only by whitespace, C will treat the combination as a single string. So the following three forms are equivalent:

```
printf("Hello, young lovers, wherever you are.");
printf("Hello, young "    "lovers" ", wherever you are.");
printf("Hello, young lovers"
        ", wherever you are.");
```

With all these methods, you should include any required spaces in the strings: "Jim" "Smith" becomes "JimSmith", but the combination "Jim ""Smith" is "Jim Smith".

Using *scanf( )*

Now let's go from output to input and examine the scanf() function. The C library contains several input functions, and scanf() is the most general of them, for it can read a variety of formats. Of course, input from the keyboard is text because the keys generate text characters: letters, digits, and punctuation. When you desire to enter, say, the integer 2002, you type the characters 2 0 0 and 2. If you want to store that as a numerical value rather than as a string, your program has to convert the string character-by-character to a numerical value. And that is what scanf() does! It converts string input into various forms: integers, floating-point numbers, characters, and C strings. It is the inverse of printf(), which converts integers, floating-point numbers, characters, and C strings to text that is to be displayed on the screen.

Like printf(), scanf() uses a control string followed by a list of arguments. The control string indicates into which formats the input is to be converted. The chief difference is in the argument list. Printf() uses variable names, constants, and expressions. Scanf() uses pointers to variables. Fortunately, you don't have to know anything about pointers to use the function. Just remember these two simple rules:

1. If you use scanf() to read a value for one of the basic variable types we've discussed, precede the variable name with an &.

2. If you use scanf() to read a string into a character array, don't use an &.

Listing 14.15 presents a short program illustrating these rules.

Listing 4.15 *input.c*

```
/* input.c -- when to use & */
#include <stdio.h>
main()
{
    int age;              /* variable */
    float assets;         /* variable */
    char pet[30];         /* string   */

    printf("Enter your age, assets, and favorite pet.\n");
    scanf("%d %f", &age, &assets); /* use the & here      */
    scanf("%s", pet);              /* no & for char array */
    printf("%d $%.0f %s\n ", age, assets, pet);
}
```

And here is a sample exchange:

```
Enter your age, assets, and favorite pet.
82
8345245.19 rhino
82 $8345245 rhino
```

The scanf() function uses whitespace (newlines, tabs, and spaces) to decide how to divide the input into separate fields. It matches up consecutive conversion specifications to consecutive fields, skipping over the whitespace in-between. Note how we spread the input over two lines. We could just as well have used one or five lines, as long as we had at least one newline, space, or tab between each entry. The only exception to this is the %c specification, which reads the very next character, even if that character is whitespace. We'll return to this topic in a moment.

The scanf() function uses pretty much the same set of conversion-specification characters as printf() does. Table 4.4 lists the main conversion specifiers as described in ANSI C.

Table 4.4 *ANSI C Conversion Specifiers for* scanf( )

Conversion Specifier	Meaning
%c	Interpret input as a character.
%d	Interpret input as a signed decimal integer.
%e, %f, %g	Interpret input as a floating-point number.
%E, %G	Interpret input as a floating-point number.
%i	Interpret input as a signed decimal integer.
%o	Interpret input as a signed octal integer.
%p	Interpret input as a pointer.
%s	Interpret input as a string; input begins with the first nonwhitespace character and includes everything up to the next whitespace character.
%u	Interpret input as an unsigned decimal integer.
%x, %X	Interpret input as a signed hexadecimal integer.

You also can use modifiers in the conversion specifiers shown in Table 4.4. The modifiers go between the percent sign and the conversion letter. If you use more than one in a specifier, they should appear in the same order as shown in Table 4.5.

As you can see, using conversion specifiers can be involved, and there are features that we have omitted. These omitted features primarily facili-

Table 4.5 *Conversion Modifiers for* scanf( )

Modifier	Meaning
*	Suppress assignment (see text). Example: "%*d"
digit(s)	Maximum field width; input stops when the maximum field width is reached or when the first whitespace character is encountered, whichever comes first. Example: "%10s"
h, l, or L	"%hd" and "%hi" indicate that the value will be stored in a short int. "%ho", "%hx", and "%hu" indicate that the value will be stored in an unsigned short int. "%ld" and "%li" indicate that the value will be stored in a long. "%lo", "%lx", and "%lu" indicate that the value will be stored in unsigned long. "%le", "%lf", and "%lg" indicate that the value will be stored in type double. Using L instead of l with e, f, and g indicates that the value will be stored in type long double. In the absence of these modifiers, d, i, o, and x indicate type int, and e, f, and g indicate type float.

tate reading selected data from highly formatted sources, such as punched cards or other data records. Since we will be using scanf() primarily as a convenient means for feeding data to a program interactively, we won't discuss such unneeded features.

The *scanf( )* View of Input

Let's look in more detail at how scanf() reads input. Suppose you use a %d specifier to read an integer. Scanf() begins reading input a character at a time. As we mentioned, it skips over whitespace characters (spaces, tabs, and newlines) until it finds a nonwhitespace character. Because it is attempting to read an integer, scanf() expects to find a digit character or, perhaps, a sign (+ or -). If it finds a digit or a sign, it saves the sign and then reads the next character. If that is a digit, it saves the digit and reads the next character. Scanf() continues reading and saving characters until it encounters a nondigit. It then concludes that it has reached the end of the integer. Scanf() places the nondigit back in the input. This means that the next time the program goes to read input, it will start at the previously rejected, nondigit character. Finally, scanf() computes the numerical value corresponding to the digits it read and places that value in the specified variable.

If you use a field width, scanf() halts at the field end or at the first whitespace, whichever comes first.

What if the first nonwhitespace character is, say, an A instead of a digit? Then scanf() stops right there and places the A (or whatever) back in the input. No value is assigned to the specified variable, and the next time the program reads input, it will start at the A again. And if your program has only %d specifiers, scanf() will never get past that A. Also, if you use a scanf() statement with several specifiers, ANSI C requires the function to stop reading input at the first failure.

Reading input using the other numeric specifiers works much the same as the %d case. The main difference is that scanf() may recognize more characters as being part of the number. For instance, the %x specifier requires that scanf() recognize the hexadecimal digits *a-f* and *A-F*. Floating-point specifiers require scanf() to recognize decimal points and E-notation.

If you use a %s specifier, any character other than whitespace is acceptable. So scanf() skips whitespace to the first nonwhitespace character and then saves up nonwhitespace characters until hitting whitespace again. This means that %s results in scanf() reading a single word, that is, a string with no whitespace in it. If you use a field width, scanf() stops at the end of the field or at the first whitespace. You can't use the field width to make scanf() read more than one word for one %s specifier. A final point: when scanf() places the string in the designated array, it adds the terminating '\0' to make the array contents a C string.

If you use a %c specifier, all input characters are fair game. If the next input character is a space or a newline, then a space or a newline is assigned to the indicated variable; whitespace is not skipped. One subtle point: if %c is preceded by a space in the format string, scanf() does skip to the first nonwhitespace character. Thus, the command scanf("%c", &ch) reads the first character encountered in input, while scanf(" %c", &ch) reads the first nonwhitespace character encountered.

Actually, scanf() is not the most commonly used input function in C. It is featured here because of its versatility (it can read all the different data types), but C has several other input functions, such as getchar() and gets() that are better suited for specific tasks, such as reading single characters or reading strings containing spaces. We will cover some of these functions in Chapters 7, 11, and 12. In the meantime, if you need an integer or decimal fraction or a string, you can use scanf().

The *scanf( )* Return Value

The scanf() function returns the number of *items* that it successfully read. If it reads no items, which will happen if you type in a nonnumeric string when it expects a number, scanf() returns the value 0. And it returns EOF when it detects the condition known as *end of file*. (EOF is a special value defined in the stdio.h file. Typically, a #define directive gives EOF the value −1.) We'll discuss end of file in Chapter 6 and make use of scanf()'s return value later in the book.

The * Modifier with *printf( )* and *scanf( )*

Both printf() and scanf() can use the * modifier to modify the meaning of a specifier, but they do so in dissimilar fashions. First, let's see what the * modifier can do for printf().

Suppose that you don't want to commit yourself to a field width in advance but that you want the program to specify it. You can do this by using * instead of a number for the field width. But you also have to use an argument to tell what the field width should be. That is, if you have the conversion specifier %*d, the argument list should include a value for * and a value for d. The technique also can be used with floating-point values to specify the precision as well as the field width. Listing 14.6 is a short example showing how this works.

Listing 14.6 *varwid.c*

```
/* varwid.c -- uses variable-width output field */
#include <stdio.h>
main()
{
   unsigned width, precision;
   int number = 256;
   double weight = 242.5;

   printf("What field width?\n");
   scanf("%d", &width);
   printf("The number is :%*d:\n", width, number);
   printf("Now enter a width and a precision:\n");
   scanf("%d %d", &width, &precision);
   printf("Weight = %*.*f\n", width, precision, weight);
}
```

The variable width provides the field width, and number is the number to be printed. Because the * precedes the d in the specifier, width comes before number in printf()'s argument list. Similarly, width and precision provide the formatting information for printing weight. Here is a sample run:

```
What field width?
6
The number is :    256:
Now enter a width and a precision:
8 3
Weight = 242.500
```

We replied to the first question with 6, so 6 was the field width used. Similarly, our second reply produced a width of 8 with 3 digits to the right of the decimal. More generally, a program could decide on values for these variables after looking at the value of weight.

The * serves quite a different purpose for scanf(). When placed between the % and the specifier letter, it causes that function to skip over corresponding input. Listing 4.17 provides an example.

Listing 4.17 *skip2.c*

```
/* skip2.c -- skips over first two integers of input */
#include <stdio.h>
main()
{
   int n;

   printf("Please enter three integers:\n");
   scanf("%*d %*d %d", &n);
   printf("The last integer was %d\n", n);
}
```

The scanf() instruction in Listing 4.17 says, "Skip two integers and copy the third into n." Here is a sample run:

```
Please enter three integers:
445 345 1212
The last integer was 1212
```

This skipping facility is useful, for example, if a program needs to read a particular column of a file that has data arranged in uniform columns.

Usage Tips

Specifying fixed field widths is useful when you want to print columns of data. Since the default field width is just the width of the number, the repeated use of, say,

```
printf("%d %d %d\n", val1, val2, val3);
```

would produce ragged columns if the numbers in a column had different sizes. For example, the output could look like this:

```
12 234 1222
4 5 23
22334 2322 10001
```

(This assumes that the value of the variables has been changed between print statements.)

The output can be cleaned up by using a sufficiently large fixed field width. For example, using

```
printf("%9d %9d %9d\n", val1, val2, val3);
```

would yield:

```
       12       234      1222
        4         5        23
    22334      2322     10001
```

Leaving a blank between one conversion specification and the next ensures that one number will never run into the next, even if it overflows its own field. This is so because the regular characters in the control string, including spaces, are printed.

On the other hand, if a number is to be embedded in a phrase, it often is convenient to specify a field as small or smaller than the expected number width. This makes the number fit in without unnecessary blanks. For example,

```
printf("Count Beppo ran %.2f miles in 3 hours.\n", distance);
```

might produce:

```
Count Beppo ran 10.22 miles in 3 hours.
```

But, changing the conversion specification to %10.2f would give:

```
Count Beppo ran      10.22 miles in 3 hours.
```

Chapter Summary

A *string* is a series of characters treated as a unit. In C, strings are represented by a series of characters terminated by the *null character*, which is the character whose ASCII code is 0. Strings can be stored in character arrays. An *array* is a series of items, or elements, all of the same type. To declare an array called `name` and having 30 elements of type `char`, do this:

```
char name[30];
```

Be sure to allot a number of elements sufficient to hold the entire string, including the null character.

String constants are represented by enclosing the string in double quotes: `"This is an example of a string."`

The `strlen()` function can be used to find the length of a string (not counting the terminating null character). The `scanf()` function, when used with the `%s` specifier, can be used to read in single-word strings.

The C preprocessor searches a source code program for *preprocessor directives*, which begin with the # symbol, and acts upon them before the program is compiled. The `#include` directive causes the processor to add the contents of another file to your file at the location of the directive. The `#define` directive lets you establish *manifest constants*, that is, symbolic representations for constants.

The `printf()` and `scanf()` functions provide versatile support for input and output. Each uses a control string containing embedded *conversion specifiers*, which indicate the number and type of data items to be read or printed. Also, you can use the conversion specifiers to control the appearance of the output: field widths, decimal places, and placement within a field.

Review Questions

1. Run Listing 4.1 again, but this time give your first and last name when it asks you for your first name. What happens? Why?

2. Assuming that each of the following examples is part of a complete program, what will each one print?

    a. `printf("He sold the painting for $%2.2f.\n", 2.345e2);`

    b. `printf("%c%c%c\n", 'H', 105, '\41');`

    c. `#define Q "His Hamlet was funny without being vulgar."`
       `printf("%s\nhas %d characters.\n", Q, strlen(Q));`

    d. `printf("Is %2.2e the same as %2.2f?\n", 1201.0, 1201.0);`

3. Suppose a program starts like this:

```
#define BOOK "War and Peace"
main()
{
float cost =12.99;
float percent = 80.0;
```

Construct a `printf()` statement that uses `BOOK` and `cost` to print the following:

```
This copy of "War and Peace" sells for $12.99.
That is 80% of list.
```

4. Which conversion specification would you use to print each of the following?

   a. An `unsigned long` integer in a field width of 15.

   b. A hexadecimal integer in the form 0x8a in a field width of 4.

   c. A floating-point number in the form 2.33E+002 that is left-justified in a field width of 12.

   d. A floating-point number in the form +232.346 in a field width of 10.

   e. The first 8 characters of a string in a field 8 characters wide.

5. For each of the following input lines, provide a `scanf()` statement to read it. Also declare any variables or arrays used in the statement.

   a. `101`

   b. `22.3    28.34E-09`

   c. `Chelsea`

   d. `catch 22`

   e. `catch 22` (but skip over `catch`)

6. Suppose that you would rather use parentheses than braces in your programs. How well would the following work?

```
#define ( {
#define ) }
```

Programming Exercises

1. Write a program that asks for your first name and then your last name, and then prints the names in the format last, first.

2. Write a program that requests your first name and does the following with it:

a. Prints it enclosed in double quotation marks.

b. Prints it in a field 20 characters wide, with the whole field in quotes.

c. Prints it at the left end of a field 20 characters wide, with the whole field enclosed in quotes.

d. Prints it in a field 3 characters wider than the name.

3. Write a program that reads in a floating-point number and prints it first in decimal-point notation and then in exponential notation. Have the output use the following formats:

a. The input is 21.3 or 2.1e+001.

b. The input is +21.290 or 2.129E+001.

4. Write a program that requests your height in inches and your name, and then displays the information in the following form:

```
Dabney, you are 6.208 feet tall.
```

Use type `float`, and use / for division.

5. Write a program that requests the user's first name and then the user's last name. Have it print the entered names on one line and the number of letters in each name on the following line. Align each letter count with the end of the corresponding name, as in the following:

```
Melissa Honeybee
      7        8
```

Next have it print the same information, but with the counts aligned with the beginning of each name:

```
Melissa Honeybee
7       8
```

5

Operators,
Expressions,
and Statements

Keyword
► while

Operators
► + − * /
► % ++ −− *(type)*

This chapter introduces you to C's multitudinous operators, including those used for common arithmetic operations. You learn about operator precedence and the meanings of the terms statement and expression. Then you encounter the handy while loop. Compound statements, automatic type conversions, and type casts are next. Finally, you see how to write functions that use arguments.

N ow that you've looked at ways to represent data, let's explore ways to process data. C provides a wealth of operations for that purpose. You can do arithmetic, compare values, modify variables, combine relationships logically, and more. We'll start with basic arithmetic: addition, subtraction, multiplication, and division.

Another aspect of processing data is organizing your programs so that they take the right steps in the right order. C provides several language features to help you with that task. One of these features is the loop, and in this chapter we'll take a first look at it. A loop lets you repeat actions and makes your programs more interesting and powerful.

Introducing Loops

Listing 5.1 shows a sample program that does a little arithmetic to calculate the length in inches of a foot that wears a size 9 (men's) shoe. This first version doesn't use loops.

Listing 5.1 *shoes1.c*

```
/* shoes1.c --converts a shoe size to inches */
#include <stdio.h>
#define OFFSET 7.64
#define SCALE 0.325
main()
{
   float shoe, foot;

   shoe = 9.0;
```

(continued)

Listing 5.1 *(continued)*

```
    foot = SCALE * shoe + OFFSET;
    printf("Shoe size (men's)    foot length\n");
    printf("%10.1f %15.2f inches\n", shoe, foot);
}
```

Here is a program with multiplication and addition. It takes your shoe size (if you wear a size 9) and tells you how long your foot is in inches. But you say you could solve this problem by hand more quickly than you could type the program? That's a good point. A one-shot program that does just one shoe size is a waste of time and effort. We could make the program more useful by writing it as an interactive program, but that still barely taps the potential of a computer.

What we need is some way to have a computer do repetitive calculations for a succession of shoe sizes. After all, that's one of the main reasons for using a computer to do arithmetic. C offers several methods to accomplish repetitive calculations, and we will outline one here. This method, called a *while loop*, will enable us to make a more interesting exploration of operators. Listing 5.2 presents our improved shoe-sizing program.

Listing 5.2 *shoe2.c*

```
/* shoe2.c -- calculates foot lengths for several sizes */
#include <stdio.h>
#define OFFSET 7.64
#define SCALE 0.325
main()
{
    float shoe, foot;

    printf("Shoe size (men's)    foot length\n");
    shoe = 3.0;
    while (shoe < 18.5)      /* starting the while loop */
    {                              /* start of block          */
        foot = SCALE*shoe + OFFSET;
        printf("%10.1f %15.2f inches\n", shoe, foot);
```

```
        shoe = shoe + 1.0;
    }                          /* end of block         */
    printf("If the shoe fits, wear it.\n");
}
```

Here is a condensed version of shoe2.c's output:

```
Shoe size (men's)    foot length
        3.0            8.61 inches
        4.0            8.94 inches
         .               .
         .               .
         .               .
       17.0           13.16 inches
       18.0           13.49 inches
If the shoe fits, wear it.
```

(Incidentally, the constants for this conversion were obtained during an incognito visit to a shoe store. The only shoe-sizer left lying around was for men's sizes. Those of you interested in women's sizes will have to make your own visit to a shoe store.)

Here is how the while loop works. When the program first reaches the while statement, it checks to see whether the condition within parentheses is true. In this case the expression is

```
shoe < 18.5
```

where the < symbol means "is less than." The variable shoe was initialized to 3.0, which certainly is less than 18.5. Thus, the condition is true and the program proceeds to the next statement, which converts the size to inches. Then it prints the results. The next statement,

```
shoe = shoe + 1.0;
```

increases shoe by 1.0, making it 4.0. At this point the program returns to the while portion to check the condition. Why at this point? Because the next line is a closing brace (}), and we have used a set of braces ({ }) to mark the extent of the while loop. The statements between the two braces are the ones that may be repeated. The section of program between and including the braces is called a *block*. Now back to our program. The value 4 is less than 18.5, so the whole cycle of embraced commands (the block) following the while is repeated. (In computerese, the program is said to "loop" through these statements.) This continues until shoe reaches a value of 19.0. Now the condition

```
shoe < 18.5
```

becomes false, since 19.0 is not less than 18.5. When this happens, control passes to the first statement following the while loop. In our case, that is the final printf() statement.

You easily can modify this program to do other conversions. For example, change SCALE to 1.8 and OFFSET to 32.0, and you have a program that converts Centigrade to Fahrenheit. Or change SCALE to 0.6214 and OFFSET to 0, and you convert kilometers to miles. If you make these changes, you should change the printed messages, too, to prevent confusion.

The while loop provides a convenient, flexible means of controlling a program. Now let us turn to the fundamental operators that we can use in our programs.

Fundamental Operators

C uses *operators* to represent arithmetic operations. For example, the + operator causes the two values flanking it to be added together. If the term "operator" seems odd to you, please reflect that those things had to be called something. "Operator" does seem to be a better choice than, say, "those things" or "arithmetical transactors." We'll look now at the operators used for basic arithmetic: =, +, −, *, and /. (C does not have an exponentiating operator. In a later chapter we will present a function to accomplish this task.)

Assignment Operator: =

In C, the equal sign does not mean "equals." Rather, it is a value-assigning operator. The statement

```
bmw = 2002;
```

assigns the value 2002 to the variable named bmw. That is, the item to the left of the = sign is the *name* of a variable, and the item on the right is the *value* assigned to the variable. We call the = symbol the *assignment operator*. Again, don't think of the line as saying, "bmw equals 2002." Instead, read it as "assign the value 2002 to the variable bmw." The action goes from right to left for this operator.

Perhaps this distinction between the name of a variable and the value of a variable seems like hair-splitting, but consider the following very common type of computer statement:

```
i = i + 1;
```

As mathematics, this statement makes no sense. If you add 1 to a finite number, the result isn't "equal to" the number you started with. But as a computer assignment statement, it is perfectly reasonable. It means "find the value of the variable whose name is i; to that value, add 1 and then assign this new value to the variable whose name is i." See Figure 5.1.

Figure 5.1 *The statement* i = i + 1;

A statement such as

```
2002 = bmw;
```

makes no sense in C (and, indeed, is invalid) because 2002 is just a constant. You can't assign a value to a constant; it already *is* its value. So when you sit down at the keyboard, remember that the item to the left of the = sign must be the name of a variable. Actually, the left-hand side must refer to a storage location. The simplest way is to use the name of a variable, but, as you will see later, a "pointer" can be used to point to a location. More generally, ANSI C uses the term *modifiable lvalue* to label those entities to which you can assign values. "Modifiable lvalue" is not, perhaps, the most intuitive phrase you've encountered, so let's look at some definitions.

Some Terminology: Data Objects, Lvalues, Rvalues, and Operands

A *data object* is a general term for a region of data storage that can be used to hold values. The data storage used to hold a variable or an array is an object, for instance. ANSI C uses the term *lvalue* to mean a name or expression that identifies a particular object. The name of a variable, for instance, is an lvalue. So *object* refers to the actual data storage, while *lvalue* is a label used to identify, or locate, that storage.

Not all objects can have their values changed, so ANSI C uses the term *modifiable lvalue* to identify objects whose value can be changed. Thus, the left side of an assignment operator should be a modifiable lvalue. Indeed, the *l* in *l*value comes from *l*eft because modifiable lvalues can be used on the left side of assignment operators.

The term *rvalue* refers to quantities that can be assigned to modifiable lvalues. For instance, consider this statement:

```
bmw = 2002;
```

Here, `bmw` is a modifiable lvalue, and 2002 is an rvalue. As you probably guessed, the *r* in *r*value comes from *r*ight. Rvalues can be constants, variables, or any other expression that yields a value.

As long as you are learning the names of things, the proper term for what we have called an "item" (as in "the item to the left of the =") is *operand*. Operands are what operators operate on. For example, you can describe eating a hamburger as applying the "eat" operator to the "hamburger" operand. Or you can say that the left operand of the = operator shall be a modifiable lvalue.

The basic C assignment operator is a little flashier than most. Try the short program in Listing 5.3:

Listing 5.3 *golf.c*

```
/* golf.c -- golf tournament scorecard */
#include <stdio.h>
main()
{
    int jane, tarzan, cheeta;

    cheeta = tarzan = jane = 68;
    printf("                  cheeta   tarzan    jane\n");
    printf("First round score %4d %8d %8d\n",cheeta,tarzan,jane);
}
```

Many languages would balk at the triple assignment made in this program, but C accepts it routinely. The assignments are made right to left: first `jane` gets the value 68, then `tarzan` does, and finally `cheeta` does. Thus, the output is

```
                  cheeta   tarzan    jane
First round score   68       68       68
```

Addition Operator: +

The *addition operator* causes the two values on either side of it to be added together. For example, the statement

```
printf("%d", 4 + 20);
```

causes the number 24 to be printed, not the expression 4 + 20.

The values (operands) to be added can be variables as well as constants. Thus, the statement

```
income = salary + bribes;
```

will cause the computer to look up the values of the two variables on the right, add them, and assign this total to the variable income.

Subtraction Operator: −

The *subtraction operator* causes the number after the − sign to be subtracted from the number before the sign. The statement

```
takehome = 224.00 - 24.00;
```

assigns the value 200.0 to takehome.

The + and − operators are termed *binary*, or *dyadic,* operators, meaning that they require *two* operands.

Sign Operators: − and +

The minus sign also can be used to indicate or to change the algebraic sign of a value. For instance, the sequence

```
rocky = -12;
smokey = -rocky;
```

gives smokey the value 12.

When the minus sign is used in this way, it is called a *unary operator*, meaning that it takes just one operand. See Figure 5.2.

The ANSI Standard adds a unary + operator to C. It doesn't alter the value or sign of its operand; it just lets you use statements like

```
dozen = +12;
```

without getting a compiler complaint. Formerly, this construction was not allowed.

Figure 5.2 *Unary and binary operators*

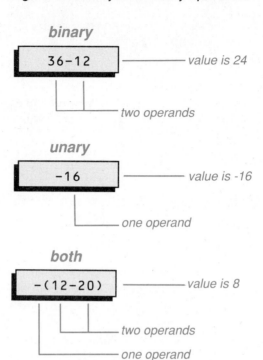

Multiplication Operator: *

Multiplication is indicated by the * symbol. The statement

```
cm = 2.54 * in;
```

multiplies the variable in by 2.54 and assigns the answer to cm.

By any chance do you want a table of squares? C doesn't have a squaring function, but, as shown in Listing 5.4, we can use multiplication to calculate squares.

Listing 5.4 *squares.c*

```
/* squares.c -- produces a table of first 20 squares */
#include <stdio.h>
main()
{
```

```
    int num = 1;

    while (num < 21)
    {
        printf("%10d %10d\n", num, num * num);
        num = num + 1;
    }
}
```

This program prints the first 20 integers and their squares, as you can verify for yourself. Let's look at a more interesting example.

Exponential Growth

You probably have heard the story of the powerful ruler who seeks to reward a scholar who has done him a great service. When the scholar is asked what he would like, he points to a chessboard and says, just one grain of wheat on the first square, two on the second, four on the third, eight on the next, and so on. The ruler, lacking mathematical erudition, is astounded at the modesty of this request, for he had been prepared to offer great riches. The joke, of course, is on the ruler, as the program in Listing 5.5 shows. It calculates how many grains go on each square and keeps a running total. Since you may not be up to date on wheat crops, we also compare the running total to a rough estimate of the annual wheat crop in the United States.

Listing 5.5 *wheat.c*

```
/* wheat.c -- exponential growth */
#include <stdio.h>
#define SQUARES 64    /* squares on a checkerboard */
#define CROP 7E14     /* US wheat crop in grains    */
main()
{
    double current, total;
    int count = 1;
```

(continued)

Listing 5.5 *(continued)*

```
printf("square   grains added   total grains   ");
printf("fraction of \n");
printf("                                       ");
printf("US total\n");
total = current = 1.0;   /* start with one grain   */
printf("%4d %15.2e %13.2e %13.2e\n", count, current,
        total, total/CROP);
while (count < SQUARES)
{
    count = count + 1;
    current = 2.0 * current;
                        /* double grains on next square */
    total = total + current;           /* update total */
    printf("%4d %15.2e %13.2e %13.2e\n", count, current,
            total, total/CROP);
}
}
```

The output begins innocuously enough:

square	grains added	total grains	fraction of US total
1	1.00e+000	1.00e+000	1.43e-015
2	2.00e+000	3.00e+000	4.29e-015
3	4.00e+000	7.00e+000	1.00e-014
4	8.00e+000	1.50e+001	2.14e-014
5	1.60e+001	3.10e+001	4.43e-014
6	3.20e+001	6.30e+001	9.00e-014
7	6.40e+001	1.27e+002	1.81e-013
8	1.28e+002	2.55e+002	3.64e-013
9	2.56e+002	5.11e+002	7.30e-013
10	5.12e+002	1.02e+003	1.46e-012

After ten squares, the scholar has acquired just a little over a thousand grains of wheat. But look what has happened by square 50!

50	5.63e+014	1.13e+015	1.61e+000

The haul has exceeded the total U.S. annual output! If you want to see what happens by the 64th square, you will have to run the program yourself.

This example illustrates the phenomenon of exponential growth. The world population growth and our use of energy resources have followed the same pattern.

Division Operator: /

C uses the / symbol to represent division. The value to the left of the / is divided by the value to the right. For example, the following gives four the value of 4.0:

```
four = 12.0/3.0;
```

Division works differently for integer types than it does for floating types. Floating-type division gives a floating-point answer, but integer division yields an integer answer. An integer has to be a whole number, which makes dividing 5 by 3 awkward, since the answer isn't a whole number. In C, any fraction resulting from integer division is discarded. This process is called *truncation*.

Try the program in Listing 5.6 to see how truncation works and how integer division differs from floating-point division.

Listing 5.6 *divide.c*

```
/* divide.c -- divisions we have known */
#include <stdio.h>
main()
{

    printf("integer division:  5/4   is %d \n", 5/4);
    printf("integer division:  6/3   is %d \n", 6/3);
    printf("integer division:  7/4   is %d \n", 7/4);
    printf("floating division: 7./4. is %1.2f \n", 7./4.);
    printf("mixed division:    7./4  is %1.2f \n", 7./4);
}
```

In Listing 5.6 we included a case of "mixed types" by having a floating-point value divided by an integer. C is a more forgiving language than some and will let you get away with this, but normally you should avoid mixing types. Now for the results:

```
integer division:   5/4    is 1
integer division:   6/3    is 2
integer division:   7/4    is 1
floating division: 7./4. is 1.75
mixed division:     7./4  is 1.75
```

Notice how integer division does not round to the nearest integer, but always truncates. And when we mixed integers with floating point, the answer came out the same as floating point. When a calculation like this has both types, the integer is converted to floating point before division.

The properties of integer division turn out to be handy for some problems, and we will give an example fairly soon. First, there is another important matter: what happens when you combine more than one operation into one statement? That is our next topic.

Operator Precedence

Consider the line:

```
butter = 25.0 + 60.0 * n / SCALE;
```

This statement has an addition, a multiplication, and a division. Which operation takes place first? Is 25.0 added to 60.0, the result of 85.0 then multiplied by n, and that result then divided by SCALE? Or is 60.0 multiplied by n, the result added to 25.0, and that answer then divided by SCALE? Or is it some other order? Let's take n to be 6.0 and SCALE to be 2.0. If you work through the statement using these values, you will find that the first approach yields a value of 255. The second approach yields 192.5. A C program must have some other order in mind, for it would give a value of 205.0 for butter.

Clearly the order of executing the various operations can make a difference, so C needs unambiguous rules for choosing what to do first. C does this by setting up an operator pecking order. Each operator is assigned a *precedence* level. Multiplication and division have a higher precedence than addition and subtraction, so they are performed first. What if two operators have the same precedence? If they share an operand, they are executed according to the order in which they occur in the statement. For most operators the order is from left to right. (The = operator was an exception to this.) Therefore, in the statement

```
butter = 25.0 + 60.0 * n / SCALE;
```

the order of operations is:

60.0 * n	the first * or / in the expression (assuming n is 6 so that 60.0 * n is 360.0)
360.0 / SCALE	then the second * or / in the expression and
25.0 + 180	finally (since SCALE is 2.0) the first + or − in the expression to yield 205.0

Many people like to represent the order of evaluation with a type of diagram called an *expression tree*. Figure 5.3 is an example of such a diagram. The diagram shows how the original expression is reduced by steps to a single value.

Figure 5.3 *Expression trees showing operators, operands, and order of evaluation*

```
SCALE=2;
n=6;
25.0+60.0*n/SCALE;
```

But what if you want, say, an addition to take place before a division. Then you can do as we have done in this line:

```
flour = (25.0 + 60.0 * n) / SCALE;
```

Whatever is enclosed in parentheses is executed first. Within the parentheses, the usual rules hold. For this example, first the multiplication takes place and then the addition. That completes the expression in the parentheses. Now the result can be divided by SCALE.

Table 5.1 summarizes the rules for the operators we've used so far. (Appendix B contains a table covering all operators.)

Notice that the two uses of the minus sign have different precedences, as do the two uses of the plus sign. The associativity column tells you how an operator associates with its operands. For example, the unary minus

Table 5.1 *Operators in Order of Decreasing Precedence*

Operators	Associativity
( )	Left to right
+ – (unary)	Left to right
* /	Left to right
+ – (binary)	Left to right
=	Right to left

sign associates with the quantity to its right, and in division the left operand is divided by the right.

Precedence and the Order of Evaluation

Operator precedence provides vital rules for determining the order of evaluation in an expression, but it doesn't necessarily determine the complete order. C leaves some choices up to the implementor. Consider this statement:

```
y = 6 * 12 + 5 * 20;
```

Precedence dictates the order of evaluation when two operators share an operand. For example, the 12 is an operand for both the * and the + operators, and precedence says that multiplication comes first. Similarly, precedence says that the 5 is to be multiplied, not added. In short, the multiplications 6 * 12 and 5 * 20 take place before any addition. What precedence does not establish is which of these two multiplications occurs first. C leaves that choice to the implementor because one choice might be more efficient for one kind of hardware, while the other choice might work better on another kind of hardware. In either case, the expression reduces to 72 + 100, so the choice doesn't affect the final value for this particular example.

"But," you say, "multiplication associates from left to right. Doesn't that mean the left-most multiplication is performed first?" (Well, maybe you don't say that, but somewhere someone does.) The association rule applies for operators that share an operand. For instance, in the expression 12 / 3 * 2, the / and * operators, which have the same precedence, share the operand 3. Thus, the left-to-right rule applies in this case, and the expression reduces to 4 * 2, or 8. (Going from right to left would give 12 / 6, or 2. Here the choice does matter.) In the previous example, the two * operators did not share a common operand, so the left-to-right rule did not apply.

Trying the Rules

Let's try these rules on a more complex example—Listing 5.7.

Listing 5.7 *rules.c*

```
/* rules.c -- precedence test */
#include <stdio.h>
main()
{
  int top, score;
  top = score = -(2 + 5) * 6 + (4 + 3 * (2 + 3));
  printf("top = %d \n", top);
}
```

What value will this program print? Figure it out; then run the program or read the following description to check your answer.

First, parentheses have the highest precedence. Whether the parentheses in -(2 + 5) * 6 or in (4 + 3 * (2 + 3)) are evaluated first depends on the implementation, as we just discussed. Either choice will lead to the same result for this example, so let's take the left one first. The high precedence of parentheses means that in the subexpression -(2 + 5) * 6, we evaluate (2 + 5) first, obtaining 7. Next, we apply the unary minus operator to 7 to obtain -7. Now, the expression is this:

```
top = score = -7 * 6 + (4 + 3 * (2 + 3))
```

The next step is to evaluate 2 + 3. The expression becomes

```
top = score = -7 * 6 + (4 + 3 * 5)
```

Next, since the * in the parentheses has priority over +, the expression becomes

```
top = score = -7 * 6 + (4 + 15)
```

and then

```
top = score = -7 * 6 + 19
```

Multiply -7 by 6 and get this expression:

```
top = score = -42 + 19
```

Then addition makes it:

```
top = score = -23
```

Now `score` is assigned the value -23, and, finally, `top` gets the value -23. Remember that the =operator associates from right to left.

Some Additional Operators

C has about forty operators, but some are used much more than others. The ones we just covered are the most common, and we would like to add four more useful operators to the list.

The *sizeof* Operator

We used the `sizeof` operator in Chapter 3. To review, the `sizeof` operator returns the size, in bytes, of its operand. The operand can be a specific data object, such as the name of a variable, or it can be a type. If it is a type, such as `float`, the operand must be enclosed in parentheses. For instance, the example in Listing 5.8 shows both forms.

Listing 5.8 *sizeof.c*

```
/* sizeof.c -- uses sizeof operator */
#include <stdio.h>
main()
{
    int n;

    printf("n has %d bytes; all ints have %d bytes.\n",
        sizeof n, sizeof (int) );
}
```

Modulus Operator: %

The *modulus operator* is used in integer arithmetic. It gives the *remainder* that results when the integer to its left is divided by the integer to its right.

For example, 13 % 5 (read as "13 modulo 5") has the value 3, since 5 goes into 13 twice, with a remainder of 3. Don't bother trying to use this operator with floating-point numbers. It just won't work.

At first glance, this operator may strike you as an esoteric tool for mathematicians, but actually it is rather practical and helpful. One common use is to help you control the flow of a program. Suppose, for example, you are working on a bill-preparing program that is designed to add in an extra charge every third month. Just have the program evaluate the month number modulo 3 (i.e., month % 3) and check to see if the result is 0. If it is, the program adds in the extra charge. After you learn about "if statements" in Chapter 7, you'll understand this better.

Listing 5.9 shows another use for the % operator.

```
Listing 5.9   min_sec.c

/* min_sec.c -- converts seconds to minutes and seconds */
#include <stdio.h>
#define SEC_PER_MIN 60          /* seconds in a minute        */
main()
{
    int sec, min, left;

    printf("Convert seconds to minutes and seconds!\n");
    printf(
      "Enter the number of seconds you wish to convert.\n");
    scanf("%d", &sec);          /* number of seconds is read in */
    min = sec / SEC_PER_MIN;  /* truncated number of minutes  */
    left = sec % SEC_PER_MIN; /* number of seconds left over  */
    printf("%d seconds is %d minutes, %d seconds.\n", sec, min,
          left);
}
```

Here is a sample output:

```
Convert seconds to minutes and seconds!
Enter the number of seconds you wish to convert.
234
234 seconds is 3 minutes, 54 seconds.
```

One problem with this interactive program is that it processes just one input value. Can you figure out a way to have the program prompt you repeatedly for new input values? We will return to this problem later in the

"Review Questions," but if you can work out a solution first, congratulations.

Increment and Decrement Operators:
++ and --

The *increment operator* performs a simple task; it increments (increases) the value of its operand by 1. This operator comes in two varieties. The first variety has the ++ come before the affected variable; this is the *prefix* mode. The second variety has the ++ after the affected variable; this is the *postfix* mode. The two modes differ with regard to the precise time that the incrementing takes place. We'll look at the similarities first and then return to that difference. The short example in Listing 5.10 shows how the increment operators work.

Listing 5.10   add_one.c

```
/* add_one.c -- incrementing: prefix and postfix */
#include <stdio.h>
main()
{   int ultra = 0, super = 0;

    while (super < 5)
    {
        super++;
        ++ultra;
        printf("super = %d, ultra = %d \n", super, ultra);
    }
}
```

Running `add_one.c` produces

```
super = 1, ultra = 1
super = 2, ultra = 2
super = 3, ultra = 3
super = 4, ultra = 4
super = 5, ultra = 5
```

The program counted to 5 twice and simultaneously. We confess that the same results could have been achieved by replacing the two increment statements with

```
super = super + 1;
ultra = ultra + 1;
```

These are simple enough statements. Why bother creating one, let alone two, abbreviations? One reason is that the compact form makes your programs neater and easier to follow. These operators give your programs an elegant gloss that cannot fail to please the eye. For instance, we can rewrite part of shoe2.c (Listing 5.2) this way:

```
shoe = 3.0;
while (shoe < 18.5)
{
    foot = SCALE*size + OFFSET;
    printf("%10.1f %20.2f inches\n", shoe, foot);
    ++shoe;
}
```

However, we still haven't taken full advantage of the increment operator. We can shorten the fragment this way:

```
shoe = 2.0;
while (++shoe < 18.5)
{
    foot = SCALE*shoe + OFFSET;
    printf("%10.1f %20.2f inches\n", shoe, foot);
}
```

Here we have combined the incrementing process and the while comparison into one expression. This type of construction is so common in C that it merits a closer look.

First, how does this construction work? Simply. The value of shoe is increased by 1 and then compared to 18.5. If it is less than 18.5, the statements between the braces are executed once. Then shoe is increased by 1 again, and the cycle is repeated until shoe gets too big. We changed the initial value of shoe from 3.0 to 2.0 to compensate for shoe being incremented before the first evaluation of foot. See Figure 5.4.

Second, what's so good about this approach? It is more compact. More important, it gathers in one place the two processes that control the loop. The first process is the test: do we continue or not? In this case, the test is checking to see whether the shoe size is less than 18.5. The second process changes an element of the test; in this case, the shoe size is increased.

Suppose you forgot to change the shoe size. Then shoe would *always* be less than 18.5, and the loop would never end. The computer would churn out line after identical line, caught in a dreaded "infinite loop." Eventually, you would lose interest in the output and have to kill the pro-

Figure 5.4 *Through the loop once*

gram somehow. Having the loop test and the loop change at one place instead of at separate locations helps you to remember to update the loop.

Another advantage of the increment operator is that it usually produces slightly more efficient machine language code, since it is similar to actual machine language instructions. However, as implementors produce better C compilers, this advantage may disappear. A smart compiler will recognize that x = x + 1 can be treated the same as ++x.

Finally, these operators have an additional feature that can be useful in certain delicate situations. To find out what this feature is, try running the program in Listing 5.11.

Listing 5.11 *post_pre.c*

```
/* post_pre.c -- postfix vs prefix */
#include <stdio.h>
main()
{
   int a = 1, b = 1;
   int aplus, plusb;

   aplus = a++;        /* postfix */
   plusb = ++b;        /* prefix  */
   printf("a    aplus    b    plusb \n");
   printf("%1d %5d %5d %5d\n", a, aplus, b, plusb);
}
```

If you and your compiler do everything correctly, you should get this result:

```
a    aplus   b   plusb
2      1     2     2
```

Both a and b were increased by 1, as promised. However, aplus has the value of a *before* a changed, while plusb has the value of b *after* b changed. This is the difference between the prefix form and the postfix form. See Figure 5.5.

```
aplus = a++;   /* postfix: a is changed after its value is used */
plusb = ++b;   /* prefix: b is changed before its value is used */
```

Figure 5.5 *Prefix and postfix*

prefix

```
q = 2*++a;
```

first, increment a by 1;
then, multiply a by 2 and assign to q

postfix

```
q = 2*a++;
```

first, multiply a by 2, assign to q
then, increment a by 1

When one of these increment operators is used by itself, as in a solitary ego++; statement, it doesn't matter which form you use. The choice does matter, however, when the operator and its operand are part of a larger expression, as in the assignment statements we just saw. In this kind of situation, you must give some thought to the result you want. For instance, recall our use of

```
while (++shoe < 18.5)
```

This test condition provided a table up to size 18. But if we had used shoe++ instead of ++shoe, the table would have gone to size 19, since shoe would have been increased after the comparison instead of before.

Of course, you could fall back on the less subtle form:

```
shoe = shoe + 1;
```

but then no one will believe that you are a true C programmer.

We suggest that you pay special attention to the examples of increment operators as you read through this book. Ask yourself if we could have used the prefix and the suffix forms interchangeably or if circumstances dictated a particular choice.

Decrementing: --

For each form of increment operator, there is a corresponding form of *decrement operator*. Instead of ++, use --.

```
-- count;    /* prefix form of decrement operator  */
count --;    /* postfix form of decrement operator */
```

Listing 5.12 illustrates that computers can be accomplished lyricists.

Listing 5.12   bottles.c

```
/* bottles.c -- counting down */
#include <stdio.h>
#define MAX 100
main()
{
  int count = MAX + 1;

  while (--count > 0) {
  printf(
     "%d bottles of beer on the wall, %d bottles of beer!\n",
     count, count);
  printf("Take one down and pass it around,\n");
  printf("%d bottles of beer!\n\n", count - 1);
  }
}
```

The output starts like this:

```
100 bottles of beer on the wall, 100 bottles of beer!
Take one down and pass it around,
99 bottles of beer!

99 bottles of beer on the wall, 99 bottles of beer!
```

```
Take one down and pass it around,
98 bottles of beer!
```

It goes on a bit and ends this way:

```
1 bottles of beer on the wall, 1 bottles of beer!
Take one down and pass it around,
0 bottles of beer!
```

Apparently our accomplished lyricist has a problem with plurals, but that could be fixed by using the conditional operators of Chapter 8.

Incidentally, the > operator stands for "is greater than." Like < ("is less than"), it is a *relational operator*. We will take a longer look at relational operators in Chapter 6. Note that you don't need to use braces to enclose the body of a while loop when it consists of just one statement, as in Listing 5.12.

Precedence

The increment and decrement operators have a very high precedence of association; only parentheses are higher. Thus, x*y++ means (x)*(y++), not (x*y)++, which is fortunate, since the latter is invalid. The increment and decrement operators affect a *variable* (or, more generally, a modifiable lvalue), and the combination x*y is not itself a variable, although its parts are.

Don't confuse precedence of these two operators with the order of evaluation. Suppose you have the following:

```
y = 2;
n = 3;
nextnum = (y + n++)*6;
```

What value does nextnum get? Substituting in values yields this:

```
nextnum = (2 + 3)*6 = 5*6 = 30
```

Only after n is used is it increased to 4. Precedence tells us that the ++ is attached only to the n, not to 2 + n. It also tells us when the value of n is used for evaluating the expression, but the nature of the increment operator determines when the value of n is changed.

When n++ is part of an expression, you can think of it as meaning "use n; then increment it." On the other hand, ++n means "increment n; then use it."

Don't Be Too Clever

You can get fooled if you try to do too much at once with the increment operators. For example, you might think that you could improve on our squares.c program (Listing 5.4) to print integers and their squares by replacing the while loop with this one:

```
while (num < 21)
    {
    printf("%10d %10d\n", num, num*num++);
    }
```

This looks reasonable. We print the number num, multiply it by itself to get the square, and then increase num by 1. In fact, this program may even work on some systems, but not all. The problem is that when printf() goes to get the values for printing, it may evaluate the last argument first and increment num before getting to the other argument. Thus, instead of printing, say,

       5   25

it may print

       6   25

In C, the compiler can choose which arguments in a function to evaluate first. This freedom increases compiler efficiency but can cause trouble if you use an increment operator on a function argument.

Another possible source of trouble is a statement like

```
ans = num/2 + 5*(1 + num++);
```

Again, the problem is that the compiler may not do things in the same order you have in mind. You would think that it would find num/2 first and then move on. But it might do the last term first, increase num, and use the new value in num/2. There is no guarantee.

Yet another troublesome case is this:

```
n = 3;
y = n++ + n++;
```

Certainly, n winds up larger by 2 after the statement is executed. But the value for y is ambiguous. A compiler can use the old value of n twice in evaluating y and then increment n twice. This gives y the value 6, and n the value 5. Or it can use the old value once, increment n once, use that value

for the second n in the expression, and then increment n a second time. This gives y the value 7, and n the value 5. Either choice is allowable.
You can easily avoid these problems:

1. Don't use increment or decrement operators on a variable that is part of more than one argument of a function.
2. Don't use increment or decrement operators on a variable that appears more than once in an expression.

Expressions and Statements

We have been using the terms "expression" and "statement" throughout these first few chapters, and now the time has come to study their meanings more closely. Statements form the basic program steps of C, and most statements are constructed from expressions. This suggests that we look at expressions first, and we will.

Expressions

An *expression* consists of a combination of operators and operands. (An *operand*, recall, is what an operator operates on.) The simplest expression is a lone operand, and you can build in complexity from there. Here are some expressions:

```
4
-6
4+21
a*(b + c/d)/20
q = 5*2
x = ++q % 3
q > 3
```

As you can see, the operands can be constants, variables, or combinations of the two. Some expressions are combinations of smaller expressions, called *subexpressions*. For instance, c/d is a subexpression of the fourth example.

Every Expression Has a Value

An important property of C is that every C expression has a value. To find the value, you perform the operations in the order dictated by operator precedence. The value of the first few expressions is clear, but what about the ones with = signs? Those expressions simply have the same value that the variable to the left of the = sign receives. Thus, the expression q=5*2 as a whole has the value 10. What about the expression q > 3? Such relational expressions have the value 1 if true and 0 if false. Here are some expressions and their values:

Expression	Value
-4 + 6	2
c = 3 + 8	11
5 > 3	1
6 + (c = 3 + 8)	17

The last expression looks strange! However, it is perfectly legal in C because it is the sum of two subexpressions, each of which has a value.

Statements

Statements are the primary building blocks of a program. A *program* is a series of statements with some necessary punctuation thrown in. A statement is a complete instruction to the computer. In C, statements are indicated by a semicolon at the end. Thus,

```
legs = 4
```

is just an expression (which could be part of a larger expression), but

```
legs = 4;
```

is a statement.

What makes an instruction complete? It has to complete an action. The expression

```
2 + 2
```

is not a complete instruction. It tells the computer to add 2 and 2, but it fails to tell the computer what to do with the answer. If we say

```
kids = 2 + 2;
```

however, we tell the computer to store the answer (4) in the memory location labeled kids. With the number 4 thus disposed of, the computer can move to the next task.

Actually, C considers any expression to be a statement if you append a semicolon. Thus, C won't object to lines like the following:

```
8;
3 + 4;
```

However, these statements do nothing for your program and can't really be considered sensible statements.

Although a statement (or, at least, a sensible statement) is a complete instruction, not all complete instructions are statements. Consider the following statement:

```
x = 6 + (y = 5);
```

In it, the subexpression y = 5 is a complete instruction, but it is only part of the statement. Because a complete instruction is not necessarily a statement, a semicolon is needed to identify instructions that truly are statements.

So far we have encountered four kinds of statements. Listing 5.13 gives a short sample that uses all four.

Listing 5.13 *addemup.c*

```
/* addemup.c -- four kinds of statements */
#include <stdio.h>
main()                       /* finds sum of first 20 integers */
{
    int count, sum;          /* declaration statement          */

    count = 0;               /* assignment statement           */
    sum = 0;                 /* ditto                          */
    while (count++ < 20)     /* while                          */
        sum = sum + count;   /*      statement                 */
    printf("sum = %d\n", sum);  /* function statement          */
}
```

Let's discuss Listing 5.13. By now you must be pretty familiar with the *declaration statement*. Nonetheless, we will remind you that it establishes the names and type of variables and causes memory locations to be set aside for them.

The *assignment statement* is the workhorse of most programs; it assigns a value to a variable. It consists of a variable name followed by the assignment operator (=) followed by an expression followed by a semicolon. Note that the `while` statement includes an assignment statement within it.

A *function statement* causes the function to do whatever it does. In our example, the `printf()` function is invoked to print some results.

A `while` statement has three distinct parts (see Figure 5.6). First is the keyword `while`. Then, in parentheses, is a test condition. Finally is the statement that is performed if the test is met. Only one statement is included in the loop. It can be a simple statement, as in this example, in which case no braces are needed to mark it off. Or the statement can be a compound statement, like some of our earlier examples, in which case braces are required. Read about compound statements just ahead.

Figure 5.6 *Structure of a simple* while *loop*

The `while` statement belongs to a class of statements sometimes called *structured statements* because they possess a structure more complex than that of a simple assignment statement. In later chapters you will encounter many other kinds of structured statements.

Compound Statements (Blocks)

A *compound statement* is two or more statements grouped together by enclosing them in braces; it is also called a *block*. We used one in our `shoe2.c` program in order to let the `while` statement encompass several statements. Compare the following program fragments:

```
/* fragment 1 */
index = 0;
while (index++ < 10)
  sam = 10 * index + 2;
printf("sam = %d\n", sam);

/* fragment 2 */
index = 0;
while (index++ < 10)
{
  sam = 10 * index + 2;
  printf("sam = %d\n", sam);
}
```

In fragment 1, only the assignment statement is included in the `while` loop. In the absence of braces, a `while` statement runs from the `while` to the next semicolon. The `printf()` function will be called just once, after the loop has been completed.

In fragment 2, the braces ensure that both statements are part of the `while` loop, and `printf()` is called each time that the loop is executed. The entire compound statement is considered to be the single statement in terms of the structure of a `while` statement. See Figure 5.7.

Figure 5.7 While *loop with a compound statement*

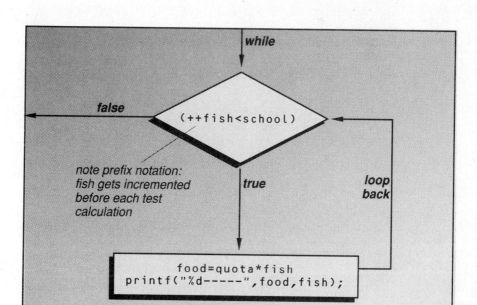

Style Tips

Look again at the two `while` fragments and notice how an indentation marks off the body of each loop. The indentation makes no difference to the compiler; it uses the braces and its knowledge of the structure of `while` loops to decide how to interpret our instructions. The indentation is there for us, so that we can see at a glance how the program is organized.

We have shown one popular style for positioning the braces for a block, or compound, statement. Another very common style is this:

```
while (index++ < 10) {
   sam = 10*index + 2;
   printf("sam = %d \n", sam);
   }
```

This style highlights the attachment of the block to the `while` loop. The other style emphasizes that the statements form a block. Again, as far as the compiler is concerned, both forms are identical.

To sum up, use indentation as a tool to point out the structure of a program to the reader.

Summary: Expressions and Statements

Expressions

An *expression* is a combination of operators and operands. The simplest expression is just a constant or a variable with no operator, such as 22 or beebop. More complex examples are 55 + 22 and vap = 2 * (vip + (vup = 4)).

Statements

A *statement* is a command to the computer. There are simple statements and compound statements. *Simple statements* terminate in a semicolon. Examples are

Declaration statement:	int toes;
Assignment statement:	toes = 12;

Function call statement:	`printf("%d\n", toes);`
Control statement:	`while (toes < 20) toes = toes + 2;`
Null statement:	`; /* does nothing */`

Compound statements, or *blocks*, consist of one or more statements (which themselves can be compound) enclosed in braces. The following `while` statement contains an example:

```
while (years < 100)
{
    wisdom = wisdom + 1;
    printf("%d %d\n", years, wisdom);
    years = years + 1;
}
```

Type Conversions

Statements and expressions normally should use variables and constants of just one type. If, however, you mix types, C doesn't stop dead in its tracks the way, say, Pascal does. Instead, it uses a set of rules to make type conversions automatically. This can be a convenience, but it also can be a danger, especially if you are mixing types inadvertently. (The `lint` program, found on many UNIX systems, checks for type "clashes." Many non-UNIX C compilers report possible type problems if you select a higher error level.) It is a good idea to have at least some knowledge of the type conversion rules.

The basic rules are these:

1. When appearing in an expression, `char` and `short`, both signed and unsigned, automatically are converted to `int` or, if necessary, to `unsigned int`. (If `short` is the same size as `int`, then `unsigned short` is larger than `int`; in that case, `unsigned short` is converted to `unsigned int`.) Under K&R C, but not under ANSI C, `float` automatically is converted to `double`. Because these are conversions to larger types, they are called *promotions*.

2. In any operation involving two types, both values are converted to the higher ranking of the two types.

3. The ranking of types, from highest to lowest, is `long double`,

double, float, unsigned long, long, unsigned int, and int. One possible exception is when long and int are the same size, in which case unsigned int outranks long. The short and char types don't appear in this list because they would have been already promoted to int or perhaps unsigned int.

4. In an assignment statement, the final result of the calculations is converted to the type of the variable that is being assigned a value. This process can result in promotion, as described in Rule 1, or *demotion*, in which a value is converted to a lower-ranking type.

5. When passed as function arguments, char and short are converted to int, and float is converted to double. This automatic promotion can be overridden by function prototyping, as discussed in Chapter 9.

Promotion usually is a smooth, uneventful process, but demotion can lead to real trouble. The reason is simple: the lower-ranking type may not be big enough to hold the complete number. A char variable can hold the integer 101 but not the integer 22334. When floating types are demoted to integer types, they are truncated, or rounded towards zero. That means 23.12 and 23.99 both are truncated to 23 and that -23.5 is truncated to -23. Listing 5.14 illustrates the working of these rules.

Listing 5.14 *convert.c*

```
/* convert.c -- automatic type conversions */
#include <stdio.h>
main()
{
    char ch;
    int i;
    float fl;

    fl = i = ch = 'A';                     /* line 8 */
    printf("ch = %c, i = %d, fl = %2.2f\n", ch, i, fl);
    ch = ch + 1;                           /* line 10 */
    i = fl + 2 * ch;                       /* line 11 */
    fl = 2.0 * ch + i;                     /* line 12 */
    printf("ch = %c, i = %d, fl = %2.2f\n", ch, i, fl);
    ch = 5212205.17;                       /* line 14 */
    printf("Now ch = %c\n", ch);
}
```

Running `convert.c` produces

```
ch = A, i = 65, fl = 65.00
ch = B, i = 197, fl = 329.00
Now ch = -
```

On our system, here is what happened:

Lines 8 and 9: The character `'A'` is stored as a 1-byte ASCII value in `ch`. The integer variable `i` receives the integer conversion of `'A'`, which is 65 stored as 2 bytes. Finally, `fl` receives the floating conversion of 65, which is 65.00.

Lines 10 and 13: The character variable `'A'` is converted to the integer 65, which then is added to the 1. The resulting 2-byte integer 66 is truncated to 1 byte and stored in `ch`. When printed using the `%c` specifier, 66 is interpreted as the ASCII code for `'B'`.

Lines 11 and 13: The value of `ch` is converted to a 2-byte integer (66) for the multiplication by 2. The resulting integer (132) is converted to floating point in order to be added to `fl`. The result (197.00) is converted to `int` and stored in `i`.

Lines 12 and 13: The value of `ch` (`'B'`, or 66) is converted to floating point for multiplication by 2.0. The value of `i` (197) is converted to floating point for the addition, and the result (329.00) is stored in `fl`.

Lines 14 and 15: Here we try a case of demotion, setting `ch` equal to a rather large number. After truncation takes place, `ch` winds up with the ASCII code for the hyphen character.

The Cast Operator

You should usually steer clear of automatic type conversions, especially of demotions. But sometimes it is convenient to make conversions, providing you exercise care. The type conversions we've discussed so far are done automatically. However, it is possible for you to demand the precise type conversion that you want. The method for doing this is called a *cast* and consists of preceding the quantity with the name of the desired type in parentheses. The parentheses and type name together constitute a *cast operator*. The general form of a cast operator is

`(type)`

where the actual type desired, such as `long`, is substituted for the word *type*.

Consider these two lines, in which `mice` is an `int` variable. The second line contains two casts to type `int`:

```
mice = 1.6 + 1.7;
mice = (int) 1.6 + (int) 1.7;
```

The first example uses automatic conversion. First `1.6` and `1.7` are added to yield `3.3`. This number is then converted through truncation to the integer `3` in order to match the `int` variable. In the second example, `1.6` is converted to an integer (`1`) before addition, as is `1.7`, so that `mice` is assigned the value `1+1`, or `2`.

Normally, you shouldn't mix types; that is why some languages don't allow it. But there are occasions when it is useful. The C philosophy is to avoid putting barriers in your way and to give you the responsibility of not abusing that freedom.

Summary: Operating in C

Here are the operators we have discussed so far.

Assignment Operator

=	Assigns the value at its right to the variable at its left.

Arithmetic Operators

+	Adds the value at its right to the value at its left.
-	Subtracts the value at its right from the value at its left.
-	As a unary operator, changes the sign of the value at its right.
*	Multiplies the value at its right by the value at its left.
/	Divides the value at its left by the value at its right. Answer is truncated if both operands are integers.
%	Yields the remainder when the value at its left is divided by the value to its right (integers only).
++	Adds 1 to the value of the variable to its right (prefix mode) or to the value of the variable to its left (postfix mode).
--	Like ++, but subtracts 1.

Miscellaneous Operators

sizeof	Yields the size, in bytes, of the operand to its right. The operand can be a type-specifier in parentheses, as in sizeof (float), or it can be the name of a particular variable or array, etc., as in sizeof foo.
(type)	As the cast operator, converts the following value to the type specified by the enclosed keyword(s). For example, (float) 9 converts the integer 9 to the floating-point number 9.0.

Function with Arguments

By now you're familiar with using function arguments. The next step along the road to function mastery is learning how to write your own functions that use arguments. Let's preview that skill now. (At this point you may wish to review the butler() function example near the end of Chapter 2; it shows how to write a function without an argument.) Listing 5.15 includes a pound() function that prints a specified number of pound signs (#). The example also illustrates some points about type conversion. *Note*: This version of the program uses the pre-ANSI function declaration instead of an ANSI prototype.

Listing 5.15 *pound.c*

```
/* pound.c -- defines a function with an argument    */
#include <stdio.h>
void pound();           /* old-fashioned style        */
                        /* function declaration       */
main()
{
  int times = 5;
  char ch = '!';        /* ASCII code is 33           */
  float f = 6.0;
```

(continued)

Listing 5.15 *(continued)*

```
    pound(times);        /* int argument              */
    pound(ch);           /* char automatically -> int */
    pound((int) f);      /* cast forces f -> int       */
}

void pound(n)            /* old-style function header  */
int n;                   /* says pound() takes one     */
{                        /* type int argument          */
    while (n-- > 0)
        printf("#");
    printf("\n");
}
```

Running the program produces this output:

```
#####
################################
######
```

First, let's examine the function heading:

```
void pound(n)
int n;
```

If the function took no arguments, the parentheses would be empty. Since the function takes one argument, we include one variable name: n. You can use any name consistent with C's naming rules. Next, on the following line, we declare the type of n. This declaration is like other declarations we've made, except that it comes before the opening brace. Argument declarations come between the function name and the opening brace.

Declaring an argument creates a variable called the *formal argument* or the *formal parameter*. In this case, we've created a type int variable called n. Making a function call like pound(10) acts to assign the value 10 to n. Or, in the case of our program, the call pound(times) serves to assign the value of times (5) to n. We say that the function call passes a value, and this value is called the *actual argument* or the *actual parameter*. So the function call pound(10) passes the actual argument 10 to the function, where 10 is assigned to the formal argument.

Variable names are private to the function. This means that a name defined in one function doesn't conflict with the same name defined elsewhere. If we used `times` instead of `n` in `pound()`, that would create a variable distinct from the `times` in `main()`. That is, we would have two variables with the same name, but the program keeps track of which is which.

Now let's look at the function calls. The first one is `pound(times)`, and, as we said, it causes the `times` value of 5 to be assigned to `n`. This causes the function to print five pound signs and a newline. The second call is `pound(ch)`. Here, `ch` is type `char`. It is initialized to the `!` character, which, on ASCII systems, means that `ch` has the numerical value 33. The automatic promotion of `char` to `int` converts this, on our system, from 33 stored in 1 byte to 33 stored in 2 bytes. So the value 33 now is in the correct form to be used as an argument to this function. The last call, `pound ((int) f)`, uses a type cast to convert `f` to the proper type for this argument.

Suppose we omit the type cast. Then the default promotion converts `f` to type `double`. On our system, this results in the function call putting an 8-byte value into the *stack*, a temporary storage area. Then the `pound()` function, expecting type `int`, reads just 2 of those bytes. The result bears little resemblance to the original value. In short, using a `float` or `double` argument when a function expects type `int` does not lead to an automatic type conversion; it leads to garbage. That's why we used an explicit type cast to convert `f` to the proper type.

The ANSI C function prototyping feature can force automatic type conversions to take place when the types appearing in a function call don't match the function's argument types. ANSI C also provides an alternative form for declaring function variables. Let's see how that is done.

First, replace the function declaration in Listing 5.15 with the following prototype:

```
void pound (int);
```

This statement tells the compiler that the program will use a function called `pound()`, which has no return value and which takes one argument, a type `int` value. Furthermore, it causes any actual arguments to `pound()` to be type-cast to type `int`. So we can make a function call like this:

```
pound(3.878);
```

With prototyping, the `3.878` is type-cast automatically to the `int` value 3, which then is passed on to the function.

The ANSI-style function header replaces

```
void pound(n)
int n;
```

with the following:

```
void pound(int n)
```

ANSI C recognizes both forms but may phase out the first someday. Chapter 9 examines prototyping in more detail.

An Example Program

Listing 5.16 is a useful program (if you're a runner or know one) that illustrates several of the ideas in this chapter. It looks long, but all the calculations are done in six lines near the end. The bulk of the program relays information between the computer and the user. We've tried using enough comments to make it nearly self-explanatory. Read through it, and when you are done, we'll clear up a few points.

Listing 5.16 *running.c*

```
/* running.c -- A useful program for runners */
#include <stdio.h>
#define S_PER_M    60    /* seconds in a minute */
#define S_PER_H  3600    /* seconds in an hour  */
#define M_PER_K 0.62137  /* miles in a kilometer */
main()
{
  float distk, distm;    /* distance run in km and in miles    */
  float rate;            /* average speed in mph               */
  int min, sec;          /* minutes and seconds of running time */
  int time;              /* running time in seconds only       */
  float mtime;           /* time in seconds for one mile       */
  int mmin, msec;        /* minutes and seconds for one mile   */
  printf("This program converts your time for a metric race\n");
  printf("to a time for running a mile and to your average\n");
  printf("speed in miles per hour.\n");
  printf("Please enter, in kilometers, the distance run.\n");
  scanf("%f", &distk);
  printf("Next enter the time in minutes and seconds.\n");
  printf("Begin by entering the minutes.\n");
  scanf("%d", &min);
  printf("Now enter the seconds.\n");
  scanf("%d", &sec);
  time = S_PER_M * min + sec;
                         /* converts time to pure seconds      */
  distm = M_PER_K * distk;
```

```
                          /* converts kilometers to miles        */
rate = distm / time * S_PER_H;
                          /* miles per sec x sec per hour = mph  */
mtime = (float) time / distm;
                          /* time/distance = time per mile       */
mmin = (int) mtime / S_PER_M;  /* find whole minutes         */
msec = (int) mtime % S_PER_M;  /* find remaining seconds     */
printf("You ran %1.2f km (%1.2f miles) in %d min, %d sec.\n",
    distk, distm, min, sec);
printf("That pace corresponds to running a mile in %d min, ",
    mmin);
printf("%d sec.\nYour average speed was %1.2f mph.\n",msec,
    rate);
}
```

Listing 5.16 utilizes the same approach that we used earlier in min_sec to convert the final time to minutes and seconds, but we also had to make type conversions. Why? Because we need integer arguments for the seconds-to-minutes part of the program, but the metric-to-mile conversion involves floating-point numbers. We have used the cast operator to make these conversions explicit.

To tell the truth, it should be possible to write the program using just automatic conversions. In fact, we did so, using mtime of type int to force the time calculation to be converted to integer form. However, that version failed to run on one of the five systems that we tried. Using type casts makes your intent clearer not only to the reader, but perhaps to the compiler as well.

Here's a sample output:

```
This program converts your time for a metric race
to a time for running a mile and to your average
speed in miles per hour.
Please enter, in kilometers, the distance run.
10.0
Next enter the time in minutes and seconds.
Begin by entering the minutes.
36
Now enter the seconds.
23
You ran 10.00 km (6.21 miles) in 36 min, 23 sec.
That pace corresponds to running a mile in 5 min, 51 sec.
Your average speed was 10.25 mph.
```

Chapter Summary

C has many operators, such as the assignment and arithmetic operators discussed in this chapter. In general, an *operator* operates on one or more operands to produce a value. Operators, such as the minus sign and sizeof, which take one operand, are termed *unary operators*. Operators requiring two operands, such as the addition and the multiplication operators, are called *binary operators*.

Expressions are combinations of operators and operands. In C, every expression has a value, including assignment expressions and comparison expressions. Rules of *operator precedence* help to determine how terms are grouped when expressions are evaluated.

Statements are complete instructions to the computer and are indicated in C by a terminating semicolon. So far we have worked with declaration statements, assignment statements, function call statements, and control statements. Statements included within a pair of braces constitute a *compound statement*, or *block*. One particular control statement is the while loop, which repeats statements as long as a test condition remains true.

In C, many *type conversions* take place automatically. The char and short types are promoted to type int whenever they appear in expressions or as function arguments. The float type is promoted to type double when used as a function argument. Under K&R C (but not ANSI C), float also is promoted to double when used in an expression. When a value of one type is assigned to a variable of a second type, the value is converted to the same type as the variable. When larger types are converted to smaller types (long to short or double to float, for example), there may be a loss of data. In cases of mixed arithmetic, smaller types are converted to larger types following the rules outlined in this chapter.

When you define a function that takes an argument, you declare a *variable*, or *formal argument*, in the function definition. Then the value passed in a function call is assigned to this variable, which can now be used in the function.

Review Questions

1. Assume all variables are of type int. Find the value of each of the following variables:

    a. x = (2 + 3) * 6;

    b. x = (12 + 6)/2*3;

    c. y = x = (2 + 3)/4;

    d. y = 3 + 2*(x = 7/2);

2. We suspect that there are some errors in the next program. Can you help us find them?

```c
main()
{
  int i = 1,
  float n;
  printf("Watch out! Here come a bunch of fractions!\n");
  while (i < 30)
    n = 1/i;
    printf(" %f", n);
  printf("That's all, folks!\n");
}
```

3. Here's a first attempt at making min_sec interactive. The program is not satisfactory; why not? How can it be improved?

```c
#include <stdio.h>
#define S_TO_M 60
main()
{
  int sec, min, left;

  printf("This program converts seconds to minutes and");
  printf("seconds.\n");
  printf("Just enter the number of seconds.\n");
  printf("Enter 0 to end the program.\n");
  while (sec > 0) {
    scanf("%d", &sec);
    min = sec/S_TO_M;
    left = sec % S_TO_M;
    printf("%d sec is %d min, %d sec. \n", sec, min, left);
    printf("Next input?\n");
    }
  printf("Bye!\n");
}
```

4. What will this program print?

```c
#include <stdio.h>
#define FORMAT "%s is a string\n"
main()
{
    int num = 0;

    printf(FORMAT,FORMAT);
    printf("%d\n", ++num);
    printf("%d\n", num++);
    printf("%d\n", num--);
```

```
        printf("%d\n", num);
    }
```

5. What will this program print?

```
#include <stdio.h>
#define TEN 10
main()
{
    int n = 0;

    while (n++ < TEN)
        printf("%5d", n);
    printf("\n");
}
```

6. If the following fragments were part of a complete program, what would they print?

a. ```
   int x = 0;

   while (++x < 3)
       printf("%4d", x);
   ```

b. ```
   int x = 100;

   while (x++ < 103)
       printf("%4d\n",x);
       printf("%4d\n",x);
   ```

c. ```
   char ch = 's';

   while (ch < 'w')
       {
       printf("%c", ch);
       ch++;
       }
   printf("%c\n",ch);
   ```

7. Construct statements that do the following:

a. Increase the variable x by 10.

b. Increase the variable x by 1.

c. Assign twice the sum of a and b to c.

d. Assign a plus twice b to c.

# Programming Exercises

1. Use a `while` loop to convert time in minutes to time in hours and minutes. Use a `#define` and a sensible method of ending the loop.
   ```

2. Write a program that asks for an integer and then prints all the integers from (and including) that value up to (and including) a value larger by 10. (That is, if the input is 5, the output runs from 5 to 15.)

3. Write a program that asks you to enter the number of days and then converts that value to weeks and days. For example, it would convert 18 days to 2 weeks, 4 days.

4. Change our program `addemup.c` (Listing 5.13) that found the sum of the first 20 integers. (If you prefer, you can think of `addemup.c` as a program that calculates how much money you get in 20 days if you receive $1 the first day, $2 the second day, $3 the third day, and so on.) Modify the program so that you can tell it interactively how far the calculation should proceed. That is, replace the 20 with a variable that is read in.

5. Now modify the program so that it computes the sum of the squares of the integers. (Or, if you prefer, how much money you receive if you get $1 the first day, $4 the second day, $9 the third day, and so on. This looks like a much better deal!) C doesn't have a squaring function, but you can use the fact that the square of n is n * n.

6. Write a program that requests a floating-point number and prints the value of the number cubed. Use a function of your own design to cube the value and print it. The `main()` program should pass the entered value to this function.

6

C Control
Statements:
Looping

Keywords
► for
► while
► do while

Operators
► < > >= <=
► != == += *=
► −= /= %=

In this chapter you learn about C's three loop structures: while, for, and do while. You use relational
operators to construct expressions to control these
loops, and you learn about several other operators,
too. Arrays, which are often used with loops, are
introduced. Finally, you take a first look at writing
functions having return values.

P owerful, intelligent, versatile, and useful! Most of us wouldn't mind being described that way. We aren't going to tell you how to earn these accolades for yourself, but, with the help of C, your programs can earn them. The trick is controlling the *flow* of a program. According to computer science (which is the science of computers and not science by computers—yet), a good language should provide these three forms of program flow:

► Executing a sequence of statements.
► Repeating a sequence of statements until some condition is met (looping).
► Using a test to decide between alternative sequences (branching).

The first form you know well; all of the previous programs have consisted of a sequence of statements. The `while` loop is one example of the second form. In this chapter, you'll take a closer look at the `while` loop along with two other loop structures: `for` and `do while`. The final form, choosing between different possible courses of action, makes a program much more "intelligent" and increases enormously the usefulness of a computer. Sadly, you'll have to wait a chapter before being entrusted with such power. We'll begin by reviewing the `while` loop.

An Initial Example

You are already somewhat familiar with the `while` loop, but let's review it with a program (Listing 6.1) that sums integers entered from the keyboard. This example makes use of the return value of `scanf()` to terminate input.

Listing 6.1 *summing.c*

```
/* summing.c -- sums integers entered interactively */
#include <stdio.h>
main()
{
   long num;
   long sum = 0L;          /* initialize sum to zero     */
   int status;

   printf("Please enter an integer to be summed. ");
   printf("Enter q to quit.\n");
   status = scanf("%ld", &num);
   while (status == 1)    /* == means "is equal to"     */
   {
        sum = sum + num;
        printf("Please enter next integer to be summed. ");
        printf("Enter q to quit.\n");
        status = scanf("%ld", &num);
   }
   printf("Those integers sum to %ld.\n", sum);
}
```

In Listing 6.1 we use type long to allow for larger numbers. For consistency, we initialize sum to 0L (type long zero) rather than to 0 (type int zero), even though C's automatic conversions allow us to use a plain 0.

Here is a sample run:

```
Please enter an integer to be summed. Enter q to quit.
20
Please enter next integer to be summed. Enter q to quit.
5
Please enter next integer to be summed. Enter q to quit.
30
Please enter next integer to be summed. Enter q to quit.
q
Those integers sum to 55.
```

Program Comments

Since we are reviewing the while loop, let's look at it first. The test condition for this loop is the following expression:

```
status == 1
```

The == operator is C's *equality operator*; that is, this expression tests to see if status is equal to 1. Don't confuse it with status = 1, which *assigns* 1 to status. With the status == 1 test condition, the loop will repeat as long as status is 1. For each cycle, the loop adds the current value of num to sum, so that sum maintains a running total. Once status gets a value other than 1, the loop terminates, and the program reports the final value of sum.

For the program to work properly, it should get a new value for num on each loop cycle, and it should reset status on each cycle. We accomplish this by using two distinct features of scanf(). First, we use scanf() to attempt to read a new value for num. Second, we use the scanf() return value to report on the success of that attempt. Recall (Chapter 4) that scanf() returns the number of items successfully read. If scanf() succeeds in reading an integer, it places the integer into num and returns the value 1, which is assigned to status. (Note that the input value goes to num, not to status.) This updates both num and the value of status, and the while loop goes through another cycle. If you respond with nonnumeric input, such as q, scanf() will fail to find an integer to read, so its return value and status will be 0. That terminates the loop.

This dual use of scanf() gets around a troublesome aspect of interactive input to a loop: how do you tell the loop when to stop? Suppose, for instance, that scanf() did not have a return value. Then the only thing that would change on each loop is the value of num. We could use the value of num to terminate the loop, using, say, num > 0 (num greater than 0) or num != 0 (num not equal to 0) as a test condition, but this prevents us from entering certain values, such as −3 or 0, as input. Or we could add new code to the loop, such as asking "Do you wish to continue? <y/n>" at each cycle and then testing to see if the user entered a y. But this is a bit clunky and slows down input. Using the return value of scanf() avoids these problems.

Now let's take a closer look at the program structure. We can summarize it thus:

> initialize sum to 0
>
> prompt user
>
> read input
>
> while the input is an integer,
>
> > add the input to sum,
> >
> > prompt user,
> >
> > then read next input
>
> when input is not an integer, print sum

This, incidentally, is an example of *pseudocode*, which is the art of expressing a program in simple English that parallels the forms of a computer language. Pseudocode is useful for working out the logic of a program. Once the logic seems right, you can translate the pseudocode to the actual programming code. The advantage of pseudocode is that it lets you concentrate on the logic and organization of a program while sparing you from simultaneously worrying about how to express the ideas in a computer language.

Anyway, because the while loop is an entry-condition loop, we have to obtain the input and check the value of status *before* we get to the body of the loop. That is why we have a scanf() before the while. But for the loop to continue, we need a read statement inside the loop so that it can find out the status of the next input. That is why we also have a scanf() statement at the end of the while loop; it readies the loop for its next iteration.

C-Style Reading Loop

Listing 6.1 could be written in Pascal or BASIC or FORTRAN along the same design displayed in the pseudocode. C, however, offers a shortcut. The construction

```
status = scanf("%ld", &num);
while (status == 1)
{
        /* loop actions */
        status = scanf("%ld", &num);
}
```

can be replaced by the following:

```
while (scanf("%ld", &num) == 1)
{
        /* loop actions */
}
```

This form uses scanf() in two different ways simultaneously. First, the function call, if successful, places a value in num. Second, the function's return value (which is 1 or 0 and not the value of num) controls the loop. Since the loop condition is tested at each iteration, scanf() is called at each iteration, providing a new num and a new test.

Now let's take a more formal look at the while statement.

The *while* Statement

The general form of the `while` loop is

```
while (expression)
    statement
```

The `statement` part can be a simple statement with a terminating semicolon, or it can be a compound statement enclosed in braces.

Our examples so far have used *relational* expressions for the expression part; that is, `expression` has been a comparison of values. More generally, you can use any expression. If `expression` is true (or, more generally, nonzero), the statement is executed once, and then the expression is tested again. This cycle of test and execution is repeated until `expression` becomes false (zero). Each cycle is called an *iteration*. See Figure 6.1.

Figure 6.1 *Structure of the* while *loop*

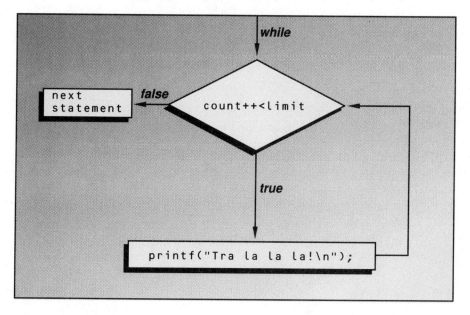

Terminating a *while* Loop

Here is a CRUCIAL point about `while` loops: when you construct a `while` loop, it must include something that changes the value of the test expression so that the expression eventually becomes false. Otherwise, the loop will never terminate. (Actually, you can use `break` and an `if` statement to terminate a loop, but you haven't learned about them yet.) Consider this example:

```
index = 1;
while (index < 5)
    printf("Good morning!\n");
```

The preceding fragment prints its cheerful message indefinitely. Why? Because nothing within the loop changes the value of `index` from its initial value of 1. Now consider this:

```
index = 1;
while (--index < 5)
    printf("Good morning!\n");
```

This last fragment isn't much better. It changes the value of `index`, but in the wrong direction! At least this version will terminate eventually when `index` drops below the most negative number that the system can handle.

When a Loop Terminates

It is important to realize that the decision to terminate the loop or to continue takes place only at the time that the test condition is evaluated. For instance, consider the program shown in Listing 6.2.

Listing 6.2 when.c

```
/* when.c -- when a loop quits */
#include <stdio.h>
main()
{
   int n = 5;

   while (n < 7)                          /* line 7 */
   {
        printf("n = %d\n", n);
```

```
        n++;                        /* line 10 */
        printf("Now n = %d\n", n);  /* line 11 */
    }
}
```

Running Listing 6.2 produces the following output:

```
n = 5
Now n = 6
n = 6
Now n = 7
```

The variable n first assumes the value 7 on line 10 during the second cycle of the loop. But the program completes the loop (line 11) and quits the loop only when the test condition on line 7 is evaluated for the third time. (The variable n was 5 for the first test and 6 for the second test.)

while—An Entry-Condition Loop

The while loop is a *conditional* loop using an *entry condition*. It is called conditional because the execution of the statement portion depends on the condition described through the test expression, such as (index < 5). The expression is an entry condition because the condition must be met *before* the body of the loop is entered. In a situation like the following, the body of the loop is never entered because the condition is false to begin with.

```
index = 10;
while (index++ < 5)
    printf("Have a fair day or better.\n");
```

Change the first line to

```
index = 3;
```

and the loop will execute.

Syntax Points

One point to keep in mind when using while is that only the single statement, simple or compound, following the test condition is part of the loop. Indentation is an aid to the reader, not the computer. Listing 6.3 shows what can happen if you forget this.

```
Listing 6.3  while1.c

/* while1.c -- watch your braces */
#include <stdio.h>
main()
{
  int n = 0;

  while (n < 3)
      printf("n is %d\n", n);
      n++;
  printf("That's all this program does\n");
}
```

Running this program produces the following output:

```
n is 0
n is 0
n is 0
n is 0
    .
    .
    .
```

Although we indented the n++; statement, we didn't enclose it and the preceding statement within braces. Thus, only the single print statement immediately following the test condition is part of the loop. The variable n is never updated, the condition n < 3 remains eternally true, and we get a loop that goes on printing n is 0 until we kill the program. This is an example of an *infinite loop*, one that does not quit without outside intervention.

Always remember that the while statement itself, even if it uses compound statements, counts syntactically as a single statement. The statement runs from the while to the first semicolon or, in the case of using a compound statement, to the terminating brace.

Be careful where you place your semicolons. For instance, consider the program in Listing 6.4.

Listing 6.4 *while2.c*

```
/* while2.c -- watch your semicolons */
#include <stdio.h>
main()
{
  int n = 0;

  while (n++ < 3);                 /* line 7 */
       printf("n is %d\n", n);     /* line 8 */
  printf("That's all this program does.\n");
}
```

This program has the following output:

```
n is 4
That's all this program does.
```

As we said earlier, the loop ends with the first statement, simple or compound, following the test condition. Since there is a semicolon immediately after the test condition on line 7, the loop ends there, for a lone semicolon counts as a statement. The print statement on line 8 is not part of the loop. So n is incremented on each loop, but it is printed only after the loop is exited.

In this example, the test condition is followed with the *null statement*, one that does nothing. In C, the lone semicolon represents the null statement. Occasionally, programmers intentionally will use the `while` statement with a null statement, either to create a time delay or because all the work gets done in the test. For example, suppose you want to skip over input to the first character that isn't whitespace or a digit. You can use a loop like this:

```
while (scanf("%d", &num) == 1)
   ;    /* skip integer input */
```

As long as `scanf()` reads an integer, it returns 1, and the loop continues. Note that for clarity we put the semicolon (the null statement) on the line below instead of on the same line. This makes it easier to see the null statement when you read a program and also reminds you that the null statement is there deliberately.

Which Is Bigger: Using Relational Operators and Expressions

Because while loops often rely on test expressions that make comparisons, comparison expressions merit a closer look. Such expressions are termed *relational expressions*, and the operators that appear in them are called *relational operators*. We have used several already, and Table 6.1 gives a complete list of C relational operators. This table pretty much covers all the possibilities for numerical relationships. (Numbers, even complex ones, are less complex than humans.)

Table 6.1 *Relational Operators*

Operator	Meaning
<	Is less than
<=	Is less than or equal to
==	Is equal to
>=	Is greater than or equal to
>	Is greater than
!=	Is not equal to

The relational operators are used to form the relational expressions used in while statements and in other C statements that we'll discuss later. These statements check to see if the expression is true or false. Here are three unrelated statements containing examples of relational expressions. The meaning, we hope, is clear.

```
while (number < 6)
{
    printf("Your number is too small.\n");
    scanf("%d", &number);
}

while (ch != '$')
{
    count++;
    scanf("%c", &ch);
}

while (scanf("%f", &num) == 1)
    sum = sum + num;
```

Note in the second example that the relational expressions can be used with characters, too. The machine code (which we have been assuming is ASCII) is used for the comparison. However, you can't use the relational operators to compare strings. Chapter 11 will show you what to use for strings.

The relational operators can be used with floating-point numbers, too. But beware, you should limit yourself to using only < and > in floating-point comparisons. The reason is that roundoff errors can prevent two numbers from being equal even though logically they should be. For example, certainly the product of 3 and ⅓ is 1.0. But if we express ⅓ as a six-place decimal fraction, the product is .999999, which is not quite equal to 1.

Each relational expression is judged to be "true" or "false" (but never "maybe"). This raises an interesting question.

What Is Truth?

We can answer this age-old question, at least as far as C is concerned. Recall that an expression in C always has a value. This is true even for relational expressions, as the example in Listing 6.5 shows. In it we print the values of two relational expressions, one true and one false.

```
Listing 6.5   t_and_f.c

/* t_and_f.c -- true and false values in C */
#include <stdio.h>
main()
{
  int true, false;

  true = (10 > 2);    /* value of a true relationship  */
  false = (10 == 2);  /* value of a false relationship */
  printf("true = %d; false = %d \n", true, false);
}
```

In Listing 6.5 we have assigned the values of two relational expressions to two variables. Being straightforward, we assigned true the value of a true expression, and false the value of a false expression. Running the program produces the following simple output:

```
true = 1; false = 0
```

Aha! For C, a true expression has the value 1, and a false expression has the value 0. Indeed, some C programs use the following construction for loops that are meant to run forever, since 1 always is true:

```
while (1)
{
    .
    .
    .
}
```

So What Else Is True?

If we can use a 1 or a 0 as a `while` statement test expression, can we use other numbers? If so, what happens? Let's experiment by trying the program in Listing 6.6.

Listing 6.6 truth.c

```
/* truth.c -- what values are true? */
#include <stdio.h>
main()
{
    int n = 3;

    while (n)
        printf("%d\n", n--);
    n = -3;
    while (n)
        printf("%2d\n", n++);

}
```

The results are

```
 3
 2
 1
-3
-2
-1
```

The first loop executes when n is **3**, **2**, and **1**, but terminates when n is **0**. Similarly, the second loop executes when n is **−3**, **−2**, and **−1**, but terminates when n is **0**. More generally, all nonzero values are regarded as "true," and only 0 is recognized as "false." C has a very tolerant notion of truth!

Alternatively, we can say that a `while` loop executes as long as its test condition evaluates to nonzero. This puts test conditions on a numeric basis instead of a true-false basis. Keep in mind that relational expressions evaluate to 1 if true and to 0 if false, so such expressions really are numeric.

Many programmers make use of this property of test conditions. For example, the phrase

```
while (goats != 0)
```

can be replaced by

```
while (goats)
```

since the expression (goats != 0) and the expression (goats) both become 0, or false, only when goats has the value 0. We think that the second form is not as clear in meaning as the first, but many C programmers prefer the second form. The popular thought has been that the second form is more efficient because it requires fewer computer processing operations when the program runs. But some compilers are clever enough to use the same efficient code for either form. The current tendency is to try for clear code and leave it to clever compilers to maximize the efficiency.

Troubles with Truth

C's tolerant notion of truth can lead to trouble. For example, let's make one subtle change in Listing 6.1, producing the program shown in Listing 6.7.

Listing 6.7 *trouble.c*

```
/* trouble.c -- misuse of = */
#include <stdio.h>
main()
{
   long num;
```

(continued)

Listing 6.7   *(continued)*

```
long sum = 0L;
int status;

printf("Please enter an integer to be summed. ");
printf("Enter q to quit.\n");
status = scanf("%ld", &num);
while (status = 1)
{
    sum = sum + num;
    printf("Please enter next integer to be summed. ");
    printf("Enter q to quit.\n");
    status = scanf("%ld", &num);
}
printf("Those integers sum to %ld\n", sum);
}
```

Running Listing 6.7 produces output like the following:

```
Please enter an integer to be summed. Enter q to quit.
20
Please enter next integer to be summed. Enter q to quit.
5
Please enter next integer to be summed. Enter q to quit.
30
Please enter next integer to be summed. Enter q to quit.
q
Please enter next integer to be summed. Enter q to quit.
Please enter next integer to be summed. Enter q to quit.
Please enter next integer to be summed. Enter q to quit.
Please enter next integer to be summed. Enter q to quit.

      .
      .
      .

(and so on until you kill the program)
```

We made a change in the `while` test condition, replacing `status == 1` with `status = 1`. The second statement is an assignment statement, so it gives `status` the value 1. Furthermore, the value of an assignment statement is the value of the left side, so `status = 1` has the same numerical value of 1. Thus, for all practical purposes, our `while` loop is the same as using `while (1)`; that is, it is a loop that never quits. We enter q, and `status` is set to 0. But the loop test resets `status` to 1 and starts another cycle.

You may wonder why, since the program keeps looping, the user doesn't get a chance to type in any more input after entering q. When `scanf()` fails to read the specified form of input, it leaves the nonconforming input in place to be read the next time. So when `scanf()` tries to read the q as an integer and fails, it leaves the q there. During the next loop cycle, `scanf()` attempts to read where it left off the last time: at the q once again. And once again `scanf()` fails to read the q as an integer. So not only does this example set up an infinite loop, it also creates a loop of infinite failure, a daunting concept. It is fortunate that computers, as yet, lack feelings. Following stupid instructions eternally is no better or worse to a computer than successfully predicting the stock market for the next ten years.

Don't use = for ==. Some computer languages (BASIC, for example) do use the same symbol for both the assignment operator and the relational equality operator, but the two operations are quite different (see Figure 6.2). The assignment operator *assigns* a value to the left-hand variable. The relational equality operator, however, checks to see if the left-hand and right-hand sides are already equal. It doesn't change the value of the left-hand variable, if one is present.

```
canoes = 5      ←assigns the value 5 to canoes
canoes == 5     ←checks to see if canoes has the value 5
```

Be careful about using the correct operator. A compiler will let you use the wrong form, yielding results other than what you expect.

Figure 6.2 *The relational operator = =*
and the assignment operator =

comparison

`canoes == 5`

== checks to see if the value of canoes is 5

assignment

`canoes = 5`

= gives canoes the value of 5

To sum up, the relational operators are used to form relational expressions. Relational expressions have the value 1 if true and 0 if false.

Statements (such as `while` and `if`) that normally use relational expressions as tests can use any expression as a test, with nonzero values recognized as "true" and zero values as "false."

Precedence of Relational Operators

The precedence of the relational operators is less than that of the arithmetic operators, including + and –, and greater than that of assignment operators. This means, for example, that

```
x > y + 2
```

means the same as

```
x > (y + 2)
```

and that

```
x = y > 2
```

means

```
x = (y > 2)
```

That is, x is assigned 1 if y is greater than 2 and is 0 otherwise; x is not assigned the value of y.

The relational operators are themselves organized into two different priorities:

Higher-priority group: `<  <=  >  =>`
Lower-priority group: `==  !=`

Like most other operators, the relational operators associate from left to right. Thus,

```
ex != wye == zee
```

is the same as

```
(ex != wye) == zee
```

First C checks to see if `ex` and `wye` are unequal. Then the resulting value of 1 or 0 (true or false) is compared to the value of `zee`. We don't anticipate using this sort of construction, but we feel that it is our duty to point out such sidelights.

Table 6.2 shows the priorities of the operators introduced so far, and Appendix B has a complete precedence ranking of all operators.

Table 6.2 *Operator Precedence*

Operators (From High to Low Precedence)	Associativity
( )	L-R
- + ++ -- sizeof *(type)* (all unary)	R-L
* / %	L-R
+ -	L-R
< > <= >=	L-R
== !=	L-R
=	R-L

Summary: The *while* Statement

Keyword

while

General Comments

The while statement creates a loop that repeats until the test *expression* becomes false, or zero. The while statement is an *entry-condition* loop; that is, the decision to go through one more pass of the loop is made *before* the loop is traversed. Thus, it is possible that the loop is never traversed. The *statement* part of the form can be a simple statement or a compound statement.

Form

```
while (expression)
        statement
```

The *statement* portion is repeated until the *expression* becomes false or zero.

(continued)

Examples

```
while (n++ < 100)
      printf(" %d %d\n",n, 2 * n + 1); /* single statement */

while (fargo < 1000)
{                                      /* compound statement */
fargo = fargo + step;
step = 2 * step;
}
```

Summary: Relational Operators and Expressions

Relational Operators

Each relational operator compares the value at its left to the value at its right.

<	Is less than
<=	Is less than or equal to
==	Is equal to
>=	Is greater than or equal to
>	Is greater than
!=	Is unequal to

Relational Expressions

A simple relational expression consists of a relational operator with an operand on each side. If the relation is true, the relational expression has the value 1. If the relation is false, the relational expression has the value 0.

Examples

5 > 2 is true and has the value 1.

(2 + a) == a is false and has the value 0.

Indefinite Loops and Counting Loops

Some of our `while` loop examples have been *indefinite* loops. This means that we don't know in advance how many times the loop will be executed before the expression becomes false. For instance, when we used an interactive loop to sum integers, we didn't know beforehand how many integers would be entered. Other of our examples, however, have been *counting* loops. They execute a predetermined number of repetitions. Listing 6.8 is a short example of a `while` counting loop.

Listing 6.8   *sweetie1.c*

```
/* sweetie1.c -- a counting loop */
#include <stdio.h>
#define NUMBER 22
main()
{
   int count = 1;                       /* initialization */

   while (count <= NUMBER)              /* test          */
     {
        printf("Be my Valentine!\n");   /* action        */
        count++;                        /* update count  */
     }
}
```

Although the form used in Listing 6.8 works fine, it is not the best choice for this situation, since the actions defining the loop are not all gathered together. Let's elaborate on that point.

Three actions are involved in setting up a loop that is to be repeated a fixed number of times.

1. A counter must be initialized.

2. The counter is compared with some limiting value.

3. The counter is incremented each time the loop is traversed.

The `while` loop condition takes care of the comparison. The increment operator takes care of the incrementing. In Listing 6.8 the incrementing is done at the end of the loop. This choice makes it possible to omit the incrementing accidentally. Thus, it would be better to combine the test and update actions into one expression by using `count++ <= NUMBER`. But the initialization of the counter still is done outside the loop, making it possible to forget to initialize a counter. Experience teaches us that what *might* happen, will happen eventually, so let's look at a control statement that avoids these problems.

The *for* Loop

The `for` loop gathers all three actions into one place. By using a `for` loop, we can replace the preceding program with the one shown in Listing 6.9.

Listing 6.9 *sweetie2.c*

```
/* sweetie2.c -- a counting loop using for */
#include <stdio.h>
#define NUMBER 22
main()
{
   int count;

   for (count = 1; count <= NUMBER; count++)
       printf("Be my Valentine!\n");
}
```

The parentheses following the keyword `for` contain three expressions separated by two semicolons. The first expression is the initialization. It is done just once, when the `for` loop first starts. The second expression is the test condition; it is evaluated before each potential execution of a loop. When the expression is false (when `count` is greater than `NUMBER`), the loop is terminated. The third expression, the change or update, is evaluated at the end of each loop. We have used it to increment the value of `count`, but it needn't be restricted to that use. The `for` statement is completed by following it with one simple or compound statement. Figure 6.3 summarizes the structure of a `for` loop.

To show another example, Listing 6.10 uses the `for` loop in a program that prints a table of cubes.

Figure 6.3 *Structure of a* for *loop*

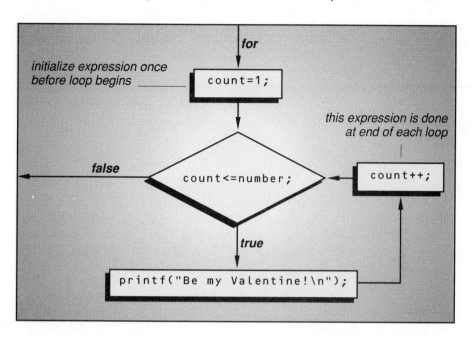

Listing 6.10 *for_cube.c*

```
/* for_cube.c -- using a for loop to make a table of cubes */
#include <stdio.h>
main()
{
  int num;

  printf("   n    n cubed\n");
  for (num = 1; num <= 6; num++)
    printf("%5d %5d\n", num, num*num*num);
}
```

Listing 6.10 prints the integers 1 through 6 and their cubes:

```
n    n cubed
1       1
```

```
2     8
3    27
4    64
5   125
6   216
```

The first line of the `for` loop tells us immediately all the information about the loop parameters: the starting value of `num`, the final value of `num`, and the amount that `num` increases on each looping.

Using *for* for Flexibility!

Although the `for` loop looks similar to the FORTRAN DO loop, the Pascal FOR loop, and the BASIC FOR . . . NEXT loop, it is much more flexible than any of these. This flexibility stems from how the three expressions in a `for` specification can be used. So far we have used the first expression to initialize a counter, the second expression to express the limit for the counter, and the third expression to increase the value of the counter by 1. When used this way, the C `for` statement is very much like the others we have mentioned. But there are many more possibilities, and here we will show you nine variations.

1. You can use the decrement operator to count down instead of up.

```
#include <stdio.h>
main()
{
   int secs;

   for (secs = 5; secs > 0; secs--)
        printf("%d seconds!\n", secs);
   printf("We have ignition!\n");
}
```

Here is the output:

```
5 seconds!
4 seconds!
3 seconds!
2 seconds!
1 seconds!
We have ignition!
```

2. You can count by twos, tens, etc., if you want.

```
#include <stdio.h>
main()
```

```
{
    int n;                   /* count by 13s */

    for (n = 2;  n < 60; n = n + 13)
        printf("%d \n", n);
}
```

This would increase n by 13 during each cycle, printing the following:

```
2
15
28
41
54
```

3. You can count by characters instead of by numbers.

```
#include <stdio.h>
main()
{
    char ch;

    for (ch = 'a'; ch <= 'z'; ch++)
        printf("The ASCII value for %c is %d.\n", ch, ch);
}
```

An abridged output looks like this:

```
The ASCII value for a is 97.
The ASCII value for b is 98.
        .
        .
        .
The ASCII value for x is 120.
The ASCII value for y is 121.
The ASCII value for z is 122.
```

The program works because characters are stored as integers, so this loop really counts by integers anyway.

4. You can test some condition other than the number of iterations. In our for_cube program, we can replace

```
for (num = 1; num <= 6; num++)
```

with

```
for (num = 1; num*num*num <= 216; num++)
```

We would use this test condition if we were more concerned with limiting the size of the cube than with limiting the number of iterations.

5. You can let a quantity increase geometrically instead of arithmetically; that is, instead of adding a fixed amount each time, you can multiply by a fixed amount.

```
#include <stdio.h>
main()
{
    float debt;

    for (debt = 100.0; debt < 150.0; debt = debt * 1.1)
        printf("Your debt is now $%.2f.\n", debt);
}
```

This program fragment multiplies debt by 1.1 for each cycle, increasing it by 10 percent each time. The output looks like this:

```
Your debt is now $100.00.
Your debt is now $110.00.
Your debt is now $121.00.
Your debt is now $133.10.
Your debt is now $146.41.
```

6. You can use any legal expression you want for the third expression. Whatever you put in will be updated for each iteration.

```
#include <stdio.h>
main()
{
    int x;
    int y = 55;

    for (x = 1; y <= 75; y = (++x * 5) + 50)
        printf("%10d %10d\n", x, y);
}
```

This loop prints the values of x and of the algebraic expression ++x * 5 + 50. The output looks like this:

```
1          55
2          60
3          65
4          70
5          75
```

Notice that the test involved y, not x. Each of the three expressions in the for loop control can use different variables. (Note that although this example is valid, it does not show good style. The program would have been clearer if we hadn't mixed the updating process with an algebraic calculation.)

7. You can even leave one or more expressions blank (but don't omit the semicolons). Just be sure to include within the loop itself some statement that will eventually cause the loop to terminate.

```
#include <stdio.h>
main()
{
  int ans, n;

  ans = 2;
  for (n = 3; ans <= 25; )
      ans = ans * n;
  printf("n = %d; ans = %d.\n", n, ans);
}
```

Here is the output:

```
n = 3; ans = 54.
```

The loop keeps the value of n at 3. The variable ans starts with the value 2, then increases to 6 and 18, and obtains a final value of 54. (The value 18 is less than 25, so the for loop goes through one more iteration, multiplying 18 by 3 to get 54.) The loop, as shown following, goes on forever, since an empty test is considered to be true:

```
for (; ; )
      printf("I want some action\n");
```

8. The first expression need not initialize a variable. It could, instead, be a printf() statement of some sort. Just remember that the first expression is evaluated or executed only once, before any other parts of the loop are executed.

```
#include <stdio.h>
main()
{
  int num;

    for (printf("Keep entering numbers!\n"); num != 6; )
          scanf("%d", &num);
  printf("That's the one I want!\n");
}
```

This fragment prints the first message once and then keeps accepting numbers until you enter a 6:

```
Keep entering numbers!
3
```

```
5
8
6
That's the one I want!
```

9. The parameters of the loop expressions can be altered by actions within the loop. For example, suppose you have the loop set up like this:

```
for(n = 1; n < 10000; n = n + delta)
```

If after a few iterations your program decides that `delta` is too small or too large, an `if` statement (Chapter 7) inside the loop can change the size of `delta`. In an interactive program, `delta` can be changed by the user as the loop runs.

In short, the freedom you have in selecting the expressions that control a `for` loop makes this loop able to do much more than just perform a fixed number of iterations. The power of the `for` loop is enhanced further by the operators we will discuss shortly.

Summary: The *for* Statement

Keyword

`for`

General Comments

The `for` statement uses three control expressions, separated by semicolons, to control a looping process. The *initialize* expression is executed once, before any of the loop statements are executed. Then the *test* expression is evaluated, and if it is true (or nonzero), the loop is cycled through once. Then the *update* expression is evaluated, and it is time to check the *test* expression again. The `for` statement is an *entry-condition* loop—the decision to go through one more pass of the loop is made *before* the loop is traversed. Thus, it is possible that the loop is never traversed. The *statement* part of the form can be a simple statement or a compound statement.

Form

```
for (initialize ; test ; update)
    statement
```

The loop is repeated until *test* becomes false or zero.

Example

```
for (n = 0;  n < 10 ; n++)
        printf(" %d %d\n", n, 2 * n + 1);
```

More Assignment Operators: +=, −=, *=, /=, %=

C has several assignment operators. The most basic one, of course, is =, which simply assigns the value of the expression at its right to the variable at its left. The other assignment operators update variables. Each is used with a variable name to its left and an expression to its right. The variable is assigned a new value equal to its old value adjusted by the value of the expression at the right. The exact adjustment depends on the operator, for example:

scores += 20	is the same as	scores = scores + 20
dimes −= 2	is the same as	dimes = dimes − 2
bunnies *= 2	is the same as	bunnies = bunnies * 2
time /= 2.73	is the same as	time = time / 2.73
reduce %= 3	is the same as	reduce = reduce % 3

In the preceding list, we used simple numbers on the right, but we could have used more elaborate expressions:

x *= 3 * y + 12	is the same as	x = x * (3 * y + 12)

The assignment operators we've just discussed have the same low priority that = does, i.e., less than that of + or *. This low priority is reflected in the last example, in which 12 is added to 3 * y before multiplying the result by x.

You are not required to use these forms. They are, however, more compact, and they may produce more efficient machine code than the longer form. They are particularly useful when you are trying to squeeze something complex into a for loop specification.

The Comma Operator

The *comma operator* extends the flexibility of the `for` loop by allowing you to include more than one initialization or update expression in a single `for` loop specification. For example, Listing 6.11 shows a program that prints first-class postage rates. (At the time of this writing, the rate is 25 cents for the first ounce and 20 cents for each additional ounce.)

Listing 6.11 *postage.c*

```
/* postage.c -- first-class postage rates */
#include <stdio.h>
#define FIRST 25
#define NEXT  20
main()
{
    int ounces, cost;

    printf(" ounces  cost\n");
    for(ounces=1, cost=FIRST; ounces<= 16; ounces++,
         cost += NEXT)
       printf("%5d %7d\n", ounces, cost);
}
```

The first four lines of output look like this:

```
ounces  cost
    1     25
    2     45
    3     65
```

We used the comma operator in the initialize and the update expressions. Its presence in the first expression causes ounces *and* cost to be initialized. Its second occurrence causes ounces to be increased by 1 and cost to be increased by 20 (the value of NEXT) for each iteration. All the calculations are done in the `for` loop specifications! See Figure 6.4.

The comma operator is not restricted to `for` loops, but that is where it is most often used. The operator has two further properties. First, it guarantees that the expressions it separates will be evaluated in a left-to-right

Figure 6.4 *The comma operator and the* for *loop*

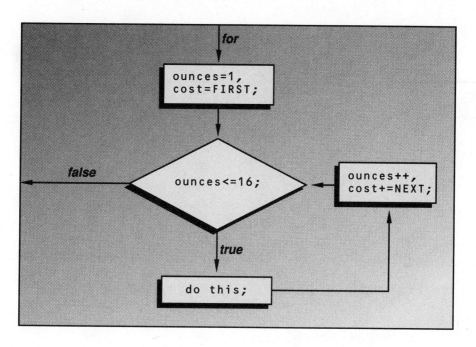

order. Thus, ounces is initialized before cost. The order is not important for this example, but it would be important if the expression for cost contained ounces. Second, the value of the whole comma expression is the value of the right-hand member. So the effect of the statement

```
x = (y = 3, (z = ++y + 2) + 5);
```

is to first assign 3 to y, increment y to 4, then add 2 to 4 and assign the resulting value of 6 to z, next add 5 to z, and finally assign the resulting value of 11 to x. Why anyone would do this is beyond the scope of this book.

The comma also is used as a separator. Thus, the commas in

```
char ch, date;
```

and

```
printf("%d %d\n", chimps, chumps);
```

are separators, not comma operators.

Summary: Our New Operators

Assignment Operators

Each of these operators updates the variable at its left by the value at its right, using the indicated operation. We use the abbreviations *R-H* for right-hand and *L-H* for left-hand.

- `+=` Adds the R-H quantity to the L-H variable
- `-=` Subtracts the R-H quantity from the L-H variable
- `*=` Multiplies the L-H variable by the R-H quantity
- `/=` Divides the L-H variable by the R-H quantity
- `%=` Gives the remainder obtained from dividing the L-H variable by the R-H quantity

Example

`rabbits *= 1.6;`   is the same as   `rabbits = rabbits * 1.6;`

The Comma Operator

The comma operator links two expressions into one and guarantees that the left-most expression is evaluated first. It is typically used to include more information in a `for` loop control expression.

Example

```
for (step = 2, fargo = 0; fargo < 1000; step *= 2)
        fargo += step;
```

Zeno Meets the *for* Loop

Let's see how the `for` loop and the comma operator can help solve an old paradox. The Greek philosopher Zeno once argued that an arrow will never reach its target. First, he said, the arrow covers half the distance to the target. Then it has to cover half of the remaining distance. Then it still has half of what's left to cover, ad infinitum. Since the journey has an infinite number of parts, Zeno argued, it would take the arrow an infinite amount of time to reach its journey's end. We doubt, however, that Zeno would have volunteered to be a target just on the strength of this argument.

Let's take a quantitative approach and suppose that it takes the arrow

1 second to travel the first half. Then it would take ½ second to travel half of what was left, ¼ second to travel half of what was left next, etc. We can represent the total time by the infinite series $1+\frac{1}{2}+\frac{1}{4}+\frac{1}{8}+\frac{1}{16}+\ldots$

The short program in Listing 6.12 finds the sum of the first few terms.

```
Listing 6.12   zeno.c

/* zeno.c -- series sum */
#include <stdio.h>
#define LIMIT 15
main()
{
 int count;
 float time, x;

 for (time=0, x=1, count=1; count <= LIMIT; count++, x *= 2.0)
 {
    time += 1.0/x;
    printf("time = %f when count = %d.\n", time, count);
 }
}
```

The output is the sum of the first 15 terms:

```
time = 1.000000 when count = 1.
time = 1.500000 when count = 2.
time = 1.750000 when count = 3.
time = 1.875000 when count = 4.
time = 1.937500 when count = 5.
time = 1.968750 when count = 6.
time = 1.984375 when count = 7.
time = 1.992188 when count = 8.
time = 1.996094 when count = 9.
time = 1.998047 when count = 10.
time = 1.999023 when count = 11.
time = 1.999512 when count = 12.
time = 1.999756 when count = 13.
time = 1.999878 when count = 14.
time = 1.999939 when count = 15.
```

You can see that although we keep adding more terms, the total seems to level out. Indeed, mathematicians have proven that the total approaches

2.0 as the number of terms approaches infinity, just as our program suggests.

What about the program itself? It shows that you can use more than one comma operator in an expression. We initialized time, x, and count. Once we set up the conditions for the loop, the program itself is extremely brief.

An Exit-Condition Loop: *do while*

The while loop and the for loop are both entry-condition loops. The test condition is checked before each iteration of the loop, so it is possible for the statements in the loop to never execute. C also has an *exit-condition* loop in which the condition is checked after each iteration of the loop, guaranteeing that statements will be executed at least once. This variety is called a do while loop. Listing 6.13 shows an example.

```
Listing 6.13   dowhile.c

/* dowhile.c -- exit condition loop */
#include <stdio.h>
main()
{
  char ch;

  do
  {
      scanf("%c", &ch);
      printf("%c", ch);
  } while (ch != '#');
}
```

The program in Listing 6.13 reads input characters and reprints them until the # character shows up. How is this program different from a while loop version such as that in Listing 6.14?

The behavioral difference appears when the # character is read. The while loop prints all the characters *up to* the first # character, and the do while loop prints all the characters *up to and including* the # character. Only after it has printed the # character does the loop check to see if a # character has shown up. In a do while loop, that action comes before the test condition.

Listing 6.14 *entry.c*

```
/* entry.c -- entry condition loop */
#include <stdio.h>
main()
{
   char ch;
   scanf("%c", &ch);
   while (ch != '#')
   {
        printf("%c", ch);
        scanf("%c", &ch);
   }
}
```

The general form of the do while loop is

```
do
     statement
while ( expression );
```

The statement can be simple or compound. Note that the do while loop itself counts as a statement and therefore requires a terminating semicolon. Also see Figure 6.5.

A do while loop always is executed at least once, since the test is made after the body of the loop has been executed. A for loop or a while loop, on the other hand, may be executed zero times, since the test is made before execution. You should restrict the use of do while loops to cases that require at least one iteration. For example, a password program could include a loop along these pseudocode lines:

```
do
{
   prompt for password
   read user input
} while (input not equal to password) ;
```

Avoid a do while structure of the type shown in the following pseudocode:

Figure 6.5 *Structure of a* do while *loop*

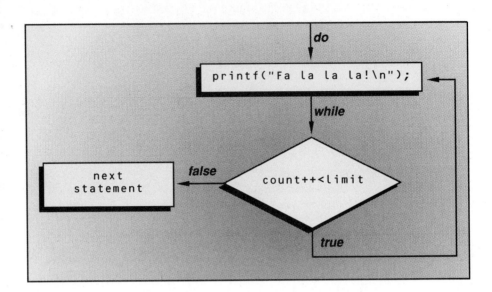

ask user if he or she wants to continue

do

some clever stuff

while (answer is yes)

Here, after the user answers "no," some clever stuff gets done anyway because the test comes too late.

Summary: The *do while* Statement

Keywords

`do, while`

General Comments

The do `while` statement creates a loop that repeats until the test *expression* becomes false or zero. The do `while` statement is an *exit-condition* loop—the decision to go through one more pass of the loop is made *after* the loop has been traversed. Thus, the loop must be executed at least once. The `statement` part of the form can be a simple statement or a compound statement.

Form

```
do
     statement
          while (expression);
```

The `statement` portion is repeated until the `expression` becomes false or zero.

Example

```
do
     scanf("%d", &number)
          while (number != 20);
```

Which Loop?

Once you decide you need a loop, which one should you use? First, decide whether you need an entry-condition loop or an exit-condition loop. Your answer should usually be an entry-condition loop. There are several reasons why computer scientists consider an entry-condition loop superior. One is the general principle that it is better to look *before* you leap (or loop) than after. A second is that a program is easier to read if the loop test is found at the beginning of the loop. Finally, in many uses, it is important that the loop be skipped entirely if the test is not initially met.

Assume you need an entry-condition loop. Should it be a `for` or a `while`? This is partly a matter of taste, since what you can do with one, you can do with the other. To make a `for` loop like a `while`, you can omit the first and third expressions. For example,

```
for ( ;test; )
```

is the same as

```
while (test)
```

To make a `while` like a `for`, preface it with an initialization and include update statements. For example,

```
      initialize;
      while (test)
      {
        body;
        update;
      }
```

is the same as

```
      for (initialize; test; update)
          body;
```

In terms of style, a `for` loop is appropriate when the loop involves initializing and updating a variable, and a `while` loop is better when the conditions are otherwise. Thus, a `while` loop is natural for the following condition:

```
      while (scanf("%ld", &num) == 1)
```

The `for` loop is a more natural choice for loops involving counting with an index:

```
      for (count = 1; count <= 100; count++)
```

Nested Loops

A *nested loop* is one loop inside another loop. A common use for nested loops is to display data in rows and columns. One loop can handle, say, all the columns in a row, and the second loop handles the rows. Listing 6.16 shows a simple example.

Listing 6.15 *rows1.c*

```
/* rows1.c -- uses nested loops */
#include <stdio.h>
#define ROWS  6
#define CHARS 6
main()
{
    int row;
```

```
    char ch;

    for (row = 0; row < ROWS; row++)              /* line 10 */
    {
        for (ch = 'A'; ch < ('A' + CHARS); ch++)  /* line 12 */
            printf("%c", ch);
        printf("\n");
    }
}
```

Running the program produces this output:

```
ABCDEF
ABCDEF
ABCDEF
ABCDEF
ABCDEF
ABCDEF
```

Discussion

The for loop beginning on line 10 is called an *outer* loop, and the loop beginning on line 12 is called an *inner* loop because it is inside the other loop. The outer loop starts with row having a value of 0 and terminates when row reaches 6. Thus, the outer loop goes through six cycles, with row having the values 0 through 5. The first statement in each cycle is the inner for loop. This loop also goes through six cycles, printing the characters A through F on the same line. The second statement of the outer loop is printf("\n");. This statement starts a new line so that the next time the inner loop is run, the output is on a new line.

Note that, with a nested loop, the inner loop runs through its full range of iterations for each single iteration of the outer loop. So, in the last example, the inner loop prints six characters to a row, and the outer loop creates six rows.

A Nested Variation

In the last example, the inner loop did the same thing for each cycle of the outer loop. But you can make the inner loop behave differently each cycle by making part of the inner loop depend on the outer loop. Listing 6.16, for example, alters the last program slightly by making the starting character of the inner loop depend on the cycle number of the outer loop.

Listing 6.16 *rows2.c*

```
/* rows2.c -- using dependent nested loops */
#include <stdio.h>
#define ROWS  6
#define CHARS 6
main()
{
    int row;
    char ch;

    for (row = 0; row < ROWS; row++)
    {
        for (ch = ('A' + row);  ch < ('A' + CHARS); ch++)
            printf("%c", ch);
        printf("\n");
    }
}
```

This time the output is as follows:

```
ABCDEF
BCDEF
CDEF
DEF
EF
F
```

Because row is added to A during each cycle of the outer loop, ch is initialized in each row to one character later in the alphabet. The test condition, however, is unaltered, so each row still ends on F. This results in one fewer character being printed in each row.

Arrays

Arrays are important features in many programs. They let you store several items of related information in a convenient fashion. In Chapter 10 we will devote the entire chapter to arrays, but because arrays often are used with loops, we want to introduce them now.

An *array* is a series of values of the same type, such as 10 `chars` or 15 `ints`, stored sequentially. The whole array bears a single name, and the individual items, or *elements*, are accessed by using an integer index. For instance, the declaration

```
float debts[20];
```

announces that `debts` is an array with 20 elements, each of which can hold a type `float` value. The first element of the array is called `debts[0]`, the second element is called `debts[1]`, etc., up to `debts[19]`. Note that the numbering of array elements starts with 0, not 1. Each element can be assigned a `float` value. For example, you can have the following:

```
debts[5] = 32.54;
debts[6] = 1.2e+21;
```

An array can be of any data type:

```
int nannies[22];    /* an array to hold 22 integers     */
char alpha[26];     /* an array to hold 26 characters    */
long big[500];      /* an array to hold 500 long integers */
```

Earlier, for example, we talked about strings, which are a special case of char arrays. (A char *array*, in general, is one whose elements are assigned `char` values. A *string* is a `char` array in which the null character, \0, is used to mark the end of the string. See Figure 6.6.)

Figure 6.6 *Character arrays and strings*

character array but not a string

character array and a string

null character

The numbers used to identify the array elements are called *subscripts, indices*, or *offsets*. The subscripts must be integers, and, as we mentioned, the subscripting begins with 0. The array elements are stored next to each other in memory, as shown in Figure 6.7.

Figure 6.7 *The* char *and* int *arrays in memory*

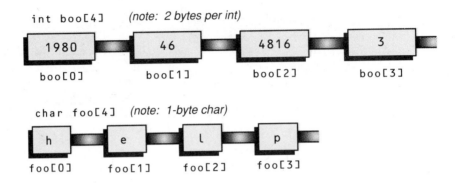

There are many, many uses for arrays. Listing 6.17 is a relatively simple one. It's a program that reads in ten scores, which will be processed later on. By using an array, we avoid inventing ten different variable names, one for each score. Also, we can use a for loop to do the reading. The program goes on to report the sum of the scores and their average.

Listing 6.17 *scores_in.c*

```
/* scores_in.c -- uses loops for array processing */
#include <stdio.h>
#define SIZE 10
main()
{
    int index, score[SIZE];
    int sum = 0;
    float average;

    printf("Enter %d scores:\n", SIZE);
    for (index = 0; index < SIZE; index++)
        scanf("%d", &score[index]);   /* read in the ten scores */
    printf("The scores read in are as follows:\n");
```

```
    for (index = 0; index < SIZE; index++)
      printf("%5d", score[index]); /* verify input        */
    printf("\n");
    for (index = 0; index < SIZE; index++)
      sum += score[index];          /* add them up         */
    average = (float) sum / SIZE;   /* time-honored method */
    printf("Sum of scores = %d, average = %.2f\n", sum, average);
    }
```

Let's see if Listing 6.17 works; then we can make a few comments. Here is the output:

```
Enter 10 scores:
76 85 62 48 98 71
66 89 70 77 99
The scores read in are as follows:
   76    85    62    48    98    71   66   89   70   77
Sum of scores = 742, average = 74.20
```

It works, so let's check out some of the details. First, note that although we typed 11 numbers, only 10 were read because the reading loop reads just 10 values. Since scanf() skips over whitespace, we can type all 10 numbers on one line or spread them over several lines.

Next, using arrays and loops is much more convenient than using 10 separate scanf() statements and 10 separate printf() statements to read in and verify the 10 scores. The for loop provides a simple and direct way to utilize the array subscripts. Notice that an element of a float array is handled like a float variable. To read the float variable fue, we would use scanf("%f", &fue). In Listing 6.17 we are reading the float element score[index], so we use scanf("%f", &score[index]).

This example illustrates several style points. First, we use a #define directive to create a manifest constant (SIZE) to specify the size of the array. We use this constant in defining the array and in setting the loop limits. If we later need to expand the program to handle 20 scores, we simply redefine SIZE to be 20. We don't have to change every part of the program that uses the array size.

Second, the idiom

```
    for (index = 0; index < SIZE; index++)
```

is a handy one for processing an array of size SIZE. It's important to get the right array limits. The first element has index 0, and the loop starts by setting index to 0. Because the numbering starts with 0, the element index for the last element is SIZE - 1. That is, the tenth element is score[9]. Using the test condition i < SIZE accomplishes this, for the last value of index used in the loop is SIZE - 1.

Third, a good practice is to have a program repeat or "echo" the values it has just read in. This helps ensure that the program is processing the data you think it is.

Finally, note that we used three separate for loops. You may wonder if this was really necessary. Could we have combined some of the operations in one loop? The answer is yes, we could have done so. That would have made the program more compact. However, we were swayed by the principle of *modularity*. The idea behind this term is that a program should be broken into separate units with each unit having one task to perform. This makes a program easier to read. Perhaps even more important, modularity makes it much easier to update or modify a program if different parts of the program are not intermingled. Once you know enough about functions, you could make each unit into a function, enhancing the modularity of the program.

A Loop Example Using a Function Return Value

For the last example in this chapter, we'll design a function that calculates the result of raising a number to an integer power. The three main tasks in this exercise are devising the algorithm for calculating the answer, expressing the algorithm in a function that returns the answer, and providing a convenient way of testing the function.

First, let's look at an algorithm. We'll keep the function simple by restricting it to positive integer powers. Then, if we want to raise a to the b power, we have to multiply a times itself b times. This is a natural task for a loop. We can set a variable pow to 1 and then multiply it by a repeatedly:

```
for(i = 1; i <= b; i++)
    pow *= a;
```

Recall that the *= operator multiplies the left side by the right side. So after the first loop cycle, pow is 1 times a, or a. After the second cycle, pow is its previous value (a) times a, or a squared, and so on. The for loop is natural in this context because the loop is executed a predetermined (once b is known) number of times.

Now that we have an algorithm, we should decide which data types to use. The exponent b, being an integer, should be type int. To allow maximum range in values for a and its power, we'll make a and pow type double.

Next, let's consider how to put the function together. We need to give the function two values, and the function should give back one. To get information to the function, we can use two arguments, one `double` and one `int`, specifying which number to raise to what power. But how do we arrange for the function to return a value to the calling program? To write a function with a return value, do the following:

1. When you define a function, state the type of value it returns.

2. Use the keyword `return` to indicate the value to be returned.

For example, we can do this:

```
double power(double a, int b)   /* power() returns type double */
{
    double pow = 1.0;
    int i;
    for(i = 1; i <= b; i++)
        pow *= a;
    return pow;                    /* return the value of pow     */
}
```

To declare the function type, preface the function name with the type, just as you do when declaring a variable. The keyword `return` causes the function to return the following value to the calling function. Here we return the value of a variable, but you can return the value of expressions, too. For instance, the following is a valid statement:

```
return 2 * x + b;
```

The function would compute the value of the expression and return it. In the calling function, the return value can be assigned to another variable, can be used as a value in an expression, or can be used as an argument to another function, as in `printf("%f", power(6.28, 3))`. Or it can be ignored.

Now let's use the function in a program. To test the function, it would be convenient to be able to feed several values to the function to see how the function reacts. This suggests setting up an input loop. The natural choice is the `while` loop. We can use `scanf()` to read in two values at a time. If successful in reading two values, `scanf()` returns the value 2, so we can control the loop by comparing the `scanf()` return value to 2. One more point: to use the `power()` function in our program, we need to declare it, just as we declare variables that the program uses. Listing 6.18 shows the program.

Listing 6.18 *power.c*

```
/* power.c -- raises numbers to integer powers */
#include <stdio.h>
double power(double, int);  /* ANSI prototype */
main()
{
  double x, xpow;
    int n;

  printf("Enter a number and the positive integer power");
  printf(" to which\nthe number will be raised. Enter q");
  printf(" to quit.\n");
  while (scanf("%lf%d", &x, &n) == 2)
  {
      xpow = power(x,n);        /* function call           */
      printf("%.3e to the power %d is %.3e\n", x, n, xpow);
  }
}

double power(double a, int b)   /* function definition     */
{
  double pow = 1;
  int i;

  for(i = 1; i <= b; i++)
      pow *= a;
  return pow;                   /* return the value of pow  */
}
```

If your compiler doesn't recognize the ANSI forms, you can use the following declaration and function header:

```
double power();                    /* declaration */

double power(a,b);                 /* header       */
double a;
int b;
```

Here is a sample run:

```
Enter a number and the positive integer power to which
the number will be raised. Enter q to quit.
```

```
2.2 5
2.200e+000 to the power 5 is 5.154e+001
8.0
8
8.000e+000 to the power 8 is 1.678e+007
144 2
1.440e+002 to the power 2 is 2.074e+004
q
```

Program Discussion

The `main()` program is an example of a *driver*, a short program designed to test a function.

The `while` loop is a generalization of a form we've used before. Entering 2.2 5 causes `scanf()` to return 2 and the loop continues. Because `scanf()` skips over whitespace, input can be spread over more than one line, as the sample output shows. But entering q produces a return value of 0 because q can't be read using the `%lf` specifier; this terminates the loop. Similarly, entering 2.8 q would produce a return value of 1; that, too, would terminate the loop.

Now let's look at the function-related matters. The `power()` function appears three times in this program. The first appearance is this:

```
double power(double, int);      /* ANSI prototype */
```

This statement announces, or declares, that the program will be using a function called `power()`. The initial keyword `double` indicates that the `power()` function returns a type `double` value. The compiler needs to know what kind of value `power()` returns so that it will know how many bytes of data to expect and how to interpret them; this is why we have to declare the function. The `double, int` within the parentheses means that `power()` takes two arguments. The first should be a type `double` value, and the second should be type `int`.

The second appearance is this:

```
xpow = power(x,n);   /* function call */
```

Here we call the function, passing it two values. The function calculates the *n*th power of x and returns it to the calling program, where the return value is assigned to the variable xpow.

The third appearance is in the head of the function definition:

```
double power(double a, int b)    /* function definition */
```

Here `power()` takes two arguments: a `double` and an `int` represented by the variables a and b. Note that power() is not followed by a semicolon when it appears in a function *definition*, but is followed by a semicolon when in a function *declaration*. After the function heading comes the code that specifies what power() does.

Recall that the function uses a for loop to calculate the value of a to the b power and assign it to pow. The following line makes the value of pow the function return value:

```
    return pow;          /* return the value of pow */
```

Using Functions with Return Values

Declaring the function, calling the function, defining the function, using the return keyword: these are the basic elements in defining and using a function with a return value.

At this point, you may have some questions. For example, if you are supposed to declare functions before you use their return values, how come we used the return value of scanf() without declaring scanf()? Or, since our definition of power() says it is type double, why do we have to declare it separately?

Let's take the second question first. The compiler needs to know what type power() is when it first encounters power() in the program. At this point, the compiler has not yet encountered the definition of power(), so it doesn't know that the definition says the return type is double. To help out the compiler, we previewed what is to come by using a *forward declaration*. This declaration informs the compiler that power() is defined elsewhere and that it will return type double. If we had placed the power() function definition ahead of main() in the file, we could have omitted the forward declaration because the compiler would have known all about power() before reaching main(). However, that is not standard C style. Since main() usually provides the overall framework for a program, it's best to show main() first. Also, functions often are kept in separate files, so a forward declaration is essential.

Next, why didn't we declare scanf()? Well, we did. The stdio.h header file has in it function declarations for scanf(), printf(), and several other I/O functions. The scanf() declaration states that it returns type int. However, if you forget to include stdio.h, the program still works. That's because C assumes that if you don't declare the type for a function, it is type int. Early C programming often relied heavily on this assumption, but modern practice is to declare the function type even if it is int.

Finally, what about main()? The ANSI Standard states that main() is type int. Since int is the default type, we have been making main() type int implicitly. From now on, however, we'll declare main() as int explicitly. To be consistent, we also should give main() a return value. we'll use a return value of 0. Many operating systems, including UNIX and PC DOS, accept return values from programs they run. These operating systems traditionally interpret a return value of 0 to mean that the program terminated normally without problems. Also, since we aren't yet using arguments for `main()`, we will use `void` in the argument list. In short, we'll use this format:

```
int main(void)
{
        .
        .
        .
        return 0;
}
```

Chapter Summary

The main topic of this chapter has been program control. C offers you many aids for structuring your programs. The `while` and the `for` statements provide *entry-condition* loops. The `for` statements are particularly suited for loops that involve initialization and updating. The *comma operator* lets you initialize and update more than one variable in a `for` loop. For the rare occasion when an *exit-condition* loop is needed, C provides the do `while` statement.

All these loops use a test condition to determine if another loop cycle is to be executed. In general, the loop continues if the test expression evaluates to a nonzero value and terminates otherwise. Often, the test condition is a *relational expression*, which is an expression formed by using a relational operator. Such an expression has a value of 1 if the relation is true and a value of 0 otherwise.

In addition to relational operators, this chapter looked at several of C's arithmetic *assignment operators*, such as += and *=. These operators modify the value of the left-hand operand by performing an arithmetic operation upon it.

Arrays were the next subject. *Arrays* are declared in the same fashion as ordinary variables, but they have a number enclosed in brackets to indicate the number of elements. The first element of an array is numbered 0; the second is numbered 1, etc. The subscripts used to number arrays can be manipulated conveniently by using loops.

Finally, the chapter showed how to write and use a function with a return value.

Review Questions

1. Find the value of `quack` after each line.

```
int quack = 2;
quack += 5;
quack *= 10;
quack -= 6;
quack /= 8;
quack %= 3;
```

2. Represent each of the following test conditions.

   a. x is greater than 5.

   b. scanf() attempts to read a single double and fails.

   c. x has the value 5.

3. We suspect that the following program is not perfect. What errors can you find?

```
main()
{                                      /* line 2  */
   int i, j, list(10);                 /* line 3  */

   for (i = 1, i <= 10,  i++)          /* line 5  */
   {                                   /* line 6  */
       list[i] = 2*i + 3;              /* line 7  */
       for (j = 1, j > = i, j++)       /* line 8  */
          printf("%d\n", list[j]);     /* line 9  */
}                                      /* line 10 */
```

4. What will each of the following programs print?

   a.
   ```
   #include <stdio.h>
   main()
   {
       int i = 0;

       while (++i < 4)
          printf("Hi! ");
       do
          printf("Bye! ");
       while (i++ < 8);
   }
   ```

   b.
   ```
   #include <stdio.h>
   main()
   {
       int i;
       char ch;

       for (i = 0, ch = 'A'; i < 4; i++, ch += 2 * i)
   ```

```
            printf("%c", ch);
    }
```

5. What will the following program print?

```
#include <stdio.h>
main()
{
    int n, m;

    n = 10;
    while (++n <= 13)
        printf("%d",n);
    do
        printf("%d",n);
    while (++n <= 12);

    printf("\n***\n");

    for (n = 1; n*n < 60; n +=3)
        printf("%d\n", n);

    printf("\n***\n");

    for (n = 1, m = 5; n < m; n *= 2, m+= 2)
        printf("%d %d\n", n, m);

    printf("\n***\n");

    for (n = 4; n > 0; n--)
    {
        for (m = 0; m <= n; m++)
            printf("+");
        printf("\n");
    }
}
```

6. Mr. Noah likes counting by twos, so he's written the following program to create an array and to fill it with the integers 2, 4, 6, 8, and so on. What, if anything, is wrong with this program?

```
#include <stdio.h>
#define SIZE 8
main()
{
   int by_twos[SIZE];
   int index;
   for (index = 1; index <= SIZE; index++)
```

```
            by_twos[index] = 2 * index;
        for (index = 1; index <= SIZE; index++)
            printf("%d ", by_twos);
        printf("\n");
    }
```

7. Define a function that takes an `int` argument and that returns, as a `long`, the square of that value.

Programming Exercises

1. Write a program that creates an array with 26 elements and stores the 26 lowercase letters in it. Also have it show the array contents.

2. Use nested loops to produce the following pattern:

```
$
$$
$$$
$$$$
$$$$$
```

3. Use nested loops to produce the following pattern:

```
F
FE
FED
FEDC
FEDCB
FEDCBA
```

4. Write a program that prints a table with each line giving an integer, its square, and its cube. Ask the user to input the lower and upper limits for the table. Use a `for` loop.

5. Write a program that reads a single word into a character array and then prints the word backwards. Hint: use `strlen()` (Chapter 4) to compute the index of the last character in the array.

6. Write a program that requests two floating-point numbers and prints the value of their difference divided by their product. Have the program loop through pairs of input values until the user enters nonnumeric input.

7. Modify Exercise 6 so that it uses a function to return the value of the calculation.

8. Write a program that reads eight integers into an array and then prints them in reverse order.

9. Daphne invests $100 at 10 percent simple interest. (That is, every year, the investment earns an interest equal to 10 percent of the original investment.) Deirdre invests $100 at 5 percent interest compounded annually. (That is, interest is 5 percent of the current balance, including previous addition of interest.) Write a program that finds how many years it takes for the value of Deirdre's investment to exceed the value of Daphne's investment. Also show the two values at that time.

7

C Control Statements: Branching and Jumps

Keywords
▶ if, else, switch, continue
▶ break, case, default, goto

Operators
▶ && || ?:

Functions
▶ getchar( ), putchar( )

In this chapter you learn how to use the `if` and `if else` statements and how to nest them. You use logical operators to combine relational expressions into more involved test expressions. You encounter C's conditional operator, study the `switch` statement, and learn about the `break`, `continue`, and `goto` jumps. And you'll use C's character I/O functions—`getchar()` and `putchar()`.

A s you grow more comfortable with C, you probably will want to tackle more complex tasks. When you do, you'll need ways to control and organize these projects. C has the tools to meet these needs. Already, you've learned to use loops to program repetitive tasks. In this chapter, you'll learn about branching structures, such as `if` and `switch`, that let a program base its actions on conditions that it checks. Also, you are introduced to C's logical operators, which let you test for more than one relationship in a `while` or `if` condition. And you'll look at C's jump statements, which shift the program flow to another part of a program. By the end of this chapter, you'll have all the basic information you need to design a program that behaves the way you want.

The *if* Statement

Let's start with a simple example of an `if` statement shown in Listing 7.1. This program reads in a list of daily low temperatures (in Celsius) and reports the total number of entries and the percentage that were below freezing. We use `scanf()` in a loop to read in the values. Once during each loop cycle we increment a counter to keep track of the number of entries. An `if` statement detects temperatures below freezing and keeps track of their number separately.

Listing 7.1 *colddays.c*

```
/* colddays.c -- finds percentage of days below freezing */
#include <stdio.h>
#define SCALE "Celsius"
#define FREEZING 0
int main(void)
```

(continued)

Listing 7.1 *(continued)*

```
{
    float temperature;
    int freezing = 0;
    int days = 0;

    printf("Enter the list of daily low temperatures.\n");
    printf("Use %s, and enter q to quit.\n", SCALE);
    while (scanf("%f", &temperature) == 1)
    {
        days++;
        if (temperature < FREEZING)
            freezing++;
    }
    if (days != 0)
        printf("%d days total: %.1f%% were below freezing.\n",
                days, 100.0 * (float) freezing / days);
    if (days == 0)
        printf("No data entered!\n");
    return 0;   /* program terminates successfully */
}
```

Here we follow the ANSI form of declaring `main()`'s type and giving `main()` a return value.

```
Enter the list of daily low temperatures.
Use Celsius, and enter q to quit.
20 11 3 -4 -6 -10 -2.5 10 8 -5 q
10 days total: 50.0% were below freezing.
```

The `while` loop test condition uses the return value of `scanf()` to terminate the loop when `scanf()` encounters nonnumeric input. By using `float` instead of `int` for `temperature`, the program is able to accept input like -2.5 as well as 8.

The new statement in the `while` block is this:

```
if (temperature < FREEZING)
    freezing++;
```

This `if` statement instructs the computer to increase `freezing` by 1 *if* the value just read (`temperature`) is less than zero. What happens if temperature is not less than zero? Then the `freezing++;` statement is skipped, and the `while` loop moves on to read the next temperature value.

We use the `if` statement two more times to control the output. If there is data, the program prints the results. If there is no data, the program reports that fact. (Soon you'll see a more elegant way to handle this part of the program.)

To avoid integer division, we used the cast to `float` when the percentage is being calculated. We don't really need the type cast, for in the expression `100.0 * freezing / days`, the subexpression `100.0 * freezing` is evaluated first and is forced into floating point by the automatic type conversion rules. But using the type cast documents our intent and protects the program from faulty compilers.

if Basics

The `if` statement is called a *branching statement* because it provides a junction at which the program has to select which of two paths to follow. The general form is this:

```
if (expression)
    statement
```

If *expression* evaluates to true (nonzero), the *statement* is executed. Otherwise, it is skipped. As with a `while` loop, *statement* can be a single statement or a single block or compound statement. The structure is very similar to that of a `while` statement. The chief difference is that, in an `if` statement, the test and (possibly) the execution are done just once; but, in the `while` loop, the test and execution may be repeated several times.

Normally, *expression* is a relational expression; that is, it compares the magnitude of two quantities, as in the expressions `x > y` and `c == 6`. If *expression* is true (x is greater than y, or c does equal 6), then the statement is executed. Otherwise, the statement is ignored. More generally, any expression can be used, and an expression with a 0 value is taken to be false.

The statement portion can be a simple statement, as in our example, or it can be a compound statement or block, marked off by braces:

```
if (score > big)
    printf("Jackpot!\n");   /* simple statement    */

if (joe > ron)
{                           /* compound statement */
    joecash++;
    printf("You lose, Ron.\n");
}
```

Note that the entire if structure counts as a single statement, even when it uses a compound statement.

Adding *else* to the *if* Statement

The simple form of an if statement gives you the choice of executing a statement (possibly compound) or skipping it. C also lets you choose between two statements by using the if else form. Let's use the if else form to fix an awkward segment from Listing 7.1.

```
if (days != 0)
  printf("%d days total: %.1f%% were below freezing.\n",
       days, 100.0 * (float) freezing / days);
if (days == 0)
  printf("No data entered!\n");
```

If the program finds that days is not unequal to 0, it should know that days must be 0 without retesting. And it does. With if else we can take advantage of that knowledge by rewriting the fragment this way:

```
if (days != 0)
  printf("%d days total: %.1f%% were below freezing.\n",
       days, 100.0 * (float) freezing / days);
else
  printf("No data entered!\n");
```

Only one test is made. If the if test expression is true, the temperature data is printed. If it's false, the warning message is printed.

Note the general form of the if else statement:

```
if (expression)
    statement1
else
    statement2
```

If *expression* is true (nonzero), *statement1* is executed. If *expression* is false or zero, the single statement following the else is executed. The statements can be simple or compound. The indentation is not required by C, but it is the standard style. It shows at a glance those statements whose execution depends on a test.

If you want more than one statement between the if and the else, you must use braces to create a single block. The following construction violates C syntax, for the compiler expects just one statement (single or compound) between the if and the else:

```
if (x > 0)
  printf("Incrementing x:\n");
     x++;
else
  printf("x < 0 \n");
```

Instead, use this:

```
if (x > 0)
{
  printf("Incrementing x:\n");
     x++;
}
else
  printf("x < 0 \n");
```

The `if` statement lets you choose whether to do one action. The `if else` statement lets you choose between two actions. Figure 7.1 compares the two statements.

Another Example: Introducing *getchar( )* and *putchar( )*

Most of our examples have used numeric input. To provide practice with other types, let's look at a character-oriented example. We can, of course, use `scanf()` and `printf()` with the `%c` specifier to read and write characters, but we won't. Instead, we'll use a pair of C functions specifically designed for character-oriented I/O: `getchar()` and `putchar()`.

The `getchar()` function takes no arguments, and it returns the next character from input. For instance, the following statement reads the next input character and assigns its value to the variable `ch`:

```
ch = getchar();
```

The `putchar()` function prints its argument. For example, the next statement prints as a character the value previously assigned to `ch`:

```
putchar(ch);
```

Because these functions deal only with characters, they are faster and more compact than the more general `scanf()` and `printf()` functions. Also, note that they don't need format specifiers. Both functions typically are defined in the `stdio.h` file. (Also, typically, they are preprocessor *macros* rather than true functions; we'll talk about function-like macros in Chapter 16.)

Figure 7.1 if *versus* if else

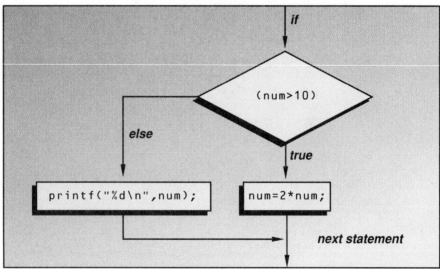

Let's see how these functions work by writing a program that repeats an input line but replaces each nonspace character with the character that follows it in the ASCII code sequence. Spaces will be reproduced as spaces. We can state the desired response this way: if the character is a space, print it; else print the next character in the ASCII sequence. Our C code looks much like this statement, as you can see in Listing 7.2.

```
Listing 7.2   cypher1.c

/* cypher1.c -- alters input, preserving spaces */
#include <stdio.h>
#define SPACE ' '                /* that's quote-space-quote */
int main(void)
{
   char ch;

   ch = getchar();              /* read a character          */
   while (ch != '\n')           /* while not end of line     */
   {
       if (ch == SPACE)         /* leave the space           */
           putchar(ch);         /* character unchanged       */
       else
           putchar(ch + 1);     /* change other characters   */
       ch = getchar();          /* get next character        */
   }
   return 0;
}
```

Here's a sample run:

```
CALL ME HAL.
DBMM NF IBM/
```

Compare this loop to the one from Listing 7.1. Listing 7.1 uses the status returned by scanf() rather than the value of the input item to determine when to terminate the loop. But Listing 7.2 uses the value of the input item itself to decide when to terminate the loop. This difference results in a slightly different loop structure, with one read statement before the loop, and one read statement at the end of each loop. C's flexible syntax, however, lets you emulate Listing 7.1 by combining reading and testing into a single expression. Listing 7.3 presents Listing 7.2 rewritten in a more typically C style:

```
Listing 7.3  cypher2.c

/* cypher2.c -- alters input, preserving spaces */
#include <stdio.h>
#define SPACE s' '              /* that's quote-space-quote */
int main(void)
{
    char ch;

    while ((ch = getchar()) != '\n')
    {
        if (ch == SPACE)        /* leave the space         */
            putchar(ch);        /*  character unchanged    */
        else
            putchar(ch + 1);    /* change other characters */
    }
    return 0;
}
```

The critical line is this:

```
while ((ch = getchar()) != '\n')
```

It demonstrates a characteristic C programming style: combining two actions in one expression. The actions are assigning a value to ch and comparing this value to the newline character. The parentheses around ch = getchar() make it the left operand of the != operator. To evaluate this expression, the computer must first call the getchar() function and then assign its return value to ch. Since the value of an assignment expression is the value of the left member, the value of ch = getchar() is just the new value of ch. Thus, after ch is read, the test condition boils down to ch != '\n', that is, to ch not being the newline character.

This particular idiom is very common in C programming. All the parentheses are necessary. Suppose we mistakenly used this:

```
while (ch = getchar() != '\n')
```

The != operator has higher precedence than =, so the first expression to be evaluated is getchar() != '\n'. Because this is a relational expression, its value is 1 or 0 (true or false). Then this value is assigned to ch. Omitting the parentheses means that ch is assigned 0 or 1 rather than the return value of getchar(); this is not desirable.

Multiple Choice: *else if*

Life often offers us more than two choices. We can extend the `if else` structure with `else if` to accommodate this fact. Let's look at a particular example. Utility companies often have charges that depend on the amount of energy the customer uses. Here are the rates that one company charges for electricity, based on kilowatt-hours (kWh):

first 240 kWh: $0.06898 per kWh

next 300 kWh: $0.12032 per kWh

over 540 kWh: $0.14022 per kWh

If you worry about your energy management, you might wish to prepare a program to calculate your energy costs. The program in Listing 7.4 is a first step in that direction.

Listing 7.4   *electric.c*

```
/* electric.c -- calculates electric bill */
#include <stdio.h>
#define RATE1 0.06898      /* rate for first 240 kwh    */
#define RATE2 0.12032      /* rate for next 300 kwh     */
#define RATE3 0.14022      /* rate for over 540 kwh     */
#define BREAK1 240.0       /* first breakpoint for rates */
#define BREAK2 540.0       /* second breakpoint for rates */
#define BASE1 (RATE1 * BREAK1)
                           /* cost for 240 kwh          */
#define BASE2 (BASE1 + (RATE2 * (BREAK2 - BREAK1)))
                           /* cost for 540 kwh          */
int main(void)
{
   float kwh;             /* kilowatt-hours used       */
   float bill;           /* charges                   */

   printf("Please enter the kwh used.\n");
   scanf("%f", &kwh);
   if (kwh <= BREAK1)
       bill = RATE1 * kwh;
   else if (kwh <= BREAK2)   /* kwh between 240 and 540    */
```

(continued)

> **Listing 7.4** *(continued)*
>
> ```
>      bill = BASE1 + (RATE2 * (kwh - BREAK1));
>  else                         /* kwh above 540           */
>      bill = BASE2 + (RATE3 * (kwh - BREAK2));
>  printf("The charge for %.1f kwh is $%1.2f.\n", kwh, bill);
>  return 0;
> }
> ```

In Listing 7.4 we used symbolic constants for the rates so that the constants are conveniently gathered in one place. If the power company changes its rates (it's possible), having the rates in one place makes it easy to update them. We also expressed the rate breakpoints symbolically. They, too, are subject to change. BASE1 and BASE2 are expressed in terms of the rates and breakpoints. Then, if the rates or breakpoints change, the bases are updated automatically. You may recall that the preprocessor does not do calculations. Where BASE1 appears in the program, it will be replaced by 0.06898 * 240.0. But don't worry; the compiler does evaluate this expression to its numerical value (16.56) so that the final program code uses 16.56 rather than a calculation.

The flow of the program is straightforward. The program selects one of three formulas, depending on the value of kwh. Figure 7.2 illustrates this flow. We should point out that the only way the program can reach the first else is if kwh is equal to or greater than 240. Thus, the else if (kwh <= BREAK2) line really is equivalent to demanding that kwh be between 240 and 540, as we noted in the program comment. Similarly, the final else can be reached only if kwh exceeds 540. Finally, note that BASE1 and BASE2 represent the total charges for the first 240 and 540 kilowatt-hours, respectively. Thus, we need add on only the additional charges for electricity in excess of those amounts.

Actually, the else if is a variation on what we already knew. For example, the core of our program is just another way of writing

```
if (kwh <=BREAK1)
    bill = RATE1 * kwh;
else
    if (kwh <=BREAK2)
        bill = BASE1 + RATE2 * (kwh - BREAK1);
    else
        bill = BASE2 + RATE3 * (kwh - BREAK2);
```

That is, the program consists of an if else statement for which the state-

Figure 7.2 *Program flow for Listing 7.4,* electric.c

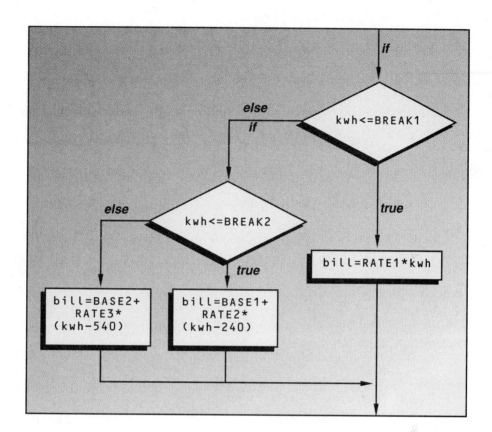

ment part of the else is another if else statement. The second if else statement is said to be *nested* inside the first. Recall that the entire if else structure counts as a single statement, which is why we didn't have to enclose the nested if else in braces. However, using braces would clarify the intent of this particular format.

These two forms are perfectly equivalent. The only differences are in where we put spaces and newlines, and these differences are ignored by the compiler. Nonetheless, the first form is better because it shows more clearly that we are making a three-way choice. This form makes it easier to skim the program and see what the choices are. Save the nested forms of indentation for when they are needed, for instance, when you must test two separate quantities. An example of such a situation would be if there were a 10-percent surcharge for kilowatt-hours in excess of 540 during the summer only.

You may string together as many else if statements as you need (within compiler limits, of course), as illustrated by this fragment:

```
if (score < 1000)
    bonus = 0;
else if (score < 1500)
    bonus = 1;
else if (score < 2000)
    bonus = 2;
else if (score < 2500)
    bonus = 4;
else
    bonus = 6;
```

(This might be part of a game program, where bonus represents how many additional photon bombs or food pellets you get for the next round.)

Pairing *else* with *if*

When you have a lot of ifs and elses, how does the computer decide which if goes with which else? For example, consider the following program fragment:

```
if (number > 6)
    if (number < 12)
        printf("You're close!\n");
else
    printf("Sorry, you lose a turn!\n");
```

When is Sorry, you lose a turn! printed? When number is less than or equal to 6, or when number is greater than 12? In other words, does the else go with the first if or the second? The answer is, the else goes with the second if. That is, you would get these responses:

Number	Response
5	none
10	You're close!
15	Sorry, you lose a turn!

The rule is that an else goes with the most recent if unless braces indicate otherwise. See Figure 7.3. We indented our example to make it look as if the else goes with the first if, but remember that the compiler ignores indentation. If we really want the else to go with the first if, we could write the fragment this way:

```
if (number > 6)
{
```

```
        if (number < 12)
            printf("You're close!\n");
    }
.else
    printf("Sorry, you lose a turn!\n");
```

Now we would get these responses:

Number	Response
5	Sorry, you lose a turn!
10	You're close!
15	none

Figure 7.3 *The rule for* if else *pairings*

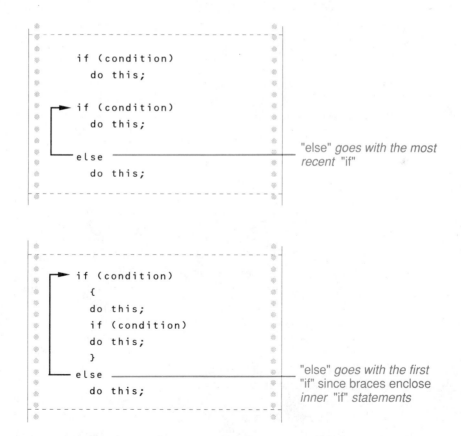

```
    if (condition)
        do this;

    if (condition)
        do this;

    else
        do this;
```
"else" *goes with the most recent* "if"

```
    if (condition)
    {
    do this;
    if (condition)
    do this;
    }
    else
    do this;
```
"else" *goes with the first* "if" *since braces enclose inner* "if" *statements*

More Nested *ifs*

You've already seen that the if...else if...else sequence is a form of nested if, one that selects from a series of alternatives. Another kind of nested if is used when choosing a particular selection leads to an additional choice. For example, a program could use an if else to select between males and females. Each branch within the if else then could contain another if else to distinguish between different income groups.

Let's apply this form of nested if to the following problem. Given an integer, print all the integers that divide into it evenly; if there are no divisors, report that the number is prime.

This problem requires some forethought before we whip out the code. First, we need an overall design for the program. For convenience, the program should use a loop to let us input numbers to be tested. That way, we don't have to run the program again each time we want to examine a new number. We've already developed a model for this kind of loop:

> prompt user
>
> while the scanf() return value is 1
>
>> analyze the number and report results
>>
>> prompt user

Recall that by using scanf() in the loop test condition, the program attempts both to read a number and to check to see if the loop should be terminated.

Next, we need a plan for finding divisors. Perhaps the most obvious approach is something like this:

```
for (div = 2; div < num; div++)
    if (num % div == 0)
        printf("%d is divisible by %d\n", num, div);
```

The loop checks all the numbers between 2 and num to see if they divide evenly into num. Unfortunately, this approach is very wasteful of computer time. We can do much better. Consider, for example, finding the divisors of 144. We find that 144 % 2 is 0, meaning 2 goes into 144 evenly. If we then actually divide 2 into 144, we get 72, which also is a divisor. So we can get two divisors instead of one divisor out of a successful num % div test. The real payoff, however, comes in changing the limits of the loop test. To see how this works, look at the pairs of divisors we get as the loop continues: 2,72 3,48 4,36 6,28 8,18 9,16 12,12 16,9 18,8 . . . Ah! Once we get past the 12,12 pair, we start getting the same divisors (in reverse order) that we already found. So, instead of running the loop to 143, we can stop after reaching 12. That saves a lot of cycles!

Generalizing this discovery, we see that we have to test only up to the square root of `num` instead of to `num`. For numbers like 9 this is not a big savings, but the difference is enormous for a number like 10000. Rather than messing with square roots, however, we can express the test condition as follows:

```
for (div = 2; (div * div) <= num; div++)
    if (num % div == 0)
            printf("%d is divisible by %d and %d.\n",
                    num, div, num / div);
```

If `num` is 144, the loop runs through `div` = 12. If `num` is 145, the loop runs through `div` = 13.

There are two reasons for using this test instead of a square root test. First, integer multiplication is much faster than extracting a square root. Second, the square root function hasn't been introduced yet.

We need to address just two more problems, and then we'll be ready to program. First, what if the test number is a perfect square? Reporting that 144 is divisible by 12 and 12 is a little clumsy. But we can use a nested `if` statement to test whether `div` equals `num / div`. If so, the program will print just one divisor instead of two.

```
for (div = 2; (div * div) <= num; div++)
{
    if (num % div == 0)
    {
        if (div * div != num)
            printf("%d is divisible by %d and %d.\n",
                num, div, num / div);
        else
            printf("%d is divisible by %d.\n", num, div);
    }
}
```

Note: Technically, the `if else` statement counts as a single statement, so the braces around it are not needed. The outer `if` is a single statement also, so the braces around it are not needed. However, when statements get long, the braces make it easier to see what is happening, and they offer protection if later you add another statement to an `if` or to the loop.

Second, how do we know if a number is prime? If `num` is prime, then program flow never gets inside the `if` statement. To solve this problem, we can set a variable to some value, say 1, outside the loop and reset the variable to 0 inside the `if` statement. Then, after the loop is completed, we can check to see if the variable is still 1. If it is, the `if` statement was never entered, and the number is prime. Such a variable often is called a *flag*.

Listing 7.5 incorporates all the ideas we've discussed. To extend the range, we've switched to type `long`.

Listing 7.5 *divisors.c*

```
/* divisors.c -- nested ifs display divisors of a number */
#include <stdio.h>
#define NO 0
#define YES 1
int main(void)
{
    long num;                        /* number to be checked */
    long div;                        /* potential divisors   */
    int prime;

    printf("Please enter an integer for analysis; ");
    printf("Enter q to quit.\n");
    while (scanf("%ld", &num) == 1)
    {
        for (div = 2, prime = YES; (div * div) <= num; div++)
        {
            if (num % div == 0)
            {
                if ((div * div) != num)
                    printf("%ld is divisible by %ld and %ld.\n",
                        num, div, num / div);
                else
                    printf("%ld is divisible by %ld.\n", num, div);
                prime = NO;           /* number is not prime  */
            }
        }
        if (prime == YES)
            printf("%ld is prime.\n", num);
        printf("Please enter another integer for analysis; ");
        printf("Enter q to quit.\n");
    }
    return 0;
}
```

Note that we used the comma operator in the `for` loop control expression to let us initialize `prime` to TRUE for each new input number.

Here's a sample run:

```
Please enter an integer for analysis; Enter q to quit.
36
36 is divisible by 2 and 18.
36 is divisible by 3 and 12.
36 is divisible by 4 and 9.
36 is divisible by 6.
Please enter another integer for analysis; Enter q to quit.
149
149 is prime.
Please enter another integer for analysis; Enter q to quit.
30077
30077 is divisible by 19 and 1583.
Please enter another integer for analysis; Enter q to quit.
q
```

Summary: Using *if* Statements for Making Choices

Keywords

`if, else`

General Comments

In each of the following forms, the `statement` can be either a simple statement or a compound statement. A "true" expression means one with a non-zero value.

Form 1

```
if (expression)
    statement
```

The `statement` is executed if the `expression` is true.

Form 2

```
if (expression)
    statement1
  else
    statement2
```

(continued)

If the *expression* is true, *statement1* is executed. Otherwise, *statement2* is executed.

Form 3

```
if (expression1)
    statement1
else if (expression2)
    statement2
else
    statement3
```

If *expression1* is true, then *statement1* is executed. If *expression1* is false but *expression2* is true, *statement2* is executed. Otherwise, if both expressions are false, *statement3* is executed.

Example

```
if (legs == 4)
     printf("It might be a horse.\n");
else if (legs > 4)
     printf("It is not a horse.\n");
else    /* case of legs < 4 */
{
     legs++;
     printf("Now it has one more leg.\n")
}
```

Let's Get Logical

You've seen how if and while statements often use relational expressions as tests. Sometimes you will find it useful to combine two or more relational expressions. For instance, suppose you want a program that counts only nonwhitespace characters (not counting the period) in an input sentence. That is, you wish to keep track of characters that are not spaces, not newline characters, and not tab characters. You can use *logical operators* to meet this need. And you can use the period character (.) to identify the end of a sentence. Listing 7.6 presents a short program illustrating the method.

Listing 7.6 *chcount.c*

```c
/* chcount.c -- counts nonwhitespace characters */
#include <stdio.h>
#define PERIOD '.'
int main(void)
{
   int ch;
   int charcount = 0;

   while ((ch = getchar()) != PERIOD)
   {
    if (ch != ' ' && ch != '\n' && ch != '\t')
           charcount++;
   }
   printf("There are %d nonwhitespace characters.\n",
charcount);

   return 0;
}
```

Here's a sample run:

```
Logical operators
combine relationships.
There are 36 nonwhitespace characters.
```

The action begins as the program reads a character and checks to see if it is a period, since the period marks the end of a sentence. Next comes something new, a statement using the logical AND operator &&. We can translate the if statement thus: If the character is not a blank AND if it is not a newline character AND if it is not a tab character, then increase charcount by 1.

All three conditions must be true if the whole expression is to be true. The logical operators have a lower priority than the relational operators, so it was not necessary to use additional parentheses to group the subexpressions.

C has three logical operators:

Operator	Meaning
&&	and
||	or
!	not

Suppose exp1 and exp2 are two simple relational expressions like cat > rat or debt == 1000. Then we can state the following:

1. exp1 && exp2 is true only if both exp1 and exp2 are true.
2. exp1 || exp2 is true if either exp1 or exp2 is true or if both are true.
3. !exp1 is true if exp1 is false and is false if exp1 is true.

Here are some concrete examples:

5 > 2 && 4 > 7 is false because only one subexpression is true.
5 > 2 || 4 > 7 is true because at least one of the subexpressions is true.
!(4 > 7) is true because 4 is not greater than 7.

The last expression, incidentally, is equivalent to the following:

```
4 <= 7
```

If you are unfamiliar or uncomfortable with logical operators, remember that

```
(practice && time) == perfection
```

Precedence

The ! operator has a very high precedence, higher than multiplication, the same as the increment operators, and just below that of parentheses. The && operator has higher precedence than ||, and both rank below the relational operators and above assignment in precedence. Thus, the expression

```
a > b && b > c || b > d
```

would be interpreted as

```
((a > b) && (b > c)) || (b > d)
```

That is, b is between a and c, or b is greater than d.

Order of Evaluation

Aside from those cases in which two operators share an operand, C ordinarily does not guarantee which parts of a complex expression will be evaluated first. For example, in the following statement the expression 5 + 3 might be evaluated before 9 + 6, or it might be evaluated afterwards:

```
apples = (5 + 3) * (9 + 6);
```

This ambiguity was left in the language to enable compiler designers to make the most efficient choice for a particular system. One exception to this rule (or lack of rule) is the treatment of logical operators. C guarantees that logical expressions are evaluated from left to right. Furthermore, it guarantees that as soon as an element is found that invalidates the expression as a whole, the evaluation stops. These guarantees make it possible to use constructions such as the following:

```
while ((c = getchar()) != ' ' && c != '\n')
```

This construction sets up a loop that reads characters up to the first space or newline character. The first subexpression gives a value to c, which then is used in the second subexpression. Without the order guarantee, the computer might try to test the second expression before finding out what value c had.

Another example is

```
if (number != 0 && 12/number == 2)
    printf("The number is 5 or 6.\n");
```

If number has the value 0, the first subexpression is false, and the relational expression is not evaluated any further. This spares the computer the trauma of trying to divide by zero. Many languages do not have this feature. After seeing that number is 0, they still plunge ahead to check the next condition.

A Word-Count Program

Now we have the tools to make a word-counting program, that is, a program that reads input and reports the number of words it finds. We may as well count characters and lines while we are at it. Let's see what such a program involves.

Summary: Logical Operators and Expressions

Logical Operators

Logical operators normally take relational expressions as operands. The !
operator takes one operand. The rest take two—one to the left, one to the
right.

Operator	Meaning
&&	and
||	or
!	not

Logical Expressions

`expression1 && expression2` is true if and only if both expressions
are true.

`expression1 || expression2` is true if either one or both expressions
are true.

`!expression` is true if the expression is false, and vice versa.

Order of Evaluation

Logical expressions are evaluated from left to right. Evaluation stops as
soon as something is discovered that renders the expression false.

Examples

`6 > 2 && 3 == 3` is true.

`! (6 > 2 && 3 == 3)` is false.

`x != 0 && (20 / x) < 5` The second expression is evaluated only if x is
nonzero.

First, the program should read input character-by-character, and it
should have some way of knowing when to stop. Second, it should be able
to recognize and count the following units: characters, lines, words. Here's
a pseudocode representation:

read a character

while there is more input

    increment character count

    if a line has been read, increment line count

    if a word has been read, increment word count

    read next character

We already have a model for the input loop:

```
while ((ch = getchar()) != STOP)
{
    .
    .
    .
}
```

Here, STOP represents some value for ch that will signal the end of the input. So far we have used the newline character and a period for this purpose, but neither is satisfactory for a general word-counting program. For the present we'll choose a character (|) that is not common in text. In Chapter 8, we'll present a better solution that also allows the program to be used with text files as well as keyboard input.

Now let's consider the body of the loop. Since the program uses getchar() for input, it can count characters by incrementing a counter during each loop cycle. To count lines, the program can check for newline characters. If a character is a newline, then the program should increment the line count.

The trickiest part is identifying words. First, we have to define what we mean by a word. We will take a relatively simple approach and define a word as a sequence of characters that contains no whitespace. Thus, "glymxck" and "r2d2" are words. A word starts, then, when a program first encounters nonwhitespace, and it ends when the next whitespace character shows up. To keep track, we can set a flag (call it wordflag) to 1 when the first character in a word is read. We also can increment the word count at that point. Then, as long as wordflag remains 1, subsequent nonwhitespace characters don't mark the beginning of a word. At the next whitespace character, we must reset the flag to 0, and the program will be ready to find the next word. Let's put that into pseudocode:

if c is not whitespace and wordflag is 0

    set wordflag to 1 and count the word if c is whitespace and wordflag is 1

    set wordflag to 0

This approach sets wordflag to 1 at the beginning of each word and to 0 at the end of each word. Words are counted only at the time the flag setting is changed from 0 to 1. Listing 7.7 translates these ideas into C.

Listing 7.7 *wordcnt.c*

```
/* wordcnt.c -- counts characters, words, lines */
#include <stdio.h>
#define STOP '|'
#define YES 1
#define NO 0
int main(void)
{
    char c;                 /* read in character       */
    long n_chars = 0L;      /* number of characters    */
    int n_lines = 0;        /* number of lines         */
    int n_words = 0;        /* number of words         */
    int wordflag = NO;      /* ==YES if c is in a word */

    while ((c = getchar()) != STOP)
    {
        n_chars++;              /* count characters    */
        if (c == '\n')
            n_lines++;          /* count lines         */
        if (c != ' ' && c != '\n' && c != '\t' && wordflag == NO)
        {
            wordflag = YES;     /* starting a new word */
            n_words++;          /* count word          */
        }
        if ((c == ' ' || c == '\n' || c == '\t') &&
            wordflag == YES)
            wordflag = NO;      /* reached end of word */
    }
    printf("characters = %ld, words = %d, lines = %d\n",
        n_chars, n_words, n_lines);
    return 0;
}
```

Here is a sample run:

```
Reason is a
powerful servant but
```

```
an inadequate master.
|
characters = 55, words = 9, lines = 3
```

Since there are three different whitespace characters, we had to use the logical operators to check for all three possibilities. Consider the line:

```
if (c != ' ' && c != '\n' && c != '\t' && wordflag == NO)
```

It says, "If c is *not* a space and *not* a newline and *not* a tab, and if we are *not* in a word." (The first three conditions together ask if c is not whitespace.) If all four conditions are met, then we must be starting a new word, and n_words is incremented. If we are in the middle of a word, then the first three conditions hold, but wordflag will be YES, and n_words is not incremented. When we reach the next whitespace character, we set wordflag equal to NO again. Check the coding to see whether the program gets confused when there are several spaces between one word and the next. In Chapter 8, we'll show how to modify this program to count words in a file.

The Conditional Operator: ?:

C offers a shorthand way to express one form of the if else statement. It is called a *conditional expression* and uses the ?: conditional operator. This is a two-part operator that has three operands. Here is an example that yields the absolute value of a number:

```
x = (y < 0) ? -y : y;
```

Everything between the = and the semicolon is the conditional expression. The meaning of the statement is this: If y is less than zero, then x = -y; otherwise, x = y. In if else terms, the statement can be expressed as

```
if (y < 0)
    x = -y;
else
    x = y;
```

The general form of the conditional expression is

expression1 ?*expression2* : *expression3*

If *expression1* is true (nonzero), then the whole conditional expression has the same value as *expression2*. If *expression1* is false (zero), the whole conditional expression has the same value as *expression3*.

You can use the conditional expression when you have a variable to which you want to assign one of two possible values. A typical example is setting a variable equal to the maximum of two values:

```
max = (a > b) ? a : b;
```

This sets max to a if it is greater than b, and to b otherwise.

Usually, an if else statement can accomplish the same end as the conditional operator. The conditional operator version, however, is more compact and, depending on the compiler, may result in more compact program code.

Let's look at a paint program example, shown in Listing 7.8. The program calculates how many cans of paint are needed to paint a given number of square feet. The basic algorithm is simple: divide the square footage by the number of square feet covered per can. But suppose the answer is 1.7 cans. Stores sell whole cans, not fractional cans, so you would have to buy 2 cans. Therefore, the program should round up to the next integer when a fractional paint can is involved. We use the conditional operator to handle that situation. We also use the conditional operator to print cans or can, as appropriate.

Listing 7.8 *paint.c*

```
/* paint.c -- uses conditional operator */
#include <stdio.h>
#define COVERAGE 200         /* square feet per paint can */
int main(void)
{
   int sq_feet;
   int cans;

   printf("Enter number of square feet to be painted:\n");
   while (scanf("%d", &sq_feet) == 1)
   {
       cans = sq_feet / COVERAGE;
       cans += ((sq_feet % COVERAGE == 0)) ? 0 : 1;
       printf("You need %d %s of paint.\n", cans,
              cans == 1 ? "can" : "cans");
   }
   return 0;
}
```

Here's a sample run:

```
Enter number of square feet to be painted:
200
You need 1 can of paint.
210
You need 2 cans of paint.
q
```

Because we're using type int, the division is truncated; that is, 210/ 200 becomes 1. Therefore, cans is rounded down to the integer part. If sq_feet % COVERAGE is 0, then COVERAGE divides evenly into sq_feet and cans is left unchanged. Otherwise, there is a remainder, so 1 is added. This is accomplished with the following statement:

```
cans += ((sq_feet % COVERAGE == 0)) ? 0 : 1;
```

It adds the value of the expression to the right of += to cans. The expression to the right is a conditional expression having the value 0 or 1, depending on whether COVERAGE divides evenly into sq_feet.

The final argument to the printf() function also is a conditional expression:

```
cans == 1 ? "can" : "cans");
```

If the value of cans is 1, then the string "can" is used. Otherwise, "cans" is used. This demonstrates that the conditional operator can use strings for its second and third operands.

Summary: The Conditional Operator

The Conditional Operator
?:

General Comments
This operator takes three operands, each of which is an expression. They are arranged as follows:

expression1 ? expression2 : expression3

(continued)

The value of the whole expression equals the value of *expression2* if *expression1* is true. Otherwise, it equals the value of *expression3*.

Examples

      (5 > 3) ? 1 : 2 has the value 1.

      (3 > 5) ? 1 : 2 has the value 2.

      (a > b) ? a : b has the value of the larger of a or b.

Loop Aids: *continue* and *break*

Normally, once the body of a loop has been entered, a program executes all the statements in the body before doing the next loop test. The continue and break statements let you skip part of a loop or even terminate it, depending on tests made in the body of the loop.

The *continue* Statement

This statement can be used in the three loop forms. When encountered, it causes the rest of an iteration to be skipped and the next iteration to be started. If the continue statement is inside nested structures, it affects only the innermost structure containing it. Let's try continue in the short program found in Listing 7.9.

Listing 7.9 skip.c

```
/* skip.c -- uses continue to skip part of loop */
#include <stdio.h>
#define MIN 0.0
#define MAX 100.0
int main(void)
{
    float score;
    float total = 0.0;
    int n;
    float min = MAX;
```

```
    float max = MIN;

    printf("Enter the scores:\n");
    while (scanf("%f", &score) == 1)
    {
        if (score < MIN || score > MAX)
        {
            printf("%0.1f is an invalid value.\n", score);
            continue;
        }
        printf("Accepting %0.1f:\n", score);
        min = (score < min)? score: min;
        max = (score > max)? score: max;
        total += score;
        n++;
    }
    if (n > 0)
    {
        printf("Average of %d scores is %0.1f.\n", n, total / n);
        printf("Low = %0.1f, high = %0.1f\n", min, max);
    }
    else
        printf("No valid scores were entered.\n");
    return 0;
}
```

In Listing 7.9 the `while` loop reads input until you enter nonnumeric data. The `if` statement within the loop screens out invalid score values. If, say, you enter 188, the program tells you that `188 is an invalid score`. Then the `continue` statement causes the program to skip over the rest of the loop, which is devoted to processing valid input. Instead, the program starts the next loop cycle by attempting to read the next input value.

Note that there are two ways that we could have avoided using `continue`. One way would have been to omit the `continue` and to make the remaining part of the loop an `else` block:

```
if (score < 0 || score > 100)
    /* printf() statement */
else
{
    /* statements */
}
```

Or we could have used this format:

```
if (score >= 0 && score <= 100)
{
    /* statements */
}
```

An advantage of using `continue` in this case is that we can eliminate one level of indentation in the main group of statements. This conciseness can be important for readability when the statements are long or are deeply nested already.

Another use for `continue` is as a placeholder. For example, the following loop reads and discards input up to, and including, the end of a line:

```
while (getchar() != '\n')
    ;
```

Such a technique is handy when a program already has read some input from a line and needs to skip to the beginning of the next line. The problem is that the lone semicolon is hard to spot. The code is much more readable if you use `continue`:

```
while (getchar() != '\n')
    continue;
```

Don't use `continue` if it complicates rather than simplifies the code. Consider the following fragment, for instance:

```
while ((ch = getchar() ) != '\n')
{
    if (ch == '\t')
        continue;
    putchar(ch);
}
```

This loop skips over the tabs and quits only when a newline character is encountered. The loop could have been expressed more economically as

```
while ((ch = getchar()) != '\n')
    if (ch != '\t')
        putchar(ch);
```

Often, as in this case, reversing an `if` test will eliminate the need for a `continue`.

You've seen that the `continue` statement causes the remaining body of a loop to be skipped. But where exactly does the loop resume? For the while and do while loops, the next action taken after the continue statement is to evaluate the loop test expression. For a for loop, the next actions are to evaluate the update expression, then the loop test expression.

The *break* Statement

A break statement in a loop causes the program to break free of the loop that encloses it and to proceed to the next stage of the program. In Listing 7.9, replacing continue with break would cause the loop to quit when, say, 188 is entered instead of just skipping to the next loop cycle. Figure 7.4 compares break and continue. If the break statement is inside nested loops, it affects only the innermost loop containing it.

Figure 7.4 break *and* continue

```
while ( (ch = getchar() ) !=EOF)
{
    blahblah(ch);
    if (ch == '\n')
        break;
    yakyak(ch);
}
blunder(n,m);
```

```
while ( (ch = getchar() ) !=EOF)
{
    blahblah(ch);
    if (ch == '\n')
        continue;
    yakyak(ch);
}
blunder(n,m);
```

Sometimes `break` is used to leave a loop when there are two separate reasons to leave. Listing 7.10 uses a loop that calculates the area of a rectangle. The loop terminates if you respond with nonnumeric input for the rectangle's length or width.

Listing 7.10 *break.c*

```
/* break.c  -- uses break to exit a loop */
#include <stdio.h>
int main(void)
{
   float length, width;

   printf("Enter the length of the rectangle:\n");
   while (scanf("%f", &length) == 1)
   {
        printf("Length = %0.2f:\n", length);
        printf("Enter its width:\n");
        if (scanf("%f", &width) != 1)
             break;
        printf("Width = %0.2f:\n", width);
        printf("Area = %0.2f:\n", length * width);
        printf("Enter the length of the rectangle:\n");
   }
   return 0;
}
```

We could have controlled the loop this way:

```
while (scanf("%f %f", &length, &width) == 2)
```

However, using `break` makes it simple to echo each input value individually.

As with `continue`, don't use `break` when it complicates code. For instance, consider the following loop:

```
while ((ch = getchar()) != '\n')
{
   if (ch == '\t')
        break;
   putchar(ch);
}
```

The logic is clearer if both tests are in one place:

```
while ((ch = getchar() ) != '\n' && ch != '\t')
        putchar(ch);
```

The `break` statement is an essential adjunct to the `switch` statement, which we study next.

Multiple Choice: *switch* and *break*

The conditional operator and the `if else` construction make it easy to write programs that choose between *two* alternatives. Sometimes, however, a program needs to choose one of *several* alternatives. We can do this by using `if else if...else`, but in many cases it is more convenient to use the C `switch` statement. Listing 7.11 is an example showing how the `switch` statement works. This program reads in a letter and then responds by printing an animal name that begins with that letter.

```
Listing 7.11   animals.c

/* animals.c -- uses a switch statement */
#include <stdio.h>
int main(void)
{
  char ch;

  printf("Give me a letter of the alphabet, and I will give ");
  printf("an animal name\nbeginning with that letter.\n");
  printf("Please type in a letter; type # to end my act.\n");
  while ((ch = getchar()) != '#')
  {
    if (ch >= 'a' && ch <= 'z') /* lowercase only */
      switch (ch)
      {
        case 'a' :
                printf("argali, a wild sheep of Asia\n");
                break;
        case 'b' :
```

(continued)

Listing 7.11 *(continued)*

```
            printf("babirusa, a wild pig of Malay\n");
            break;
        case 'c' :
            printf("coati, racoonlike mammal\n");
            break;
        case 'd' :
            printf("desman, aquatic, molelike critter\n");
            break;
        case 'e' :
            printf("echidna, the spiny anteater\n");
            break;
        default :
            printf("That's a stumper!\n");
    } /* end of switch */
  else
    printf("I recognize only lowercase letters.\n");
  while (getchar() != '\n')
    continue;              /* skip rest of input line */
  printf("Please type another letter or a #.\n");
  }                        /* while loop end           */
  return 0;
}
```

We got a little lazy and stopped at e, but we could have continued in the same manner. Let's look at a sample run before explaining the program further.

```
Give me a letter of the alphabet, and I will give an animal name
beginning with that letter.
Please type in a letter; type # to end my act.
a [enter]
argali, a wild sheep of Asia
Please type another letter or a #.
dab [enter]
desman, aquatic, molelike critter
Please type another letter or a #.
r [enter]
That's a stumper!
```

```
Please type another letter or a #.
Q [enter]
I recognize only lowercase letters.
Please type another letter or a #.
# [enter]
```

The program's two main features are its use of the `switch` statement and its handling of input. We'll look first at how `switch` works.

Using the *switch* Statement

The expression in the parentheses following the word `switch` is evaluated. In this case it has whatever value we last entered for `ch`. Then the program scans the list of *labels* (here, `case 'a' :`, `case 'b' :`, etc.) until it finds one matching that value. The program then jumps to that line. What if there is no match? If there is a line labeled `default :`, the program jumps there. Otherwise, the program proceeds to the statement following the `switch`.

What about the `break` statement? It causes the program to break out of the `switch` and skip to the next statement after the switch (see Figure 7.5). Without the `break` statement, every statement from the matched label to the end of the `switch` would be processed. For example, if we removed all the `break` statements from our program and then ran the program using the letter `d`, we would get this exchange:

```
Give me a letter of the alphabet, and I will give an animal name
beginning with that letter.
Please type in a letter; type # to end my act.
d [enter]
desman, aquatic, molelike critter
echidna, the spiny anteater
That's a stumper!
Please type another letter or a #.
# [enter]
```

All the statements from `case 'd' :` to the end of the switch were executed.

Incidentally, a `break` statement works with loops and with `switch`, but `continue` works just with loops. However, `continue` can be used as part of a `switch` statement if the statement is in a loop. In that situation, as with other loops, `continue` causes the program to skip over the rest of the loop, including other parts of the `switch`.

If you are familiar with Pascal, you will recognize the `switch` statement as being similar to the Pascal `case` statement. The most important

Figure 7.5 *Program flow in switches, with and without breaks*

```
switch(number)
{
case 1:   statement 1;
          break;
case 2:   statement 2;
          break;
case 3:   statement 3;
          break;
default:  statement 4;
}
statement 5;
```

```
switch(number)
{
case 1:   statement 1;
case 2:   statement 2;
case 3:   statement 3;
default:  statement 4;
}
statement 5;
```

in each case, number has the value 2

difference is that the switch statement requires the use of a break if you want only the labeled statement to be processed.

The switch test expression in the parentheses should be one with an integer value (including type char). The case labels must be integer-type (including char) constants or integer constant expressions (expressions containing only integer constants). You can't use a variable for a case label. This, then, is the structure of a switch:

```
switch (integer expression)
    {
case constant1:
        statements;   ←optional
case constant2:
```

```
        statements;      ←optional
    ⋮
default :                ←optional
        statements;      ←optional
}
```

Reading Only the First Character of a Line

The other new feature incorporated into `animals.c` is how it reads input. As you may have noticed in the sample run, when `dab` was entered, only the first character was processed. Often this behavior is desirable in interactive programs looking for single-character responses. The code responsible for this behavior is the following:

```
while (getchar() != '\n')
    continue;              /* skip rest of input line */
```

This loop reads characters from input up to and including the newline character generated by the Enter key. Note that the function return value is not assigned to `ch`. Thus, the characters are merely read and discarded. Because the last character discarded is the newline character, the next character to be read will be the first character of the next line. It gets read by `getchar()` and assigned to `ch` in the outer `while` loop.

If you omit this loop, the program runs into a bit of trouble. Suppose, for instance, you respond with the letter `a`. Entering `a` involves pressing the Enter key, so you actually send the sequence `a` followed by the newline character. After the program processes the `a`, it reads the newline character and prints "I recognize only lowercase letters." Thus, each letter entered causes the program to run through the outer `while` loop twice, which is disconcerting to the user.

Another approach to the newline problem is to skip only newlines rather than the entire rest of the line. You can do that by using the following code as the first statement in the large `while` loop:

```
if (ch == '\n')
    continue;
```

Multiple Labels

You can use multiple `case` labels for a given statement, as shown in Listing 7.12.

Listing 7.12 *vowels.c*

```
/* vowels.c -- uses multiple labels */
#include <stdio.h>
int main(void)
{
  char ch;
  int a_ct, e_ct, i_ct, o_ct, u_ct;

  a_ct = e_ct = i_ct = o_ct = u_ct = 0;

  printf("Enter some text; enter # to quit.\n");
  while ((ch = getchar()) != '#')
  {
      switch (ch)
      {
        case 'a' :
        case 'A' :  a_ct++;
                    break;

        case 'e' :
        case 'E' :  e_ct++;
                    break;

        case 'i' :
        case 'I' :  i_ct++;
                    break;

        case 'o' :
        case 'O' :  o_ct++;
                    break;

        case 'u' :
        case 'U' :  u_ct++;
                    break;
        default :   break;
      }                                   /* end of switch */
  }                                       /* while loop end */
  printf("number of vowels:   A    E    I    O    U\n");
  printf("                  %4d %4d %4d %4d %4d\n",
        a_ct, e_ct, i_ct, o_ct, u_ct);
  return 0;
}
```

If ch is, say, the letter i, the switch statement goes to the location labeled case 'i' :. Because there is no break associated with that label, program flow goes to the next statement, which is i_ct++;. If ch is I, program flow goes directly to that statement. In essence, both labels refer to the same statement.

Here's a sample run:

```
Enter some text; enter # to quit.
I see under the overseer.#
number of vowels:   A   E   I   O   U
                    0   7   1   1   1
```

Summary: Multiple Choice with *switch*

Keyword

`switch`

General Comments

Program control jumps to the `case` label bearing the value of *expression*. Program flow then proceeds through all the remaining statements unless redirected again with a `break` statement. Both *expression* and `case` labels must have integer values (type `char` is included), and the labels must be constants or expressions formed solely from constants. If no `case` label matches the expression value, control goes to the statement labeled `default`, if present. Otherwise, control passes to the next statement following the `switch` statement.

Form

```
switch (expression)
{
    case label1 : statement1
    case label2 : statement2
    default     : statement3
}
```

There can be more than two labeled statements, and the `default` case is optional.

Example

```
switch (choice)
```

(continued)

```
        {
        case 1 :
        case 2 : printf("Darn tootin'!\n");  break;
        case 3 : printf("Quite right!\n");
        case 4 : printf("Good show!\n"); break;
        default  : printf("Have a nice day.\n");
        }
```

If `choice` has the integer value 1 or 2, the first message is printed. If it is 3, the second and third messages are printed. (Flow continues to the following statement because there is no `break` statement after `case 2`.) If it is 4, the third message is printed. Other values print only the last message.

switch and if else

When should you use a `switch` and when should you use the `else-if` construction? Often you don't have a choice. You can't use a `switch` if your choice is based on evaluating a `float` variable or expression. Nor can you conveniently use a `switch` if a variable must fall into a certain range. It is simple to write the following:

```
if (integer < 1000 && integer > 2)
```

Unhappily, covering this range with a `switch` would involve setting up case labels for each integer from 3 to 999. However, if you can use a `switch`, often your program will run a little faster and take less code.

The *goto* Statement

The `goto` statement, bulwark of the older versions of BASIC and FORTRAN, is available in C. However, C, unlike those two languages, can get along quite well without it. Kernighan and Ritchie refer to the `goto` statement as "infinitely abusable" and suggest that it "be used sparingly, if at all." First, we will show you how to use `goto`. Then, we will show why you usually don't need to.

The `goto` statement has two parts: the `goto` and a label name. The label is named following the same conventions used in naming a variable. An example is

```
goto part2;
```

For the preceding statement to work, the function must contain another statement bearing the `part2` label. This is done by beginning a statement with the label name followed by a colon.

```
part2: printf("Refined analysis:\n");
```

Avoiding *goto*

In principle, you never need to use the `goto` statement in a C program. But if you have a background in FORTRAN or BASIC, both of which require its use, you may have developed programming habits that depend on using the `goto`. To help you get over that dependence, we will outline some familiar `goto` situations and then show you a more C-like approach.

1. Handling an `if` situation that requires more than one statement:

```
if (size > 12)
    goto a;
goto b;
a: cost = cost * 1.05;
   flag = 2;
b: bill = cost * flag;
```

In old-style BASIC and FORTRAN, only the single statement immediately following the `if` condition is attached to the `if`. No provision is made for blocks or compound statements. We have translated that pattern into the equivalent C. The standard C approach of using a compound statement or block is much easier to follow:

```
if (size > 12)
{
    cost = cost * 1.05;
    flag = 2;
}
bill = cost * flag;
```

2. Choosing from two alternatives:

```
if (ibex > 14)
    goto a;
sheds = 2;
goto b;
a: sheds = 3;
b: help = 2 * sheds;
```

Having the `if else` structure available allows C to express this choice more cleanly:

```
if (ibex > 14)
    sheds = 3;
else
    sheds = 2;
help = 2 * sheds;
```

Indeed, newer versions of BASIC and FORTRAN have incorporated the else into their syntax.

3. Setting up an indefinite loop:

```
readin: scanf("%d", &score);
if (score < 0)
    goto stage2;
lots of statements;
goto readin;
stage2: more stuff;
```

Use a while loop instead:

```
scanf("%d", &score);
while (score >= 0)
{
    lots of statements;
    scanf("%d", &score);
}
more stuff;
```

4. Skipping to the end of a loop: use continue instead.

5. Leaving a loop: use break instead. Actually, break and continue are specialized forms of a goto. The advantages of using them are that their names tell you what they are supposed to do and that, since they don't use labels, there is no danger of putting a label in the wrong place.

6. Leaping madly about to different parts of a program: DON'T!

There is one use of goto that is tolerated by many C practitioners: getting out of a nested set of loops if trouble shows up. (A single break gets you out of the innermost loop only.)

```
while (funct > 0)
    {
    for (i = 1, i <= 100; i++)
        {
        for (j= 1; j <= 50; j++)
            {
            statements galore;
            if (big trouble)
```

```
            goto help;
        statements;
        }
    more statements;
    }
    yet more statements;
    }
and more statements;
help : bail out;
```

As you can see from our other examples, the alternative forms are clearer than the `goto` forms. This difference grows even greater when you mix several of these situations. Which `goto`s are helping `if`s, which are simulating `if else`s, which are controlling loops, which are just there because you have programmed yourself into a corner? Using `goto`s excessively lets you create a labyrinth of program flow. If you aren't familiar with `goto`s, keep it that way. If you are used to using them, try to train yourself not to. Ironically, C, which doesn't need a `goto`, has a better `goto` than most languages because it lets you use descriptive words for labels instead of numbers.

Summary: Program Jumps

Keywords

`break, continue, goto`

General Comments

These three instructions cause program flow to jump from one location of a program to another location.

The *break* Command

The `break` command can be used with any of the three loop forms and with the `switch` statement. It causes program control to skip the rest of the loop or the `switch` containing it and to resume with the next command following the loop or `switch`.

(continued)

Example

```
switch (number)
{
     case  4:  printf("That's a good choice.\n");
               break;
     case  5:  printf("That's a fair choice.\n");
               break;
     default:  printf("That's a poor choice.\n");
}
```

The *continue* Command

The continue command can be used with any of the three loop forms but not with a switch. It causes program control to skip the remaining statements in a loop. For a while or for loop, the next loop cycle is started. For a do while loop, the exit condition is tested and then, if necessary, the next loop cycle is started.

Example

```
while ((ch = getchar())  != EOF)
{
     if (ch == ' ')
          continue;
     putchar(ch);
     chcount++;
}
```

This fragment echoes and counts nonspace characters.

The *goto* Command

A goto statement causes program control to jump to a statement bearing the indicated label. A colon is used to separate a labeled statement from its label. Label names follow the rules for variable names. The labeled statement can come either before or after the goto.

Form

```
goto label;
     .
     .
     .
label : statement
```

(continued)

Example
```
top : ch = getchar();
        .
        .
        .

if (ch != 'y')
        goto top;
```

Chapter Summary

The `if` statement uses a test condition to control whether or not a program executes the single simple statement or block following the test condition. Execution occurs if the test expression has a nonzero value and doesn't occur if the value is zero. The `if else` statement lets you select from two alternatives. If the test condition is nonzero, the statement before the `else` is executed. If the test expression evaluates to zero, the statement following the `else` is executed. By using another `if` statement to immediately follow the `else`, you can set up a structure that chooses between a series of alternatives.

The test condition often is a *relational expression*, that is, an expression formed by using one of the relational operators discussed in Chapter 6. By using C's logical operators, you can combine relational expressions. For example, you can test to see if x is greater than 0 and less than 20.

The *conditional operator* (*operand1* ? *operand2* : *operand3*) creates an expression whose value is governed by its first operand and is given by one of the next two operands. If the first operand is nonzero, the whole expression has the value of *operand2*; otherwise, the value is that of *operand3*.

The `switch` statement lets you select from a series of statements labeled with integer values. If the integer value of the test condition following the `switch` keyword matches a label, execution goes to the statement bearing that label. Execution then proceeds through the statements following the labeled statement unless you use a `break` statement.

The `break`, `continue`, and `goto` are *jump statements* that cause program flow to jump to another location in a program. A `break` statement causes the program to jump to the next statement following the end of the loop or `switch` containing the `break`. The `continue` statement causes the program to skip the rest of the containing loop and to start the next cycle.

The control statements presented in these last two chapters will let you tackle programs much more powerful and ambitious than those you worked with before. As proof, just compare some of the examples in these chapters to those of the earlier chapters.

Review Questions

1. Determine which expressions are true and which are false.

   a. 100 > 3 && 'a' > 'c'

   b. 100 > 3 | | 'a' > 'c'

   c. !(100 > 3)

2. The following program has unnecessarily complex relational expressions as well as some outright errors. Simplify and correct it.

```
#include <stdio.h.
int main(void)                                  /* 1  */
{                                               /* 2  */
   int weight, height;  /* weight in lbs, height in inches */
                                                /* 4  */
   scanf("%d, weight, height);                  /* 5  */
   if (weight < 100)                            /* 6  */
      if (height >= 72)                         /* 7  */
         printf("You are very tall for your weight.\n");
      else if (height < 72 && > 64)             /* 9  */
         printf("You are tall for your weight.\n");
   else if (weight > 300 && !(weight <= 300))   /* 11 */
      if (!(height >= 48)                       /* 12 */
         printf(" You are quite short for your weight.\n");
   else                                         /* 14 */
      printf("Your weight is ideal.\n");        /* 15 */
                                                /* 16 */

   return 0;
}
```

3. What is the numerical value of each of the following expressions?

   a. 5 > 2

   b. 3+4 > 2 && 3 < 2

   c. x >= y | | y > x

4. What will the following program print?

```
#include <stdio.h>
int main(void)
{
   int num;
```

```
    for (num = 1; num <= 11; num++)
    {
        if (num % 3 == 0)
            putchar('$');
        else
            putchar('*');
            putchar('#');
        putchar('%');
    }
    putchar('\n');
    return 0;
}
```

5. What's wrong with this program?

```
#include <stdio.h>
int main(void)
{
    char ch;
    int lc = 0;    /* lowercase char count
    int uc = 0;    /* uppercase char count
    int oc = 0;    /* other char count

    while ((ch = getchar()) != '#')
    {
        if ('a' <= ch >= 'z')
            lc++;
        else if (!(ch < 'A') || !(ch > 'Z')
            uc++;
        oc++;
    }
    printf(%d lowercase, %d uppercase, %d other, lc, uc, oc);
    return 0;
}
```

6. What will the following program print when given this input?

```
q
c
g
b

#include <stdio.h>
int main(void)
{
    char ch;

    while ((ch = getchar()) != '#')
```

```
{
    if (ch == '\n')
        continue;
    printf("Step 1\n");
    if (ch == 'c')
        continue;
    else if (ch == 'b')
        break;
    else if (ch == 'g')
        goto laststep;
    printf("Step 2\n");
laststep:  printf("Step 3\n");
}
printf("Done\n");
return 0;
}
```

Programming Exercises

1. Write a program that reads input until encountering the # character and then reports the number of spaces read, the number of newline characters read, and the number of all other characters read.

2. Write a program that reads input until encountering #. Have the program print each input character and its ASCII decimal code. Print eight character-code pairs per line. Suggestion: use a character count and the modulus operator (%) to print a newline character for every eight cycles of the loop.

3. Using if else statements, write a program that reads input up to #, replaces each period with an exclamation mark, replaces each exclamation mark initially present with two exclamation marks, and reports at the end the number of substitutions it has made.

4. Redo Exercise 3, but use a switch.

5. Write a program that reads input up to # and reports the number of times that the sequence ei occurs. *Note*: The program will have to "remember" the preceding character as well as the current character. Test it with input like "Receive your eieio award."

6. Write a program that requests the hours worked in a week and then prints the gross pay, the taxes, and the net pay. Assume the following:

   a. Basic pay rate = $10.00/hr

   b. Overtime (in excess of 40 hours) = time and a half

   c. Tax rate =

                  15% of the first $300
                  20% of the next $150
                  25% of the rest

    Use #define constants, and don't worry if the example does not conform to current tax law.

7. Modify assumption a in Exercise 6 so that the program presents a menu of pay rates to choose from. Use a switch to select the pay rate. The beginning of a run should look something like this:

```
*****************************************************************
Enter the number corresponding to the desired pay rate or
action:
1) $8.75/hr                         2) $9.33/hr
3) $10.00/hr                        4) $11.20/hr
5) quit
*****************************************************************
```

If choices 1 through 4 are selected, then the program should request the hours worked. The program should recycle until 5 is entered. If something other than choices 1 through 5 is entered, the program should remind the user what the proper choices are and then recycle. Use #defined constants.

8. Write a program that accepts an integer as input and then displays all the prime numbers smaller than or equal to that number.

8

Character Input/
Output and
Redirection

In this chapter you learn more about input, output, and the differences between buffered and unbuffered input. You learn how to simulate the end-of-file condition from the keyboard and how to use redirection to connect your programs to files. Finally, you gain some experience in making the user interface friendlier.

I n the computing world, we use the words *input* and *output* in several ways. We speak of input and output devices, such as keyboards, disk drives, and laser printers. Or we talk about the data used for input and output. And we discuss the functions that perform input and output. This chapter concentrates on the functions used for input and output (*I/O* for short).

I/O functions transport information to and from your program; printf(), scanf(), getchar(), and putchar() are examples. You've seen these functions in previous chapters, and now you'll be able to look at their conceptual basis. Along the way, you'll see how to improve the program-user interface.

Originally, input/output functions were not part of the definition of C. Their development was left to the implementors of C. In practice, the UNIX implementation of C has served as a model for these functions. The ANSI C library, recognizing past practice, contains a large number of these UNIX I/O functions, including the ones we've used. Because such standard functions must work in a wide variety of computer environments, they seldom take advantage of features peculiar to a particular system. Thus, many C vendors supply additional I/O functions that do make use of special features, such as the 8086 microprocessor I/O ports or the Macintosh ROM routines. These specialized functions let you write programs that utilize a particular computer more effectively. Unfortunately, they often can't be used on other computer systems. Consequently, we'll concentrate on the standard I/O functions available on all systems, for they allow you to write portable programs that can be moved easily from one system to another.

Single-Character I/O: *getchar()* and *putchar()*

As you saw in Chapter 7, getchar() and putchar() perform input and output one character at a time. That may strike you as a rather silly way of doing things. After all, you can easily read groupings larger than a single character. But this method does suit the ability of a computer. Furthermore, this approach is the heart of most programs that deal with text, that is, with ordinary words. To remind yourself of how these functions work, examine Listing 8.1, a very simple example. All it does is fetch characters from keyboard input and send them to the screen. We call this process *echoing the input*. We use a `while` loop that terminates when the # character is encountered.

Listing 8.1 *echo.c*

```
/* echo.c -- repeats input */
#include <stdio.h>
int main(void)
{
    char ch;

    while ((ch = getchar()) != '#')
        putchar(ch);
    return 0;
}
```

On most systems the definitions of `getchar()` and `putchar()` are found in the system file `stdio.h`, which is why we have included that file in the program. (Typically, `getchar()` and `putchar()` are not true functions but are defined using preprocessor macros, a topic we'll cover in Chapter 16.) Using this program produces exchanges like this:

```
Hello, there. I would[enter]
Hello, there. I would
like a #3 bag of potatoes.[enter]
like a
```

The [enter] is our way of indicating that you press the Enter key (or the Return key).

After watching this program run, you may wonder why you must type a whole line before the input is echoed. You also may wonder if there is a better way to terminate input. Using a particular character, such as #, to terminate input prevents you from using that character in the text. To answer these questions, we have to look at how C programs handle keyboard input. In particular, we need to examine buffering and the concept of a standard input file.

Buffers

When you run the previous program on some systems, the text that you input is echoed immediately. That is, a sample run would look like this:

```
HHeelloo,,  tthheerree..  II  wwoouulldd[enter]

lliikkee  aa  #
```

The preceding behavior is the exception. On most systems, nothing happens until you press Enter, as in the first example. The immediate echoing of input characters is an instance of *unbuffered* (or *direct*) input, meaning that the character you type is immediately made available to the waiting program. The delayed echoing, on the other hand, illustrates *buffered* input, in which the characters you type are collected and stored in an area of temporary storage called a *buffer*. Pressing Enter causes the block of characters (or single character, if that is all you typed) to be made available to your program. Figure 8.1 compares these two kinds of input.

Figure 8.1 *Buffered versus unbuffered input*

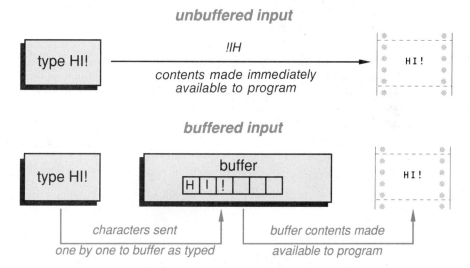

Why have buffers? First, it is less time-consuming to transmit several characters as a block than one by one. Second, if you mistype, you can use your keyboard correction facilities to fix your mistake. When you finally press Enter, the corrected version can be transmitted.

Unbuffered input, on the other hand, is desirable for some interactive programs. In a word processor, for instance, you would like each command to take place as soon as you press a key. Thus, both buffered and unbuffered input have their uses.

Buffering comes in two varieties: *fully buffered* I/O and *line-buffered* I/O. For fully buffered input, the buffer is flushed (the contents are sent to their destination) when the buffer is full. This kind of buffering usually occurs with file input. The buffer size depends on the system, but 512 bytes and 4096 bytes are common values. With line-buffered I/O, the buffer is flushed whenever a newline character shows up. Keyboard input normally is line-buffered so that pressing Enter flushes the buffer.

Which kind of input do you have: buffered or unbuffered? You can find out by running the echo.c program and seeing which behavior results. Some C compilers give you a choice. On our microcomputer system, for example, getchar() provides buffered input, while getche() provides direct input. Also, some operating systems provide a choice. On UNIX, for instance, the stty command and the ioctl() function let you specify the type of input that you want. In ANSI C, the setbuf() and setvbuf() functions (Chapter 12) supply some control over buffering, but the inherent limitations of some systems can restrict the effectiveness of these functions. In this book, with apologies to our unbuffered friends, we assume that you are using buffered input.

Terminating Keyboard Input

Our program halts when # is entered, which is convenient as long as we exclude that character from normal input. But, as you've seen, # can show up in normal input. Ideally, we'd like a terminating character that normally does not show up in text. Such a character won't pop up accidentally in the middle of some input, stopping the program before we want it to stop. C has an answer to this need, but, to understand it, you need to know how C handles files.

Files, Streams, and Keyboard Input

A *file* is an area of memory in which information is stored. Normally a file would be kept in some sort of permanent memory, such as a floppy disk, a hard disk, or a tape. You doubtless are aware of the importance of files to computer systems. For instance, your C programs are kept in files. And the programs used to compile your programs are kept in files. This last example points out that some programs need to be able to access particular files. When you compile a program stored in a file called echo.c, the compiler *opens* the echo.c file and *reads* its contents. When the compiler finishes, it *closes* the file. Other programs, such as word processors, not only open, read, and close files, they also *write* to them.

C, being powerful, flexible, and so on, provides many library functions for opening, reading, writing, and closing files. On one level, it can deal with files using the basic file tools of the host operating system. This is called *low-level I/O*. Because of the many differences among computer systems, it is impossible to create a standard library of universal low-level I/O functions, and ANSI C does not attempt to do so. But C also deals with files on a second level called the *standard I/O package*. This involves creating a standard model and a standard set of I/O functions for dealing with files. At this higher level, differences between systems are handled by specific C implementations so that you deal with a uniform interface.

What sort of differences are we talking about? Different systems, for example, store files differently. Some store the file contents in one place and information about the file elsewhere. Some build a description of the file into the file itself. In dealing with text, some systems use a single newline character to mark the end of a line. Others may use the combination of the carriage return and linefeed characters to represent the end of a line. Some systems measure file sizes to the nearest byte; some measure in blocks of bytes.

When you use the standard I/O package, you are shielded from these differences. Thus, to check for a newline, you can use `if (ch == '\n')`. If the system actually uses the carriage-return/linefeed combination, the I/O functions automatically translate back and forth between the two representations.

Conceptually, the C program deals with a stream instead of directly with a file. A *stream* is an idealized flow of data to which the actual input or output is mapped. This means that various kinds of input with differing properties are represented by streams with more uniform properties. The process of opening a file then becomes one of associating a stream with the file, and reading and writing take place via the stream.

Chapter 12 discusses files in greater detail. For this chapter, simply note that C treats input and output devices the same as it treats regular files on storage devices. In particular, the keyboard and the display device are treated as files that are opened automatically by every C program. Keyboard input is represented by a stream called `stdin`, and output to the screen (or teletype, or other output device) is represented by a stream called `stdout`. The `getchar()`, `putchar()`, `printf()`, and `scanf()` functions all are members of the standard I/O package, and they deal with these two streams.

One implication of all this is that you can use the same techniques with keyboard input as you do with files. For example, a program reading a file needs a way to detect the end of the file so that it knows where to stop reading. Therefore, C input functions come equipped with a built-in end-of-file detector. Since keyboard input is treated like a file, you should be able to use that end-of-file detector to terminate keyboard input, too. Let's see how this is done, beginning with files.

The End of File

A computer operating system needs some way to tell where each file begins and ends. One method to detect the end of a file is to place a special character in the file to mark the end. This is the method used, for example, in CP/M, IBM-DOS, and MS-DOS text files. These operating systems use (or once used) the Control-Z character to mark the ends of files. (Control-Z is the character generated by holding down the Control key while typing the Z key.) Figure 8.2 illustrates this approach.

Figure 8.2 *A file with an end-of-file marker*

prose:

Ishphat the robot

slid open the hatch

and shouted his challenge.

prose in a file:

Ishphat the robot\n slid open the hatch\n and shouted his challenge.\n ^Z

A second approach is for the operating system to store information on the size of the file. If a file has 3000 bytes and a program has read 3000 bytes, then the program has reached the end. MS-DOS and its relatives use this approach for binary files, since this method allows the files to hold all characters, including Control-Z. Newer versions of DOS also use this approach for text files. UNIX uses this approach for all files.

C handles this variety of methods by having the getchar() function return a special value when the end of a file is reached, regardless of how the operating system actually detects the end of file. The name given to this value is EOF (end of file). Thus, the return value for getchar() when it detects an end of file is EOF. The scanf() function also returns EOF upon detecting the end of a file. Typically, EOF is defined in the stdio.h file as follows:

```
#define EOF (-1)
```

Why −1? Normally, getchar() returns a value in the range 0 through 127, since those are values corresponding to the standard character set. Or it might return values from 0 through 255 if the system recognizes an extended character set. In either case, the value −1 does not correspond to any character, so it can be used to signal the end of file.

Some systems may define EOF to be a value other than −1. But the definition always will be different from a return value produced by a legitimate input character. If you include the stdio.h file and use the EOF symbol, you don't have to worry about the numeric definition. The important point is that EOF represents a value which signals that the end of a file was detected; it is not a symbol actually found in the file.

Okay, how can you use EOF in a program? Compare the return value of getchar() with EOF. If they are different, you have not yet reached the end of a file. In other words, you can use an expression like this:

```
while ((ch = getchar()) != EOF)
```

But what if you are reading keyboard input and not a file? Most systems provide a way to simulate an end-of-file condition from the keyboard. Knowing that, we can rewrite our basic read and echo program as shown in Listing 8.2.

Listing 8.2 *echo_eof.c*

```
/* echo_eof.c -- repeats input to end of file */
#include <stdio.h>
int main(void)
{
   int ch;

   while ((ch = getchar()) != EOF)
        putchar(ch);
   return 0;
}
```

Note these points:

▶ You don't have to define EOF because stdio.h takes care of that.

▶ You don't have to worry about the actual value of EOF because the #define statement in stdio.h lets you use the symbolic representation EOF.

▶ The variable ch is changed from type char to type int because char variables may be represented by unsigned integers in the range 0 to 255, but EOF may have the numeric value −1. That is an impossible value for an unsigned char variable, but not for an int. Fortunately, getchar() is actually of type int itself, so it can read the EOF character. Implementations that use a signed char type may

291

get by with declaring ch as type char, but it is better to use the more general form.

► The fact that ch is an integer doesn't faze putchar(). It still prints the character equivalent.

► To use this program on keyboard input, you need a way to type the EOF character. No, you can't just type the letters *E-O-F*, and you can't just type −1. (Typing −1 would transmit two characters: a hyphen and the digit 1.) Instead, you have to find out what your system requires. On most UNIX systems, for example, typing Control-D at the beginning of a line causes the end-of-file signal to be transmitted. Many microcomputing systems recognize a Control-Z typed anywhere on a line as an end-of-file signal.

Here is a buffered example of running echo_eof.c:

```
She walks in beauty, like the night
She walks in beauty, like the night
  Of cloudless climes and starry skies...
  Of cloudless climes and starry skies...
              Lord Byron
              Lord Byron
[Control-D]
```

Each time you press Enter, the characters stored in the buffer are processed, and a copy of the line is printed. This continues until you simulate the end of file, UNIX-style.

Let's stop for a moment and think about the possibilities for echo_eof.c. It copies onto the screen whatever input you feed it. Suppose you could somehow feed a file to it. Then it would print the contents of the file onto the screen, stopping when it reached the end of the file, for it would find an EOF signal then. Or suppose instead that you could find a way to direct the program's output to a file. Then you could enter data from the keyboard and use echo_eof.c to store in a file what you type. Or suppose you could do both simultaneously: direct input from one file into echo_eof.c and send the output to another file. Then you could use echo_eof.c to copy files. Thus, our little program has the potential to look at the contents of files, to create new files, and to make copies of files— pretty good for such a short program! The key is to control the flow of input and output, and that is our next topic.

Redirection and Files

Input and output involve functions, data, and devices. Consider, for instance, our echo_eof.c program. It uses the input function getchar().

The input device (we have assumed) is a keyboard, and the input data stream consists of individual characters. Suppose you want to keep the same input function and the same kind of data, but wish to change where the program looks for data. A good question to ask (and to answer) is "How does a program know where to look for its input?"

By default, a C program using the standard I/O package looks to the standard input as its source for input. This is the stream identified earlier as stdin. It is whatever has been set up as the usual way for reading data into the computer. It could be magnetic tape, punched cards, a teletype, or (as we will continue to assume) your keyboard. A modern computer is a suggestible tool, however, and you can influence it to look elsewhere for input. In particular, you can tell a program to seek its input from a file instead of from a keyboard.

There are two ways to get a program to work with files. One way is to explicitly use special functions that open files, close files, read files, write in files, and so forth. That we'll save for Chapter 12. The second way is to use a program designed to work with keyboard and screen, but to *redirect* input and output along different channels, to and from files, for example. In other words, you reassign the stdin stream to file. The getchar() program continues to get its data from the stream, not really caring from where the stream gets its data. This approach is more limited in some respects than the first, but it is much simpler to use. It is the one that we will use now.

One major problem with redirection is that it is associated with the operating system, not C. But the most popular C environments (UNIX and DOS 2.0 and later) feature redirection, and some C implementations simulate it on systems lacking the feature. We'll look at the UNIX and DOS versions.

UNIX and DOS Redirection

UNIX and current DOS versions let you redirect both input and output. Redirecting input enables your program to use a file instead of the keyboard for input, and redirecting output enables it to use a file instead of the screen for output.

Redirecting Input

Suppose you have compiled our echo_eof.c program and placed the executable version in a file called echo_eof (or echo_eof.exe on DOS systems). To run the program, you just type the executable file's name:

```
echo_eof
```

The program runs as we described earlier, taking its input from the keyboard. Now suppose that you wish to use the program on a text file called words. A *text file* is one containing text, that is, data stored as human-readable characters. It could be an essay or a program in C, for example. A file containing machine language instructions, such as the file holding the executable version of a program is *not* a text file. Since our program works with characters, it should be used with text files. All you need do is enter this command instead of the previous one:

```
echo_eof < words
```

The < symbol is a UNIX (and DOS) redirection operator. It causes the words file to be associated with the stdin stream, channelling the file contents into the echo_eof program. The echo_eof program itself doesn't know (or care) that the input is coming from a file instead of the keyboard. All it knows is that a stream of characters is being fed to it, so it reads them and prints them one character at a time until the end of file shows up. Because C puts files and I/O devices on the same footing, the file is now the I/O *device*. Try it!

Redirection Sidelights

With UNIX and DOS, the spaces on either side of the < are optional. Some systems, such as AmigaDOS, support redirection but don't allow a space between the redirection symbol and the filename. You can't use redirection from within some integrated environments. In such cases, you must create an executable file and run it in the standard environment.

Here is a sample run for one particular words file; the $ is one of the two standard UNIX prompts. On a DOS system, you would see the DOS prompt, perhaps an A> or C>.

```
$ echo_eof < words
The world is too much with us: late and soon,
Getting and spending, we lay waste our powers:
Little we see in Nature that is ours;
We have given our hearts away, a sordid boon!
$
```

Well, that time we got our words' worth.

Redirecting Output

Now suppose that you wish to have echo_eof send your keyboard input to a file called mywords. Then you can enter the following and begin typing:

```
echo_eof > mywords
```

The > is a second redirection operator. It causes a new file called mywords to be created for your use, and then it redirects the output of echo_eof (that is, a copy of the characters you type) to that file. The redirection reassigns stdout from the display device (your screen) to the mywords file instead. If you already have a file with the name mywords, normally it would be erased and then replaced by the new one. (Some UNIX systems, however, give you the option of protecting existing files.) All that appears on your screen are the letters as you type them, and the copies go to the file instead. To end the program, type Control-D (UNIX) or Control-Z (DOS) at the beginning of a line. Try it. If you can't think of anything to type, just imitate the next example. In it we use the $ UNIX prompt. Remember to end each line by pressing Enter to send the buffer contents to the program.

```
$ echo_eof > mywords
You should have no problem recalling which redirection
operator does what. Just remember that each operator points
in the direction the information flows. Think of it as a
funnel.
[Control-D]
$
```

Once the Control-D or Control-Z is processed, the program terminates and your system prompt returns. Did the program work? The UNIX ls command or DOS dir command, which lists filenames, should show you that the file mywords now exists. You can use the UNIX cat or DOS type command to check the contents, or you can use echo_eof again, this time redirecting the file *to* the program.

```
$ echo_eof < mywords
You should have no problem recalling which redirection
operator does what. Just remember that each operator points
in the direction the information flows. Think of it as a
funnel.
$
```

Combined Redirection

Now suppose you want to make a copy of the file `mywords` and call it `savewords`. Just issue this next command

```
echo_eof < mywords > savewords
```

and the deed is done. The following command would have served as well, since the order of redirection operations doesn't matter:

```
echo_eof > savewords < mywords
```

But beware. Don't use the same file for both input and output to the same command:

```
echo_eof < mywords > mywords    ←WRONG
```

The reason is that `> mywords` causes the original `mywords` to be truncated to zero length before it is ever used as input.

In brief, here are the rules governing the use of the two redirection operators < and > with UNIX or DOS:

1. A redirection operator connects an *executable* program (including standard UNIX commands) with a data file. It cannot be used to connect one data file to another, nor can it be used to connect one program to another program.

2. Input cannot be taken from more than one file, nor can output be directed to more than one file using these operators.

3. Normally, spaces between the names and operators are optional, except occasionally when some characters with special meaning to the UNIX shell or DOS are used. We could, for example, have used `echo_eof<words`.

You have already seen several proper examples. Here are some wrong examples, with `addup` and `count` as executable programs and `fish` and `beets` as text files:

```
fish > beets            ←violates Rule 1
addup < count           ←violates Rule 1
addup < fish < beets    ←violates Rule 2
count > beets fish      ←violates Rule 2
```

UNIX and DOS also feature the >> operator, which lets you add data to the end of an existing file, and the pipe operator (|), which lets you connect the output of one program to the input of a second program. See a UNIX book such as *UNIX Primer Plus* (Waite, Prata, and Martin, Indianapolis: Howard W. Sams) for more information on all these operators.

Comment

Redirection enables you to use keyboard-input programs with files. But for this to work, the program has to test for end of file. For example, Chapter 7 presented a word-counting program that counted words up to the first | character. Change `ch` from type `char` to type `int`, and replace `'|'` with `EOF` in the loop test, and you can use the program to count words in text files.

Summary: How to Redirect Input and Output

With most C systems you can use redirection, either for all programs through the operating system or else just for C programs, courtesy of the C compiler. In the following, let `prog` be the name of the executable program and let `file1` and `file2` be names of files.

Redirecting Output to a File

>

```
prog >file1
```

Redirecting Input from a File

<

```
prog <file2
```

Combined Redirection

```
prog <file2 >file1
prog >file1 <file2
```

Both forms use `file2` for input and `file1` for output.

(continued)

Spacing

Some systems require a space to the left of the redirection operator and no space to the right. Other systems (UNIX, for example) will accept either spaces or no spaces on either side.

A Graphic Example

You can use `getchar()` and `putchar()` to produce geometric patterns using characters. Listing 8.3 shows such a program. It reads a character and then prints it a number of times, the number depending on the character's ASCII value. The program also prints a sufficient number of spaces to center each line.

Listing 8.3 *patterns.c*

```
/* patterns.c -- produces a symmetric pattern of characters */
#include <stdio.h>
int main(void)
{
   int ch;                  /* read character                      */
   int index;
   int chnum;

   while ((ch = getchar()) != '\n')
   {
      chnum = ch % 26;      /* produces a number from 0 to 25 */
      index = 0;
      while (index++ < (30 - chnum))
         putchar(' ');      /* spaces to center pattern         */
      index = 0;
      while (index++ < (2 * chnum + 1))
         putchar(ch);       /* print ch several times           */
      putchar('\n');
   }
   return 0;
}
```

Listing 8.3 uses nested loops. The outer `while` loop gathers input characters. The first inner `while` loop prints leading spaces to center the text, and the second `while` loop prints the character multiple times. The number of characters printed is determined from the numeric value for the character. What you get depends on what you enter. If, for example, you type

    What's up?

then the response is

                   wwwwwwwwwwwwwwwwww
                           h
        aaaaaaaaaaaaaaaaaaaaaaaaaaaaaaaaaaaaaaaa
                 tttttttttttttttttttttttttt
                    ''''''''''''
                 ssssssssssssssssssssssss

              uuuuuuuuuuuuuuuuuuuuuuuuuuuuu
                 ppppppppppppppppppp
              ?????????????????????????

What can you do with this program? You can ignore it. You can tinker with it to change the kinds of patterns it makes. You can try to find combinations of input characters that produce a pretty pattern. For example, the input

    hijklmnopqrstuiii

produces:

                        h
                       iii
                      jjjjj
                     kkkkkkk
                    lllllllll
                   mmmmmmmmmmm
                  nnnnnnnnnnnnn
                 ooooooooooooooo
                pppppppppppppppppp
               qqqqqqqqqqqqqqqqqqqq
              rrrrrrrrrrrrrrrrrrrrrr
             ssssssssssssssssssssssss
            tttttttttttttttttttttttttt
           uuuuuuuuuuuuuuuuuuuuuuuuuuuuu
                       iii
                       iii
                       iii

Creating a Friendlier User Interface

Most of us have on occasion written programs that are awkward to use. Fortunately, C gives us the tools to make input a smoother, more pleasant process. Unfortunately, learning these tools may, at first, lead to new problems. Our goal in this section is to guide you through some of these problems to a friendlier user interface, one that eases data entry and smooths over the effects of faulty input.

Working with Buffered Input

Buffered input is often a convenience to the user, but it can be bothersome to the programmer when character input is used. The problem, as you've seen in some earlier examples, is that buffered input requires you to press the Enter key to transmit your input. This act also transmits a newline character which the program must handle. Let's examine this and other problems with a guessing program. You pick a number, and the computer tries to guess it. The computer uses a plodding method, but we are concentrating on I/O, not algorithms. See Listing 8.4 for the starting version of the program.

Listing 8.4 *guess.c*

```
/* guess.c -- an inefficient number-guesser */
#include <stdio.h>
int main(void)
{
  int guess = 1;
  char response;

  printf("Pick an integer from 1 to 100. I will try to guess ");
  printf("it.\nRespond with a y if my guess is right and with");
  printf("\nan n if it is wrong.\n");
  printf("Uh...is your number %d?\n", guess);
  while ((response = getchar()) != 'y')      /* get response */
  printf("Well, then, is it %d?\n", ++guess);
  printf("I knew I could do it!\n");
  return 0;
}
```

Here's a sample run:

```
Pick an integer from 1 to 100. I will try to guess it.
Respond with a y if my guess is right and with
an n if it is wrong.
Uh...is your number 1?
n
Well, then, is it 2?
Well, then, is it 3?
n
Well, then, is it 4?
Well, then, is it 5?
y
I knew I could do it?
```

Out of consideration for the program's pathetic guessing algorithm, we chose a small number. Note that the program makes two guesses every time we enter n. What's happening is that the program reads our n response as a denial that the number is 1 and then reads the newline character as a denial that the number is 2.

One solution is to use a `while` loop to discard the rest of the input line, including the newline character. This has the additional merit of treating responses such as no or no way the same as a simple n. The version in Listing 8.4 treats no as two responses. Here is a revised loop that fixes the problem:

```
while ((response = getchar()) != 'y')     /* get response */
{
printf("Well, then, is it %d?\n", ++guess);
while (getchar() != '\n')
    continue;                    /* skip rest of input line    */
}
```

Using this loop produces responses like the following:

```
Pick an integer from 1 to 100. I will try to guess it.
Respond with a y if my guess is right and with
an n if it is wrong.
Uh...is your number 1?
n
Well, then, is it 2?
no
Well, then, is it 3?
no sir
Well, then, is it 4?
forget it
```

```
Well, then, is it 5?
y
I knew I could do it?
```

So there are no more problems with the newline character. But, as a purist, you may not like f being treated as meaning the same as n. To eliminate that defect, we can use an if statement to screen out other responses. Change the loop to this:

```
while ((response = getchar()) != 'y')        /* get response */
{
    if (response == 'n')
        printf("Well, then, is it %d?\n", ++guess);
    else
        printf("Sorry, I understand only y or n.\n");
    while (getchar() != '\n')
        continue;                      /* skip rest of input line */
}
```

Now the program's response looks like this:

```
Pick an integer from 1 to 100. I will try to guess it.
Respond with a y if my guess is right and with
an n if it is wrong.
Uh...is your number 1?
n
Well, then, is it 2?
no
Well, then, is it 3?
no sir
Well, then, is it 4?
forget it
Sorry, I understand only y or n.
n
Well, then, is it 5?
y
I knew I could do it?
```

When you write interactive programs, you should try to anticipate ways in which users will fail to follow instructions. Then you should design your program to handle user failures gracefully. Tell them when they are wrong, and give them another chance.

You should, of course, provide clear instructions to the user. But no matter how clear you make them, someone will always misinterpret them and then blame you for poor instructions.

Mixing Numeric and Character Input

Typically, you use getchar() to read input one character at a time and you use scanf() to read numbers or strings. This mixture can create problems because getchar() reads every character, including spaces, tabs, and newlines. In contrast, scanf(), when reading numbers, skips over spaces, tabs, and newlines. (However, when reading characters using the %c specifier, scanf() behaves like getchar().)

To illustrate a representative problem, Listing 8.5 presents a program that reads in a character and two numbers as input. It then prints the character using the number of rows and columns specified in the input.

Listing 8.5 *showchar1.c*

```
/* showchar1.c -- program with an I/O problem */
#include <stdio.h>
void display(char c, int lines, int width);
int main(void)
{
    int ch;            /* character to be printed   */
    int rows, cols;    /* number of rows and columns */

    printf("Enter a character and two integers:\n");
    while ((ch = getchar()) != EOF)
    {
      scanf("%d %d", &rows, &cols);
      display(ch, rows, cols);
      printf("Enter another character and two integers;\n");
      printf("Simulate eof to quit.\n");
    }
    return 0;
}

void display(char c, int lines, int width)
{
    int row, col;

    for (row = 1; row <= lines; row++)
    {
        for (col = 1; col <= width; col++)
```

(continued)

> **Listing 8.5** (continued)
>
> ```
>               putchar(c);
>         putchar('\n');    /* end line and start a new one */
>     }
> }
> ```

The program is set up so that `main()` gets the data, and the `display()` function does the printing. Let's look at a sample run to see what the problem is.

```
Enter a character and two integers:
a 2 3
aaa
aaa
Enter another character and two integers;
Simulate eof to quit.
 b 1 2
```

```
Enter another character and two integers;
Simulate eof to quit.
bb
Enter another character and two integers;
Simulate eof to quit.
^Z
```

```
Enter another character and two integers;
Simulate eof to quit.
^Z
```

The program starts off fine. We enter a 2 3, and it prints two rows of three a characters, as expected. Then we enter b 1 2, and it prints one row with two b characters. But in between it prints eight blank lines! What's wrong? It's that newline character again, this time the one immediately following the 3 on the first input line. Since getchar() doesn't skip over newline characters, this newline character is read by getchar() during the next cycle of the loop, becoming the character to be displayed.

Then scanf() has a turn at exposing our poor programming. Because getchar() reads the newline, the next input is the b character. The scanf() function attempts to read it as an integer and fails. So rows retains its previous value of 2. (At least, that is how our system behaves on a failed match; ANSI C doesn't require any particular behavior in that instance.) Then scanf() tries to read the cols value. Input is still stuck on the b, so that read fails, too, and cols remains at 3. The net result is that the program tells display() to print two rows of three newline characters. But each newline character generates a new line, giving a total of eight blank lines. Then the next loop cycle begins, and getchar() finally gets to read the b. This clears the way for scanf() to read the next two numbers. Similarly, the newline following this line forces us to enter Control-Z twice to end the program. (We're assuming the program is run on a DOS system.)

To clear up this problem, the program has to skip over any newlines or spaces between the last number typed for one cycle of input and the character typed at the beginning of the next line. Also, it would be nice if the program could be terminated at the scanf() stage in addition to the getchar() test. The next version, shown in Listing 8.6, accomplishes this.

Listing 8.6 *showr2.c*

```
/* showchar2.c -- prints characters in rows and columns */
#include <stdio.h>
void display(char c, int lines, int width);
int main(void)
{
    int ch;          /* character to be printed   */
    int rows, cols;  /* number of rows and columns */

    printf("Enter a character and two integers:\n");
    while ((ch = getchar()) != EOF)
    {
        if (ch != '\n' && ch != ' ' && ch != '\t')
        {
            if (scanf("%d %d",&rows, &cols) != 2)
                break;
```

(continued)

Listing 8.6 *(continued)*

```
        display(ch, rows, cols);
        printf("Enter another character and two integers;\n");
        printf("Simulate eof to quit.\n");
     }
   }
   return 0;
}

void display(char c, int lines, int width)
{
    int row, col;

    for (row = 1; row <= lines; row++)
    {
        for (col = 1; col <= width; col++)
            putchar(c);
        putchar('\n');   /* end line and start a new one */
    }
}
```

The if statement causes the program to skip over the scanf() and display() statements if ch is whitespace. This means we can enter data fairly freely:

```
a 2 3
aaa
aaa
b 1 2 c 3 5
bb
ccccc
ccccc
ccccc
[Control-Z]
```

By using an if statement with a break, we terminate the program if the return value of scanf() is not 2. This occurs if one or both input values are not integers or if end-of-file is encountered.

By using the if statement to skip spaces as well as newlines, the program can handle the second input line. If we omit the space skipping, the input line would have to look like this: ·

```
b 1 2c 3 5
```

Otherwise, a space between the 2 and c would be read into `ch`, and `scanf()` would try to read c as an integer.

Character Sketches

Now let's look at something a little more decorative. Our plan is to create a program allowing you to draw rough, filled-in figures using characters. Each line of output consists of an unbroken row of characters. You choose the character and the starting and stopping positions for printing the character in the row. The program, shown in Listing 8.7, keeps reading your choices until it finds EOF. This program illustrates several programming techniques, which, of course, we'll discuss soon.

Listing 8.7 *sketcher.c*

```
/* sketcher.c  -- this program makes solid figures */
#include <stdio.h>
#define TRUE 1
#define FALSE 0
#define MAXLENGTH 80
int badlimits(int begin, int end, int limit);
void display(char c, int first, int last);
int main(void)
{
    int ch;                /* character to be printed      */
    int start, stop;       /* starting and stopping points */
    int badlimits();       /* returns TRUE for bad limits  */

    while ((ch = getchar()) != EOF) /* read in character    */
    {
        if (ch == '\n' || ch == ' ' || ch == '\t')
            continue;        /* skip newlines, spaces */
        if (scanf("%d %d", &start, &stop) != 2)  /* read limits */
```

(continued)

Listing 8.7 *(continued)*

```
            break;
        if (badlimits(start, stop, MAXLENGTH) == TRUE)
            printf("Inappropriate limits were entered.\n");
        else
            display(ch, start, stop);
    }
    return 0;
}

int badlimits(int begin, int end, int limit)
{
    if (begin > end || begin < 1 || end > limit)
        return TRUE;
    else
        return FALSE;
}

void display(char c, int first, int last)
{
    int column;

    for (column = 1; column < first; column++)
        putchar(' ');      /* print blanks to starting point */
    for (column = first; column <= last; column++)
        putchar(c);        /* print char to stopping point   */
    putchar('\n');         /* end line and start a new one    */
}
```

The general structure is similar to that of Listing 8.6. The three main differences are these:

► We use a `continue` statement to skip to the end of the loop if `ch` is whitespace, rather than isolating the relevant code with an `if` statement.

► The `display()` function has been rewritten to display the character in a different manner. Here `first` represents the first column and `last` represents the last column for displaying the character.

► We've added a `badlimits()` function to screen out bad input values.

Suppose we call the executable program `sketcher`. To run the program, we type its name. Then we enter a character and two numbers. The program responds, we enter another set of data, and the program responds again until we provide an EOF signal. On a UNIX system using the **%** prompt, an exchange could look like this:

```
% sketcher
B 10 20
          BBBBBBBBBBB
Y 12 18
            YYYYYYY
[Control-D]
%
```

The program printed the character B in columns 10 to 20, and it printed Y in columns 12 to 18. Unfortunately, when we use the program interactively, our commands are interspersed with the output. A more satisfactory way to use this program is to create a file containing suitable data and then use redirection to feed the file to the program. Suppose, for example, the file `fig` contains the following data:

```
_ 30 50
| 30 50
| 30 50
| 30 50
| 30 50
| 30 50
= 20 60
: 31 49
: 30 49
: 29 49
: 27 49
: 25 49
: 30 49
: 30 49
/ 30 49
: 35 48
: 35 48
```

Then the command `sketcher < fig` produces the output shown in Figure 8.3. (*Note*: Printers and screens have different values for the vertical-to-horizontal ratio for characters. This difference causes figures of this sort to look more compressed vertically when printed than when displayed on a screen.)

Figure 8.3 *Output of character sketch program*

Analyzing the Program

The sketcher.c program is short, but it is more involved than the examples we have given before. Let's look at some of its elements.

Line Length

We limited the program to print no farther than the 80th column, since 80 characters is the standard width of many video monitors and of regular-width paper. However, you can redefine the value of MAXLENGTH if you wish to use the program with a device having a different output width.

Program Structure

We've followed a modular approach, using separate functions (modules) to verify input and to manage the display. The larger a program is, the more vital it is to use modular programming.

The main() function acquires the data:

```
while ((ch = getchar()) != EOF)
{
    if (ch == '\n' || ch == ' ' || ch == '\t')
        continue;                    /* skip newlines, spaces */
    if (scanf("%d %d", &start, &stop) != 2)  /* read limits */
        break;
    .
    .
    .
}
```

With Listing 8.6, we discussed the rationale for skipping whitespace. Next the program checks to see if the input makes sense:

```
if (badlimits(start, stop, MAXLENGTH) == TRUE)
    printf("Inappropriate limits were entered.\n");
else
    .
    .
    .
```

The purpose of the if else statement is to let the program skirt any values of start and stop that would lead to trouble. We will discuss the details of the badlimits() function later. The important point here is that it returns a value of TRUE if the data fails to pass the testing procedure. In that case, the computer prints a message and skips over the else part, which is the display output.

The display() function uses one for loop to print spaces up to where the character is first to appear. The second for loop then prints the character from the start column to the end column. Finally, it prints a newline to end the line.

```
void display(char c, int first, int last)
{
    int column;

    for (column = 1; column < first; column++)
        putchar(' ');       /* print blanks to starting point */
    for (column = first; column <= last; column++)
        putchar(c);         /* print char to stopping point  */
    putchar('\n');          /* end line and start a new one  */
}
```

Error-Checking

Getting the user to provide data in a form that the computer can use properly is a pervasive problem. One technique is to use *error-checking*. In this technique the computer checks the data to see if it is okay before using it. We have included a beginning effort at error-checking in this program with the badlimits() function:

```
int badlimits(int begin, int end, int limit)
{
    if (begin > end || begin < 1 || end > limit)
        return TRUE;
    else
        return FALSE;
}
```

What is the badlimits() function protecting against? First, there's no sense having the starting position come after the final position. Terminals normally print from left to right, not vice versa, so the expression begin > end checks for that possible error. Second, the first column on a screen is column 1. We can't write to the left of the left margin. The begin > 1 expression guards against making an error there. Finally, the expression end > limit checks to see that we don't try to print past the right margin.

Are there any other erroneous values we could give to begin and end? Well, we could try to make begin greater than limit. Would that pass our test? No. It is true that we don't check for this error directly. However, suppose that begin is greater than limit. Then, either end is also greater than limit—in which case that error is caught—or else end isn't greater than limit. But if end is less than limit, it must also be less than begin. Thus, this case gets caught by the first test. Another possible error is that end is less than 1. We leave it to you to make sure that this error doesn't sneak through, either.

We kept the test pretty simple. If you design a program for serious use, you should put more effort than we did into this part of the program. For instance, you should put in error messages to identify which values are wrong and why, perhaps injecting your personality into the messages. Here are some possibilities:

```
Your value of 897654 for stop exceeds the screen width.
Oh my! Your START is bigger than your STOP. Please try again.
THE START VALUE SHOULD BE BIGGER THAN 0, HONORED USER.
```

The personality you inject, of course, is up to you.

Another input problem occurs if letters show up when scanf() expects numbers. As the program is set up, letters cause the program to terminate, which is preferable to it getting stuck or misinterpreting input. It's also possible to have scanf() skip over data it can't read; we'll show the technique later in the book.

Chapter Summary

Many programs use getchar() to read input character by character. Typically, systems use *line-buffered* input, meaning that input is transmitted to the program when you press Enter. Pressing Enter also transmits a newline character that may require programming attention.

C features a family of functions, called the *standard I/O package*, that treats different file forms on different systems in a uniform manner. The getchar() and scanf() functions belong to this family. Both functions return the value EOF (defined in the stdio.h header) when they detect the end of a file. UNIX systems let you simulate the end-of-file condition from the keyboard by typing Control-D at the beginning of a line; DOS systems use Control-Z for the same purpose.

Many operating systems, including UNIX and DOS, feature *redirection*, which lets you use files instead of the keyboard and screen for input and output. Programs that read input up to EOF can then be used either with keyboard input and simulated end-of-file signals or with redirected files.

Interspersing calls to getchar() with calls to scanf() can cause problems when scanf() leaves a newline character in the input just before a call to getchar(). By being aware of this problem, however, you can program around it.

When you are writing a program, plan the user interface thoughtfully. Try to anticipate the sort of errors that users are likely to make and then design your program to handle them.

Review Questions

1. putchar(getchar()) is a valid expression; what does it do? Is getchar(putchar()) also valid?

2. Suppose you have a program count that counts the characters in its input. Devise a command that counts the number of characters in the file essay and stores the result in a file named essayct.

3. What is EOF?

4. What is the output of each of the following fragments for the indicated input (assume that ch is type int and that the input is buffered):

   a. The input is as follows:

      If you quit, I will.[enter]

      The fragment is as follows:

      ```
      while ((ch = getchar()) != 'i')
          putchar(ch);
      ```

   b. The input is as follows:

      Harhar[enter]

      The fragment is as follows:

      ```
      while ((ch = getchar()) != '\n')
      {
          putchar(ch++);
      ```

```
        putchar(++ch);
    }
```

5. How does C deal with the fact that different computers systems have different file and newline conventions?

Programming Exercises

1. Devise a program that counts the number of characters in its input up to the end of file.

2. Modify the program in Exercise 1 so that it beeps each time that it counts a character. Insert a short delay loop (a loop that does nothing but increment a counter) to separate one beep from the next. Do not use it on long files.

3. Write a program that reads input until encountering EOF. Have the program print each input character and its ASCII decimal value. Note that characters preceding the space character in the ASCII sequence are nonprinting characters. Treat them specially. If the nonprinting character is a newline or tab, print \n or \t, respectively. Otherwise, use control-character notation. For instance, ASCII 1 is Control-A, which can be displayed as ^A. Note that the ASCII value for A is the value for Control-A plus 64. A similar relation holds for the other nonprinting characters. Print ten pairs per line, except start a fresh line each time that a newline character is encountered.

4. Write a program that reads input until encountering EOF. Have it report the number of uppercase letters and the number of lowercase letters in the input. Assume that the numeric values for the lowercase letters are sequential, and assume the same for uppercase.

5. Write a program that reads input until encountering EOF. Have it report the average number of letters per word. Don't count whitespace as being letters in a word. Actually, punctuation shouldn't be counted either, but don't worry about that now.

6. Modify the guessing program of Listing 8.4 so that it uses a more intelligent guessing strategy. For example, have the program initially guess 50, and have it ask the user whether the guess is high, low, or correct. If, say, the guess is low, have the next guess be halfway between 50 and 100, that is, 75. If that guess is high, let the next guess be halfway between 75 and 50, and so on. Using this *binary search* strategy, the program quickly zeros in on the correct answer, at least if the user does not cheat.

9

Functions

In this chapter you learn about functions: how to define them, how to use arguments and return values, and how to use pointer variables as function arguments. You find out about function types, ANSI C prototypes, and recursion.

H ow do you organize a program? C's design philosophy is to use functions as building blocks. You've already relied on the standard C library for functions such as printf(), scanf(), getchar(), putchar(), and strlen(). Now you're ready for a more active role: creating your own functions. You've previewed several aspects of that process in earlier chapters, and this chapter consolidates your earlier information and expands on it.

Review

First, what is a function? A *function* is a self-contained unit of program code designed to accomplish a particular task. A function in C plays the same role that functions, subroutines, and procedures play in other languages, although the details may differ. Some functions cause action to take place. For example, printf() causes data to be printed on your screen. Some functions find a value for a program to use. For instance, strlen() tells a program how long a certain string is. In general, a function can both produce actions and provide values.

Why should you use functions? For one, they save you from repetitious programming. If you have to do a certain task several times in a program, you need write an appropriate function only once. The program can then use that function wherever needed. Or you can use the same function in different programs, just as you have used putchar() in many programs. Two, even if you do a task just once in just one program, using a function is worthwhile because functions make a program more modular, hence easier to read and easier to change or fix. Suppose, for example, you want to write a program that does the following:

    Read in a list of numbers

    Sort the numbers

    Find their average

    Print a bar graph

You could use this program:

```
#include <stdio.h>
#define SIZE 50
main()
{
  float list[SIZE];

  readlist(list, SIZE);
  sort(list, SIZE);
  average(list, SIZE);
  bargraph(list, SIZE);
}
```

Of course, you would also have to write the four functions `read-list()`, `sort()`, `average()`, and `bargraph()` . . . mere details. Descriptive function names make it quite clear what the program does and how it is organized. You then can work with each function separately until it does its job right. And if you make the functions general enough, you can use them in other programs.

Many programmers like to think of a function as a "black box" defined in terms of the information that goes in (its input) and the value or action that it produces (its output). What goes on inside the black box is not our concern, unless we are the ones who have to write the function. For example, when you use `printf()`, you know that you have to give it a control string and, perhaps, some arguments. You also know what output `printf()` should produce. You never had to think about the programming that went into creating `printf()`. Thinking of functions in this manner helps you concentrate on the overall design of the program rather than on the details. Think carefully about what the function should do and how it relates to the program as a whole before worrying about writing the code.

What do you need to know about functions? You need to know how to define them properly, how to call them up for use, and how to set up communication between functions. To refresh your memory on these points, we will begin with a very simple example and then bring in more features until we have the full story.

Creating and Using a Simple Function

Our modest first goal is to create a function that types 65 asterisks in a row. To give our function a context, we will include it in a program that prints a simple letterhead. Listing 9.1 presents the complete program. It consists of the functions `main()` and `starbar()`.

Listing 9.1 *lethead1.c*

```
/* lethead1.c */
#include <stdio.h>
#define NAME "MEGATHINK, INC."
#define ADDRESS "10 Megabuck Plaza"
#define PLACE "Megapolis, CA 94904"
#define LIMIT 65
int main(void)
{
    void starbar(void);  /* prototype the function */
    starbar();
    printf("%s\n", NAME);
    printf("%s\n", ADDRESS);
    printf("%s\n", PLACE);
    starbar();
    return 0;
}

/* define the starbar() function */
void starbar(void)
{
    int count;

    for (count = 1; count <= LIMIT; count++)
        putchar('*');
    putchar('\n');
}
```

Here is the output:

```
*****************************************************************
MEGATHINK, INC.
10 Megabuck Plaza
Megapolis, CA 94904
*****************************************************************
```

There are several major points to note about this program:

► We use the starbar identifier in three separate contexts: a function prototype that tells the compiler what sort of function starbar()

is, a function call that causes the function to be executed, and a function definition that specifies exactly what the function does.

▶ Like variables, functions have types. Any program that uses a function should declare the type for that function before it is used. Therefore, `main()` contains this ANSI C prototype:

```
void starbar(void);
```

The parentheses indicate that `starbar` is a function name. The first `void` is a function type; the `void` type indicates that the function does not return a value. The second `void` (the one in the parentheses) indicates that the function takes no arguments. The semicolon indicates that we are declaring the function, not defining it. That is, this line announces that the program uses a type `void` function called `starbar()` and that the compiler should expect to find the definition for this function elsewhere. For compilers that don't recognize ANSI C prototyping, just declare the type:

```
void starbar();
```

Note that some very old compilers don't recognize the `void` type. In that case, use type `int` for functions that don't have return values.

▶ We placed the prototype inside `main()`; it can go before `main()`, instead. Either way is fine.

▶ We called (invoked, summoned) the function `starbar()` from `main()` by using its name followed by parentheses and a semicolon, creating a statement:

```
starbar();
```

This is one form for calling up a function, but it isn't the only one. Whenever the computer reaches a `starbar();` statement, it looks for the `starbar()` function and follows the instructions there. When finished with the code within `starbar()`, the computer returns to the next line of the *calling function*—`main()`, in this case. See Figure 9.1.

▶ We followed the same form in defining `starbar()` as we did in defining `main()`. We started with the type, name, and parentheses. Then we supplied the opening brace, a declaration of variables used, the defining statements of the function, and then the closing brace (see Figure 9.2). Note that this instance of `starbar()` is not followed by a semicolon. The lack of a semicolon tells the compiler that we are *defining* `starbar()` rather than calling or prototyping it.

▶ We included `starbar()` and `main()` in the same file. We could have used two separate files. The single-file form is slightly easier to compile. Two separate files make it simpler to use the same function in different programs. If we do place the function in a separate file, then we would also place the necessary #define and #include directives in that file. We will discuss using two or more files later. For now, we will keep all our functions together. The closing brace of main() tells the compiler where that function ends, and the following starbar() header tells the compiler that starbar() is a function.

The variable count in starbar() is a *local* variable. This means it is known only to starbar(). You can use the name count in other functions, including main(), and there will be no conflict. You simply wind up with separate, *independent* variables having the same name.

Figure 9.1 *Control flow for* lethead1.c *(Listing 9.1)*

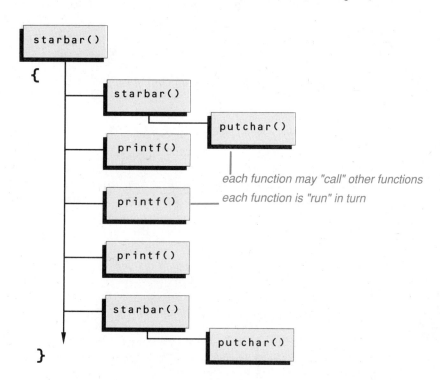

If you think of starbar() as a black box, its action is printing a line of stars. It doesn't have any input because it doesn't need to use any information from the calling function. It doesn't provide (return) any information to main(), so starbar() doesn't have a return value. In short, starbar() doesn't require any communication with the calling function.

Let's create a case where communication *is* needed.

Figure 9.2 *Structure of a simple function*

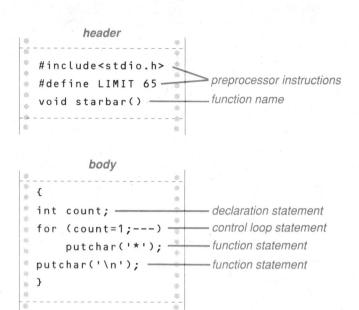

Function Arguments

The letterhead shown earlier would look a little nicer if the text were centered. We can center text by printing the correct number of leading spaces before printing the text. This is similar to the starbar() function, which printed a certain number of asterisks. But now we want to print a certain number of spaces. Rather than writing separate functions for each task, we'll follow the C philosophy and write a single, more general function that does both. We'll call the new function n_chars(). Instead of having the display character and number of repetitions built into the function, we will use function arguments to convey those values.

Let's get more specific. Our bar of stars is 65 characters wide, and the function call n_chars('*', 65) should print that. What about spaces? MEGATHINK, INC. is 15 spaces wide. Thus, in our first version, there were 50 spaces following the heading. To center it, we should lead off with 25 spaces, which will result in 25 spaces on either side of the phrase. Therefore, we could use the call n_chars(' ', 25).

Aside from using arguments, the n_char() function will be quite similar to starbar(). One difference is that it won't add a newline the way starbar() does because we may want to print other text on the same line. Listing 9.2 shows the revised program. To emphasize how arguments work, the program uses a variety of argument forms.

Listing 9.2 *lethead2.c*

```
/* lethead2.c */
#include <stdio.h>
#define NAME "MEGATHINK, INC."
#define ADDRESS "10 Megabuck Plaza"
#define PLACE "Megapolis, CA 94904"
#define LIMIT 65
#define SPACE ' '
int main(void)
{
  int spaces;
  void n_char(char, int);

  n_char('*', LIMIT);        /* using constants as arguments */
  putchar('\n');
  n_char(SPACE, 25);         /* using constants as arguments */
  printf("%s\n", NAME);
  spaces = (65 - strlen(ADDRESS)) / 2;
                             /* we let the program calculate */
                             /* how many spaces to skip      */
  n_char(SPACE, spaces);   /* use a variable as argument   */
  printf("%s\n", ADDRESS);
  n_char(SPACE, (65 - strlen(PLACE)) / 2);
                             /* an expression as argument    */
  printf("%s\n", PLACE);
  n_char('*', LIMIT);
  putchar('\n');
  return 0;
}

/* here is n_char() */
void n_char(char ch, int num)
{
  int count;

  for (count = 1; count <= num; count++)
  putchar(ch);
}
```

Here is the result of running the program:

```
*****************************************************************
                       MEGATHINK, INC.
                      10 Megabuck Plaza
                      Megapolis, CA 94904
*****************************************************************
```

Now let's review how to set up a function that takes arguments. After that, we'll look at how the function is used.

Defining a Function with an Argument: Formal Arguments

Our function definition begins with this ANSI C declaration:

```
void n_char(char ch, int num)
```

This line informs the compiler that n_char() uses two arguments called ch and num, that ch is type char, and that num is type int. Both the ch and num variables are called *formal arguments*. Like variables defined inside the function, formal arguments are local variables, private to the function. This means that you don't have to worry about duplicating variable names used in other functions.

Note that the ANSI C form requires that each variable be preceded by its type. That is, unlike the case with regular declarations, you can't use a list of variables of the same type:

```
void dibs(int x, y, z)          /* invalid function header */
void dubs(int x, int y, int z)  /* valid function header   */
```

ANSI C also recognizes the pre-ANSI form:

```
void n_char(ch, num)
char ch;
int num;
```

Here, the parentheses contain the list of argument names, but the types are declared afterwards. Note that the arguments are declared *before* the brace that marks the start of the function's body, while ordinary local variables are declared after the brace. This form does allow you to use comma-separated lists of variable names if the variables are of the same type:

```
void dibs(x, y, z)
int x, y, z;           /* valid */
```

Although the n_char() function accepts values from main(), it doesn't return a value. Thus, n_char() is type void.

Now let's see how this function is used.

Prototyping a Function with Arguments

We used an ANSI prototype to declare the function before it is used:

```
void n_char(char, int);
```

When a function takes arguments, the prototype indicates their number and type by using a comma-separated list of the types. If you like, you can use variable names in the prototype:

```
void n_char(char ch, int num);
```

Using names in this way doesn't actually create variables. It merely clarifies the fact that `char` means a `char` variable, and so on.

Again, ANSI C also recognizes the older form of declaring a function, which is without an argument list:

```
void n_char();
```

Later, we'll look at the advantages of using the prototype format.

Calling a Function with an Argument:
Actual Arguments

We give `ch` and `num` values by using *actual arguments* in the function call. Consider our first use of `n_char()`:

```
n_char(SPACE, 65);
```

The actual arguments are the space character and 65. These *values* are assigned to the corresponding formal arguments in `n_char()`—the variables `ch` and `num`. In short, the formal argument is a variable in the *called* function, and the actual argument is the particular value assigned to that variable by the calling function. As we showed in our example, the actual argument can be a constant, a variable, or an even more elaborate expression. Regardless of which it is, the actual argument is evaluated, and its value is sent to the function. For instance, consider our final use of `n_char()`:

```
n_char(SPACE, (65 - strlen(PLACE)) / 2);
```

The long expression forming the second actual argument is evaluated to 23.

Then the value 23 is assigned to the variable num. The function neither knows nor cares whether that number came from a constant, a variable, or a more general expression. Again, the actual argument is a specific value that is assigned to the variable known as the formal argument (see Figure 9.3).

Figure 9.3 *Formal arguments and actual arguments*

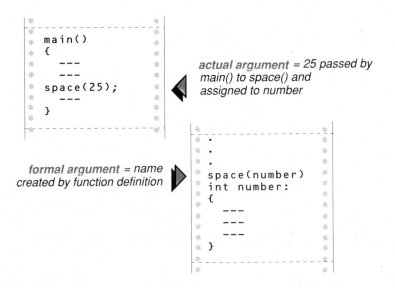

The Black Box Viewpoint

Taking a black box viewpoint of n_char(), the input is the character to be displayed and the number of spaces to be skipped. The resulting action is printing the character the specified number of times. The input is communicated to the function via arguments. This information is enough to tell you how to use the function in main(). Also, it serves as a design specification for writing the function.

The fact that ch, num, and count are local variables private to the n_char() function is an essential aspect of the black box approach. If we were to use variables with the same names in main(), they would be separate, independent variables. That is, if main() had a count variable, changing its value wouldn't change the value of count in n_char(), and vice versa. What goes on inside the black box is hidden from the calling function.

Returning a Value from a Function with *return*

You have seen how to communicate information from the calling function to the called function. To send information in the other direction, you use the function return value. To refresh your memory on how that works, we'll construct a function that returns the smaller of its two arguments. We'll call the function `imin()` because it's designed to handle `int` values. Also, we will create a simple `main()` whose sole purpose is to check to see if `imin()` works. A program designed to test functions this way sometimes is called a *driver*. The driver takes a function for a spin. If the function pans out, then it can be installed in a more noteworthy program. Listing 9.3 shows our driver and our minimum value function.

Listing 9.3 *lesser.c*

```
/* lesser.c -- finds the lesser of two evils */
#include <stdio.h>
int main(void)
{
    int evil1, evil2;
    int imin(int, int);

    while (scanf("%d %d", &evil1, &evil2) == 2)
        printf("The lesser of %d and %d is %d.\n",
               evil1, evil2, imin(evil1,evil2));
    return 0;
}

int imin(int n,int m)
{
    int min;

    if (n < m)
        min = n;
    else
        min = m;
    return min;
}
```

Here is a sample run:

```
88 92
The lesser of 88 and 92 is 88.
q
```

The keyword `return` causes the value of the following expression to be the return value of the function. In this case, the function returns the value that was assigned to `min`. Because `min` is type `int`, so is the `imin()` function.

The variable `min` is private to `imin()`, but the value of `min` is communicated back to the calling function with `return`. The effect of a statement like the next one is to assign the value of `min` to `lesser`:

```
lesser = imin(n,m);
```

Could we say the following instead?

```
imin(n,m);
lesser = min;
```

No, for the calling function doesn't even know that `min` exists. Remember that `imin()`'s variables are local to `imin()`. The function call `imin(evil1, evil2)` copies the values of one set of variables to another set.

Not only can the returned value be assigned to a variable, it can be used as part of an expression. You can do this, for example:

```
answer = 2 * imin(z, zstar) + 25;
printf("%d\n", imin(-32 + answer, LIMIT));
```

The return value can be supplied by any expression, not just a variable. For example, we can shorten our program to the following:

```
/* minimum value function, second version */
imin(int n,int m)
{
     return (n < m) ? n : m;
}
```

The conditional expression is evaluated to either `n` or `m`, whichever is smaller, and that value is returned to the calling function. If you prefer for clarity or style to enclose the return value in parentheses, you may, though parentheses are not required.

Using `return` has one other effect. It terminates the function and returns control to the next statement in the calling function. This occurs even if the `return` statement is not the last in the function. Thus, we could have written `imin()` this way:

```
/* minimum value function, third version */
imin(int n,int m)
{
   if (n < m)
        return (n);
   else
```

```
        return (m);
    }
```

Many, but not all, C practitioners deem it better to use `return` just once and at the end of a function in order to make it easier for someone to follow the control flow through the function. However, it's no great sin to use multiple `returns` in a function as short as this one. Anyway, to the user, all three versions are the same, since all take the same input and produce the same output. Just the innards are different. Even this version works the same:

```
/* minimum value function, fourth version */
imin(n, m)
int n, m;    /* pre-ANSI form for declaring arguments */
{
    if (n < m)
        return(n);
    else
        return(m);
     printf("Professor Fleppard is a fopdoodle.\n")
}
```

The `return` statements prevent the `printf()` statement from ever being reached. Professor Fleppard can use the compiled version of this function in his own programs and never learn the true feelings of his student programmer.

You can use a statement like this, too:

```
return;
```

It causes the function to terminate and return control to the calling function. Because no expression follows `return`, no value is returned, and this form should be used in a type `void` function.

Function Types

Functions should be declared by type. A function with a return value should be declared the same type as the return value. Functions with no return value should be declared as type `void`. If no type is given for a function, C assumes that the function is type `int`. This convention stems from the early days of C when most functions were type `int` anyway.

The type declaration is part of the function definition. Keep in mind that it refers to the return value, not to the function arguments. For instance, the following function heading indicates that we are defining a function that takes two type `int` arguments but that returns a type `double` value:

```
double klink(int a, int b)
```

To use a function correctly, a program needs to know the function type before the function is used for the first time. One way to accomplish this is to place the complete function definition ahead of its first use. However, this may make the program harder to read. Also, the functions may be part of the C library or in some other file. Thus, we generally inform the compiler about functions by declaring them in advance. For example, the `main()` function in Listing 9.3 contains these lines:

```
#include <stdio.h>
int main(void)
{
   int evil1, evil2, lesser;
   int imin(int, int);
```

The last line establishes that `imin` is the name of a function that returns a type `int` value. Now the compiler will know how to treat `imin()` when it appears later in the program.

We've placed the advance function declarations *inside* the function using them. They also can be placed *outside* the function. For example, we can rewrite the beginning of `lesser.c` as follows:

```
#include <stdio.h>
int imin(int, int);     /* imin() declaration */
int main(void)
{
   int evil1, evil2, lesser;
```

In either case, your chief concern should be that the function declaration appear *before* the function is used.

In the ANSI C standard library, functions are grouped into families, each having its own *header file*. These header files contain, among other things, the declarations for the functions in the family. For instance, the `stdio.h` header contains function declarations for the standard I/O library functions, such as `printf()` and `scanf()`. The `math.h` header contains function declarations for a variety of mathematical functions. For example, it will contain

```
double sqrt(double);
```

(or a pre-ANSI equivalent) to tell the compiler that the `sqrt()` function returns a type `double` value. Don't confuse these declarations with definitions. A *function declaration* informs the compiler which type the function is, but the *function definition* supplies the actual code. Including the `math.h` header file tells the compiler that `sqrt()` returns type `double`, but the code for `sqrt()` resides in a separate file of library functions.

ANSI C Function Prototyping

The traditional, pre-ANSI C scheme for declaring functions was deficient in that it declared a function's return type but not its arguments. Let's look at the kinds of problems that arise when the old form of function declarations is used.

The following pre-ANSI declaration informs the compiler that `imin()` returns a type `int` value:

```
int imin();
```

However, it says nothing about the number or type of `imin()`'s arguments. Thus, if you use `imin()` with the wrong number or type of arguments, the compiler doesn't catch the error.

The Problem

Let's look at some examples involving `imax()`, a close relation to `imin()`. Listing 9.4 shows a program that declares `imax()` the old-fashioned way and then uses `imax()` incorrectly.

Listing 9.4 *misuse.c*

```
/* misuse.c -- uses a function incorrectly */
#include <stdio.h>
int imax();        /* old-style declaration */
int main(void)
{
   printf("The maximum of %d and %d is %d.\n",
       3, 5, imax(3));
   printf("The maximum of %d and %d is %d.\n",
       3, 5, imax(3.0, 5.0));
```

(continued)

Listing 9.4 *(continued)*

```
   return 0;
}

int imax(n, m)
int n, m;
{
   int max;
   if (n > m)
        max = n;
   else
        max = m;
   return max;
}
```

The first call to `printf()` omits an argument to `imax()`, and the second call uses floating-point arguments instead of integers. Despite these errors, the program compiles and runs.

Here's the output using Microsoft's QuickC compiler:

```
The maximum of 3 and 5 is 130.
The maximum of 3 and 5 is 0.
```

With Turbo C, we got values of 273 and 0. The two compilers work fine; they merely are following the older C standards.

What's happening? The mechanics may differ among systems, but here's what goes on with a PC or VAX. The calling function places its arguments in a temporary storage area called the *stack*, and the called function reads those arguments off the stack. These two processes are *not* coordinated with one another. The calling function decides which type to pass based on the actual arguments in the call, and the called function reads values based on the types of its formal arguments. Thus, the call `imax(3)` places *one* integer on the stack. When the `imax()` function starts up, it reads *two* integers off the stack. Only one was actually placed on the stack, so the second value read is whatever value happened to be sitting in the stack at the time.

The second time we use `imax()` in the example, we pass it `float` values. This places two `double` values on the stack. (Recall that a `float` is promoted to `double` when passed as an argument.) On our system, that's two 8-byte values, so 16 bytes of data are placed on the stack. When `imax()` reads two `int`s from the stack, it reads the first 4 bytes on the stack. These happen to be all zeros, so `imax()` wound up with n and m set to 0.

The ANSI Solution

The ANSI Standard's solution to the problems of mismatched arguments is to permit the function declaration to declare the variable types, too. The result is a *function prototype*, a declaration that states the return type, the number of arguments, and the types of those arguments. To indicate that `imax()` requires two `int` arguments, we can declare it with either of the following prototypes:

```
int imax(int, int);
int imax(int a, int b);
```

The first form uses a comma-separated list of types. The second adds variable names to the types. The variable names, recall, are dummy names and don't have to match the names used in the function definition.

With this information at hand, the compiler can check to see if the function call matches the prototype. Are there the right number of arguments? Are they the correct type? If there is a type mismatch, the compiler does a type cast to convert the actual arguments to the same type as the formal arguments. For example, `imax(3.0, 5.0)` becomes `imax((int) 3.0, (int) 5.0)`. We've modified Listing 9.4 to use a function prototype. The result is shown in Listing 9.5.

Listing 9.5 *proto1.c*

```
/* proto1.c -- uses a function prototype */
#include <stdio.h>
int imax(int, int);          /* prototype */
int main(void)
{
  printf("The maximum of %d and %d is %d.\n",
      3, 5, imax(3));
  printf("The maximum of %d and %d is %d.\n",
```

(continued)

```
Listing 9.5  (continued)

        3, 5, imax(3.0, 5.0));
    return 0;
}

int imax(int n, int m)
{
    int max;

    if (n > m)
        max = n;
    else
        max = m;
    return max;
}
```

When we tried to compile Listing 9.5, one compiler gave an error message stating that the call to `imax()` had too few parameters. A second compiler gave a warning to the same effect. (The difference between an error and a warning is that an error prevents compilation, while a warning permits compilation.) In both cases, the compiler now checked to see whether the correct number of arguments were present.

What about the type errors? To investigate those, we replaced `imax(3)` with `imax(3, 5)` and tried compilation again. This time there were no messages, and we ran the program. Here is the resulting output:

```
The maximum of 3 and 5 is 5.
The maximum of 3 and 5 is 5.
```

As promised, the `3.0` and `5.0` of the second call were converted to 3 and 5 so that the function could handle the input properly. One interesting point is that both compilers made this type cast without telling us. Most programmers object to this "silent" correction. By resetting the warning level on the compilers we used, we can have the compilers warn us whenever they have to make a type conversion. Our compilers allow us to select a higher warning level that causes the compilers to report when they make type conversions. However, the ANSI Standard does not require compilers to provide that feature.

No Arguments and Unspecified Arguments

Suppose you give a prototype like this:

```
void print_name();
```

An ANSI C compiler will assume that you have decided to forego function prototyping, and it will not check arguments. To indicate that a function really has no arguments, use the `void` keyword within the parentheses:

```
void print_name(void);
```

ANSI C interprets the preceding expression to mean that `print_name()` takes no arguments. It then will check to see that you, in fact, do not use arguments when calling this function.

A few functions, such as `printf()` and `scanf()`, take a variable number of arguments. In `printf()`, for instance, the first argument is a string, but the remaining arguments are fixed in neither type nor number. ANSI C allows partial prototyping for such cases. We could, for example, use this prototype for `printf()`:

```
int printf(char *, ...);
```

This prototype says that the first argument is a string (Chapter 11 will elucidate that point) and that there may be further arguments of an unspecified nature.

Recursion

C permits a function to call itself. This process is termed *recursion*. Recursion is a sometimes tricky, sometimes convenient tool. It's tricky to get recursion to end, for a function that calls itself tends to do so indefinitely unless the programming includes a conditional test to terminate recursion.

Recursion Revealed

To see what's involved, let's look at an example. The function `main()` in Listing 9.6 calls the `up_and_down()` function. We'll term this the first level of recursion. Then `up_and_down()` calls itself; we'll term that the second level of recursion. The second level calls the third level, and so on. This example is set up to go four levels.

Listing 9.6 *recur.c*

```
/* recur.c -- recursion illustration */
#include <stdio.h>
void up_and_down(int);
int main(void)
{
  up_and_down(1);
  return 0;
}

void up_and_down(int n)
{
  printf("Level %d\n", n);      /* print #1 */
  if (n < 4)
      up_and_down(n+1);
  printf("LEVEL %d\n", n);      /* print #2 */
}
```

The output looks like this:

```
Level 1
Level 2
Level 3
Level 4
LEVEL 4
LEVEL 3
LEVEL 2
LEVEL 1
```

Let's trace through the program to see how recursion works. First, main() calls up_and_down() with an argument of 1. As a result, the formal argument n in up_and_down() has the value 1, so print statement #1 prints Level 1. Then, because n is less than 4, up_and_down() (Level 1) calls up_and_down() (Level 2) with an argument of n + 1, or 2. This causes n in the Level 2 call to be assigned the value 2, so print statement #1 prints Level 2. Similarly, the next two calls lead to the printing of Level 3 and Level 4.

Once Level 4 is reached, n is 4, so the if test fails. The up_and_down() function is not called again. Instead, the Level 4 call proceeds to print statement #2, which prints LEVEL 4, since n is 4. Then it reaches the return statement. At this point, the Level 4 call ends, and control passes back to the function that called it, the Level 3 call. The last statement executed in the Level 3 call was the call to Level 4 in the if statement. Therefore, Level 3 resumes with the following statement, which is print statement #2. This causes LEVEL 3 to be printed. Then Level 3 ends, passing control to Level 2, which prints LEVEL 2, and so on.

Recursion Fundamentals

Recursion can be confusing at first, so we'll look at a few basic points that will help you understand the process.

First, each level of function call has its own variables. That is, the n of Level 1 is a different variable from the n of Level 2. So our program created four separate variables, each called n, but each having a distinct value. When the program finally returned to the first level call of up_and_down(), the original n still had the value 1 it started with. See Figure 9.4.

Figure 9.4 *Recursion variables*

variables:	n	n	n	n
after level 1 call	1			
after level 1 call	1	2		
after level 1 call	1	2	3	
after level 1 call				
after return from level 4	1	2	3	4
after return from level 3	1	2	3	
after return from level 2	1	2		
after return from level 1	1			
	(all gone)			

Second, each function call is balanced with a return. When program flow reaches the return at the end of the last recursion level, control passes to the previous recursion level. The program does not jump all the way back to the original call in main(). Instead, it must move back through each recursion level.

Third, statements in a recursive function that come before the recursive call are executed in the same order that the functions are called. For instance, in Listing 9.6 print statement #1 comes before the recursive call. It was executed four times in the order of the recursive calls: Level 1, Level 2, Level 3, and Level 4.

Fourth, statements in a recursive function that come after the recursive call are executed in the opposite order from which the functions are called. For example, print statement #2 comes after the recursive call, and it was executed in this order: Level 4, Level 3, Level 2, Level 1. This feature of recursion is useful for programming problems involving reversals of order. We'll see an example soon.

Finally, although each level of recursion has its own set of variables, the code itself is not duplicated. The code is a sequence of instructions, and a function call is a command to go to the beginning of that set of instructions. Thus, a recursive call returns the program to the beginning of that instruction set. Aside from the fact that recursive calls create new variables on each call, they are much like a loop. Indeed, sometimes recursion can be used instead of loops, and vice versa.

Tail Recursion

In the simplest form of recursion, the recursive call is at the end of the function, just before the `return` statement. It is called *tail recursion*, or *end recursion*, because the recursive call comes at the end. Tail recursion is the simplest form because it acts like a loop.

Let's look at both a loop version and a tail recursion version of a function to calculate factorials. The factorial of an integer is the product of the integers from 1 through that number. For example, 3 factorial (written 3!) is 1*2*3. The 0! is taken to be 1, and factorials are not defined for negative numbers. Listing 9.7 presents a function that uses a `for` loop to calculate factorials.

Listing 9.7 *factor.c*

```
/* factor.c -- uses loops to calculate factorials */
#include <stdio.h>
int main(void)
{
   int num;
   long fact(int n);
   while (scanf("%d", &num) == 1)
   {
        if (num < 0)
              printf("No negative numbers, please.\n");
```

```
        else if (num > 15)
                printf("Keep input under 16.\n");
        else
                printf("%d factorial = %ld\n", num, fact(num));
  }
  return 0;
}
long fact(int n)              /* loop finds factorial */
{
  long ans;

  for (ans = 1; n > 1; n--)
        ans *= n;
  return ans;
}
```

The test driver program limits input to the integers 0–15. It turns out that 15! is slightly over 2 billion, which makes 16! much larger than `long` on our system. To go beyond 15!, we would have to use a type `double` function.

The loop initializes ans to 1 and then multiplies it by the integers from n down to 2. Technically, we should multiply by 1, but that doesn't change the value. Here's a sample run:

```
3
3 factorial = 6
10
10 factorial = 3628800
q
```

Now let's try a recursive version. The key is that n! = n x (n−1)!. This follows since (n−1)! is the product of all the positive integers through n−1. Thus, multiplying by n gives the product through n. This suggests a recursive approach. If we call the function rfact(), then rfact(n) is n * rfact(n−1). We can thus evaluate rfact(n) by having it call rfact(n−1), as in Listing 9.8. Of course, we have to end the recursion at some point, and we can do this by setting the return value to 1 when n is 0.

Listing 9.8 rfactor.c

```
/* rfactor.c -- uses recursion to calculate factorials */
#include <stdio.h>
int main(void)
{
  int num;
  long rfact(int n);

  while (scanf("%d", &num) == 1)
  {
      if (num < 0)
          printf("No negative numbers, please.\n");
      else if (num > 15)
          printf("Keep input under 16.\n");
      else
          printf("%d factorial = %ld\n", num, rfact(num));
  }
  return 0;
}
long rfact(int n)      /* recursive function */
{
  long ans;

  if (n > 0)
      ans= n * rfact(n-1);
  else
      ans = 1;
  return ans;
}
```

The recursive version of Listing 9.8 produces the same output as the previous version. Note that although the recursive call to `rfact()` is not the last line in the function, it is the last statement executed when n > 0, so it is tail recursion.

Recursion and Reversal

Now let's look at a problem in which recursion's ability to reverse order is handy. The problem is this: write a function that prints the binary equivalent of an integer. Binary notation represents numbers in terms of powers of 2. Just as 234 in decimal means $2 \times 10^2 + 3 \times 10^1 + 4 \times 10^0$, so 101 in binary means $1 \times 2^2 + 0 \times 2^1 + 1 \times 2^0$. Binary numbers use only the digits 0 and 1.

We need a method. How can we, say, find the binary equivalent of 5? Well, odd numbers must have a binary representation ending in 1. Even numbers end in 0. So we can determine if the last digit is a 1 or a 0 by evaluating 5 % 2. If the result is 1, then 5 is odd, and the last digit is 1. In general, if n is a number, the final digit is n % 2. So the first digit we find is the last digit we want to print. This suggests using a recursive function in which n % 2 is calculated before the recursive call but in which it is printed after the recursive call. That way, the first value calculated is the last value printed.

To get the next digit, divide the original number by 2. This is the binary equivalent to moving the decimal point one place to the left so that we can examine the next binary digit. If this value is even, the next binary digit is 0. If it is odd, the binary digit is 1. For example, 5/2 is 2 (integer division), so the next digit is 0. This gives 01 so far. Now repeat the process. Divide 2 by 2 to get 1. Evaluate 1 % 2 to get 1, so the next digit is 1. This gives 101. When do we stop? We stop when the result of dividing by 2 is less than 2 because as long as it is 2 or greater, there is one more binary digit. Each division by 2 lops off one more binary digit until we reach the end. (If this seems confusing to you, try working through the decimal analogy. The remainder of 628 divided by 10 is 8, so 8 is the last digit. Integer division by 10 yields 62, and the remainder from dividing 62 by 10 is 2, so that's the next digit. And so on.) Listing 9.9 implements this approach.

Listing 9.9 *binary.c*

```
/* binary.c -- prints integer in binary form */
#include <stdio.h>
void to_binary(int n);
int main(void)
{
   int number;

   while (scanf("%d", &number) == 1)
   {
        to_binary(number);
        putchar('\n');
   }
```

(continued)

Listing 9.9 *(continued)*

```
   return 0;
}
void to_binary(int n)    /* recursive function */
{
   int r;

   r = n % 2;
   if (n >= 2)
        to_binary(n / 2);
   putchar('0' + r);
   return;
}
```

In Listing 9.9 the expression '0' + r evaluates to the character '0' if r is 0 and to the character '1' if r is 1. This assumes that the numeric code for the '1' character is one greater than the code for the '0' character. Both the ASCII and the EBCDIC codes satisfy that assumption.

Here's a sample run:

```
5
101
255
1111111
256
10000000
q
```

All C Functions Are Created Equal

Each C function in a program is on equal footing with the others. Each can call any other function or be called by any other function. This makes the C function somewhat different from Pascal and Modula-2 procedures because those procedures can be nested within other procedures. Procedures in one nest will be ignorant of procedures in another nest.

Isn't the function main() special? Yes, it is a little special in that when a program of several functions is put together, execution starts with the first statement in main(). But that is the limit of its preference. Even main() can be called by itself recursively or by other functions, although this is rarely done.

Compiling Programs with Two or More Functions

The simplest approach to using several functions is to place them in the same file. Then just compile that file as you would a single-function file. Other approaches are more system dependent, as the next few sections illustrate.

UNIX

Suppose that file1.c and file2.c are two files containing C functions. Then the following command will compile both files and produce an executable file called a.out:

```
cc file1.c file2.c
```

In addition, two object files called file1.o and file2.o are produced. If you later change file1.c but not file2.c, you can compile the first and combine it with the object code version of the second file using the command

```
cc file1.c file2.o
```

Microsoft C Versions 4.0–5.1

Use the CL command to compile the two files:

```
cl file1.c file2.c
```

Compiling produces two object code files (file1.obj and file2.obj) and an executable file named file1.exe. The base name of the first file in the list is used for the executable file. If you reedit just file2.c, you can recompile using this command:

```
cl file1.obj file2.c
```

QuickC

Use the Set Program List ... entry from the File menu (version 1.0) or from the Make menu (version 2.0) to create a .mak file indicating which files belong to the program. Use the Edit Program List ... entry to modify this list. QuickC will compile the files in the current program list.

Turbo C

Create a text file with a .prj extension (for project) and enter the names of the files used for the program. For instance, the file file1.prj can contain the following text:

```
file1.c
file2.c
```

Use the Project menu to select the desired project file; then select the Run or Compile menu.

Using Header Files

Often you will have used the C preprocessor to define constants used in a program. Such definitions hold only for the file containing the #define directives. Thus, if you place the functions of a program into separate files, you also have to make the #define directives available to each file. The most direct way is to retype the directives for each file, but this is time-consuming and increases the possibility for error. Also, it poses a maintenance problem: if you revise a #define value, you have to remember to do so for each file.

A better solution is to place the #define directives in a header file and then use the #include directive in each source code file. Let's examine a programming example. Suppose you manage a chain of four hotels. Each hotel charges a different room rate, but all the rooms in a given hotel go for the same rate. For people who book multiple nights, the second night goes for 95 percent of the first night, the third night goes for 95 percent of the second night, and so on. (Don't worry about the economics of such a policy.) You want a program that lets you specify the hotel and the number of nights and gives you the total charge. You'd like the program to have a menu that lets you continue entering data until you choose to quit.

Listings 9.10, 9.11, and 9.12 show what you might come up with. The first listing contains the `main()` function, which provides the overall organization for the program. The second listing contains the supporting functions, which we assume are kept in a separate file. Finally, Listing 9.12 shows a header file that contains the defined constants and function prototypes for all the source files of the program. Recall that in UNIX and DOS environments, the double quotes in the directive `#include "hotels.h"` indicate that the `include` file is in the current working directory (typically the directory containing the source code).

Listing 9.10 hotel1.c

```
/* hotel1.c -- room rate program, continued in Listing 9.11 */
#include <stdio.h>
#include "hotels.h" /* defines constants, declares functions */
int main(void)
{
    double nights, hotel;
    int code;

    while ((code = menu()) != QUIT)
    {
        switch(code)
        {
        case 1 : hotel = HOTEL1;
                 break;
        case 2 : hotel = HOTEL2;
                 break;
        case 3 : hotel = HOTEL3;
                 break;
        case 4 : hotel = HOTEL4;
                 break;
        default: hotel = 0.0;
                 printf("Oops!\n");
                 break;
        }
        nights = getnights();
        showprice(hotel, nights);
    }
    return 0;
}
```

Listing 9.11 *hotel2.c*

```c
/* hotel2.c -- rest of hotel program */
#include <stdio.h>
#include "hotels.h"
int menu(void)
{
    int code, status;

    printf("\n%s%s\n", STARS, STARS);
    printf("Enter the number of the desired hotel:\n");
    printf("1) Fairfield Arms          2) Hotel Olympic\n");
    printf("3) Chertworthy Plaza       4) The Stockton\n");
    printf("5) quit\n");
    printf("%s%s\n", STARS, STARS);
    while ((status = scanf("%d", &code)) != 1  ||
             (code < 1 || code > 5))
    {
        if (status != 1)
            scanf("%*s");
        printf("Enter an integer from 1 to 5, please.\n");
    }
    return code;
}
int getnights(void)
{
    int nights;

    printf("How many nights are needed? ");
    while (scanf("%d", &nights) != 1)
    {
        scanf("%*s");
        printf("Please enter an integer, such as 2.\n");
    }
    return nights;
}
void showprice(double hotel, int nights)
{
    int n;
    double total = 0.0;
    double factor = 1.0;
```

```
      for (n = 1; n <= nights; n++, factor *= DISCOUNT)
    total += hotel * factor;
      printf("The total cost will be $%0.2f.\n", total);
}
```

Listing 9.12 *hotels.h*

```
/* hotels.h -- constants and declarations for hotel.c */
#define QUIT      5
#define HOTEL1    50.00
#define HOTEL2    55.00
#define HOTEL3    80.00
#define HOTEL4    100.00
#define DISCOUNT  0.95
#define STARS "**********************************"

int menu(void);
int getnights(void);
void showprice(double, int);
```

Here's a sample run:

```
****************************************************************
Enter the number of the desired hotel:
1) Fairfield Arms        2) Hotel Olympic
3) Chertworthy Plaza     4) The Stockton
5) quit
****************************************************************
3
How many nights are needed? 1
The total cost will be $80.00.

****************************************************************
Enter the number of the desired hotel:
1) Fairfield Arms        2) Hotel Olympic
3) Chertworthy Plaza     4) The Stockton
5) quit
****************************************************************
```

```
4
How many nights are needed? 3
The total cost will be $285.25.

*****************************************************************
Enter the number of the desired hotel:
1) Fairfield Arms          2) Hotel Olympic
3) Chertworthy Plaza       4) The Stockton
5) quit
*****************************************************************
5
```

Incidentally, the program itself has some interesting features. In particular, the `menu()` and `getnights()` functions skip over nonnumeric data by testing the return value of `scanf()` and by using the `scanf("%*s")` call to skip to the next whitespace. Note how `menu()` checks for both nonnumeric input and out-of-limits numerical input:

```
while ((status = scanf("%d", &code)) != 1  ||
       (code < 1 || code > 5))
```

The preceding example uses C's guarantee that logical expressions are evaluated from left to right and that evaluation ceases the moment the statement is clearly false. In this instance, the values of `code` are checked only after it is determined that `scanf()` succeeded in reading an integer value.

Assigning separate tasks to separate functions encourages this sort of refinement. A first pass at `menu()` or `getnights()` might use a simple `scanf()` without the data verification features we've added. Then, once the basic version works, you can begin improving each module.

Finding Addresses: The & Operator

One of the most important C concepts (and sometimes one of the most perplexing) is the *pointer*. A pointer is a variable used to store an *address*. You've already seen that `scanf()` uses addresses for arguments. More generally, any C function that modifies a value in the calling function without using a `return` value uses addresses. We'll look at this topic next, beginning with the unary & operator.

The unary & operator gives you the address at which a variable is stored. If pooh is the name of a variable, then &pooh is the address of the variable. You can think of the address as a location in memory. Suppose you have the following statement:

```
pooh = 24;
```

And suppose that the address where pooh is stored is 12126. Then the statement

```
printf("%d %u\n", pooh, &pooh);
```

would produce this:

```
24 12126
```

In Listing 9.13, let's use this operator to see where variables of the same name—but in different functions—are kept.

Listing 9.13 *loccheck.c*

```
/* loccheck.c  -- checks to see where variables are stored */
#include <stdio.h>
void mikado(int);                       /* declare function */
int main(void)
{
    int pooh = 2, bah = 5;

    printf("In main(), pooh = %d and &pooh = %p\n",
        pooh, &pooh);
    printf("In main(), bah = %d and &bah = %p\n",
      bah, &bah);
    mikado(pooh);
    return 0;
}
void mikado(int bah)                    /* define function  */
{
    int pooh = 10;

    printf("In mikado(), pooh = %d and &pooh = %p\n",
        pooh, &pooh);
    printf("In mikado(), bah = %d and &bah = %p\n",
      bah, &bah);
}
```

Listing 9.13 used the %p format for printing the addresses. This format specifier is used for displaying addresses but is not available on some systems. If your system lacks %p, try %u or, perhaps, %lu. On our system, the output of this little exercise is this:

```
In main(), pooh = 2 and &pooh = FFD8
In main(), bah = 5 and &bah = FFDA
In mikado(), pooh = 10 and &pooh = FFD0
In mikado(), bah = 2 and &bah = FFD6
```

The way that %p represents addresses varies between implementations. This one (Turbo C on a PC) displays the address in hexadecimal form.

What does this output show? First, the two poohs have different addresses. The same is true for the two bahs. Thus, as promised, the computer considers these to be four separate variables. Second, the call mikado(pooh) did convey the value (2) of the actual argument (pooh of main()) to the formal argument (bah of mikado()). Note that just the value was transferred. The two variables involved (pooh of main() and bah of mikado()) retain their distinct identities.

We raise the second point because it is not true for all languages. In a FORTRAN subroutine, for example, the subroutine affects the original variable in the calling routine. The subroutine's variable may have a different name, but the address is the same. C doesn't do this. Each function uses its own variables. This is preferable because it prevents the original variable from being altered mysteriously by some side effect of the called function. However, it can make for some difficulties, too, as the next section shows.

Altering Variables in the Calling Function

Sometimes you will want one function to make changes in the variables of a different function. For example, a common task in sorting problems is interchanging the values of two variables. Suppose you have two variables called x and y and you wish to swap their values. The simple sequence

```
x = y;
y = x;
```

does not work because, by the time the second line is reached, the original value of x has already been replaced by the original y value. An additional line is needed to store temporarily the original value of x:

```
temp = x;
x = y;
y = temp;
```

Now that the method works, you can put it into a function and construct a driver to test it. To make clear which variables belong to `main()` and which belong to the `interchange()` function, Listing 9.14 uses `x` and `y` for the first, and `u` and `v` for the second.

Listing 9.14 *swap1.c*

```
/* swap1.c -- 1st attempt at a swapping function */
#include <stdio.h>
void interchange(int u, int v); /* declare function */
int main(void)
{
    int x = 5, y = 10;

    printf("Originally x = %d and y = %d.\n", x , y);
    interchange(x, y);
    printf("Now x = %d and y = %d.\n", x, y);
    return 0;
}
void interchange(int u, int v)  /* define function  */
{
    int temp;

    temp = u;
    u = v;
    v = temp;
}
```

Running the program gives these results:

```
Originally x = 5 and y = 10.
Now x = 5 and y = 10.
```

Oops! The values didn't get switched! Let's put some print statements into `interchange()` to see what's gone wrong (Listing 9.15).

```
Listing 9.15   swap2.c

/* swap2.c -- researching swap1.c */
#include <stdio.h>
void interchange(int u, int v);
int main(void)
{
    int x = 5, y = 10;

    printf("Originally x = %d and y = %d.\n", x , y);
    interchange(x, y);
    printf("Now x = %d and y = %d.\n", x, y);
    return 0;
}
void interchange(int u, int v)
{
    int temp;

    printf("Originally u = %d and v = %d.\n", u , v);
    temp = u;
    u = v;
    v = temp;
    printf("Now u = %d and v = %d.\n", u, v);
}
```

Here is the new output:

```
Originally x = 5 and y = 10.
Originally u = 5 and v = 10.
Now u = 10 and v = 5.
Now x = 5 and y = 10.
```

Well, nothing is wrong with `interchange()`; it does swap the values of u and v. The problem is in communicating the results to `main()`. As we pointed out, `interchange()` uses different variables from `main()`, so interchanging the values of u and v has no effect on x and y! Can we somehow use `return`? Well, we could finish `interchange()` with the line

```
return(u);
```

and change the call in `main()` to

```
x = interchange(x,y);
```

This change gives x its new value, but it leaves y in the cold. With `return` you can send just *one* value back to the calling function. But we need to communicate *two* values. It can be done! All we have to do is use *pointers*.

Pointers: A First Look

Pointers? What are they? Basically, a *pointer* is a variable whose value is an address. Just as a `char` variable has a character as a value and an `int` variable has an integer as a value, the pointer variable has an address as a value. If we give a particular pointer variable the name `ptr`, then we can have statements like

```
ptr = &pooh;  /* assigns pooh's address to ptr */
```

We say that `ptr` "points to" pooh. The difference between `ptr` and `&pooh` is that `ptr` is a variable, while `&pooh` is a constant. If we wish, we can make `ptr` point elsewhere:

```
ptr = &bah;  /* make ptr point to bah instead of to pooh */
```

Now the value of `ptr` is the address of bah.
To create a pointer variable, you need to be able to declare its type. Suppose you want to declare `ptr` so that it can hold the address of an `int`. To make this declaration, you need to use a new operator. Let's examine that operator now.

The Indirection Operator: *

Suppose you know that `ptr` points to bah:

```
ptr = &bah;
```

Then you can use the *indirection operator* `*` (also called the *dereferencing operator*) to find the value stored in bah. (Don't confuse this *unary* indirection operator with the *binary* `*` operator of multiplication.)

```
val = *ptr;  /* finding the value ptr points to */
```

The statements `ptr = &bah;` and `val = *ptr;` taken together amount to the following statement:

```
val = bah;
```

Using the address and indirection operators is a rather indirect way of accomplishing this result, hence the name "indirection operator."

Summary: Pointer-Related Operators

The Address Operator

&

General Comments
When followed by a variable name, & gives the address of that variable.

Example

&nurse is the address of the variable nurse.

The Indirection Operator

*

General Comments
When followed by a pointer name or an address, * gives the value stored at the pointed-to address.

Example
```
nurse = 22;
ptr = &nurse;   /* pointer to nurse */
val = *ptr;
```

The net effect is to assign the value 22 to val.

Declaring Pointers

You already know how to declare int variables and other fundamental types. How do you declare a pointer variable? You might guess that the form is like this:

```
pointer ptr;      /* not the way to declare a pointer */
```

Why not? Because it is not enough to say that a variable is a pointer. You also have to say what kind of variable the pointer points to. The reason for this is that different variable types take up different amounts of storage, and some pointer operations require knowledge of that storage size. Also, the program has to know what kind of data is stored at the address. A `long` and a `float` may use the same amount of storage, but they store numbers quite differently. Here's how pointers are declared:

```
int *pi;          /* pi is a pointer to an integer variable  */
char *pc;         /* pc is a pointer to a character variable */
float *pf, *pg;   /* pf, pg are pointers to float variables   */
```

The type specification identifies the type of variable pointed to, and the asterisk (*) identifies the variable itself as a pointer. The declaration `int *pi;` says that `pi` is a pointer and that `*pi` is type `int`. See Figure 9.5.

Figure 9.5 *Declaring and using pointers*

Similarly, the value (`*pc`) of what `pc` points to is of type `char`. What of `pc` itself? We describe it as being of type "pointer to `char`." Its value, being an address, is an unsigned integer on most systems. Thus, on most systems, you can use the `%u` format to print the value of `pc`. But, as we mentioned earlier, that need not hold true universally, so ANSI C provides the `%p` form specifically for pointers.

Using Pointers to Communicate Between Functions

We have touched only the surface of the rich and fascinating world of pointers, but our concern here is using pointers to solve our communication problem. Listing 9.16 shows a program that uses pointers to make the interchange() function work. Let's look at it, run it, and then try to understand how it works.

```
Listing 9.16   swap3.c

/* swap3.c -- using pointers to make swapping work */
#include <stdio.h>
void interchange(int *u, int *v);
int main(void)
{
    int x = 5, y = 10;

    printf("Originally x = %d and y = %d.\n", x, y);
    interchange(&x, &y);  /* send addresses to function  */
    printf("Now x = %d and y = %d.\n", x, y);
    return 0;
}
void interchange(int *u, int *v)
{
    int temp;

    temp = *u;         /* temp gets value that u points to */
    *u = *v;
    *v = temp;
}
```

After all this trouble, does Listing 9.16 really work?

```
Originally x = 5 and y = 10.
Now x = 10 and y = 5.
```

Yes, it works.

Now, let's see how Listing 9.16 works. First, our function call looks like this:

```
interchange(&x, &y);
```

Instead of transmitting the *values* of x and y, we are transmitting their *addresses*. This means that the formal arguments u and v appearing in

```
void interchange(u, v)
```

will have addresses as their values. Therefore, they should be declared as pointers. Since x and y are integers, u and v are pointers to integers; so we declare them as follows:

```
void interchange (int *u, int *v)
```

Next, in the body of the function, we declare

```
int temp;
```

to provide the temporary storage we need. We want to store the value of x in temp. Therefore, we say:

```
temp = *u;
```

Remember, u has the value &x, so u points to x. This means that *u gives us the value of x, which is what we want. We *don't* want to write

```
temp = u;    /* NO */
```

because that would assign temp the *address* of x rather than its *value*; and we are trying to interchange values, not addresses.

Similarly, to assign the *value* of y to x, we use

```
*u = *v;
```

which translates to

```
x = y;
```

Let's summarize what we did. We wanted a function that would alter the values x and y. By passing the function the addresses of x and y, we gave interchange() access to those variables. Using pointers and the * operator, the function could examine the values stored at those locations and change them.

There are a couple of variants that you should know about. The pre-ANSI form for the function heading is this:

```
void interchange(u, v)
int *u, *v;
```

You can omit the variable names in the ANSI prototype. Then the prototype declaration looks like this:

```
void interchange(int *, int *);
```

More generally, you can communicate two kinds of information about a variable to a function. If you use a call of the form

```
function1(x);
```

you transmit the *value* of x. If you use a call of the form

```
function2(&x);
```

you transmit the *address* of x. The first form requires that the function definition include a formal argument of the same type as x:

```
int function1(int num)
```

The second form requires that the function definition include a formal argument that is a pointer to the right type:

```
int function2(int *ptr)
```

Use the first form if the function needs a value for some calculation or action. Use the second form if the function needs to alter variables in the calling function. You have been doing this all along with the scanf() function. When you want to read in a value for a variable num, for example, you use scanf("%d", &num). That function reads a value and then uses the address you give it to store the value.

Pointers let you get around the fact that the variables of interchange() were local. They let that function reach out into main() and alter what was stored there.

Pascal and Modula-2 users may recognize the first form as being the same as Pascal's value parameter and the second form as being similar (but not identical) to Pascal's variable parameter. BASIC users may find the whole setup a bit unsettling. If this section seems strange to you, be assured that a little practice will make at least some uses of pointers seem simple, normal, and convenient. See Figure 9.6.

Figure 9.6 *Names, addresses, and values in a byte-addressable system, such as the IBM PC*

```
52000 52001 52002 52003 52004 52005 . . .       52009 52010 ── machine address
e|byte|byte|byte|byte|byte|byte|byte|byte|byte|byte|by
```

| | G | 7776 | 1942 | 2.015x10³⁰ | q | – – – | value in memory |

ch   feet   date   sunmass   quit ───── variable name

&ch = 52000
&feet = 52001   "float" *type variable*
&date = 52003   *takes 4 bytes*
&sunmass = 52005
&quit = 52009

address operator

Variables: Names, Addresses, and Values

The preceding discussion of pointers has hinged on the relationships between the names, addresses, and values of variables. Let's discuss these matters further.

When you write a program, you think of a variable as having two attributes: a name and a value. (There are other attributes, including type, but that's another matter.) After the program has been compiled and loaded, the computer also thinks of the same variable as having two attributes: an address and a value. An address is the computer's version of a name.

In many languages, the address is the computer's business, concealed from the programmer. In C, however, you can access the address through the & operator:

&barn is the address of the variable barn.

You can get the value from the name just by using the name:

printf("%d\n", barn) prints the value of barn.

You can get the value from the address by using the * operator:

Given pbarn = &barn;, then *pbarn is the value stored at address &barn.

Although you can print an address to satisfy your curiosity, that is not the main use for the & operator. More important, using &, *, and pointers lets you manipulate addresses and their contents symbolically, as in swap3.c (Listing 9.16).

Summary: Functions

Form

A typical function definition has this form:

```
name(argument list)
argument declarations
function body
```

The presence of the argument list and declarations is optional. Variables other than the arguments are declared within the body, which is bounded by braces.

ANSI C encourages the following form:

```
name(argument declaration list)
function body
```

The argument declaration list is a comma-separated list of variable declarations.

Examples

```
int diff(x,y)          /* function name and argument list */
int x,y;               /* declare arguments               */
{                      /* begin function body             */
   int z;              /* declare local variable          */

   z = x - y;
   return z;
}                      /* end function body               */

int diff(int x,int y)     /* ANSI version                 */
{                         /* begin function body          */
  int z;                  /* declare local variable       */

  z = x - y;
  return z;
}                         /* end function body            */
```

Communicating Values

Arguments are used to convey values from the calling function to the function. If variables a and b have the values 5 and 2, then the call

```
c = diff(a,b);
```

transmits 5 and 2 to the variables x and y. The values 5 and 2 are called *actual arguments*, and the diff() variables x and y are called *formal arguments*. The keyword return communicates one value from the function to the calling function. In our example, c receives the value of z, which is 3. A function ordinarily has no effect on the variables in a calling function. To directly affect variables in the calling function, use pointers as arguments. This may be necessary if you wish to communicate more than one value back to the calling function.

Function Type

Functions must have the same type as the value they return. Functions are assumed to be type int. If a function is another type, it must be declared as such in the calling function and in the function definition.

Example

```
int main(void)
{
  double q, x, duff();  /* declare in calling function   */
  int n;
  .
  .
  .
  q = duff(x,n);
  .
  .
  .
}
double duff(u, k)       /* declare in function definition */
double u;
int k;
{
  double tor;
```

(continued)

```
          .
          .
          .
    return tor;          /* returns a double value          */
}
```

Chapter Summary

Use *functions* as building blocks for larger programs. Each function should have a single, well-defined purpose. Use *arguments* to communicate values to a function, and use the keyword `return` to communicate back a value. If the function returns a value not of type `int`, then you must specify the function type in the function definition and in the declaration section of the calling function. If you want the function to affect variables in the calling function, use *addresses* and *pointers*.

ANSI C offers *function prototyping*, a powerful C enhancement that allows compilers to verify that the proper number and types of arguments are used in a function call.

A C function can call itself; this is called *recursion*.

Review Questions

1. What is the difference between an actual argument and a formal argument?

2. Write function headings (K&R style and the new ANSI C style) for the functions described below. Note that you need write only the headings, not the body.

    a. `n_to_char()` takes an `int` argument and returns a `char`.

    b. `digits()` takes a `double` argument and an `int` argument and returns an `int`.

    c. `random()` takes no argument and returns an `int`.

3. Devise a function that returns the sum of two `double` arguments.

4. Is anything wrong with this function definition?

```
void salami(num)
```

```
{
    int num, count;

    for (count = 1; count <= num; num++)
        printf(" O salami mio!\n");
}
```

5. Given the following output

```
Please choose one of the following:
1) copy files          2) move files
3) remove files        4) quit
Enter the number of your choice:
```

    a. Write a function that displays a menu of four numbered choices and asks you to choose one. (The output should look like the preceding.)

    b. Write a function that has two `int` arguments: a lower limit and an upper limit. The function should read an integer from input. If the integer is outside the limits, the function should print a menu (using the function from part a of this question) and get a new value. When an integer in the proper limits is entered, the function should return that value to the calling function.

    c. Write a minimal program using the functions from parts a and b of this question. By minimal, we mean it need not actually perform the actions promised by the menu; it should just show the choices and get a valid response.

Programming Exercises

1. Devise a function `min(x,y)` that returns the smaller of two `double` values, and test the function with a simple driver.

2. Devise a function `chline(ch,i,j)` that prints the requested character in columns i through j. Test it in a simple driver.

3. Write a function that takes three arguments: a character and two integers. The character is to be printed. The first integer specifies the number of times that the character is to be printed on a line, and the second integer specifies the number of lines that are to be printed. Write a program that makes use of this function.

4. The harmonic mean of two numbers is obtained by taking the inverses of the two numbers, averaging them, and taking the inverse of the result. Write a function that takes two `double` arguments and returns the harmonic mean of the two numbers.

5. Write a function that replaces the contents of two variables with two new values: the sum and the difference of the original contents.

6. Write a program that reads characters from the standard input to end-of-file. For each character, have the program report whether it is a letter. If it is a letter, also report its numerical location in the alphabet. For example, *c* and *C* would each be letter 3. Incorporate a function that takes a character as an argument and returns the numerical location if the character is a letter and that returns −1 otherwise.

7. In Chapter 6 (Listing 6.18) we wrote a `power()` function that returned the result of raising a type `double` number to a positive integer value. Improve the function so that it correctly handles negative powers. Also, build into the function that 0 to any power is 0 and that any number to the 0 power is 1. Use a loop. Test the function in a program.

8. Redo Exercise 7, but this time use a recursive function.

9. Generalize the `to_binary()` function of Listing 9.13 so that it takes a second argument in the range 2–10. It then prints the number that is its first argument to the number base given by the second argument.

10

Arrays and Pointers

Keyword
- ➤ static

Operators
- ➤ &   * (unary)

In this chapter you learn how to create and initialize arrays. Along the way, you strengthen your knowledge of pointers and see how they relate to arrays. You write functions that process arrays and explore two-dimensional arrays.

eople turn to computers for tasks like tracking monthly expenses or daily rainfall or quarterly sales or weekly weights. As a programmer, you inevitably will have to deal with large quantities of related data. Often, arrays offer the best way to handle such data in an efficient, convenient manner. Chapter 6 introduced arrays, and this chapter takes a more thorough look. In particular, it examines how to write array-processing functions. Such functions will allow you to extend the advantages of modular programming to arrays. In doing so, you'll see the intimate relationship between arrays and pointers.

Arrays

Recall that an *array* is composed of a series of elements of one data type. You use *declarations* to tell the compiler when you want an array. An *array declaration* tells the compiler how many elements the array contains and what the type is for these elements. Armed with this information, the compiler can set up the array properly. Array elements can have the same types as ordinary variables. Consider the following example of array declarations:

```
/* some array declarations */
int main(void)
{
    float candy[365];      /* array of 365 floats */
    char code[12];         /* array of 12 chars   */
    int states[50];        /* array of 50 ints    */
    :
    :

}
```

The brackets ([]) identify candy and the rest as arrays, and the number enclosed in the brackets indicates the number of elements in the array.

To access elements in an array, you identify an individual element by using its subscript number, also called an *index*. The numbering starts with

0. Hence, `candy[0]` is the first element of the `candy` array, and `candy[364]` is the 365th and last element.

This is rather old hat; let's learn something new.

Initialization and Storage Classes

Arrays are often used to store data needed for a program. For example, a 12-element array can store the number of days in each month. In cases such as these, it would be convenient to initialize the array at the beginning of a program. We can. Let's see how it is done.

You know that you can initialize single-valued variables (sometimes called *scalar* variables) in a declaration with expressions like

```
int fix = 1;
float flax = PI * 2;
```

where, we hope, `PI` was defined earlier as a macro. Can you do something similar with arrays? The answer is that old favorite, yes and maybe. It's yes for ANSI C and maybe for K&R C. If the array is an *external* array or a *static* array, it can be initialized. If it is an *automatic* array, it can be initialized under ANSI C but not under the older K&R definition of the language. We'll cover these new terms in Chapter 13, but we'll preview them now.

The terms *external, static*, and *automatic* describe different *storage classes* that C allows. The storage class determines how widely known a data item is to various functions in a program and for how long it is kept in memory. Until now, we have used only automatic variables. Let's look at these three storage classes.

Automatic Variables and Arrays

An automatic variable or array is one defined *inside* a function (this includes formal arguments). As we've emphasized, a variable defined in a function is private to that function, even if it reuses a name appearing in another function. As we haven't mentioned, such a variable exists only for the duration of the function call. When a function finishes and returns to the calling function, the space used to hold its variables is freed.

ANSI C allows us to initialize automatic arrays:

```
int main(void)
{
    int powers[8] = {1,2,4,6,8,16,32,64}; /* ANSI only */
        .
        .
        .
}
```

Because the array is defined inside `main()`, it is an automatic array. It is initialized by using a comma-separated list of values enclosed in braces. You can use spaces between the values and the commas, if you wish. The first element (`powers[0]`) is assigned the value 1, and so on.

K&R C, however, does not allow this. The only way to give values to an automatic array in K&R is to assign values to the elements individually, perhaps by using a loop.

External Variables and Arrays

An external variable or array is one defined *outside* a function. Here, for example, we define an external variable and an external array:

```
int report;
int sows[5] = {12, 10, 8, 9, 6};   /* ok in ANSI and K&R */
int main(void)
{

    .
    .
    .

}
int feed(n)
int n;
{

    .
    .
    .

}
```

External variables and arrays differ from their automatic cousins in three respects. First, they are known to all functions following them in a file. Thus, in our example, both `main()` and `feed()` can use and modify the `int` variable `report` and the array `sows`. Second, external variables and arrays persist as long as the program runs. Because they are not defined in a particular function, they don't expire when a particular function terminates. Third, external variables and arrays are initialized to zeros by default, so `report` is initialized to 0.

Static Variables and Arrays

You can define a static variable or array inside a function by beginning the definition with the keyword `static`:

```
int account(n, m)
int n, m;
{
```

```
        static int beans[2] = {343, 332}; /* ok in ANSI, K&R */
            .
            .
            .
    }
```

This creates an array that, like an automatic array, is local to the function
account(). However, like an external array, a static array retains its values
between function calls and is initialized to zeros by default.

Storage Classes: Comments

C offers multiple storage classes to meet different programming needs. In
Chapter 13 we'll investigate the uses of each type. For most cases, automatic variables and arrays are the best choice. However, because K&R
doesn't allow automatic arrays to be initialized, many programs use external or static arrays instead. We'll use external and static arrays so that our
examples will work with pre-ANSI compilers as well as with ANSI compilers. That said, let's learn a bit more about array initialization.

More Array Initialization

Listing 10.1 presents a short program that prints the number of days per
month.

Listing 10.1 day_mon1.c

```
/* day_mon1.c -- prints the days for each month */
#include <stdio.h>
#define MONTHS 12
int days[MONTHS] = {31,28,31,30,31,30,31,31,30,31,30,31};
int main(void)
{
   int index;
   extern int days[];  /* optional declaration */

   for (index = 0; index < MONTHS; index++)
      printf("Month %d has %d days.\n", index + 1,
             days[index]);
   return 0;
}
```

The output looks like this:

```
Month 1 has 31 days.
Month 2 has 28 days.
Month 3 has 31 days.
Month 4 has 30 days.
Month 5 has 31 days.
Month 6 has 30 days.
Month 7 has 31 days.
Month 8 has 31 days.
Month 9 has 30 days.
Month 10 has 31 days.
Month 11 has 30 days.
Month 12 has 31 days.
```

Not quite a superb program, but it's wrong only one month in every four years. By defining `days[]` outside the function, we made it external. We initialized it with a list of comma-separated values enclosed in braces. Inside the function, the optional declaration

```
extern int days[];
```

uses the keyword `extern` to remind us that the `days` array is defined elsewhere in the program as an external array. Because the array is defined elsewhere, we needn't give its size here. (See Chapter 13 for more on `extern`.) Omitting this entire declaration statement has no effect on how this program works. Indeed, it's a common practice to define external variables at the top of a file and to omit the optional `extern` declarations.

The number of items in the list should match the size of the array. What if we count wrong? Let's try the last example again, as shown in Listing 10.2, with a list that is two too short.

Listing 10.2 *day_mon2.c*

```
/* day_mon2.c -- initializes 10 out of 12 elements */
#include <stdio.h>
#define MONTHS 12
int days[MONTHS] = {31,28,31,30,31,30,31,31,30,31};
```

(continued)

Listing 10.2   *(continued)*

```
int main(void)
{
  int index;
  extern int days[];  /* optional declaration */

  for (index = 0; index < MONTHS; index++)
    printf("Month %d has %d days.\n", index + 1,
           days[index]);
  return 0;
}
```

This time the output looks like this:

```
Month 1 has 31 days.
Month 2 has 28 days.
Month 3 has 31 days.
Month 4 has 30 days.
Month 5 has 31 days.
Month 6 has 30 days.
Month 7 has 31 days.
Month 8 has 31 days.
Month 9 has 30 days.
Month 10 has 31 days.
Month 11 has 0 days.
Month 12 has 0 days.
```

As you can see, the compiler had no problem. When it ran out of values from the list, it initialized the remaining elements to 0. This initializing to 0 holds for external and static arrays. However, uninitialized elements of automatic arrays, like uninitialized ordinary variables, get garbage values.

The compiler is not so forgiving if you have too many list values. This overgenerosity is considered an error. There is no need, however, to expose yourself to the ridicule of your compiler. Instead, you can let the compiler match the array size to the list by omitting the size from the braces (Listing 10.3).

Listing 10.3 *day_mon3.c*

```
/* day_mon3.c -- initializes 10 out of 12 elements */
#include <stdio.h>
int days[] = {31,28,31,30,31,30,31,31,30,31};
int main(void)
{
  int index;
  extern int days[];  /* optional declaration */

  for (index = 0; index < sizeof days / sizeof (int); index++)
    printf("Month %d has %d days.\n", index + 1,
            days[index]);
  return 0;
}
```

There are two main points to note in the program:

► When you use empty brackets to initialize an array, the compiler will count the number of items in the list and make the array that large.

► Notice what we did in the `for` loop control statement. Lacking faith (justifiably) in our ability to count correctly, we let the computer give us the size of the array. The `sizeof` operator gives the size, in bytes, of the object or type following it. On our system, each `int` element occupies 2 bytes, so we divide the total number of bytes by 2 to get the number of elements. Other systems may have a different size `int`. Therefore, to be general, we divide by `sizeof` (int).

Here is the result of running this program:

```
Month 1 has 31 days.
Month 2 has 28 days.
Month 3 has 31 days.
Month 4 has 30 days.
Month 5 has 31 days.
Month 6 has 30 days.
Month 7 has 31 days.
Month 8 has 31 days.
```

```
Month 9 has 30 days.
Month 10 has 31 days.
```

Oops! We put in just ten values. But our method of letting the program find the array size kept us from trying to print past the end of the array. This points out a potential disadvantage of automatic counting: errors in the number of elements may pass unnoticed.

There is one more short method of initializing arrays. Since it works only for character strings, however, we will save it for the next chapter.

Assigning Array Values

You can *assign* values to array members, regardless of storage class. For example, the following fragment assigns even numbers to an automatic array:

```
/* array assignment */
#include <stdio.h>
#define SIZE 50
int main(void)
{
    int counter, evens[SIZE];

    for (counter = 0; counter < SIZE; counter++)
        evens[counter] = 2 * counter;
    .
    .
    .
}
```

Note that this assignment is element by element. C doesn't let you assign one array to another as a unit. Nor can you use the list-in-braces form except when initializing:

```
/* nonvalid array assignment */
#define SIZE 5
int main(void)
{
    int oxen[SIZE] = {5,3,2,8};      /* ok here       */
    int yaks[SIZE];

    yaks = oxen;                     /* not allowed   */
    yaks[SIZE] = oxen[SIZE];         /* invalid       */
    yaks[SIZE] = {5,3,2,8};          /* doesn't work */
}
```

Pointers to Arrays

Pointers, as you may recall from Chapter 9, provide a symbolic way to use addresses. Since the hardware instructions of computing machines rely heavily on addresses, pointers allow you to express yourself in a way that is close to the way the machine expresses itself. This makes programs with pointers efficient. In particular, pointers offer an efficient way to deal with arrays. Indeed, as we shall see, array notation is simply a disguised use of pointers.

An example of this disguised use is that an array name is also the address of the first element of an array. That is, if flizny is an array, then the following is true:

```
flizny == &flizny[0]
```

Both flizny and &flizny represent the memory address of that first element. (Recall that & is the address operator.) Both are *constants*, for they remain fixed for the duration of the program. However, they can be assigned as values to a pointer *variable*, and we can change the value of a variable, as Listing 10.4 shows. Notice what happens to the value of a pointer when we add a number to it.

```
Listing 10.4  pnt_add.c

/* pnt_add.c -- pointer addition */
#include <stdio.h>
#define SIZE 4
int main(void)
{
   int dates[SIZE], *pti, index;
   float bills[SIZE], *ptf;

   pti = dates;    /* assign address of array to pointer */
   ptf = bills;
   for (index = 0; index < SIZE; index ++)
        printf("pointers + %d: %10u %10u\n",
              index, pti + index, ptf + index);
   return 0;
}
```

Here is the output:

```
pointers + 0:      56014      56026
pointers + 1:      56016      56030
pointers + 2:      56018      56034
pointers + 3:      56020      56038
```

The first line prints the beginning addresses of the two arrays, and the next line gives the result of adding 1 to the address, and so on. What?

```
56014 + 1 = 56016?
56026 + 1 = 56030?
```

Pretty dumb? Like a fox! Our system is addressed by individual bytes, but type `int` uses 2 bytes and type `float` uses 4 bytes. What is happening here is that when you say "add 1 to a pointer," C adds one *storage unit*. For arrays, this means that the address is increased to the address of the next *element*, not just the next byte (see Figure 10.1). This is one reason we have to declare what sort of object a pointer points to. The address is not enough because the computer needs to know how many bytes are used to store the object. (This is true even for pointers to scalar variables; otherwise, the *pt operation to fetch the value wouldn't work correctly.)

Figure 10.1 *An array and pointer addition*

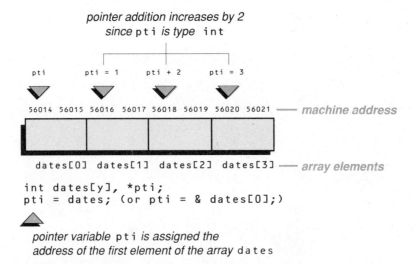

```
int dates[y], *pti;
pti = dates; (or pti = & dates[0];)
```

pointer variable `pti` *is assigned the address of the first element of the array* `dates`

Now we can define more clearly what is meant by pointer-to-`int` or pointer-to-`float` or pointer to any other data object:

▶ The value of a pointer is the address of the object to which it points. How the address is represented internally is hardware dependent. Many computers, including PCs and VAXs, are *byte addressable*, meaning that each byte in memory is numbered sequentially. Here, the address of a large object, such a type double variable, typically is the address of the first byte of the object.

▶ Applying the * operator to a pointer yields the value stored in the pointed-to object.

▶ Adding 1 to the pointer increases its value by the size, in bytes, of the pointed-to object.

As a result of this cleverness of C, we have the following equalities:

```
dates + 2 == &dates[2]       /* same address */
*(dates + 2) == dates[2]     /* same value   */
```

These relationships sum up the close connection between arrays and pointers. They mean that we can use a pointer to identify an individual element of an array and to get its value. In essence, we have two different notations for the same thing. Indeed, the C language standard describes array notation in terms of pointers, so the pointer approach is the more basic of the two.

Incidentally, don't confuse *(dates+2) with *dates+2. The indirection operator (*) binds more tightly (has higher precedence) than +, so the latter means (*dates)+2:

```
*(dates + 2)     /* value of the 3rd element of dates        */
*dates + 2       /* 2 added to the value of the 1st element */
```

The relationship between arrays and pointers means that we can often use either approach when writing a program. Listing 10.5, for instance, produces the same output as Listing 10.1 when compiled and run.

Listing 10.5 *day_mon4.c*

```
/* day_mon4.c -- uses pointer notation */
#include <stdio.h>
#define MONTHS 12
int days[MONTHS] = {31,28,31,30,31,30,31,31,30,31,30,31};
int main(void)
```

(continued)

Listing 10.5 *(continued)*

```
{
   int index;
   extern int days[];  /* optional declaration */

   for (index = 0; index < MONTHS; index++)
      printf("Month %d has %d days.\n", index + 1,
             *(days + index));
   return 0;
}
```

Here, `days` is the address of the first element of the array, `days + index` is the address of element `days[index]`, and `*(days + index)` is the value of that element, just as `days[index]` is. The loop references each element of the array in turn and prints the contents of what it finds.

In some cases you don't have a choice between pointers and arrays, and you have to use pointers. One such case is when you have a function with an array as an argument.

Functions, Arrays, and Pointers

Suppose you wish to write a function that operates on an array. For instance, suppose you want a function that returns the sum of the elements of an array. Listing 10.6 shows a program that does this. To point out an interesting fact about array arguments, the program also prints the size of the relevant arrays.

Listing 10.6 *sum_arr1.c*

```
/* sum_arr1.c -- sums the elements of an array */
#include <stdio.h>
#define SIZE 10
long sum(int ar[], int n);
int main(void)
{
```

```
        static int marbles[SIZE] = {20,10,5,39,4,16,19,26,31,20};
        long answer;

        answer = sum(marbles, SIZE);
        printf("The total number of marbles is %ld.\n", answer);
        printf("The size of marbles is %d bytes.\n",
             sizeof marbles);
        return 0;
   }


long sum(int ar[], int n)      /* how big an array? */
{
        int i;
        long total = 0;

        for( i = 0; i < n; i++)
             total += ar[i];
        printf("The size of ar is %d bytes.\n", sizeof ar);
        return total;
   }
```

Recall that the += operator adds the value of the operand on its right to the operand on its left. Thus, total is a running sum of the array elements. The output on our system looks like this:

```
The size of ar is 2 bytes.
The total number of marbles is 190.
The size of marbles is 20 bytes.
```

Array Names as Arguments

Well, the function does successfully sum the number of marbles. But what is ar? From the function argument declarations, you might expect that ar is a new array into which are copied the values found in marbles—the actual argument to the function. After all, the formal argument n is assigned the value of its corresponding actual argument. Yet ar is only 2 bytes, so it couldn't be assigned the 20 bytes of data in marbles. Thus, ar is not an array of 10 ints.

The reason that ar is not an array is that C does not allow arrays to be passed as function arguments. Look at the function call:

```
sum(marbles, SIZE);
```

The first argument is `marbles`, the name of an array. And the name of an array, recall, is the *address* of the first element of the array. That is, the identifier `marbles` is not an array; it is the address of an `int`, `marbles[0]`. So the function call `sum(marbles,SIZE)` passes two numbers: an address and an integer. This means that the formal arguments to `sum()` should be a pointer-to-`int` and an `int`. The function heading should look like this:

```
int sum(int *ar, int n)
```

Indeed, if you replace the heading in Listing 10.6 with this heading, the program works exactly the same as before. When you declare a formal argument (and *only* when you declare a formal argument) in C, the forms

```
int *ar;
```

and

```
int ar[];
```

are exactly equivalent. Both state that `ar` is a pointer-to-`int`. That is why `sizeof ar` is 2—our system uses 2-byte pointers.

If `ar` is a pointer, why can we use the expression `ar[i]` in `sum()`? In C, remember, `ar[i]` is the same as `*(ar + i)`. Both represent the value stored at address `ar + i`. This is true if `ar` is the name of an array, and it is true if `ar` is the name of a pointer variable. Thus, we can use pointer notation to process an array, and we can use array notation with a pointer variable. In this instance, `ar` starts out pointing to the first element of the `marbles` array. Increasing `i` then makes `ar + i` point to each element in turn. Because we also pass the size of the array, the `sum()` function knows when the end of the array is reached.

In short, when you use an array name as a function argument, you pass the address of the first element of the array to the function. The function then uses a pointer set to that address to access the original array in the calling program.

Incidentally, we designed the function to use an argument representing the array size. This lets us use the same function for differently sized arrays. Note that the only way the function can know the array size is if we tell it. As the example shows, applying the `sizeof` operator to an array name yields the size of an array, but applying `sizeof` to a pointer variable yields the size of the pointer, not the size of the object that is pointed to. Another way to indicate the size is to build it into the function. That is, instead of using the `n` argument in `sum()`, we could have made the loop test be `i < 10`. However, such a function would be limited to working with 10-element arrays.

Using Pointer Arguments

The fact that `ar` is a variable offers an alternative way to write the `sum()` function. Rather than adding `i` to a fixed value `ar`, we can alter the value of `ar` itself. Listing 10.7 illustrates this approach.

Listing 10.7 *sum_arr2.c*

```
/* sum_arr2.c -- sums the elements of an array */
#include <stdio.h>
#define SIZE 10
long sump(int *ar, int n);
int main(void)
{
   static int marbles[SIZE] = {20,10,5,39,4,16,19,26,31,20};
   long answer;

   answer = sump(marbles, SIZE);
   printf("The total number of marbles is %ld.\n", answer);
   return 0;
}

long sump(int *ar, int n)     /* use pointer arithmetic    */
{
   int i;
   long total = 0;

   for (i = 0; i < n; i++)
   {
      total += *ar;      /* add value to total              */
      ar++;              /* advance pointer to next element */
   }
   return total;
}
```

Again, `ar` starts out pointing to the first element of `marbles`, so the assignment expression `total += *ar` adds the value of the first element (20) to `total`. Then the expression `ar++` increments the pointer variable `ar` so that it points to the next element in the array. Since `ar` points to type `int`, C increments the value of `ar` by the size of `int`.

Alternatively, we can condense the body of the loop to one line:

```
total += *ar++;
```

The unary operators * and ++ have the same precedence but associate from right to left. This means that the ++ applies to ar, not to *ar. That is, the pointer is incremented, not the value pointed to. The fact that we use the postfix form (ar++ rather than ++ar) means that the pointer is not incremented until after the pointed-to value is added to total. If we used *++ar, then the order would be: increment the pointer; then use the value pointed to. But if we used (*ar)++, the program would use the value of ar and then increment the value, not the pointer. That would leave the pointer pointing to the same element, but the element would contain a new number. Although the *ar++ notation is commonly used, you may prefer to use *(ar++) for clarity. Listing 10.8 illustrates these niceties of precedence.

Listing 10.8 order.c

```
/* order.c -- precedence in pointer operations */
#include <stdio.h>
int data[2] = {100, 300};
int moredata[2] = {100, 300};
int main(void)
{
   int *p1, *p2, *p3;

   p1 = p2 = data;
   p3 = moredata;
   printf("%d %d %d\n", *p1++, *++p2, (*p3)++);
   printf("%d %d %d\n", *p1, *p2, *p3);
   return 0;
}
```

Here is its output:

```
100 300 100
300 300 101
```

The only operation that altered an array value is (*p3)++. We made it point to a different array from the other pointers so that the data array would be unchanged.

Comment: Pointers and Arrays

As you have seen, functions that process arrays actually use pointers as arguments. But you do have a choice between array notation and pointer notation for writing array-processing functions. Using array notation, as in Listing 10.6, makes it more obvious that the function is working with arrays. Also, array notation has a more familiar look to programmers versed in other languages, such as FORTRAN, Pascal, Modula-2, or BASIC. Other programmers may be more accustomed to working with pointers and may find the pointer notation more natural.

As far as C goes, the two notations are equivalent in meaning. Pointer notation, particularly when used with the increment operator, is closer to machine language and, with some compilers, leads to more efficient code. Many programmers, however, feel that the programmer's main concerns should be correctness and clarity and that code optimization should be left to the compiler.

Pointer Operations

Just what can you do with pointers? C offers five basic operations that you can perform on pointers, and the next program demonstrates these possibilities. To show the results of each operation, we will print the value of the pointer (which is the address it points to), the value stored in the pointed-to address, and the address of the pointer itself. (If your compiler supports the %p specifier, use it instead of %u for printing the addresses.)

Listing 10.9 pt_ops.c

```
/* pt_ops.c -- pointer operations */
#include <stdio.h>
int main(void)
{
  static int urn[3] = {100,200,300};
  int *ptr1, *ptr2;

  ptr1 =urn;          /* assign an address to a pointer */
  ptr2 = &urn[2];     /* ditto                          */
```

(continued)

Listing 10.9 *(continued)*

```
printf("ptr1 = %u, *ptr1 =%d, &ptr1 = %u\n",
    ptr1, *ptr1, &ptr1);
ptr1++;              /* increment a pointer          */
printf("ptr1 = %u, *ptr1 =%d, &ptr1 = %u\n",
    ptr1, *ptr1, &ptr1);
                     /* dereference a pointer and take */
                     /* the address of a pointer       */
printf("ptr2 = %u, *ptr2 =%d, &ptr2 = %u\n",
    ptr2, *ptr2, &ptr2);
++ptr2;   /* going past end of the array */
printf("ptr2 = %u, *ptr2 =%d, &ptr2 = %u\n",
    ptr2, *ptr2, &ptr2);
printf("ptr2 - ptr1 = %u\n", ptr2 - ptr1);
                     /* pointer subtraction          */
return 0;
}
```

Here is the output:

```
ptr1 = 234, *ptr1 =100, &ptr1 = 3606
ptr1 = 236, *ptr1 =200, &ptr1 = 3606
ptr2 = 238, *ptr2 =300, &ptr2 = 3604
ptr2 = 240, *ptr2 =1910, &ptr2 = 3604
ptr2 - ptr1 = 2
```

Listing 10.9 shows the five basic operations that can be performed with or on pointer variables:

1. *Assignment.* You can assign an address to a pointer. Typically you do this by using an array name or by using the address operator (&). In the example, ptr1 is assigned the address of the beginning of the array urn. This address happens to be memory cell number 234. (On our system, static variables are stored in low memory locations.) The variable ptr2 gets the address of the third and last element, urn[2].

2. *Value-finding (dereferencing).* The * operator gives the value stored in the pointed-to location. Thus, *ptr1 initially is 100, the value stored at location 234.

3. *Taking a pointer address.* Like all variables, pointer variables have

an address and a value. The & operator tells us where the pointer itself is stored. In our example, `ptr1` is stored in memory location 3606. The content of that memory cell is 234, the address of `urn`.

4. *Incrementing a pointer.* You can do this by regular addition or by using the increment operator. Incrementing a pointer to an array element makes it move to the next element of an array. Thus, `ptr1++` increases the numerical value of `ptr1` by 2 (2 bytes per `int`) and makes `ptr1` point to `urn[1]` (see Figure 10.2). Now `ptr1` has the value 236 (the next array address) and `*ptr1` has the value 200, the value of `urn[1]`. Note that the address of `ptr1` itself remains 3606. After all, a variable doesn't move around just because it changes value!

Of course, you can also decrement a pointer. There are some cautions to note when incrementing or decrementing a pointer, however. The computer does not keep track of whether a pointer still points to an array element. The operation `++ptr2` in our example caused `ptr2` to move up another 2 bytes, and now it points to whatever happened to be stored after the array. Also, you can use the increment or decrement operators for pointer variables but not for address constants, such as array names, just as you can't use the increment operator on regular constants. However, you can use simple addition, as in `urn + 2`, for address constants.

```
Given:
int urn[3];
int *ptr1, *ptr2;
int x, y;
```

Valid	Invalid
ptr1++;	urn++;
x++;	3++;
ptr2 = ptr1 + 2;	ptr2 = urn++;
ptr2 = urn + 1;	x = y + 3++;

5. *Differencing.* You can find the difference between two pointers. Normally you do this for two pointers to elements that are in the same array to find out how far apart the elements are. The result is in the same units as the type size. For instance, in the output from Listing 10.9, `ptr2 - prt1` has the value 2, meaning these pointers point to objects separated by 2 `int`s, not by 2 bytes.

These operations open many possibilities. C programmers create arrays of pointers, pointers to functions, arrays of pointers to pointers, arrays of pointers to functions, and so on. But relax, we'll stick to the basic uses we have already unveiled. The first basic use for pointers is to communicate information to and from functions. You already know that you

Figure 10.2 *Incrementing a type* int *pointer*

ptr1 is the value of the address
234, which is currently 100

```
ptr1=urn;
ptr1 sets to 234
```
then
```
ptr1++ sets ptr1 to 236
```
etc.

must use pointers if you want a function to affect variables in the calling function. The second use is in functions designed to manipulate arrays. Let's look at a programming example using functions and arrays.

Another Example

In the program shown in Listing 10.10, one function displays an array and one function multiplies each element of an array by a given value. The second function emphasizes the fact that array functions operate on the original array, not on a copy. To provide some variety, we use array notation for one function and pointer notation for the other.

Listing 10.10 *arf.c*

```c
/* arf.c -- array functions */
#include <stdio.h>
#define SIZE 5
void show_array(double ar[], int n);
void mult_array(double mult, double ar[], int n);
int main(void)
```

```
{
    static double dip[SIZE] = {20.0, 17.66, 8.2, 15.3, 22.22};

    show_array(dip, SIZE);
    mult_array(2.5, dip, SIZE);
    show_array(dip, SIZE);
    return 0;
}
void show_array(double ar[], int n)
{
    int i;

    for (i = 0; i < n; i++)
        printf("%8.3f ", ar[i]);
    putchar('\n');
}


/* multiplies each array member by the same multiplier */
void mult_array(double mult, double ar[], int size)
{
    int i;

    for (i = 0; i < size; i++)
        *(ar++) *= mult;
}
```

Here is the output:

```
20.000    17.660     8.200    15.300    22.220
50.000    44.150    20.500    38.250    55.550
```

Note that both functions are type void. The mult_array() function does provide new values to the dip array, but not by using the return mechanism.

Multidimensional Arrays

Tempest Cloud, a weather person who takes her subject cirrusly, wants to analyze 5 years of monthly rainfall data. One of her first decisions is how to represent the data. One choice is to use 60 variables, one for each data item. (We mentioned this choice once before, and it is as senseless now as it was then.) Using an array with 60 elements would be an improvement, but it would be nicer still if she could keep each year's data separate. She could use 5 arrays, each with 12 elements, but that is clumsy and could get really awkward if Tempest decides to study 50 years' worth of rainfall instead of 5. She needs something better.

The better approach is to use an array of arrays. The master array would have 5 elements, one for each year. Each of those elements, in turn, would be a 12-element array, one for each month. This is how to declare such an array:

```
static float rain[5][12];
```

You also can visualize this `rain` array as a two-dimensional array consisting of 5 rows, each of 12 columns, as shown in Figure 10.3. By changing the second subscript, we move along a row, month by month. By changing the first subscript, we move vertically along a column, year by year.

Figure 10.3 *Two-dimensional array*

```
static float rain[5][12];
```

The two-dimensional view is merely a convenient way of visualizing an array with two indices. Internally, such an array is stored sequentially, beginning with the first 12-element array, followed by the second 12-element array, and so on.

Let's use this two-dimensional array in a weather program. Our program goal will be to find the total rainfall for each year, the average yearly rainfall, and the average rainfall for each month. To find the total rainfall for a year, we have to add all the data in a given row. To find the average rainfall for a given month, we have to add all the data in a given column.

The two-dimensional array makes it easy to visualize and execute these activities. Listing 10.11 shows the program.

```
Listing 10.11  rain.c

/* rain.c  -- finds yearly totals, yearly average, and monthly
                   average for several years of rainfall data */
#include <stdio.h>
#define MONTHS 12    /* number of months in a year */
#define YRS    5     /* number of years of data    */
int main(void)
{
  /* initializing rainfall data for 1970 - 1974 */
  static float rain[YRS][MONTHS] = {
  {10.2, 8.1, 6.8, 4.2, 2.1, 1.8, 0.2, 0.3, 1.1, 2.3, 6.1, 7.4},
  {9.2, 9.8, 4.4, 3.3, 2.2, 0.8, 0.4, 0.0, 0.6, 1.7, 4.3, 5.2},
  {6.6, 5.5, 3.8, 2.8, 1.6, 0.2, 0.0, 0.0, 0.0, 1.3, 2.6, 4.2},
  {4.3, 4.3, 4.3, 3.0, 2.0, 1.0, 0.2, 0.2, 0.4, 2.4, 3.5, 6.6},
  {8.5, 8.2, 1.2, 1.6, 2.4, 0.0, 5.2, 0.9, 0.3, 0.9, 1.4, 7.2}
  };
  int year, month;
  float subtot, total;

  printf(" YEAR    RAINFALL  (inches)\n");
  for (year = 0, total = 0; year < YRS; year++)
  {              /* for each year, sum rainfall for each month */
    for (month = 0, subtot = 0; month < MONTHS; month++)
            subtot += rain[year][month];
    printf("%5d %15.1f\n", 1970 + year, subtot);
    total += subtot;                  /* total for all years */
  }
  printf("\nThe yearly average is %.1f inches.\n\n", total/YRS);
  printf("MONTHLY AVERAGES:\n\n");
  printf(" Jan Feb Mar Apr May Jun Jul Aug Sep Oct ");
  printf(" Nov Dec\n");

  for (month = 0; month < MONTHS; month++)
  {              /* for each month, sum rainfall over years */
    for (year = 0, subtot =0; year < YRS; year++)
          subtot += rain[year][month];
```

(continued)

Listing 10.11 *(continued)*

```
    printf("%4.1f ", subtot/YRS);
}
printf("\n");
return 0;
}
```

Here is the output:

```
YEAR        RAINFALL (inches)
1970            50.6
1971            41.9
1972            28.6·
1973            32.2
1974            37.8

The yearly average is 38.2 inches.

MONTHLY AVERAGES:

Jan  Feb  Mar  Apr  May  Jun  Jul  Aug  Sep  Oct  Nov  Dec
7.8  7.2  4.1  3.0  2.1  0.8  1.2  0.3  0.5  1.7  3.6  6.1
```

As you study this program, concentrate on the initialization and on the computation scheme. The initialization is the more involved of the two, so we will look at the computation first.

To find the total for a given year, we kept `year` constant and let `month` go over its full range. This is the inner `for` loop of the first part of the program. Then we repeated the process for the next value of `year`. This is the outer loop of the first part of the program. A nested loop structure like this is natural for handling a two-dimensional array. One loop handles the first subscript, and the other loop handles the second subscript.

The second part of the program has the same structure, but now we change `year` with the inner loop and `month` with the outer. Remember, each time the outer loop cycles once, the inner loop cycles its full allotment. Thus, this arrangement cycles through all the years before changing months. We get a five-year total for the first month, then a five-year total for the second month, and so on.

Initializing a Two-Dimensional Array

For the initialization we included five embraced lists of numbers, all enclosed by one outer set of braces. The data in the first interior set of braces is assigned to the first row of the array, the data in the second interior set goes to the second row, and so on. The rules we discussed about mismatches between data and array sizes apply to each row. That is, if the first inner set of braces encloses 10 numbers, only the first 10 elements of the first row are affected. The last two elements in that row then are initialized by default to zero. If there are too many numbers, it is an error; the numbers do not get shoved into the next row.

We could have left out the interior braces and just retained the two outermost braces. As long as we have the right number of entries, the effect is the same. If we are short of entries, however, the array is filled sequentially row by row until the data runs out. Then the remaining elements are initialized to 0. Figure 10.4 shows both ways of initializing an array.

Figure 10.4 Two methods of initializing an array

```
N  v:
static int sq[2][3]={
                        {5,6},
                        {7,8}
                     };
```

```
static int sq[2][3]={5,6,7, 8};
```

More Dimensions

Everything we have said about two-dimensional arrays can be generalized to three-dimensional arrays and further. You can declare a three-dimensional array this way:

```
int box[10][20][30];
```

You can visualize this array as 10 two-dimensional arrays (each 20 × 30) stacked atop each other. Or you can think of it as an array of arrays of arrays. That is, it is a 10-element array, each element of which is a 20-element array. Each 20-element array then has elements that are 30-element arrays. Or you can simply think of arrays in terms of the number of indices needed. We'll stick to two dimensions in our examples.

Pointers and Multidimensional Arrays

How do pointers relate to multidimensional arrays? We'll look at some examples now to find the answer. To simplify the discussion, we'll examine an array that is much smaller than rain. Suppose we have this declaration:

```
int zippo[4][2];  /* an array of arrays of ints */
```

Then zippo, being the name of an array, is the address of the first element of the array. In this case, the first element of zippo is itself an array of two ints, so zippo is the address of an array of two ints. Let's analyze that further in terms of pointer properties:

▶ Since zippo is the address of the array's first element, zippo equals &zippo[0]. Next, zippo[0] is itself an array of two integers, so zippo[0] equals &zippo[0][0], the address of its first element, an int. In short, zippo[0] is the address of an int-sized object, and zippo is the address of a two-int-sized object. Because both the integer and the array of two integers begin at the same location, both zippo and zippo[0] have the same value.

▶ Adding 1 to a pointer or address yields a value larger by the size of the referred-to object. In this respect, zippo and zippo[0] differ, for zippo refers to an object two ints in size, while zippo[0] refers to an object one int in size. Thus, zippo + 1 and zippo[0] + 1 do not have the same value.

▶ Dereferencing a pointer or an address (applying the * operator) yields the value represented by the referred-to object. Because zippo[0] is the address of its first element zippo[0][0], *(zippo[0]) represents the value stored in zippo[0][0], an int value. Similarly, *zippo represents the value of its first element, zippo[0]. But zippo[0] itself is the address of an int; it's the address &zippo[0][0]. Since it is equivalent to zippo[0] and since *(zippo[0]) is zippo[0][0], then **zippo also is zippo[0][0], an int. In short, zippo is the address of an address and must be dereferenced twice to get an ordinary value. An address of an address or a pointer to a pointer is an example of *double indirection.*

Clearly, increasing the number of array dimensions increases the complexity of the pointer view. At this point, most students of C begin realizing why pointers are considered one of the more difficult aspects of the language. You may wish to study the preceding points carefully and see how they are borne out by the following examples. Listing 10.12 is a program that prints addresses.

Listing 10.12 *zippo1.c*

```
/* zippo1.c -- addresses */
#include <stdio.h>
int main(void)
{
    int zippo[4][2];

    printf("zippo = %u, zippo[0] = %u, &zippo[0][0] = %u, ",
            zippo, zippo[0], &zippo[0][0]);
    printf("*zippo = %u\n", *zippo);
    return 0;
}
```

And here is the output:

```
zippo = 3512, zippo[0] = 3512, &zippo[0][0] = 3512, *zippo = 3512
```

The output shows that the address of the two-dimensional array zippo and the address of the one-dimensional array zippo[0] are the same. Each is the address of the corresponding array's first element, and this is the same numerically as &zippo[0][0]. Also, note that zippo and *zippo have the same value.

Nonetheless, there is a difference. On our system, int is 2 bytes. So, as discussed earlier, zippo[0] and *zippo point to a 2-byte data object. Adding 1 to either should produce a value larger by 2. The name zippo is the address of an array of two ints, so it identifies a 4-byte data object. Thus, adding 1 to zippo should produce an address 4 bytes larger. Let's modify the program, as shown in Listing 10.13, to check that.

Listing 10.13 *zippo2.c*

```
/* zippo2.c -- more zippo info */
#include <stdio.h>
int main(void)
{
    int zippo[4][2];
```

(continued)

Listing 10.13 *(continued)*

```
    printf("zippo = %u, zippo[0] = %u, &zippo[0][0] = %u\n",
    zippo, zippo[0], &zippo[0][0]);
    printf("*zippo = %u\n", *zippo);

    printf("zippo + 1 = %u, zippo[0] + 1 = %u\n",
    zippo + 1, zippo[0] + 1);
    printf("&zippo[0][0] + 1 = %u, *zippo + 1 = %u\n",
    &zippo[0][0] + 1, *zippo + 1);
    printf("*(zippo + 1) = %u\n", *(zippo + 1));
    return 0;
}
```

Here is the new output:

```
zippo = 3512, zippo[0] = 3512, &zippo[0][0] = 3512
*zippo = 3512
zippo + 1 = 3516, zippo[0] + 1 = 3514
&zippo[0][0] + 1 = 3514, *zippo + 1 = 3514
*(zippo + 1) = 35166
```

The results are as we predicted. Adding 1 to zippo moves us from one two-int array to the next array, while adding 1 to zippo[0] moves us from one int to the next. See Figure 10.5. Also, note what happens if we add 2 to zippo[0] (or, equivalently, to *zippo). We would go past the end of the first two-int array to the beginning of the next. The last two examples illustrate that zippo[0], &zippo[0][0], and *zippo are but three different notations for the same thing. All are addresses of the same int.

Note the difference between *zippo + 1 and *(zippo + 1). The former applies the * first and then adds, while the latter adds and then dereferences. In the first case, because *zippo is the address of an int, adding 1 increases the value by 2 bytes on our system. In the second case, because zippo is the address of a two-int object, 4 is added. This means that zippo + 1 is the address of the second two-int array element, and applying the * operator yields the address of the first element of that array. Thus, *(zippo + 1) is the address of an int. In particular, it's the address of the element zippo[1][0]. The expression *zippo + 1 also is the address of an int, but it's the address of zippo[0][1]. In short, dereferencing, then adding, moves the address along a row (changes the second index); adding, then dereferencing, moves the address along a column (changes the first index).

Figure 10.5 *An array of arrays*

Another point to note is that *each* element of zippo is an array and hence the address of a first element. Thus, we have these relationships:

```
zippo[0] == &zippo[0][0] == *zippo
zippo[1] == &zippo[1][0] == *(zippo + 1)
zippo[2] == &zippo[2][0] == *(zippo + 2)
zippo[3] == &zippo[3][0] == *(zippo + 3)
```

Applying the * operator to each gives the following results:

```
*zippo[0] == zippo[0][0] == **zippo
*zippo[1] == zippo[1][0] == *(*(zippo + 1))
*zippo[2] == zippo[2][0] == *(*(zippo + 2))
*zippo[3] == zippo[3][0] == *(*(zippo + 3))
```

More generally, we can represent individual elements using array notation and pointer notation as follows:

```
zippo[m][n] == *(*(zippo + m) + n)
```

The value m, being the index associated with zippo, is added to zippo. The value n, being the index associated with the subarray zippo[m], is added to zippo[m], which is *(zippo + m) in array notation. This makes *(zippo + m) + n the address of element zippo[m][n], and applying the * operator yields the contents at that address.

Now suppose we want to declare a pointer variable pz that is compatible with zippo. Such a pointer could be used, for example, in writing a function to deal with zippo-like arrays. Will the type pointer-to-int suffice? No. That type is compatible with zippo[0], which points to a single int, but we want pz to point to an array of ints. Here is what we can do:

```
int (*pz)[2];
```

This statement says that pz is a pointer to an array of two ints. Why the parentheses? Well, [] has a higher precedence than *. Thus, with a declaration like

```
int *pax[2];
```

we apply the brackets first, making pax an array of two somethings. Next, we apply the *, making pax an array of two pointers. Finally, we use the int, making pax an array of two pointers to int. Thus, this declaration creates two pointers. But our original version uses parentheses to apply the * first, creating one pointer to an array of two ints.

Functions and Multidimensional Arrays

You may be wondering if you really have to learn about pointers to pointers. If you want to write functions that process two-dimensional arrays, the answer is yes. Mainly you need to understand pointers well enough to make the proper declarations for function arguments. In the function body itself, you usually can get by with array notation.

Suppose, then, that you want to write a function to deal with two-dimensional arrays. You have several choices. You can use a function written for one-dimensional arrays on each subarray. Or you can use the same function on the whole array, but treat the whole array as one-dimensional instead of two-dimensional. Or you can write a function that explicitly deals with two-dimensional arrays. To illustrate these three approaches, let's take a small two-dimensional array and apply each of the approaches to double the magnitude of each element.

Applying a One-Dimensional Function to Subarrays

To keep things simple, we'll declare junk to be a static array of arrays so that we can initialize it. We'll write a function that takes an array address and an array size as arguments and doubles the indicated elements. We'll use a for loop to apply this function to each subarray of junk. And we'll print the array contents. Listing 10.14 shows the program.

Listing 10.14 *dubarr1.c*

```
/* dubarr1.c -- doubles array elements */
#include <stdio.h>
void dub(int ar[], int size);
```

```
int main(void)
{
    static int junk[3][4] = {
           {2,4,5,8},
           {3,5,6,9},
           {12,10,8,6}
    };
    int i, j;

    for (i = 0; i < 3 ; i++)
       dub(junk[i], 4);

    for (i = 0; i < 3; i++)
    {
       for (j = 0; j < 4; j++)
          printf("%5d", junk[i][j]);
       putchar('\n');
    }
    return 0;
}

void dub (int ar[], int size)   /* or int *ar */
{
    int i;

    for (i = 0; i < size; i++)
       ar[i] *= 2;
}
```

The first `for` loop in `main()` uses `dub()` to process the subarrays `junk[0]`, `junk[1]`, and so on. This approach works because `junk[0]`, `junk[1]`, etc., *are* each one-dimensional arrays. Note that we pass `dub()` a size parameter of 4, since that is the number of elements in each subarray. Here is the output:

```
    4    8    10    16
    6    10    12    18
   24    20    16    12
```

Applying a One-Dimensional Function to a Two-Dimensional Array

In the preceding example, we looked at `junk` as being an array of 3 arrays of 4 `int`s. For most C implementations, we also can look at `junk` as being an array of 12 `int`s. Suppose, for instance, we pass `dub()` the value `junk[0]` as an argument. This act initializes the pointer `ar` in `dub()` to the

address of junk[0][0]. As a result, ar[0] corresponds to junk[0][0], and
ar[3] corresponds to junk[0][3]. What about ar[4]? It represents the
element following junk[0][3], which is junk[1][0], the first element of
the next subarray. In other words, we've finished one row and have gone to
the beginning of the next. The program in Listing 10.15 continues in this
fashion to cover the whole array, with ar[11] representing junk[2][3].

Listing 10.15 dubarr2.c

```
/* dubarr2.c -- doubles array elements */
#include <stdio.h>
void dub(int ar[], int size);
int main(void)
{
    static int junk[3][4] = {
            {2,4,5,8},
            {3,5,6,9},
            {12,10,8,6}
    };
    int i, j;

    dub(junk[0], 3*4);

    for (i = 0; i < 3; i++)
    {
        for (j = 0; j < 4; j++)
            printf("%5d", junk[i][j]);
        putchar('\n');
    }
    return 0;
}

void dub (int ar[], int size)  /* or int *ar; */
{
    int i;

    for (i = 0; i < size; i++)
        ar[i] *= 2;
}
```

In Listing 10.15, note that dub() is unchanged from Listing 10.14. We
merely changed the limit to 3*4 (or 12) and used one call to dub() instead

of three. (We wrote the limit as **3*4** to emphasize that it is the total number of elements calculated by multiplying the number of rows times the number of columns.) Does it work? Here is the output:

```
 4    8   10   16
 6   10   12   18
24   20   16   12
```

Applying a Two-Dimensional Function

Both of the approaches so far lose track of the column-and-row information. In this application (doubling each element), that information is unimportant. But suppose each row represented a year and each column a month. Then you might want a function to, say, total up individual columns. In that case, the function should have the row and column information available. This can be accomplished by declaring the right kind of formal variable so that the function can pass the array properly. In this case, the array `junk` is an array of 3 arrays of 4 `int`s. As our earlier discussion has implied, this means that `junk` is a pointer to an array of four `int`s. And a variable of this type can be declared in this way:

```
int (*pj)[4];
```

Alternatively, if `pj` is a formal argument to a function, we can declare it this way:

```
int pj[][4];
```

Note that the first set of brackets is empty. The empty brackets identify `pj` as being a pointer. Such a variable can then be used in the same way as `junk`. That is what we have done in the next example, shown in Listing 10.16.

Listing 10.16 *dubarr3.c*

```
/* dubarr3.c -- doubles array elements */
#include <stdio.h>
void dub2 (int ar[][4], int size);
int main(void)
{
```

(continued)

Listing 10.16 *(continued)*

```
    static int junk[3][4] = {
            {2,4,5,8},
            {3,5,6,9},
            {12,10,8,6}
    };
    int i, j;

    dub2(junk,3);
    for (i = 0; i < 3; i++)
    {
        for (j = 0; j < 4; j++)
            printf("%5d", junk[i][j]);
        putchar('\n');
    }
    return 0;
}

void dub2 (int ar[][4], int size)    /* or int (*ar)[4] */
{
    int i, j;

    for (i = 0; i < size; i++)
        for (j = 0; j < 4; j++)
            ar[i][j] *= 2;
}
```

In Listing 10.16 we pass as arguments junk, which is a pointer to the first array, and 3, the number of rows. The dub2() function then treats ar as an array of arrays of 4 ints. The number of columns is built into the function, but the number of rows is left open. The same function will work with, say, a 12-by-4 array if 12 is passed as the number of rows. That's because size is the number of elements; but, since each element is an array, or row, size becomes the number of rows.

Note that ar is used in the same fashion as junk is used in main(). This is possible because ar and junk are the same type: pointer to array-of-four-ints.

Here is the output:

```
 4    8   10   16
 6   10   12   18
24   20   16   12
```

Be aware that the following declaration will not work properly:

```
int ar[][]; /* faulty declaration */
```

Recall that the compiler converts array notation to pointer notation. This means, for example, that ar[1] will become ar+1. But for the compiler to evaluate this, it needs to know what size of object ar points to. The declaration

```
int ar[][4];
```

says that ar points to an array of 4 ints, hence to an object 8 bytes long on our system. So ar+1 means "add 8 bytes to the address." With the empty-bracket version, the compiler would not know what to do.

You can also include a size in the other bracket pair, but it is ignored:

```
void dub2(ar, n)
int ar[3][4];     /* the 3 is ignored */
int n;
```

In general, to declare a pointer corresponding to an *N*-dimensional array, you must provide values for all but the left-most set of brackets.

Planning a Program

Now that you've seen the mechanics of writing array functions, let's try a more programming-oriented example. Our self-appointed task is to write a program that reads numbers into an array, prints the entered numbers, and reports the average. To make the program more realistic, we'll require that it allow the user to terminate input, if desired, before the array is filled. This will enable the program to process any number of items up to a maximum determined by the array size. Also, we'll want to avoid calculating the average if no numbers are entered.

General Plan

Conceptually, we expect the program to perform three major tasks: reading in a set of numbers, printing the set of numbers, and calculating the average. Now that you know how to process arrays with functions, let's use functions to modularize the work. As a first pass, we can visualize the program as shown in Listing 10.17.

Listing 10.17 *draft1.c*

```
/* draft1.c -- first draft of program skeleton */
#include <stdio.h>
#define MAX 25
void read_array(double ar[]);
void show_array(double ar[]);
double mean(double ar[]);
int main(void)
{
   double data[MAX];

   read_array(data);
   show_array(data);
   printf("The average is %.2lf.\n", mean(data));
   return 0;
}
```

Now we have a modular program, but this draft doesn't handle data communication well. For instance, the read_array() function should know the maximum number of items that it is allowed to read. Thus, it should also take MAX as an argument. Incidentally, the fact that data is a pointer means that the read_array() function will modify the data array in main() directly, which is exactly what we want for this function.

Similarly, the show_array() and mean() functions should know how big an array they are using. Thus, they each need an additional argument. But, in general, this argument should not be MAX, since the user may enter fewer numbers. We can use a variable size to represent the actual number of items entered; it can be the second argument to these two functions.

This raises a new problem: How does main() know what size is? One solution is to have the read_array() function return that value. That is, it takes as arguments the array to be filled and the maximum number of values that the array holds. It then reads data into the array and returns the actual number of items read. If this number is zero, we can skip the rest of the program. This line of thought leads to a second draft for the skeleton, which we show in Listing 10.18.

Listing 10.18 draft2.c

```c
/* draft2.c -- second top-level draft for the program */
#include <stdio.h>
#define MAX 25
int read_array(double ar[], int limit);
void show_array(double ar[], int n);
double mean(double ar[], int n);
int main(void)
{
  double data[MAX];
  int size;
  double average;

  size = read_array(data, MAX);
  if (size == 0)
      printf("No data. Bye.\n");
  else
  {
      printf("The following numbers were entered:\n\n");
      show_array(data, size);
      printf("\nThe average of these values is %.2f.\n",
          mean(data, size));
  }
  return 0;
}
```

Note that we changed the prototype for read_array() to reflect that it now has a return value. Now we have the overall design for the program and its data flow, and we can turn to the individual functions.

The *read_array( )* Function

The read_array() function is the most ambitious of the three. It should read in values until the array is filled or until the user wants to stop, whichever occurs first. The main question is how to let the user inform the program that he or she is finished. We can use the properties of scanf() to help here. Recall that scanf() returns the number of values successfully read. Nonnumeric input or end of file causes it to return 0 or EOF, respectively. Therefore, we can terminate input if scanf() doesn't return the value 1. Also, we can use a counter to keep track of the number of entries so that we can terminate input if the counter exceeds the size of the array. Here's one approach:

```
int read_array(double ar[], int limit)
{
   int i = 0;

   printf("Enter up to %d numbers. To terminate\n", limit);
   printf("earlier, enter a letter or EOF.\n");
   while (i < limit && scanf("%lf", &ar[i]) == 1)
        i++;
   return i;
}
```

This approach looks simple enough, but there are two subtle points to note. The first is that the test i < limit comes first. Recall that the && operator guarantees that the second operand is not evaluated if the first operand is false. This means that if i equals limit, the expression scanf("%lf", &ar[i]) == 1 is not evaluated. This, in turn, means that the scanf() function is not called, which is good. Suppose that we'd used the opposite order:

```
while ( scanf("%lf", &ar[i]) == 1 && i < limit)
```

In this case, scanf() reads a value into ar[limit] before finding out that it has gone too far. Remember, because array numbering begins with 0, ar[limit] is one position past the end of the array. You don't want to put data there!

The second subtle point is that the loop increments i after reading a value into ar[i]. This makes i one greater than the index of the last array element filled. Because indexing begins with 0, i at that point equals the number of array items, not the array index. This is convenient because the number of array items is the value we wish to return.

If you like, you can use pointers more explicitly. For instance, you could use the following input loop:

```
while (i < limit && scanf("%lf", ar++) == 1)
      i++;
```

Recall that scanf() requires the address of the location that is to receive the data. Initially, ar holds the address of the first element of the array, so the first time through the loop scanf() places a number in the first element of the array. Then the increment operator increases ar so that it points to the next element of the array, thus preparing for the next loop cycle.

The *show_array( )* Function

Next, we want a function to display the array values. We already have written one for Listing 10.10. A problem with that function, however, is that it prints everything on one line. Here we have more data, so we would like to insert some newline characters.

One scheme is to use a `for` loop as before and to print a newline after every sixth value. We can do this by using the modulus operator (**%**):

```
void show_array(double ar[], int n)
{
  int i;

  for (i = 0; i < n; i++)
  {
      printf("%10.2f ", ar[i]);
      if (i % 6 == 5)
          putchar('\n');
  }
  if (i % 6 != 0)
      putchar('\n');
}
```

Since i starts at 0, i % 6 first becomes 5 after six values have been printed. The expression subsequently becomes 5 after each additional six values have been printed.

The `if (i % 6 != 0)` test causes a newline to be printed after all the values have been printed, unless the last value printed was already at the end of a line—in which case the loop itself prints a newline. If i % 6 is 5 inside the loop, the i++ operation at loop's end causes i % 6 to be 0 after leaving the loop.

The *mean( )* Function

Finding the mean is a simple problem. We can use a `for` loop to sum the numbers and then divide by the total number of items to get the average.

```
double mean(double ar[], int n)
{
  int i;
  double total = 0;

  for (i = 0; i < n ; i++)
      total += ar[i];
  return (total / n);
}
```

The only potential trouble spot is if n is 0 because dividing by 0 is a no-no. The `main()` function shields `mean()` from this possibility.

The Result

Putting the parts together results in the program shown in Listing 10.19.

Listing 10.19 *mean.c*

```
/* mean.c -- finds the mean of a set of numbers */
#include <stdio.h>
#define MAX 25
int read_array(double ar[], int limit);
void show_array(double ar[], int n);
double mean(double ar[], int n);
int main(void)
{
  double data[MAX];
  int size;
  double average;

  size = read_array(data, MAX);
  if (size == 0)
      printf("No data. Bye.\n");
  else
  {
      printf("The following numbers were entered:\n\n");
      show_array(data, size);
      printf("\nThe average of these values is %.2f.\n",
          mean(data, size));
  }
  return 0;
}
int read_array(double ar[], int limit)
{
  int i = 0;

  printf("Enter up to %d numbers. To terminate\n", limit);
  printf("earlier, enter a letter or EOF.\n");
  while (i < limit  && scanf("%lf", &ar[i]) == 1)
      i++;
  return i;
}
```

```
void show_array(double ar[], int n)
{
  int i;

  for (i = 0; i < n; i++)
  {
      printf("%10.2f ", ar[i]);
      if (i % 6 == 5)
          putchar('\n');
  }
  if (i % 6 != 0)
      putchar('\n');
}
double mean(double ar[], int n)
{
  int i;
  double total = 0;

  for (i = 0; i < n ; i++)
      total += ar[i];
  return (total/n);
}
```

Here's a sample run:

```
Enter up to 25 numbers. To terminate
earlier, enter a letter or EOF.
1 2 3 4 5 6 7 8 9 10 q
The following numbers were entered:
      1.00       2.00       3.00      4.00      5.00      6.00
      7.00       8.00       9.00     10.00
The average of these values is 5.50.
```

Chapter Summary

An *array* is a set of elements all having the same data type. Array elements are stored sequentially in memory and are accessed by using an integer index (or offset). In C, the first element of an array has an index of 0, so the final element in an array of n elements has an index of n - 1.

To declare a simple *one-dimensional array*, use this form:

```
type name[size];
```

Here, `type` is the data type for each and every element, `name` is the name of the array, and `size` is the number of elements.

C interprets the name of an array to be the address of the first element of the array. In other terms, the name of an array is equivalent to a pointer to the first element. In general, arrays and pointers are closely connected. If `ar` is an array, then the expressions `ar[i]` and `*(ar + i)` are equivalent.

C does not allow entire arrays to be passed as function arguments, but you can pass the address of an array. The function then can use this address to manipulate the original array. You can use either array notation or pointer notation in the called function. In either case, you're actually using a pointer variable.

Adding an integer to a pointer or incrementing a pointer changes the value of the pointer by the number of bytes of the object being pointed to. That is, if `pd` points to an 8-byte `double` value in an array, adding 1 to `pd` increases its value by 8 so that it will point to the next element of the array.

Two-dimensional arrays represent an array of arrays. For instance, the declaration

```
double sales[5][12];
```

creates an array `sales` having 5 elements, each of which is an array of 12 `floats`. The first of these one-dimensional arrays can be referred to as `sales[0]`, the second as `sales[1]`, and so on, with each being an array of 12 `ints`. Use a second index to access a particular element in these arrays. For instance, `sales[2][5]` is the sixth element of `sales[2]`, and `sales[2]` is the third element of `sales`.

We've used `int` arrays and `double` arrays in this discussion, but the same concepts apply to other types. Character strings, however, have many special rules. This stems from the fact that the terminal null character in a string provides a way for functions to detect the end of a string without being passed a size. We will look at character strings in detail in Chapter 11.

Review Questions

1. What will this program print?

```
#include <stdio.h>
char ref[] = { 'D', 'O', 'L', 'T'};
int main(void)
```

```
{
    char *ptr;
    int index;

    for (index = 0, ptr = ref; index < 4; index++, ptr++)
        printf("%c %c\n", ref[index], *ptr);
}
```

2. In Question 1, of what is `ref` the address? What about `ref + 1`? What does `++ref` point to?

3. What is the value of `*ptr` and of `*(ptr + 2)` in each case?

   a. ```
      int *ptr;
      static int torf[2][2] = {12, 14, 16};
      ptr = torf[0];
      ```

   b. ```
      int *ptr;
      static int fort[2][2] = { {12}, {14,16} };
      ptr = fort[0];
      ```

4. Create an appropriate declaration for each of the following variables:

   a. `digits` is an array of 10 `int`s.

   b. `rates` is an array of 6 `float`s.

   c. `mat` is an array of 3 arrays of 5 integers.

   d. `pstr` is a pointer to an array of 20 `char`s.

   e. `psa` is an array of 20 pointers to `char`.

5. What is the index range for a 10-element array?

Programming Exercises

1. Modify the rain program in Listing 10.11 so that it does the calculations using pointers instead of subscripts. (You still have to declare and initialize the array.)

2. Write a program that initializes an array and then copies the contents of the array into two other arrays. (All three arrays should be declared in the main program.) To make the first copy, use a function with array notation. To make the second copy, use a function with pointer notation and pointer incrementing. Have each function take as arguments the name of the source array, the name of the target array, and the number of elements to be copied.

3. Write a function that returns the largest value stored in an array. Test the function in a simple program.

4. Write a function that returns the index of the largest value stored in an array. Test the function in a simple program.

5. Write a function that returns the difference between the largest and smallest elements of an array. Test the function in a simple program.

6. Write a program that initializes a two-dimensional array and uses one of the copy functions from Exercise 2 to copy it to a second two-dimensional array. (Since a two-dimensional array is an array of arrays, a one-dimensional copy function can be used with each subarray.)

7. Use a copy function from Exercise 2 to copy the 3rd through 5th elements of a 7-element array into a 3-element array. The function itself need not be altered; just choose the right actual arguments. (The actual arguments need not be an array name and array size. They only have to be the address of an array element and a number of elements to be processed.)

8. Write a function that sets each element in an array to the sum of the corresponding elements in two other arrays. That is, if array 1 has the values 2, 4, 5, 8 and array 2 has the values 1, 0, 4, 6, the function assigns array 3 the values 3, 4, 9, 12. The function should take three array names and an array size as arguments. Test the function in a simple program.

9. Write a program that declares a 3-by-5 array and initializes it to some values of your choice. Have the program print the values, double all the values, and then display the new values. Write a function to do the displaying and a second function to do the doubling. Have the functions take the array name and the number of rows as arguments.

10. Rewrite the rain program in Listing 10.11 so that the main tasks are performed by functions instead of in `main()`.

11. Write a program that prompts the user to enter three sets of five `double` numbers each. The program should accomplish all of the following:

   a. Store the information in a 3-by-5 array.
   b. Compute the average of each set of 5 values.
   c. Compute the average of the values.
   d. Determine the largest value of the 15 values.
   e. Report the results.

   Each major task should be handled by a separate function.

11

Character Strings and String Functions

Functions

▶ gets( ), puts( ), strcat( ), stremp( )

▶ strcpy( ), sprint( ), strchr( ), isalnum( )

▶ isalpha( ), iscntrl( ), isdigit( ), isgraph( )

▶ islower( ), isprint( ), ispunct( ), isspace( )

▶ isupper( ), isxdigit( )

In this chapter you learn more about creating and using strings. You use several string and character functions from the C library and practice creating your own string functions. Also, you learn how to use command-line arguments.

Charater strings are one of the most useful and important data
types in C. You have been using character strings all along, but
there still is much to learn about them. Of course, you already
know the most basic fact: a *character string* is a char array terminated with a null character (\0). This chapter discusses the nature of
strings, how to declare and initialize strings, how to get them into and out
of programs, and how to manipulate strings.

Listing 11.1 presents a busy program that illustrates several ways to set
up strings, read them, and print them. It uses two new functions: gets(),
which reads a string, and puts(), which prints a string. (You probably
notice a family resemblance to getchar() and putchar().) The rest of the
program should look fairly familiar.

Listing 11.1 *strings.c*

```
/* strings.c -- stringing the user along */
#include <stdio.h>
#define MSG "You must have many talents. Tell me some."
                          /* a symbolic string constant */
#define LIM  5
#define LINELEN 81         /* maximum string length + 1  */
char m1[] = "Just limit yourself to one line's worth.";
                          /* initializing an external  */
                          /* character array           */
char *m2 = "If you can't think of anything, fake it.";
                          /* initializing an external  */
                          /* character pointer         */
int main(void)
{
   char name[LINELEN];
```

(continued)

Listing 11.1 *(continued)*

```
    static char talents[LINELEN];
    int i;
    int count = 0;
    char *m3 = "\nEnough about me -- what's your name?";
                        /* initializing a pointer      */
    static char *mytal[LIM] = {  "Adding numbers swiftly",
        "Multiplying accurately", "Stashing data",
        "Following instructions to the letter",
        "Understanding the C language"};
                            /* initializing an array of   */
                            /* strings                    */

    printf("Hi! I'm Clyde the Computer. I have many talents.\n");

    printf("Let me tell you some of them.\n");
    puts("What were they? Ah, yes, here's a partial list.");
    for (i = 0; i < LIM; i++)
        puts(mytal[i]);  /* print list of computer talents */
    puts(m3);
    gets(name);
    printf("Well, %s, %s\n", name, MSG);
    printf("%s\n%s\n", m1, m2);
    gets(talents);
    puts("Let's see if I've got that list:");
    puts(talents);
    printf("Thanks for the information, %s.\n", name);
    return 0;
}
```

To show you what this program does, here is a sample run:

```
Hi! I'm Clyde the Computer. I have many talents.
Let me tell you some of them.
What were they? Ah, yes, here's a partial list.
Adding numbers swiftly
Multiplying accurately
Stashing data
Following instructions to the letter
Understanding the C language
```

```
Enough about me -- what's your name?
Nigel Barntwit
Well, Nigel Barntwit, You must have many talents. Tell me some.
Just limit yourself to one line's worth.
If you can't think of anything, fake it.
Fencing, yodeling, malingering, cheese tasting, and sighing.
Let's see if I've got that list:
Fencing, yodeling, malingering, cheese tasting, and sighing.
Thanks for the information, Nigel Barntwit.
```

Let's see how Listing 11.1 works. However, rather than go through it line by line, we will take a more encompassing approach. First, we will look at ways of defining a string within a program. Then we will see what is involved in reading a string into a program. Finally, we will study ways to output a string.

Defining Strings within a Program

As you probably noticed when you read Listing 11.1, there are many ways to define a string. We are going to look at the principal ways now: using string constants, using char arrays, using char pointers, and using arrays of character strings. A program should make sure that there is a place to store a string, and we will take up that topic, too.

Character String Constants

A *string constant* is anything enclosed in double quotation marks. The enclosed characters, plus a terminating \0 character automatically provided by the compiler, are stored in memory as a character string. Our program uses several such character string constants, most often as arguments for the printf() and puts() functions. Note, too, that we can #define character string constants.

If you want to use a double quotation mark within a string, precede the quotation mark with a backslash:

```
printf("\"Run, Spot, run!\" exclaimed Dick.\n");
```

This produces the output:

```
"Run, Spot, run!" exclaimed Dick.
```

Character string constants are placed in the *static storage* class. Static storage means that if you use a string constant in a function, the string is stored just once and lasts for the duration of the program, even if the function is called several times. The entire quoted phrase acts as a pointer to where the string is stored. This action is analogous to the name of an array acting as a pointer to the array's location. If this is true, what kind of output should the program in Listing 11.2 produce?

Listing 11.2 *quotes.c*

```
/* quotes.c -- strings as pointers */
#include <stdio.h>
int main(void)
{
    printf(" %s, %u, %c\n", "We", "love", *"figs");
    return 0;
}
```

The %s format should print the string We. The %u format produces an unsigned integer. Thus, if the phrase "love" is an address, then %u should print the address of the first character in the string. (Type unsigned is not guaranteed to be large enough to hold addresses, so you may prefer to use the ANSI C %p specifier for pointers.) Finally, *"figs" should produce the value of the address pointed to, which should be the first character of the string "figs". Does this really happen? Well, here is the output:

```
We, 3798, f
```

Character String Arrays and Initialization

When you define a character string array, you must let the compiler know how much space is needed. One way to do this is to initialize the array with a string constant. Since automatic arrays cannot be initialized in older C implementations, you must use static or external arrays for this purpose. For example, the following declaration initializes the external array m1 to the characters of the indicated string:

```
char m1[] = "Just limit yourself to one line's worth.";
```

This form of initialization is short for the standard array initialization form:

```
char m1[] = { 'J', 'u', 's', 't', ' ', 'l', 'i', 'm', 'i',
```

```
    't', ' ', 'y', 'o', 'u', 'r', 's', 'e', 'l',
    'f', ' ', 't', 'o', ' ', 'o', 'n', 'e', ' ',
    'l', 'i', 'n', 'e', '\"', 's', ' ', 'w', 'o', 'r',
    't', 'h', '.', '\0'
};
```

Note the closing null character. Without it, you have a character array, but not a string. For either form (and we do recommend the first), the compiler counts the characters and sizes the array accordingly. Initializing character arrays is one case when it really does make sense to let the compiler determine the array size.

Just as for other arrays, the array name m1 yields the address of the first element of the array:

```
m1 == &m1[0] , *m1 == 'J', and *(m1+1) == m1[1] == 'u'
```

Indeed, you can use pointer notation to set up a string. For example, we used this declaration:

```
char *m3 = "\nEnough about me -- what's your name?";
```

This declaration is very nearly the same as:

```
static char m3[] = "\nEnough about me -- what's your name?"
```

Both declarations amount to saying that m3 is a pointer to the indicated string. In both cases, the string itself determines the amount of storage set aside for the string. Nonetheless, the forms are not identical.

Array versus Pointer

What is the difference, then, between an array and a pointer form? The array form (m3[]) causes an array of 38 elements (one for each character plus one for the terminating '\0') to be created in static storage. Each element is initialized to the corresponding character. Hereafter, the compiler will recognize the name m3 as a synonym for the address of the first array element, &m3[0]. One important point here is that in the array form, m3 is an address *constant*. You can't change m3 because that would mean changing the location (address) where the array is stored. You can use operations like m3+1 to identify the next element in an array, but ++m3 is not allowed. The increment operator can be used only with the names of variables, not with constants.

The pointer form (*m3) also causes 38 elements in static storage to be set aside for the string. In addition, it sets aside one more storage location for the pointer *variable* m3. This variable initially points to the first character of the string, but the value can be changed. Thus, you can use the increment operator. For instance, ++m3 would point to the second character (E). Note that *m3 does not have to be declared as static. The reason is that you are not initializing an array of 38 elements; rather, you are initializing a single pointer variable. There are no storage class restrictions for initializing ordinary, nonarray variables, either in K&R C or in ANSI C.

Are these differences important? Often they are not, but it depends on what you try to do. See the following discussion for some examples.

Array and Pointer Differences

Let's examine the differences between initializing a character array to hold a string and initializing a pointer to point to a string. (By "pointing to a string," we really mean pointing to the first character of a string.) For example, consider these two declarations:

```
static char heart[] = "I love Tillie!";
char *head = "I love Millie!";
```

The chief difference is that the array name heart is a constant, while the pointer head is a variable. What practical difference does this make?

First, both can use pointer addition:

```
for (i = 0; i < 6; i++)
    putchar(*(heart + i));
putchar('\n');
for (i = 0; i < 6; i++)
    putchar(*(head + i));
putchar('\n');
```

The output is

```
I love
I love
```

Only the pointer version, however, can use the increment operator:

```
while (*(head) != '\0') /* stop at end of string          */
    putchar(*(head++);  /* print character, advance pointer */
```

This produces

```
I love Millie!
```

Suppose you want head to agree with heart. You can say this:

```
head = heart;   /* head now points to the array heart */
```

But you cannot say this:

```
heart = head;   /* illegal construction */
```

The situation is analogous to x = 3; versus 3 = x;. The left side of the as-signment statement must be a variable or, more generally, an lvalue, such as *p_int. Incidentally, head = heart; does not make the Millie string vanish; it just changes the address stored in head. But, unless you've saved the address of "I love Millie!" elsewhere, you won't be able to access that string once head points to another location.

There is a way to alter the heart message—go into the array itself:

```
heart[7]= 'M';
```

or

```
*(heart + 7) = 'M';
```

The *elements* of an array are variables, but the *name* is not a variable.

Specifying Storage Explicitly

Another way to set up storage is to be explicit. In the external declaration, we could have said

```
char m1[44] = "Just limit yourself to one line's worth.";
```

instead of

```
char m1[] = "Just limit yourself to one line's worth.";
```

Just be sure that the number of elements is at least one more (that null character again) than the string length. As with other static or external arrays, any unused elements are automatically initialized to 0 (which in char form is the null character, not the zero digit character). See Figure 11.1.

Note that in our program we had to assign a size for the array name:

```
char name[81];
```

Since the contents for name are to be read when the program runs, the compiler has no way of knowing in advance how much space to set aside unless we tell it. There is no string constant present whose characters the

Figure 11.1 *Initializing an array*

```
static char pets[12] = "nice cat.";
```

compiler can count. So we gambled that 80 characters would be enough to hold the user's name. Incidentally, the array size must evaluate to an integer constant. You can't use a variable that gets set at run time. The array size is locked into the program.

Arrays of Character Strings

Often it is convenient to have an array of character strings. Then you can use a subscript to access several different strings. We used this example in Listing 11.1:

```
static char *mytal[LIM] = {"Adding numbers swiftly",
        "Multiplying accurately", "Stashing data",
        "Following instructions to the letter",
        "Understanding the C language"};
```

Let's study this declaration. Because LIM is 5, we can say that mytal is an array of 5 pointers-to-char. The first pointer is mytal[0], and it points to the first character of the first string. The second pointer is mytal[1], and it points to the beginning of the second string. In general, each pointer points to the first character of the corresponding string:

```
*mytal[0] == 'A', *mytal[1] == 'M', *mytal[2] == 'S'
```

and so on. You can think of mytal[0] as representing the first string and *mytal[0] as the first character of the first string. Because of the relationship between array notation and pointers, you also can use mytal[0][0] to represent the first character of the first string, even though mytal is not defined as a two-dimensional array.

The initialization follows the rules for arrays. The braced portion is equivalent to

```
{{...}, {...},...,{...} };
```

where the ellipses indicate the stuff we were too lazy to type in. The main point is that the first set of double quotation marks corresponds to a brace-pair and thus is used to initialize the first character string pointer. The next set of double quotation marks initializes the second pointer, and so on. A comma separates adjacent strings.

Again, we could have been explicit about the size of the character strings by using a declaration like this:

```
static char mytal_2[LIM][LINLIM];
```

One difference is that this second choice sets up a *rectangular* array with all the rows of the same length. The following choice, however, sets up a *ragged* array, with each row's length determined by the string it was initialized to:

```
static char *mytal[LIM];
```

This ragged array doesn't waste any storage space. Figure 11.2 shows the two kinds of arrays.

Another difference is that `mytal` and `mytal_2` have different types; `mytal` is an array of pointers-to-`char`, while `mytal_2` is an array of arrays of `char`. In short, `mytal` holds 5 addresses, while `mytal_2` holds 5 complete character arrays.

Pointers and Strings

Perhaps you noticed an occasional reference to pointers in our discussion of strings. Most C operations for strings actually work with pointers. Consider, for example, the instructive program shown in Listing 11.3.

Listing 11.3 p_and_s.c

```
/* p_and_s.c -- pointers and strings */
#include <stdio.h>
int main(void)
{
   static char *mesg = "Don't be a fool!";
   static char *copy;
```

(continued)

Listing 11.3 *(continued)*

```
copy = mesg;
printf("%s\n", copy);
printf("mesg = %s; &mesg = %u; value = %u\n",
    mesg, &mesg, mesg);
printf("copy = %s; &copy = %u; value = %u\n",
    copy, &copy, copy);
return 0;
}
```

Note: Use %p instead of &u if your compiler supports that form.

Figure 11.2 *Rectangular versus ragged array*

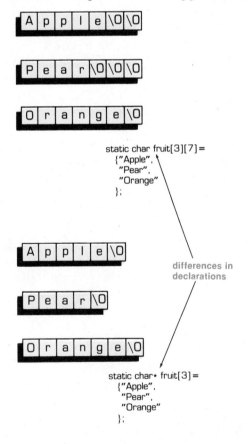

Looking at this program, you might think that it makes a copy of the string "Don't be a fool!", and your first glance at the output might seem to confirm this guess:

```
Don't be a fool!
mesg = Don't be a fool!; &mesg = 32; value = 14
copy = Don't be a fool!; &copy = 34; value = 14
```

But study the `printf()` output. First, `mesg` and `copy` are printed as strings (`%s`). No surprises here; all the strings are "Don't be a fool!".

The next item on each line is the address of the specified pointer. The two pointers `mesg` and `copy` are stored in locations `32` and `34`, respectively.

Now notice the final item, the one we called `value`. It is the value of the specified pointer. The value of the pointer is the address it contains. We see that `mesg` points to location `14`, and so does `copy`. Thus, the string itself was never copied. All that `copy = mesg;` does is produce a second pointer pointing to the very same string.

Why all this pussyfooting around? Why not just copy the whole string? Well, ask yourself, which is more efficient: copying one address or copying, say, 50 separate elements? Often, the address is all that is needed to get the job done.

Now that we have discussed defining strings within a program, let's turn to strings that are read in.

String Input

If you wish to read a string into a program, you must first set aside space to store the string and then use an input function to fetch the string.

Creating Space

The first order of business is setting up a place to put the string once it is read. As we mentioned earlier, this means that you need to allot sufficient storage to hold whatever strings you expect to read. Don't expect the computer to count the string length as it is read and then allot space for it. The computer won't (unless you write a function to do so). For example, if you try something like this,

```
static char *name;

scanf("%s", name);
```

it probably will get by the compiler. But when the name is read, the name will be written over data or code in your program. Most programmers regard this as highly humorous, but only in other people's programs.

The simplest course is to include an explicit array size in the declaration:

```
char name[81];
```

Another possibility is to use the C library functions that allocate memory, and we'll touch on those in Chapter 16. In our program, we used an automatic array for name. You can do that even under K&R C, since you don't have to initialize the array.

Once you have set aside space for the string, you can read the string. The C library provides a trio of functions that can read strings: scanf(), gets(), and fgets(). The last is file oriented, and we'll defer discussion of it until Chapter 12. The scanf() and gets() functions both can read strings. The more commonly used is gets(), which we discuss first.

The *gets( )* Function

The gets() (*get* string) function is very handy for interactive programs. It gets a string from your system's standard input device, normally your keyboard. Since a string has no predetermined length, gets() needs a way to know when to stop. Its method is to read characters until it reaches a newline (\n) character, which you generate by pressing the Enter key. It takes all the characters up to (but not including) the newline, tacks on a null character (\0), and gives the string to the calling program. The newline character itself is read and discarded so that the next read will begin at the start of the next line. Listing 11.4 shows a simple means of using gets().

Listing 11.4   name1.c

```
/* name1.c -- reads a name */
#include <stdio.h>
#define MAX 81
int main(void)
{
   char name[MAX];          /* allot space             */

   printf("Hi, what's your name?\n");
```

```
    gets(name);                 /* place string into name array */
    printf("Nice name, %s.\n", name);
    return 0;
}
```

Listing 11.4 will accept any name (including spaces) up to 80 characters. (Remember to reserve one space for the \0.) Note that we want gets() to affect something (name) in the calling function. This means that we should use an address as an argument; and, of course, the name of an array *is* an address.

The gets() function is more sophisticated than this last example suggests. Look at Listing 11.5.

Listing 11.5 *name2.c*

```
/* name2.c -- reads a name */
#include <stdio.h>
#define MAX 81
int main(void)
{
    char name[MAX];
    char *ptr, *gets(char *);

    printf("Hi, what's your name?\n");
    ptr = gets(name);
    printf("%s? Ah! %s!\n", name, ptr);
    return 0;
}
```

Here is a sample interchange:

```
Hi, what's your name?
Tony de Tuna
Tony de Tuna? Ah! Tony de Tuna!
```

The `gets()` function gets input in two ways:

► It uses an address to feed the string into `name`.

► It uses the `return` keyword to return the address of the string, and the program assigns that address to `ptr`. Notice that `ptr` is a pointer to `char`. This means that `gets()` must return a value that is a pointer to `char`. In the declaration section, you can see that we correctly declared `gets()`.

The declaration form

```
char *gets(char *);
```

says that `gets()` is a function (hence the parentheses) of type pointer-to-char (hence the * and `char`). We got away without this declaration in `name1` because we never tried to use the return value of `gets()`. The prototype also indicates that `gets()` takes a string argument.

ANSI C mandates that the `stdio.h` header file include a declaration for `gets()`. Thus, with newer implementations, you need not declare the function yourself as long as you remember to include that header file.

The design of a `gets()` function could look something like this:

```
char *gets(char *s)
{
    .
    .
    .
    return(s);
}
```

Note that `gets()` returns the same pointer that was passed to it. There is but one copy of the input string—the one placed at the address passed as a function argument. The actual design is slightly more complicated because `gets()` has two possible returns. If everything goes well, then it returns the address of the read string, as we have said. If something goes wrong or if `gets()` encounters EOF, it returns a null, or zero, address. This null address is called the *null pointer* and is represented in `stdio.h` by the defined constant `NULL`. Thus, `gets()` incorporates a bit of error-checking, making it convenient to use constructions like this:

```
while (gets(name) != NULL)
```

Such a construction allows you to both check for EOF and read a value. If EOF is encountered, nothing is read into `name`. This two-pronged approach is more compact than that allowed by `getchar()`, which has a `return` but no argument:

```
while ((ch = getchar()) != EOF)
```

By the way, don't confuse the NULL pointer with the null character. The NULL pointer is an address, while the null character is a type char data object with the value zero.

One weakness of gets() is that it doesn't check to see if the input actually fits into the reserved storage area. Extra characters simply overflow into the adjoining memory. The fgets() function (Chapter 12) improves on this questionable behavior by letting you specify an upper limit for the number of characters to be read.

The *scanf( )* Function

You've used scanf() with the %s format before to read a string. The chief difference between scanf() and gets() lies in how they decide when they have reached the end of the string: scanf() is more of a "get word" than a "get string" function. The gets() function, as you've seen, takes in all the characters up to the first newline. The scanf() function has two choices. For either choice, the string starts at the first nonwhitespace character encountered. If you use the %s format, the string runs up to (but not including) the next whitespace character (blank, tab, or newline). If you specify a field width, as in %10s, the scanf() collects up to 10 characters or up to the first whitespace character, whichever comes first. See Figure 11.3.

Figure 11.3 *Field widths and* scanf( )

Input Statement	Original Input Queue*	Name Contents	Remaining Queue
scanf("%s", name);	Fleebert☐Hup	Fleebert Hup	☐Hup
scanf("%5s", name);	Fleebert☐Hup	Fleeb	ert☐Hup
scanf("%5s", name);	Ann☐Ular	Ann	☐Ular

the ☐ represents the space character

Recall that the scanf() function returns an integer value that equals the number of items successfully read or returns EOF if it encounters the end of file.

Listing 11.6 illustrates how scanf() works when you specify a field width.

```
Listing 11.6   scan_str.c

/* scan_str.c -- using scanf() */
#include <stdio.h>
int main(void)
{
    static char name1[11], name2[11];
    int count;

    printf("Please enter 2 names.\n");
    count = scanf("%5s %10s",name1, name2);
    printf("I read the %d names %s and %s.\n",
            count, name1, name2);
    return 0;
}
```

Here are three runs:

```
Please enter 2 names.
Jesse Jukes
I read the 2 names Jesse and Jukes.

Please enter 2 names.
Liza Applebottham
I read the 2 names Liza and Applebotth.

Please enter 2 names.
Portensia Callowit
I read the 2 names Porte and nsia.
```

In the first example, both names fell within the allowed size limits. In the second example, only the first 10 characters of Applebottham were read because we used a %10s format. In the third example, the last four letters of Portensia went into name2 because the second call to scanf() resumed reading input where the first ended; in this case, that was still inside the word Portensia.

You are better off using gets() to read text from the keyboard. It is easier to use, faster, and more compact. The typical use for scanf() would be reading and converting a mixture of data types in some standard form. For example, if each input line contained the name of a tool, the number in stock, and the cost of the item, you might use scanf(). Or you might throw together a function of your own that did some entry error-checking.

Now let's discuss how to print strings.

String Output

Again, we will use library functions. C recognizes three standard library functions for printing strings. One, `fputs()`, is file oriented, and we'll look at it in Chapter 12. The other two are `puts()` and `printf()`.

The *puts( )* Function

The `puts()` function is very easy to use. Just give it the address of a string for an argument. Listing 11.7 illustrates some of the many ways to do this.

Listing 11.7 *put_out.c*

```
/* put_out.c -- using puts() */
#include <stdio.h>
#define DEF "I am a #defined string."
int main(void)
{
   static char str1[] = "An array was initialized to me.";
   char *str2 = "A pointer was initialized to me.";

   puts("I'm an argument to puts().");
   puts(DEF);
   puts(str1);
   puts(str2);
   puts(&str1[4]);
   puts(str2+4);
   return 0;
}
```

The output is

```
I'm an argument to puts().
I am a #defined string.
An array was initialized to me.
A pointer was initialized to me.
rray was initialized to me.
inter was initialized to me.
```

This example reminds us that phrases in double quotation marks are string constants and are treated as addresses. Also, the names of character array strings are treated as addresses. The expression &str1[4] is the address of the fifth element of the array str1. That element contains the character 'r', and that is what puts() uses for its starting point. Similarly, str2+4 points to the memory cell containing the 'i' of "pointer," and the printing starts there.

How does puts() know when to stop? It stops when it encounters the null character, so there had better be one. Don't try the program in Listing 11.8!

```
Listing 11.8   nono.c

/* nono.c -- no! */
#include <stdio.h>
int main(void)
{
    static c1 = 'A';
    static char dont[] = {'H', 'I', '!', '!' };
    static c2 = 'B';

    puts(dont);    /* dont is not a string */
    return 0;
}
```

Because dont lacks a closing null character, it is not a string, so puts() won't know where to stop. It will just keep printing from memory following dont until it finds a null somewhere. There usually are lots of nulls in memory, and if you're lucky, puts() may find one soon, but don't count on it.

Notice that each string displayed by puts() begins a new line. When puts() finally finds the closing null character, it replaces it with a newline character.

The *printf( )* Function

We discussed printf() pretty thoroughly in Chapter 4. Like puts(), it takes a string address as an argument. The printf() function is less convenient to use than puts(), but it is more versatile because it formats various data types.

One difference is that printf() does not automatically print each string on a new line. Instead, you must indicate where you want new lines. Thus,

```
printf("%s\n", string);
```

has the same effect as

```
puts(string);
```

As you can see, the first form takes more typing. It also takes longer for the computer to execute. On the other hand, `printf()` makes it simple to combine strings for one line of printing. For example,

```
printf("Well, %s, %s\n", name, MSG);
```

combines `Well,` with the user's name and a `#defined` character string, all on one line.

The Do-It-Yourself Option

You aren't limited to the standard C library options for input and output. If you don't have these options or don't like them, you can prepare your own versions, building on `getchar()` and `putchar()`. Suppose you lack a `puts()` function or merely want to try your own hand at writing that function. Listing 11.9 shows one way to do it.

***Listing 11.9** put1.c*

```
/* put1.c -- prints a string */
#include <stdio.h>
void put1(char *string)
{
    while (*string != '\0')
        putchar(*string++);
    putchar('\n');
}
```

The `char` pointer `string` initially points to the first element of the called argument. After the contents of that element are printed, the pointer increments and points to the next element. This goes on until the pointer points to an element containing the null character. Then a newline is tagged on at the end. Remember, the higher precedence of ++ compared to * means that putchar(*string++) prints the value pointed to by string but increments string itself, not the character it points to.

Many C programmers would use the following test for the while loop:

```
while (*string)
```

When string points to the null character, *string has the value 0, which terminates the loop. This approach certainly takes less typing than the previous version. If you are not familiar with C practice, it is less obvious. It may result in more efficient code, depending on the compiler. Regardless of its merits, this idiom is widespread.

Suppose you have a puts(), but you want a new function that also tells you how many characters are printed. As Listing 11.10 demonstrates, it's easy to add that feature.

Listing 11.10 put2.c

```c
/* put2.c -- prints a string and counts characters */
#include <stdio.h>
int put2(char *string)
{
    int count = 0;
    while (*string != '\0')
    {
        putchar(*string++);
        count++;
    }
    putchar('\n');              /* newline not counted */
    return(count);
}
```

The following call prints the string pizza:

```
put2("pizza");
```

The next call also returns a character count that is assigned to num, in this case, the value 5.

```
num = put2("pizza");
```

Listing 11.11 presents a driver using put s1() and put s2(), and showing nested functions.

Listing 11.11   put_put.c

```
/* put_put.c -- nested functions */
#include <stdio.h>
void put1(char *);
int put2();
main(char *)
{
    put1("If I'd as much money as I could spend,");
    printf("I count %d characters.\n",
        put2("I never would cry old chairs to mend."));
    return 0;
}
```

We assume that you'll place the put1() and put2() functions in the same file. Note that we used #include stdio.h because on our system putchar() is defined there, and our new functions use putchar().

Hmm, we are using printf() to print the value of put2(), but in the act of finding the value of put2() the computer first must run it, causing the string to be printed. Here's the output:

```
If I'd as much money as I could spend,
I never would cry old chairs to mend.
I count 37 characters.
```

String Functions

The C library supplies several string-handling functions. We'll look at five of the most useful and common ones: strlen(), strcat(), strcmp(), strcpy(), and sprintf().

The *strlen( )* Function

The strlen() function, as you already know, finds the length of a string. We use it in the next example, a function that shortens lengthy strings:

```
/* fit.c -- procrustean function */
void fit(string,size)
char *string;
int size;
{
    if (strlen(string) > size)
        *(string + size) = '\0';
}
```

Try the fit() function in the test program of Listing 11.12.

Listing 11.12 *test.c*

```
/* test.c -- try the string-shrinking function */
#include <stdio.h>
#include <string.h> /* contains string function declarations */
void fit(char *, int);
int main(void)
{
    static char mesg[] = "Hold on to your hats, hackers.";

    puts(mesg);
    fit(mesg,7);
    puts(mesg);
    return 0;
}
void fit(char *string, int size)
{
    if (strlen(string) > size)
        *(string + size) = '\0';
}
```

The output is this:

```
Hold on to your hats, hackers.
Hold on
```

Our fit() function placed a '\0' character in the eighth element of the array, replacing a blank. The rest of the array is still there, but puts() stops at the first null character and ignores the rest of the array.

The string.h file contains function declarations for the C family of string functions, so we will include it in our examples. *Note*: Some pre-

ANSI systems use `strings.h` instead, while others may lack a string header file entirely.

The *strcat( )* Function

Listing 11.13 illustrates what `strcat()` can do.

Listing 11.13 *str_cat.c*

```
/* str_cat.c -- joins two strings */
#include <stdio.h>
#include <string.h>   /* declares the strcat() function */
#define SIZE 80
int main(void)
{
    static char flower[SIZE];
    static char addon[] = "s smell like old shoes.";

    puts("What is your favorite flower?");
    gets(flower);
    strcat(flower, addon);
    puts(flower);
    puts(addon);
    return 0;
}
```

The output is

```
What is your favorite flower?
Rose
Roses smell like old shoes.
s smell like old shoes.
```

As you can see, `strcat()` (for *str*ing con*cat*enation) takes two strings for arguments. A copy of the second string is tacked onto the end of the first, and this combined version becomes the new first string. The second string is not altered.

Caution! This function does not check to see if the second string will fit in the first array. If you fail to allot enough space for the first array, you will run into problems as excess characters overflow into adjacent memory locations. Of course, you can use `strlen()` to look before you leap, as shown in Listing 11.14.

Listing 11.14 *join_chk.c*

```
/* join_chk.c -- joins two strings, check size first */
#include <stdio.h>
#include <string.h>
#define SIZE 30
int main(void)
{
    static char flower[SIZE];
    static char addon[] = "s smell like old shoes.";

    puts("What is your favorite flower?");
    gets(flower);
    if ((strlen(addon) + strlen(flower) + 1) <= SIZE)
        strcat(flower, addon);
    puts(flower);
    return 0;
}
```

In Listing 11.14 note that we add 1 to the combined lengths to allow space for the null character. Function `strcat()` is type `char *`, that is, a pointer to `char`. It returns the value of its first argument—the address of the first character of the string to which the second string is appended.

The *strcmp()* Function

Suppose you wish to compare someone's response to a stored string, as shown in Listing 11.15.

Listing 11.15 *nogo.c*

```
/* nogo.c -- will this work? */
#include <stdio.h>
#define ANSWER "Grant"
int main(void)
```

```
{
    char try[40];

    puts("Who is buried in Grant's tomb?");
    gets(try);
    while (try != ANSWER)
    {
        puts("No, that's wrong. Try again.");
        gets(try);
    }
    puts("That's right!");
    return 0;
}
```

As nice as this program may look, it will not work correctly. ANSWER and try really are pointers, so the comparison try != ANSWER doesn't check to see if the two strings are the same. Rather, it checks to see if the two strings have the same address. Since ANSWER and try are stored in different locations, the two addresses never are the same, and the user is forever told that he or she is wrong. Such programs tend to discourage people.

What we need is a function that compares string contents, not string addresses. We could devise one, but the job has been done for us with strcmp() (for *string comp*arison). Our revised program is shown in Listing 11.16.

Listing 11.16 *compare.c*

```
/* compare.c -- this will work */
#include <stdio.h>
#include <string.h>    /* declares strcmp() */
#define ANSWER "Grant"
#define MAX 40
int main(void)
{
    char try[MAX];

    puts("Who is buried in Grant's tomb?");
```

(continued)

437

Listing 11.16 (continued)

```
    gets(try);
    while ((strcmp(try,ANSWER) != 0))
    {
        puts("No, that's wrong. Try again.");
        gets(try);
    }
    puts("That's right!");
    return 0;
}
```

Note: Since any nonzero value is "true," some programmers would abbreviate the `while` statement to `while (strcmp(try,ANSWER))`.

From Listing 11.16 you may correctly deduce that `strcmp()` takes two string pointers as arguments and returns a value of 0 if the two strings are the same. Good for you for so deducing.

One of the nice features of `strcmp()` is that it compares strings, not arrays. Thus, although the array `try` occupies 40 memory cells and `"Grant"` only 6 (one for the null character), the comparison looks only at the part of `try` up to its first null character. Thus, `strcmp()` can be used to compare strings stored in arrays of different sizes.

But what if the user answers `"GRANT"` or `"grant"` or `"Ulysses S. Grant"`? The user is told that he or she is wrong. To make a friendlier program, you have to anticipate all possible correct answers. There are some tricks. You can `#define` the answer as `"GRANT"` and write a function that converts all input to uppercase. That eliminates the problem of capitalization, but you still have the other forms to worry about. We leave that as an exercise for you.

What value does `strcmp()` return if the strings are not the same? Listing 11.17 shows a sample.

Listing 11.17 *compback.c*

```
/* compback.c -- strcmp returns */
#include <stdio.h>
#include <string.h>
int main(void)
```

```
{
    printf("%d\n", strcmp("A", "A"));
    printf("%d\n", strcmp("A", "B"));
    printf("%d\n", strcmp("B", "A"));
    printf("%d\n", strcmp("C", "A"));
    printf("%d\n", strcmp("apples", "apple"));
    return 0;
}
```

Here is the output on one system:

```
0
-1
1
1
1
```

Comparing "A" to itself returns a 0. Comparing "A" to "B" gives a -1, and reversing the comparison gives a 1. These results suggest that strcmp() returns a negative number if the first string precedes the second alphabetically and that it returns a positive number if the order is the other way. Thus, comparing "C" to "A" gives a 1. Other systems may return 2—the difference in ASCII code values. The ANSI Standard says that strcmp() returns a negative number if the first string comes before the second alphabetically, returns a 0 if they are the same, and returns a positive number if the first string follows the second alphabetically. The exact numerical values, however, are left open to the implementation.

What if the initial characters are identical? In general, strcmp() moves along until it finds the first pair of disagreeing characters. It then returns the corresponding code. For instance, in the very last example, "apples" and "apple" agree until the final s of the first string. This matches up with the sixth character in "apple", which is the null character, ASCII 0. Since the null character is the very first character in the ASCII sequence, s comes after it, and the function returns a positive value.

The last comparison points out that strcmp() compares all characters, not just letters. So instead of saying the comparison is alphabetic, we should say that strcmp() goes by the machine *collating sequence*. This means that characters are compared according to their numeric representation, typically the ASCII values. In ASCII, the codes for uppercase letters precede those for lowercase letters. Thus, strcmp("A", "a") is negative.

Most often, you won't care about the exact value returned. You just want to know if it is zero or nonzero, that is, whether there is a match or not. Or you may be trying to sort the strings alphabetically, in which case you want to know if the comparison is positive, negative, or zero.

In Listing 11.18, we can use the `strcmp()` function for checking to see if a program should stop reading input.

```
Listing 11.18  input.c

/* input.c -- beginning of some program */
#include <stdio.h>
#include <string.h>
#define SIZE 81
#define LIM 100
#define STOP ""  /* a null string */
int main(void)
{
   static char input[LIM][SIZE];
   int ct = 0;

   while (ct < LIM && gets(input[ct]) != NULL &&
          strcmp(input[ct],STOP) != 0)
   {
      .
      .
      .
      ct++;
   }
   return 0;
}
```

This program quits reading input when it encounters an EOF character (`gets()` returns `NULL` in that case), or when you press the Enter key at the beginning of a line (you feed in an empty string), or when you reach the limit `LIM`. Entering the empty line gives the user an easy way to terminate the entry phase. Alternatively, `STOP` could be redefined to be some other string, such as `"stop"` or `"quit"`.

The *strcpy( )* Function

We've said that if `pts1` and `pts2` are both pointers to strings, then the expression

```
    pts2 = pts1;
```

copies only the address of a string, not the string itself. Suppose, though, that you do want to copy a string. Then you can use the strcpy() function. It works as shown in Listing 11.19.

Listing 11.19 *copy1.c*

```
/* copy1.c -- strcpy() demo */
#include <stdio.h>
#include <string.h>  /* declares strcpy() */
#define WORDS  "Please reconsider your last entry."
#define SIZE 40
int main(void)
{
    static char *orig = WORDS;
    static char copy[SIZE] = "reserved space";

    puts(orig);
    puts(copy);
    strcpy(copy, orig);
    puts(orig);
    puts(copy);
    return 0;
}
```

Here is the output:

```
Please reconsider your last entry.
reserved space
Please reconsider your last entry.
Please reconsider your last entry.
```

You can see that the string pointed to by the second argument (orig) is copied into the array pointed to by the first argument (copy). The copy is called the *target*, and the original string is called the *source*. You can remember the order of the arguments by noting that it is the same as the order in an assignment statement: the target string is on the left. Note that strcpy() writes over any existing contents of the target string.

It is your responsibility to ensure that the destination array has enough room to copy the source. That is why we used the declaration

```
       static char copy[SIZE];
```

and not

```
       static char *copy;    /* allots no space for string */
```

In short, `strcpy()` takes two string pointers as arguments. The second pointer, which points to the original string, can be a declared pointer, an array name, or a string constant. But the first pointer, which points to the copy, should point to a data object, such as an array, roomy enough to hold the string.

The `strcpy()` function has two more properties that you may find useful. First, it is type `char *`. It returns the value of its first argument—the address of a character. Second, the first argument need not point to the beginning of an array. Listing 11.20 illustrates both these points.

Listing 11.20 *copy2.c*

```
/* copy2.c -- strcpy() demo */
#include <stdio.h>
#include <string.h>                /* declares strcpy() */
#define WORDS  "beast"
#define SIZE 40
int main(void)
{
    static char *orig = WORDS;
    static char copy[SIZE] = "Be the best that you can be.";
    char *ps;

    puts(orig);
    puts(copy);
    ps = strcpy(copy + 7, orig);
    puts(copy);
    puts(ps);
    return 0;
}
```

Here is the output:

```
beast
Be the best that you can be.
```

```
Be the beast
beast
```

Note that strcpy() copies the null character from the source string. In this example, the null character overwrites the t in that in copy so that the new string ends with beast. See Figure 11.4. Also note that ps points to the eighth element (index of 7) of copy because the first argument is copy + 7. Therefore, puts(ps) prints the string starting at that point.

Figure 11.4 strcpy( ) *uses pointers*

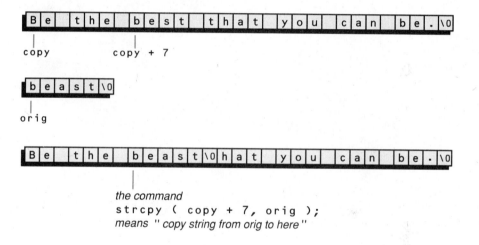

The *sprintf( )* Function

The sprintf() function is declared in stdio.h instead of string.h. It works like printf(), but it writes to a string instead of writing to a display. Thus, it provides a way to combine several elements into a single string. The first argument to sprintf() is the address of the target string. The remaining arguments are the same as for printf()—a conversion specification string followed by a list of items to be written.

One use for sprintf() is to generate a system command. The C library has a system() function that allows a program to execute operating system commands. For example, you could have a program solicit information from the user about copying a file and then use the system() command to have the operating system do the copying. This command takes a string argument indicating which command to execute. Listing 11.21 is a simple example using the MS-DOS COPY command. Change copy to cp for UNIX.

Listing 11.21 *command.c*

```
/* command.c -- generate a command string */
#include <stdio.h>
#include <stdlib.h> /* ANSI C: declares the system() function */
#define MAX 20
int main(void)
{
    char source[MAX];
    char target[MAX];
    char command[2 * MAX + 5];

    puts("Enter the name of the file you wish to copy:");
    gets(source);
    puts("Enter the desired name for the copy:");
    gets(target);
    sprintf(command, "copy %s %s", source, target);
    printf("Executing the following command: %s\n", command);
    system(command);
    return 0;
}
```

Here's a sample run:

```
Enter the name of the file you wish to copy:
taxing.c
Enter the desired name for the copy:
taxing1.c
Executing the following command: copy taxing.c taxing1.c
1 File(s) copied
```

The `sprintf()` command copied the string `"copy taxing.c tax-ing1.c"` into the `command` array. Next, the `printf()` command showed the contents of that string. Then the `system()` call executed the command specified by the string. The final line of output was produced by the operating system, not our program, after the operating system ran the COPY command.

Other String Functions

The ANSI C library includes sixteen string-handling functions, including `strchr()`, which finds the first occurrence of a character in a string, and `strrchr()`, which finds the last occurrence of a character in a string.

(Some pre-ANSI implementations call these functions `index()` and `rindex()`, respectively.) Many implementations provide additional functions beyond those required by the ANSI Standard. You should check the documentation for your implementation to see what is available.

Now that we have outlined some string functions, let's look at a full program that handles strings.

A String Example: Sorting Strings

Let's tackle the practical problem of sorting strings alphabetically. This task can show up in preparing name lists, in making up an index, and in many other situations. One of the main tools in such a program is `strcmp()`, since it can be used to determine the order of two strings. Our general plan will be to read an array of strings, sort them, and print them. A little while ago we presented a scheme for reading strings, and we will start the program that way. Printing the strings is no problem. We'll use a standard sorting algorithm that we'll explain later. We will do one slightly tricky thing—see if you can spot it. Listing 11.22 presents the program.

Listing 11.22 *sort_str.c*

```
/* sort_str.c -- reads in strings and sorts them */
#include <stdio.h>
#include <string.h>
#define SIZE 81          /* string length limit, including \0 */
#define LIM 20           /* maximum number of lines to be read */
#define HALT ""          /* null string to stop input          */
void stsrt(char *strings[], int num);  /* string-sort function */
int main(void)
{
    static char input[LIM][SIZE];  /* array to store input     */
    char *ptstr[LIM];              /* array of pointer variables */
    int ct = 0;                    /* input count              */
    int k;                         /* output count             */

    printf("Input up to %d lines, and I will sort them.\n",LIM);
    printf("To stop, press the Enter key at a line's start.\n");
    while (ct < LIM && gets(input[ct]) != NULL &&
```

(continued)

Listing 11.22 *(continued)*

```
        strcmp(input[ct],HALT) != 0)
  {
     ptstr[ct] = input[ct];       /* set ptrs to strings    */
     ct++;
  }
  stsrt(ptstr, ct);               /* string sorter          */
  puts("\nHere's the sorted list:\n");
  for (k = 0; k < ct; k++)
     puts(ptstr[k]) ;             /* sorted pointers         */
  return 0;
}
/* string-pointer-sorting function */
void stsrt(char *strings[], int num)
{
  char *temp;
  int top, seek;

  for (top = 0; top < num-1; top++)
     for (seek = top + 1; seek < num; seek++)
        if (strcmp(strings[top],strings[seek]) > 0)
        {
            temp = strings[top];
            strings[top] = strings[seek];
            strings[seek] = temp;
        }
}
```

We fed Listing 11.22 an obscure nursery rhyme to test it:

```
Input up to 20 lines, and I will sort them.
To stop, press the Enter key at a line's start.
O that I was where I would be,
Then would I be where I am not;
But where I am I must be,
And where I would be I can not.
```

Here's the sorted list:

```
And where I would be I can not.
But where I am I must be,
O that I was where I would be,
Then would I be where I am not;
```

Hmm, the nursery rhyme doesn't seem to suffer much from being alphabetized.

The tricky part of the program is that instead of rearranging the strings themselves, we just rearranged *pointers* to the strings. Let us explain. Originally, ptrst[0] is set to input[0], and so on. This means that the pointer ptrst[i] points to the first character in the array input[i]. Each input[i] is an array of 81 elements, and each ptrst[] is a single variable. The sorting procedure rearranges ptrst, leaving input untouched. If, for example, input[1] comes before input[0] alphabetically, the program switches ptrsts, causing ptrst[0] to point to the beginning of input[1] and causing ptrst[1] to point to the beginning of input[0]. This is much easier than using, say, strcpy() to interchange the contents of the two input strings. See Figure 11.5 for another view of this process.

Figure 11.5 *Sorting string pointers*

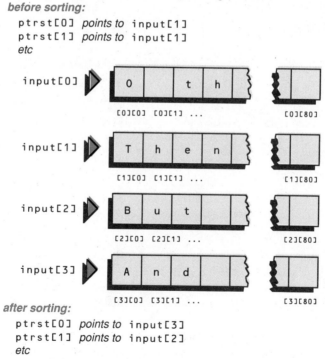

before sorting:

```
ptrst[0] points to input[1]
ptrst[1] points to input[1]
etc
```

after sorting:

```
ptrst[0] points to input[3]
ptrst[1] points to input[2]
etc
```

Sorting

To sort the pointers, we use the *selection sort* algorithm. The idea is to use a `for` loop to compare each element in turn with the first element. If the compared element precedes the current first element, the program swaps the two. Thus, by the time the program reaches the end of the loop, the first element contains a pointer to whichever string is first in the machine collating sequence. Then the outer `for` loop repeats the process, this time starting with the second element of `input`. When the inner loop completes, the pointer to the second-ranking string ends up in the second element of `ptrst`. The process continues until all the elements have been sorted. We'll take a more detailed look at this algorithm in Chapter 13.

The *ctype.h* Character Functions

ANSI C, as well as many pre-ANSI implementations, provides a family of character-related functions declared in the `ctype.h` header file. Several of these functions analyze the nature of a character, returning a true (non-zero) value if the character belongs to a particular class, and false (zero) otherwise. Table 11.1 lists these functions.

Table 11.1 *Character-Testing Functions*

Name	True If Argument Is
isalnum()	Alphanumeric (alphabetic or numeric)
isalpha()	Alphabetic
iscntrl()	A control character, e.g., Control-B
isdigit()	A digit
isgraph()	Any printing character other than a space
islower()	A lowercase character
isprint()	A printing character
ispunct()	A punctuation character (any printing character other than a space or an alphanumeric character)
isspace()	A whitespace character: space, newline, formfeed, carriage return, vertical tab, horizontal tab, or, possibly, other implementation-defined characters
isupper()	An uppercase character
isxdigit()	A hexadecimal-digit character

There also are two character-mapping functions: `toupper()` maps lowercase characters to uppercase, and `tolower()` maps uppercase characters to lower. Listing 11.23 presents a program that transforms an input line by reversing the case of the letters.

Listing 11.23 *invert.c*

```c
/* invert.c -- modifies a string */
#include <stdio.h>
#include <string.h>
#include <ctype.h>
#define LIMIT 80
void modify(char *);
int main(void)
{
  char line[LIMIT];

  puts("Please enter a line:");
  gets(line);
  modify(line);
  puts(line);
  return 0;
}

void modify(char *str)
{
  while (*str != '\0')
  {
      if (isupper(*str))
          *str = tolower(*str);
      else if (islower(*str))
          *str = toupper(*str);
      str++;
  }
}
```

The `while (*str != '\0')` loop processes each character in the string pointed to by `str` until the null character is reached. Here is a sample run:

```
Please enter a line:
Hello, Mr. Potato Head!
hELLO, mR. pOTATO hEAD!
```

In modify(), we use isupper() to be sure that a character is upper-case before trying to convert it to lowercase. Under ANSI C, this isn't necessary because tolower() returns the original character if it is not uppercase to begin with. However, not all older implementations offer that protection, so for maximum portability we checked first.

Incidentally, the ctype.h functions usually are implemented as *macros*. These are C preprocessor constructions that act much like functions but have some important differences. We'll cover macros in Chapter 16.

Next, let's try to fill an old emptiness in our lives, namely, the void between the parentheses in main().

Command-Line Arguments

The *command line* is the line you type to run your program. Suppose you have a program in a file named fuss. Then the command line to run it might look like this:

```
% fuss
```

or perhaps this:

```
A> fuss
```

Command-line arguments are additional items on the same line:

```
% fuss -r Ginger
```

A C program can read those additional items for its own use (see Figure 11.6). It does this by using arguments to main(). Listing 11.24 shows a typical example.

Listing 11.24   echo.c

```
/* echo.c -- main() with arguments */
int main(int argc, char *argv[])
{
    int count;

    for (count = 1; count < argc; count++)
```

```
    printf("%s ", argv[count]);  /* process each argument */
    printf("\n");
    return 0;
}
```

Figure 11.6 *Command-line arguments*

*executable file
called "echo"*

Compile this program into an executable file called echo, and this is what happens when you run it:

```
A> echo I could use a little help.
I could use a little help.
```

You can see why it is called echo, but you may wonder how it works. We'll explain now.

C compilers provide main() with two arguments. The first argument is the number of strings in the command line. By tradition (but not necessity), this int argument is called argc for *arg*ument *c*ount. The system uses spaces to tell when one string ends and the next begins. Thus, our echo example has seven strings, including the command name, and our fuss example had three. The second argument is an array of pointers to strings. Each string on the command line is stored in memory and has a pointer assigned to point to it. By convention, this array of pointers is called argv, for *arg*ument *v*alues. When possible (some operating systems don't allow

451

this), `argv[0]` is assigned the name of the program itself. Then `argv[1]` is assigned the first following string, etc. For our example, we have the following relationships:

`argv[0]`	points to	echo (for most systems)
`argv[1]`	points to	I
`argv[2]`	points to	could
`argv[3]`	points to	use
`argv[4]`	points to	a
`argv[5]`	points to	little
`argv[6]`	points to	help

The program in Listing 11.24 uses a `for` loop to print each string in turn. Recall that the `printf()` `%s` specifier expects the address of a string to be provided as an argument. Each element, `argv[0]`, `argv[1]`, etc., is just such an address.

With pre-ANSI C, use the form

```
main(argc, argv)
int argc;
char *argv[];
```

to declare `argc` and `argv`. The form is the same as for any other function having formal arguments. Many programmers use a different declaration for `argv`:

```
int main(int argc, char **argv)
```

This alternative declaration for `argv` really is equivalent to `char *argv[]`. It says that `argv` is a pointer to a pointer to `char`. Our example comes down to the same thing. We had an array with seven elements. The name of the array is a pointer to the first element. Thus, `argv` points to `argv[0]`, and `argv[0]` is a pointer to `char`. Hence, even with the original definition, `argv` is a pointer to a pointer to `char`. You can use either form, but we think that the first more clearly suggests that `argv` represents a set of strings.

Incidentally, many environments, including UNIX, let you use quotation marks to lump several words into a single argument. For example, the command

```
echo "I am hungry" now
```

would assign the string "I am hungry" to `argv[1]` and the string "now" to `argv[2]`.

Command-Line Arguments
in Integrated Environments

Integrated environments like QuickC and Turbo C don't use command lines to run programs. However, both have menu selections that let you specify a command-line argument. In QuickC 2.0, you open the Options menus, select Run/Debug, and enter the argument(s) into the Command Line box. With QuickC 1.0, you open the Run menu and select Set Run-time Options to get the Command Line box. In Turbo C, you open the Options menu, select Args, and enter the argument(s).

String to Number Conversions

Numbers can be stored either as strings or in numeric form. Storing a number as a string means storing the digit characters. For instance, the number 213 can be stored in a character string array as the digits `'2'`, `'1'`, `'3'`, `'\0'`. Storing 213 in numeric form means storing it as, say, an `int`.

C requires numeric forms for numeric operations, such as addition and comparison. But displaying numbers on your screen requires a string form because a screen displays characters. The `printf()` and `sprintf()` functions, through their `%d` and other specifiers, convert numeric forms to string forms. C also has functions that convert string forms to numeric forms.

Suppose, for example, we want our program to use a numeric command-line argument. Unfortunately, command-line arguments are read as strings. Therefore, to use the numeric value, we first must convert the string to a number. If the number is an integer, we can use the `atoi()` function (for *a*lphanumeric *to* *i*nteger). It takes a string as an argument and returns the corresponding integer value. Listing 11.25 shows a sample use.

Listing 11.25 *hello.c*

```
/* hello.c -- converts command-line argument to number */
#include <stdio.h>
#include <stdlib.h>
int main(int argc, char *argv[])
{
    int i, times;
```

(continued)

> **Listing 11.25** *(continued)*
>
> ```c
>     if (argc < 2 || (times = atoi(argv[1])) < 1)
>         printf("Usage: %s positive-number\n", argv[0]);
>     else
>         for (i = 0; i < times; i++)
>             puts("Hello, good looking!");
>     return 0;
> }
> ```

Here's a sample run:

```
% hello 3
Hello, good looking!
Hello, good looking!
Hello, good looking!
```

The % is a UNIX prompt. The command-line argument of 3 was stored as the string '3''\0'. The atoi() function converted this string to the integer value 3, which was assigned to times. This then determined the number of for loop cycles executed.

If you run the program without a command-line argument, the argc < 2 test aborts the program and prints a usage message. The same thing happens if test is 0 or negative. C's order-of-evaluation rule for logical operators guarantees that if argc < 2, then atoi(argv[1]) is not evaluated.

What if the command line is something like hello what?. On the implementations we've used, the atoi() function returns a value of 0 if its argument is not recognizable as a number. However, the ANSI Standard does not require that behavior.

We include the stdlib.h header because, under ANSI C, it contains the function declaration for atoi(). That header file also includes declarations for atof() and atol(). The atof() function converts a string to a type double value, and the atol() function converts a string to a type long value. They work analogously to atoi(), so they are type double and long, respectively.

Many implementations have itoa() and ftoa() functions for converting integers and floating-point values to strings. However, they are not part of the ANSI C library; use sprintf(), instead, for greater compatibility.

Chapter Summary

A C *string* is a series of `char`s terminated by the null character, `'\0'`. A string can be stored in a character array. A string also can be represented with a *string constant*, in which the characters, aside from the null character, are enclosed in double quotation marks. The compiler supplies the null character. Thus, `"joy"` is stored as the four characters j, o, y, and \0. The length of a string, as measured by `strlen()`, doesn't count the null character.

String constants can be used to initialize character arrays. In pre-ANSI C, only external and static arrays can be initialized, but ANSI C permits automatic arrays to be initialized, too. The array size should be at least one greater than the string length in order to accommodate the terminating null character. String constants also can be used to initialize pointers of type pointer-to-`char`.

Functions use pointers to the first character of a string to identify which string to act upon. Typically, the corresponding actual argument is an array name, a pointer variable, or a quoted string. In each case, the address of the first character is passed. In general, it is not necessary to pass the length of the string, since the function can use the terminating null character to locate the end of a string.

The `gets()` and `puts()` functions fetch a line of input and print a line of output, respectively. They are part of the `stdio.h` family of functions.

The C library includes several *string-handling* functions. Under ANSI C, these functions are declared in the `string.h` file. The library also has several *character-processing* functions; they are declared in the `ctype.h` file.

You can give a program access to *command-line arguments* by providing the proper two formal variables to the `main()` function. The first argument, traditionally called `argc`, is an `int` and is assigned the count of command-line words. The second argument, traditionally called `argv`, is a pointer to an array of pointers of `char`. Each pointer-to-`char` points to one of the command-line argument strings, with `argv[0]` pointing to the command name, `argv[1]` pointing to the first command-line argument, and wso on.

The `atoi()`, `atol()`, and `atof()` functions convert string representations of numbers to type `int`, `long`, and `double` forms, respectively.

Review Questions

    1. What's wrong with this attempted declaration of a character string?

```
int main(void)
```

```
{
    char name[] = {'F', 'e', 's', 's' };
        .
        .
        .
}
```

2. What will this program print?

```
#include <stdio.h>
#include <string.h>
int main(void)
{
    static char food[] = "Yummy";
    char *ptr;

    ptr = food + strlen(food);
    while (--ptr >= food)
        puts(ptr);
}
```

3. Here is an exercise providing practice with strings, loops, pointers, and pointer incrementing. First, suppose you have this function definition:

```
#include <stdio.h>
char *pr (char *str);
{
    char *pc;

    pc = str;
    while (*pc)
        putchar(*pc++);
    do {
        putchar(*--pc);
        } while (pc - str);
    return (pc);
}
```

Consider the following function call:

```
x = pr("Ho Ho Ho!");
```

   a. What is printed?

   b. What type should x be?

   c. What value does x get?

   d. What does the expression *--pc mean, and how is it different from --*pc?

   e. What would be printed if *--pc were replaced with *pc--?

f. What do the two `while` expressions test for?

g. What happens if `pr()` is supplied with a null string as an argument?

h. What must be done in the calling function so that `pr()` can be used as shown?

4. What does the following program print?

```c
#include <stdio.h>
#include <string.h>
#define M1   "How are ya, sweetie? "
char M2[40] = "Beat the clock.";
char *M3  = "chat";
int main(void)
{
    char words[80];
    printf(M1);
    puts(M1);
    puts(M2);
    puts(M2 + 1);
    strcpy(words,M2);
    strcat(words, " Win a toy.");
    puts(words);
    words[4] = '\0';
    puts(words);
    while (*M3)
        puts(M3++);
    puts(--M3);
    puts(--M3);
    M3 = M1;
    puts(M3);
}
```

5. The `strlen()` function takes a pointer to a string as an argument and returns the length of the string. Write your own version of this function.

6. Design a function that takes a string pointer as argument and returns a pointer to the first space character in the string on or after the pointed-to position. Have it return a null pointer if it finds no spaces.

Programming Exercises

1. Design a function that fetches the next n characters from input, including blanks, tabs, and newlines.

2. Modify the function in Exercise 1 so that it stops after n characters or after the first blank, tab, or newline, whichever comes first. (And don't just use scanf().)

3. Design a function that fetches the first word from a line of input and discards the rest of the line. Define a word as a sequence of characters with no blanks, tabs, or newlines in it.

4. Design a function that searches the specified string for the first occurrence of a specified character. Have the function return a pointer to the character if successful, and a null if the character is not found in the string. (This duplicates the way that the library strchr() function works.)

5. Write a function is_within() that takes a character and a string pointer as arguments. Have the function return a nonzero value (true) if the character is in the string and zero (false) otherwise.

6. The strncpy(s1,s2,n) function copies exactly n characters from s2 to s1, truncating s2 or padding it with extra null characters as necessary. The target string may not be null-terminated if the length of s2 is n or more. The function returns s1. Write your own version of this function.

7. Write a function string_in() that takes two string pointers as arguments. If the second string is contained in the first string, have the function return the address at which the contained string begins. For instance, string_in("hats", "at") would return the address of the a in hats. Otherwise, have the function return the NULL pointer.

8. Write a function that replaces the contents of a string with the string reversed.

9. Write a program that reads in up to 10 strings or to EOF, whichever comes first. Have it offer the user a menu with five choices: print the original list of strings, print the strings in ASCII collating sequence, print the strings in order of increasing length, print the strings in order of the length of the first word in the string, and quit. Have the menu recycle until the user enters the quit request. The program, of course, should actually perform the promised tasks.

10. Write a program that reads input up to EOF and reports the number of words, the number of uppercase letters, the number of lowercase letters, the number of punctuation characters, and the number of digits. Use the ctype.h family of functions.

11. Write a program that echoes the command-line arguments in reverse word order. That is, if the command-line arguments are see you later, the program should print later you see.

12. Write a power-law program that works on a command-line basis.

The first command-line argument should be the type `double` number to be raised to a power, and the second argument should be the integer power.

13. Use the character classification functions to prepare an implementation of `atoi()`.

12

File Input/Output

Functions

- ▶ fopen( ), getc( ), putc( ), exit( ), fclose( )
- ▶ fprintf( ), fscanf( ), fgets( ), fputs( )
- ▶ rewind( ), fseek( ), ftell( ), fflush( )
- ▶ ungetc( ), setvbuf( ), fread( ), fwrite( )

In this chapter you learn how to process files using C's standard I/O family of functions. You learn about text modes and binary modes, text and binary formats, and buffered and nonbuffered I/O. You practice using functions that can access files both sequentially and randomly.

iles are essential to today's computer systems. They are used to store programs, documents, data, correspondence, forms, graphics, and myriad other kinds of information. As a programmer, you will have to write programs that create files, write into files, and read from files. In this chapter we show you how.

Communicating with Files

Often you need programs that can read information from files or can write results into a file. One such form of program-file communication is file redirection, as you saw in Chapter 8. This method is simple but limited. For instance, suppose you wish to write an interactive program that asks you for book titles and then saves the complete listing in a file. If you use redirection, as in

```
books > bklist
```

your interactive prompts are redirected into bklist. Not only does this put unwanted text into bklist, it prevents you from seeing the questions you are supposed to answer.

Fortunately, C offers more powerful methods of communicating with files. It lets you open a file from within a program and then use special I/O functions to read from or write to that file. Before investigating these methods, however, let's review briefly the nature of a file.

What Is a File?

A *file* is a named section of storage, usually on a disk. We think of stdio.h, for instance, as the name of a file containing some useful information. To the operating system, however, a file is a bit more complicated. A large file, for example, may wind up stored in several scattered fragments. Or a file may contain additional data that allows the operating system to determine what kind of file it is. But these are the operating system's concerns, not ours (unless we are writing operating systems). Our concern is how files appear to a C program.

C views a file as a continuous sequence of bytes, each of which can be read individually. This corresponds to the file structure in the UNIX environment, where C grew up. Because other environments may not correspond exactly to this model, ANSI C provides two ways to view files.

The Text View and the Binary View

The two ANSI-mandated views of a file are *binary* and *text*. In the binary view, each and every byte of the file is accessible to a program. In the text view, what the program sees can differ from what is in the file. With the text view, the local environment's representation of such things as the end of a line are mapped to the C view when a file is read. Similarly, the C view is mapped to the local representation of output. By way of example, MS-DOS text files represent the end of a line with the carriage-return, linefeed combination: \r\n. C programs represent the end of a line with just \n. Thus, when a C program takes the text view of an MS-DOS text file, it converts \r\n to \n when reading from a file, and it converts \n to \r\n when writing to a file.

You aren't restricted to using only the text view for an MS-DOS text file. You can also use the binary view of the same file. If you do, your program sees both the \r and the \n characters in the file; no mapping takes place. See Figure 12.1. MS-DOS distinguishes between text and binary *files*, while C provides for text and binary *views*. Normally, you use the text view for text files, and the binary view for binary files. However, you can use either view of either type file, though a text view of a binary file works poorly.

Although ANSI C provides for both a binary and a text view, these views can be implemented identically. For instance, since UNIX uses just one file structure, both views are the same for UNIX implementations.

Levels of I/O

In addition to selecting the view of a file, you can, in most cases, choose between two levels of I/O, that is, between two levels of handling access to files. *Low-level I/O* uses the fundamental I/O services provided by the operating system. *Standard high-level I/O* uses a standard package of C library functions and stdio.h header file definitions. ANSI C supports only the standard I/O package because there is no way to guarantee that all operating systems can be represented by the same low-level I/O model. Because ANSI C establishes the portability of the standard I/O model, we will concentrate on it.

Figure 12.1 *Binary view and text view*

an MS-DOS
text file

```
Rebecca clutched the\r\n
jewel-encrusted scarab\r\n
to her heaving bosun.\r\n
^Z
```

```
Rebecca clutched the\r\n
jewel-encrusted scarab\r\n
to her heaving bosun.\r\n
^Z
```

the way it looks to a C
program when opened in
the binary mode

```
Rebecca clutched the\n
jewel-encrusted scarab\n
to her heaving bosun.\n
```

the way it looks to a C program when opened
in the text mode

Standard Files

C programs automatically open three files on your behalf. They are termed the *standard input*, the *standard output*, and the *standard error output*. The standard input, by default, is the normal input device for your system, usually your keyboard. Both the standard output and the standard error output, by default, are the normal output device for your system, usually your display screen.

The standard input, naturally, provides input to your program. It's the file that is read by getchar(), gets(), and scanf(). The standard output is where normal program output goes. It is used by putchar(), puts(), and printf(). Redirection, as you learned in Chapter 8, causes other files to be recognized as the standard input or standard output. The purpose of the standard error output file is to provide a logically distinct place to send error messages. If, for example, you use redirection to send output to a file instead of to the screen, output sent to the standard error output still goes to the screen. This is good because if the error messages were routed to the file, you would not see them until you viewed the file.

Standard I/O

The standard I/O package has two advantages, besides portability, over low-level I/O. First, it has many specialized functions that simplify the handling of various I/O problems. For instance, printf() converts various forms of data to string output suitable for terminals. Second, input and output are *buffered*. That is, information is transferred in large chunks (typically 512 bytes at a time or more) instead of a byte at a time. When a program reads a file, for example, a chunk of data is copied to a buffer—an intermediate storage area. This buffering greatly increases the data transfer rate. The program then can examine individual bytes in the buffer. The buffering is handled behind the scenes, so you have the illusion of character-by-character access. (You can also buffer low-level I/O, but you have to do much of the work yourself.) Listing 12.1 shows how to use standard I/O to read a file and count the number of characters in the file. We'll discuss the features of Listing 12.1 in the next several sections.

Listing 12.1 *count.c*

```
/* count.c -- using standard I/O */
#include <stdio.h>
#include <stdlib.h> /* ANSI C exit() prototype              */
int main(int argc, char *argv[])
{
    int ch;        /* place to store each character as read */
    FILE *fp;      /* "file pointer"                        */
    long count = 0;

    if (argc != 2)
    {
        printf("Usage: %s filename\n", argv[0]);
        exit(1);
    }
    if ((fp = fopen(argv[1], "r")) == NULL)
    {
        printf("Can't open %s\n", argv[1]);
        exit(1);
    }
    while ((ch = getc(fp)) != EOF)
    {
        putc(ch,stdout);
        count++;
```

```
    }
    fclose(fp);
    printf("File %s has %ld characters\n", argv[1], count);
    return 0;
}
```

Checking for Command-Line Arguments

First, the program in Listing 12.1 checks the value of `argc` to see if there is a command-line argument. If there isn't, the program prints a usage message and exits. The string `argv[0]` is the name of the program. Using `arv[0]` instead of the program name explicitly causes the error message to change automatically if you change the name of the executable file. This feature also is handy in environments like UNIX that permit multiple names for a single file. But beware, some operating systems, such as pre MS-DOS 3.0, don't recognize `argv[0]`, so this usage is not completely portable.

The `exit()` function causes the program to terminate, closing any open files. The argument to `exit()` is passed on to some operating systems, including UNIX, where it can be used by other programs. The UNIX convention is to pass a value of 0 for programs that terminate normally and to pass nonzero values for abnormal termination. Different exit values can be used to distinguish between different causes of failure.

Under ANSI C, using `return` in the initial call to `main` has the same effect as calling `exit()`. Thus, the following statement

```
    return 0;
```

which we've been using all along, is equivalent in effect to:

```
    exit(0);
```

Note, however, the qualifying phrase "the initial call." If you make `main()` into a recursive program, `exit()` still terminates the program, but `return` passes control to the previous level of recursion until the original level is reached. Then `return` terminates the program.

Under ANSI C, the `stdlib.h` header file contains the prototype for `exit()`. You can omit this file on pre-ANSI systems.

The *fopen( )* Function

Next, the program uses `fopen()` to open the file. This function is declared in `stdio.h`. Its first argument is the name of the file to be opened; more exactly, it is the address of a string containing that name. The second argument is a string identifying the mode in which the file is to be opened. The C library provides for several possibilities, as shown in Table 12.1.

Table 12.1 *Mode Strings for* fopen( )

Mode String	Meaning
"r"	Open a text file for reading
"w"	Open a text file for writing, truncating an existing file to zero length, or creating the file if it does not exist
"a"	Open a text file for writing, appending to the end of an existing file, or creating the file if it does not exist
"r+"	Open a text file for update, i.e., for both reading and writing
"w+"	Open a text file for update (reading and writing), first truncating the file to zero length if it exists or creating the file if it does not exist
"a+"	Open a text file for update (reading and writing), appending to the end of an existing file, or creating the file if it does not yet exist; the whole file can be read, but writing can only be appended
"rb", "wb", "ab", "ab+", "a+b", "wb+", "w+b", "ab+", "a+b"	Like the preceding modes, except using binary mode instead of text mode

For systems like UNIX, which have just one file type, the modes with the b are equivalent to the corresponding modes lacking the b. *Caution*: If you use any of the "w" modes for an existing file, the file contents are truncated so that your program can start with a clean slate.

Once your program successfully opens a file, fopen() returns a *file pointer*, which the other I/O functions then can use to specify the file. The file pointer, fp in our example, is of type pointer-to-FILE, where FILE is a derived type defined in stdio.h. The pointer fp doesn't point to the actual file. Instead, it points to a data package containing information about the file, including information about the buffer used for the file's I/O. Since the I/O functions in the standard library use a buffer, they need to know where the buffer is. They also need to know how full the buffer is and which file is being used. This enables the functions to refill or empty the buffer when necessary. The data package pointed to by fp has all that information. (This data package is an example of a C structure, a topic we discuss in Chapter 14.)

The fopen() function returns the NULL pointer (also defined in stdio.h) if it cannot open the file. Our program exits if fp is NULL. The fopen() function can fail because the disk is full, because the name is illegal, because access is restricted, or because of a hardware problem, to name just a few reasons. So check for trouble: a little error-trapping can go a long way.

The *getc( )* and *putc( )* Functions

The two functions getc() and putc() work very much like getchar() and putchar(). The difference is that you must tell these newcomers which file to use. Thus, our old standby

```
ch = getchar();
```

means get a character from the standard input, but

```
ch = getc(fp);
```

means get a character from the file identified by fp.
Similarly,

```
putc(ch, fpout);
```

means put the character ch into the file identified by the FILE pointer fpout. In the putc() argument list, the character comes first, then the file pointer.

In Listing 12.2, we use stdout for the second argument of putc(). It is defined in stdio.h as being the file pointer associated with the standard output. So putc(ch,stdout) is the same as putchar(ch). Indeed, the latter function normally is defined as being the former. Similarly, getchar() is defined as being getc() using the standard input.

The *fclose( )* Function

The fclose(fp) closes the file identified by fp, flushing buffers as needed. For a program less casual than this one, we would check to see if the file had been closed successfully. The function fclose() returns a value of 0 if successful, and EOF if not:

```
if (fclose(fp) != 0)
  printf("Error in closing file %s\n", argv[1]);
```

The fclose() function can fail, for example, if the disk is full, if the diskette has been removed, or if there has been an I/O error.

Standard Files

The stdio.h file associates three file pointers with the three standard files automatically opened by C programs:

Standard File	File Pointer	Normally
Standard input	stdin	Your keyboard
Standard output	stdout	Your screen
Standard error	stderr	Your screen

These pointers are all type pointer-to-FILE, so they can be used as arguments to the standard I/O functions, just as fp was in our example. Let's move on to an example that creates a new file and writes to it.

A Simple-Minded File-Condensing Program

In this next program we'll copy selected data from one file to another. Thus, we'll open two files simultaneously, using the "r" mode for one and the "w" mode for the other. The program (Listing 12.2) condenses the contents of the first file by the brutal expedient of retaining only every third character. Finally, it places the condensed text into the second file. The name for the second file is the old name with .red (for reduced) appended. Command-line arguments, opening more than one file simultaneously, and filename appending are quite useful techniques generally. This particular form of condensing is of more limited appeal, but it can have its uses, as you will see.

Listing 12.2 *reducto.c*

```
/* reducto.c -- reduces your files by two-thirds ! */
#include <stdio.h>
```

```
#include <stdlib.h>
int main(int argc, char *argv[])
{
    FILE  *in, *out;    /* declare two FILE pointers     */
    int ch;
    char name[40];      /* storage for output filename   */
    int count = 0;
    if (argc < 2)       /* check for an input file       */
    {
        fprintf(stderr, "Usage: %s filename\n", argv[0]);
        exit(1);
    }
    if ((in = fopen(argv[1], "r")) == NULL)
    {
        fprintf(stderr, "I couldn't open the file \"%s\"\n",
                argv[1]);
        exit(2);
    }
    strcpy(name,argv[1]);   /* copy filename into array   */
    strcat(name,".red");    /* append .red to name        */
    if ((out = fopen(name, "w")) == NULL)
    {                           /* open file for writing      */
        fprintf(stderr,"Can't create output file.\n");
        exit(3);
    }
    while ((ch = getc(in)) != EOF)
        if (count++ % 3 == 0)
            putc(ch, out);  /* print every 3rd char       */
    if (fclose(in) != 0 || fclose(out) != 0)
        fprintf(stderr,"Error in closing files\n");
        return 0;
}
```

Our executable file is called `reducto`. We applied it to a file called eddy, which contained the single line:

```
So even Eddy came oven ready.
```

The command was

```
reducto eddy
```

and the output was written to a file called `eddy.red`. Displaying that file revealed the following:

```
Send money
```

Here are some program notes.

The `fprintf()` function is like `printf()` except that it requires a file pointer as its first argument. We've used the `stderr` pointer to send our error messages to the standard error; this is a standard C practice.

To construct the new name for the output file, we used `strcpy()` to copy the name `eddy` into the array `name`. Then we used the `strcat()` function to combine that name with `.red`, producing `eddy.red`. We also checked to see if the program succeeded in opening a file by that name. This is particularly important in the DOS environment since a filename like, say, `strange.c.red` is invalid; you can't add extensions to extensions under DOS. (The proper MS-DOS approach would be to replace any existing extension with `.red`, so that the reduced version of `strange.c` would be `strange.red`.)

This program had two files open simultaneously, so we declared two `FILE` pointers. Note that each file is opened and closed independently of the other. There are limits to how many files you can have open at one time. The limit depends on your system and implementation; the range is often 10 to 20. You can use the same file pointer for different files, providing those files are not open at the same time.

File I/O: *fprintf(), fscanf(), fgets(),* and *fputs()*

For each of the I/O functions in the preceding chapters, there is a similar file I/O function. The main distinction is that you need to use a `FILE` pointer to tell the new functions which file to work with. Like `getc()` and `putc()`, these functions require that you identify a file by using a pointer-to-`FILE` such as `stdout` or that you use the return value of `fopen()`.

The *fprintf( )* and *fscanf( )* Functions

The file I/O functions `fprintf()` and `fscanf()` work just like `printf()` and `scanf()`, except that they require an additional first argument to identify the proper file. We've already used `fprintf()`. Listing 12.3 illustrates both of these file I/O functions along with the `rewind()` function.

Listing 12.3 *addaword.c*

```
/* addaword.c -- uses fprintf(), fscanf(), and rewind() */
#include <stdio.h>
#include <stdlib.h>
#define MAX 20
int main(void)
{
    FILE *fp;
    char words[MAX];

    if ((fp = fopen("words", "a+")) == NULL)
    {
        fprintf(stdin,"Can't open \"words\" file.\n");
        exit(1);
    }
    puts("Enter words to add to the file; press the Enter");
    puts("key at the beginning of a line to terminate.");
    while (gets(words) != NULL  && words[0] != '\0')
        fprintf(fp, "%s ", words);
    puts("File contents:");
    rewind(fp);              /* go back to beginning of file */
    while (fscanf(fp,"%s",words) == 1)
        puts(words);
    if (fclose(fp) != 0)
        fprintf(stderr,"Error closing file\n");
    return 0;
}
```

This program lets you add words to a file. By using the "a+" mode, the program can both read and write in the file. The first time the program is used, it creates the words file and lets you place words in it. When you use the program subsequently, it lets you add (append) words to the prior contents. The append modes only let you add material to the end of the file, but the "a+" mode does let you read the whole file. The rewind() command takes the program to the file beginning so that the final while loop can print the file contents. Note that rewind() takes a file pointer argument.

If you enter an empty line, gets() places a null character in the first element of the array. We use that fact to terminate the loop.

Here's a sample run from a DOS environment:

```
C>addaword
Enter words to add to the file; press the Enter
key at the beginning of a line to terminate.
See the canoes[enter]
[enter]
File contents:
See
the
canoes
C>addaword
Enter words to add to the file; press the Enter
key at the beginning of a line to terminate.
on the[enter]
sea[enter]
[enter]
File contents:
See
the
canoes
on
the
sea
```

As you can see, fprintf() and fscanf() work like printf() and scanf(). Unlike putc(), the fprintf() and fscanf() functions take the FILE pointer as the first argument instead of as the last argument.

The *fgets( )* and *fputs( )* Functions

The fgets() function takes three arguments to gets()'s one. The first argument, as with gets(), is the address (type char *) where input should be stored. The second argument is an integer representing the maximum size of the input string. The final argument is the file pointer identifying the file to be read. Thus, a function call looks like this:

```
fgets(buf, MAX, fp);
```

Here, buf is the name of a char array, MAX is the maximum size of the string, and fp is the pointer-to-FILE.

The fgets() function reads input through the first newline character or until one fewer than the upper limit of characters is read or until the end of file is found; fgets() then adds a terminating null character to form a string. Thus, the upper limit represents the maximum number of characters plus the null character. If fgets() reads in a whole line before running into the character limit, it adds the newline character marking the end of

the line into the string, just before the null character. Here it differs from
`gets()`, which reads the newline but discards it.

Like `gets()`, `fgets()` returns the value `NULL` when it encounters EOF.
This lets you check for the end of a file. Otherwise, it returns the address
passed to it.

The `fputs()` function takes two arguments: first, an address of a
string, then a file pointer. It writes the string found at the pointed-to location into the indicated file. Unlike `puts()`, `fputs()` does not append a newline when it prints. A function call looks like this:

```
fputs(buf, fp);
```

Here, `buf` is the string address, and `fp` identifies the target file.

Because `fgets()` keeps the newline and `fputs()` doesn't add one,
they work well in tandem. Listing 12.4 shows an echo program using these
two functions.

Listing 12.4 *echo.c*

```
/* echo.c -- using fgets() and fputs() */
#include <stdio.h>
#define MAXLINE 20
int main(void)
{
    char line[MAXLINE];

    while (fgets(line, MAXLINE, stdin) != NULL &&
        line[0] != '\n')
    fputs(line, stdout);
    return 0;
}
```

When you press the Enter key at the beginning of a line, `fgets()`
reads the newline and places it into the first element of the array `line`. We
use that fact to terminate the input loop. Encountering end of file also
terminates it. (In Listing 12.3 we tested for `'\0'` instead of `'\n'` because
`gets()` discards the newline.)

Here is a sample run. Do you notice anything odd?

```
It is Spring.
It is Spring.
The hills are green and the sea is sparkling.
```

```
The hills are green and the sea is sparkling.
[enter]
```

The program works fine. This should seem surprising because the second line we entered contains 45 characters, and the line array holds only 20, including the newline character! What happened? When fgets() read the second line, it read just the first 19 characters, through the second e in green. These were copied into line, which fputs() printed. Because fgets() hadn't reached the end of a line, line did not contain a newline character, so fputs() didn't print a newline. The third call to fgets() resumed where the second call left off. Thus, it read the next 19 characters into line beginning with the n in green. This next block replaced the previous contents of line and, in turn, was printed on the same line as the output. Remember, the last output didn't have a newline. In short, fgets() read the second line in chunks of 19 characters, and fputs() printed it in the same-size chunks.

This program also terminates input if a line has exactly 19 characters. In that case, fgets() stops reading input after the 19 characters, so the next call to fgets() starts with the newline at the end of the line. This newline becomes the first character read, thus terminating the loop.

You may be wondering why the program didn't print the first 19 characters of the second line as soon as we typed them. That is where screen buffering comes in. The second line wasn't sent to the screen until the newline character had been reached.

Commentary: *gets( )* and *fgets( )*

Because fgets() can be used to prevent storage overflow, it is a better function than gets() for serious programming. Because it does read a newline into a string and because puts() appends a newline to output, fgets() should be used in conjunction with fputs(), not puts(). Otherwise, one newline in input can become two on output.

The six I/O functions we have just discussed should give you tools aplenty for reading and writing text files. So far, we have used them only for *sequential access*, that is, processing the file contents in order. Next, we look at *random access*, that is, accessing the contents in any desired order.

Adventures in Random Access: *fseek( )* and *ftell( )*

The fseek() function lets you treat a file like an array and move directly to any particular byte in a file opened by fopen(). To see how it works, let's create a program (Listing 12.5) that displays a file in reverse order. Borrowing from our earlier examples, it uses a command-line argument to obtain the name of the file that it will read. Note that fseek() has three arguments and returns an int value. The ftell() function returns the current position in a file as a long value.

Listing 12.5 *reverse.c*

```c
/* reverse.c -- displays a file in reverse order */
#include <stdio.h>
#include <stdlib.h>
#define CNTL_Z '\032'   /* eof marker in DOS text files */
int main(int argc, char *argv[])
{
   char ch;
   FILE *fp;
   long count, last;

   if (argc != 2)
   {
   printf("Usage: reverse file\n");
      exit(1);
   }
   if ((fp = fopen(argv[1],"rb")) == NULL)
   {                          /* read-only and binary modes */
      printf("reverse can't open %s\n", argv[1]);
      exit(1);
   }
   fseek(fp, 0L, SEEK_END);          /* go to end of file */
   last = ftell(fp);
   for (count = 1L; count <= last; count++)
   {
   fseek(fp, -count, SEEK_END);   /* go backward       */
      ch = getc(fp);
      if (ch != CNTL_Z && ch != '\r')
         putchar(ch);
   }
   fclose(fp);
   return 0;
}
```

Here is the output for a sample file:

```
.C ni eno naht ylevol erom margorp a
ees reven llahs I taht kniht I
```

We need to discuss three topics: how `fseek()` and `ftell()` work, how to use a binary stream, and how to make the program portable.

How *fseek( )* and *ftell( )* Work

The first of the three arguments to `fseek()` is a `FILE` pointer to the file being searched. The file should have been opened by using `fopen()`.

The second argument to `fseek()` is called the *offset*. This argument tells how far to move from the starting point (see the following list of mode starting points). The argument must be a `long` value. It can be positive (move forward) or negative (move backward) or zero (stay put).

The third argument is the *mode*, and it identifies the starting point. Under ANSI, the `stdio.h` header file specifies the following manifest constants for the mode:

Mode	Measure Offset from
SEEK_SET	Beginning of file
SEEK_CUR	Current position
SEEK_END	End of file

Older implementations may lack these definitions and, instead, use the numeric values `0L`, `1L`, and `2L`, respectively, for these modes. Recall that the `L` suffix identifies type `long` values. Or the implementation may have the constants defined in a different header file. When in doubt, consult your usage manual or the on-line manual.

The value returned by `fseek()` is `0` if everything is okay, and −1 if there is an error, such as attempting to move past the bounds of the file.

The `ftell()` function is type `long`, and it returns the current file location. Under ANSI, it is declared in `stdio.h`. As originally implemented in UNIX, `ftell()` specifies the file position by returning the number of bytes from the beginning, with the first byte being byte 0, and so on. Under ANSI C, this definition applies to files opened in the binary mode, but not necessarily to files opened in the text mode. That is one reason why we used the binary mode for Listing 12.5.

Now we can explain the basic elements of Listing 12.5. First, the statement

```
fseek(fp, 0L, SEEK_END);
```

takes us to an offset of 0 bytes from the file end. That is, it takes us to the end of the file. Next, the statement

```
        last = ftell(fp);
```

assigns to `last` the number of bytes from the beginning to the end of the file.

Then, we have this loop:

```
for (count = 1L; count <= last; count++)
{
    fseek(fp, -count, SEEK_END);     /* go backward */
        ch = getc(fp);

          .
          .
          .

}
```

The first cycle positions the program at the first character before the end of the file, that is, at the final character of the file. Then the program prints that character. The next loop positions the program at the preceding character and prints it. This continues until the first character is reached and printed.

Binary versus Text Mode

We designed Listing 12.5 to work in both the UNIX and the MS-DOS environments. UNIX has only one file format, so no special adjustments are needed. MS-DOS, however, does require extra attention. Many MS-DOS editors mark the end of a text file with the character Control-Z. When such a file is opened in the text mode, C recognizes this character as marking the end of the file. When the same file is opened in the binary mode, however, the Control-Z character is just another character in the file, and the actual end-of-file comes later. It may come immediately after the Control-Z, or the file may be padded with null characters to make the size a multiple of, say, 256. Null characters don't print under DOS, and we included code to prevent the program from trying to print the Control-Z character.

Another difference is one we've mentioned before: MS-DOS represents a text file newline with the \r\n combination. A C program opening the same file in a text mode "sees" \r\n as a simple \n. But, when using the binary mode, the program sees both characters. Thus, we included coding to suppress the printing of \r.

Because a UNIX text file normally contains neither Control-Z nor \r, this extra coding does not affect most UNIX text files.

The `ftell()` function may work differently in the text mode than in the binary mode. Many systems have text file formats that are different enough from the UNIX model that a byte count from the beginning of the file is not a meaningful quantity. ANSI C states that, for the text mode, `ftell()` returns a value that can be used as the second argument to

fseek(). For MS-DOS, for example, ftell() can return a count that sees
\r\n as a single byte.

Portability

Ideally, fseek() and ftell() should conform to the UNIX model. However, differences in real systems sometimes make this impossible. Therefore, ANSI provides lowered expectations for these functions. Here are
some limitations:

▶ In the binary mode, implementations need not support the
SEEK_END mode. (Thus, Listing 12.5 is not guaranteed to be
portable.)

▶ In the text mode, the only calls to fseek() that are guaranteed to
work are these:

fseek(file, 0L, SEEK_SET)	Go to beginning of file
fseek(file, 0L, SEEK_CUR)	Stay at current position
fseek(file, 0L, SEEK_END)	Go to file end
fseek(file, ftell-pos, SEEK_SET)	Go to position *ftell-pos* from the beginning, where *ftell-pos* is a value returned by ftell()

Fortunately, many common environments allow stronger implementations of these functions. Let's look at a text mode example.

Using Random-Access in a Text Mode

Our goal is to write a program that takes a list of filenames from the command line and prints the name of each file followed by the last line of that
file. Lest we get too rusty, let's use the modular approach to structure the
program. Listing 12.6 shows the result.

Listing 12.6 *lastline.c*

```
/* lastline.c -- prints last lines of files */
#include <stdio.h>
void show_end(char *name, FILE *file);
int main(int argc, char *argv[])
{
```

```
    FILE *fp;
    int file;

    if (argc < 2)
    {
        printf("Usage: %s file(s)\n", argv[0]);
        exit(1);
    }
    for (file = 1; file < argc; file++)
    {
        if ((fp = fopen(argv[file],"r")) == NULL)
            fprintf(stderr,"%s can't open %s\n", argv[0],
                argv[file]);
        else
        {
            show_end(argv[file],fp);
            fclose(fp);
        }
    }
    return 0;
}

void show_end(char *name, FILE *file)
{
    int ch;
    int newlines = 0;
    long count, start, last;

    printf("%s:\n", name);
    start = ftell(file);
    fseek(file, 0L, SEEK_END);          /* go to end of file */
    last = ftell(file);
    for (count = 1L; count <= last; count++)
    {
        fseek(file, -count, SEEK_END);   /* go backward       */
        ch = getc(file);
        if (ch == '\n')
            newlines++;
        if (newlines == 2)               /* or maybe 3        */
        {
```

(continued)

```
Listing 12.6  (continued)

        start = ftell(file);
                          /* or maybe ftell(file) - 1    */
        break;
     }
  }
  fseek(file, start, SEEK_SET);
  while ((ch = getc(file)) != EOF)
     putchar(ch);
}
```

We let `main()` handle the command-line arguments and the opening
and closing of files. The `show_end()` function takes care of finding and
displaying the final line.

Here is a sample run from the MS-DOS environment:

```
C>lastline prose prod produce
prose:
a program more lovely than one in C.
lastline can't open prod
produce:
red potatoes
C>
```

The `main()` program contains a loop for processing the command-
line arguments. Recall that `argc` includes the command name in the count,
so it is one greater than the number of command-line arguments. Also,
since `argv[0]` is the command name, `argv[count-1]` is the last argument.
Thus, the loop cycles through all the arguments. If the argument is the
name of a file that the program can open, the file is processed. Otherwise,
the loop prints an error message and goes to the next argument. You can
use this form for any program that is expected to handle a list of files.

The `show_last()` function assumes that the text file ends with a newline. It searches backward from the end of the file until it finds a second
newline character. This would mark the end of the next-to-last line. By
reading the character, we move to the next character, which would be the
first character on the final line. The fragment

```
if (newlines == 2)              /* or maybe 3   */
{
  start = ftell(file);
```

```
                    /* or maybe ftell(file) - 1 */
      break;
   }
```

saves the location of this character and breaks the `for` loop. The file may have only one line, causing the test `newlines == 2` to never become true. In that case, the loop runs to completion, examining all the characters in the file. Then the program prints the entire file, using the value of `start` that was set before the loop was entered.

Portability

In testing this program in diverse environments, we found that the era of complete portability has not yet arrived. Each of the three environments required some changes.

The files are opened in text mode, so we shouldn't have to worry about detecting the `\r` character. However, with Turbo C 2.0, we had to use 3 instead of 2 for the number of newlines. The reason is that while this version of Turbo C correctly transforms `\r\n` to `\n` when moving forward through a file, it transforms `\r\n` to `\n \n` when moving backward. Apparently the `\n` is passed as `\n`. Then the `\r` is detected. Turbo C notes that it is immediately followed by a `\n`, so it maps the combination to a second `\n`.

With Microsoft C and QuickC, we sometimes had to subtract 1 from `start`; otherwise, the first letter of the final line was omitted. Sometimes? Yes, the behavior depended on which text editor created the files! If the file had a terminal Control-Z, the subtraction of 1 was needed; otherwise, it wasn't.

The UNIX system we use is not yet ANSI compliant. Therefore, to run the program on UNIX, we had to define `SEEK_END`, etc., to be the corresponding numeric values. Also, we couldn't use the ANSI C prototypes and function declarations.

So, with some modifications, the program works in the UNIX and MS-DOS environments, but it does go beyond the ANSI guarantees for `fseek()`. For example, we use offsets from the file end, and the offsets are not values returned by `ftell()`. All in all, you'll be better off using the binary mode rather than the text mode for random-access programs.

Behind the Scenes with Standard I/O

Now that you've seen some of the features of the standard I/O package, let's examine a representative conceptual model to see how standard I/O works.

Normally, the first step in using standard I/O is to use `fopen()` to open a file. (But recall that the `stdin`, `stdout`, and `stderr` files are opened automatically.) The `fopen()` function not only opens a file but sets up a buffer (two buffers for read-write modes), and it sets up a data structure containing data about the file and about the buffer. Also, `fopen()` returns a pointer to this structure so that other functions will know where to find it. We'll assume that this value is assigned to a pointer variable named `fp`. The `fopen()` function is said to open a *stream*. If the file is opened in the text mode, we get a text stream, and if the file is opened in the binary mode, we get a binary stream.

The data structure typically includes a *file position indicator* to specify the current position in the stream. It also has indicators for errors and end-of-file, a pointer to the beginning of the buffer, a file identifier, and a count for the number of bytes actually copied into the buffer.

Let's concentrate on file input. Usually, the next step is to call upon one of the input functions declared in `stdio.h`, such as `fscanf()`, `getc()`, or `fgets()`. Calling any one of these functions causes a chunk of data to be copied from the file to the buffer. The buffer size is implementation dependent, but it typically is 512 bytes or some multiple thereof. In addition to filling the buffer, the initial function call sets values in the structure pointed to by `fp`. In particular, the current position in the stream, and the number of bytes copied into the buffer are set. Usually the current position starts at byte 0.

Once the data structure and buffer are initialized, the input function reads the requested data from the buffer. As it does so, the file position indicator is set to point to the character following the last character read. Because all the input functions from the `stdio.h` family use the same buffer, a call to any one function resumes where the previous call to any of the functions stopped.

When an input function finds that it has read all the characters in the buffer, it requests that the next buffer-sized chunk of data be copied from the file into the buffer. In this manner, the input functions can read all the file contents up to the end of the file. After a function reads the last character of the final buffer's worth of data, it sets the end-of-file indicator to true. The next call to an input function then returns EOF.

In a similar manner, output functions write to a buffer. When the buffer is filled, the data is copied to the file.

Other Standard I/O Functions

The ANSI standard library contains over three dozen functions in the standard I/O family. Although we don't cover them all here, we will briefly describe a few more to give you a better idea of what is available. We'll list each function by its ANSI C prototype to indicate its arguments and return values. Of those functions we discuss here, all but `setvbuf()` are also available in pre-ANSI implementations. Appendix F lists the full ANSI C standard I/O package.

*int ungetc(int c, FILE *fp)*

The `int ungetc(int c, FILE *fp)` function pushes the character specified by `c` back onto the input stream. If you push a character onto the input stream, the next call to a standard input function will read that character. See Figure 12.2. Suppose, for example, you want a function to read characters up to, but not including, the next colon. You can use `getchar()` or `getc()` to read characters until a colon is read and then use `ungetc()` to place the colon back in the input stream. The ANSI C Standard guarantees only one pushback at a time. If an implementation permits you to push back several characters in a row, the input functions will read them in the reversed order of pushing.

Figure 12.2 *The* ungetc( ) *function*

*int fflush(FILE *fp)*

Calling the `int fflush(FILE *fp)` function causes any unwritten data in the buffer to be sent to the output file identified by `fp`. This process is called *flushing a buffer*. If `fp` is the NULL pointer, all output buffers are flushed.

*int setvbuf(FILE *fp, char *buf, int mode, size_t size)*

The `int setvbuf(FILE *fp, char *buf, int mode, size_t size)` function sets up an alternative buffer to be used by the standard I/O functions. It is called after the file has been opened and before any other operations have been performed on the stream. The pointer `fp` identifies the stream, and `buf` points to the storage to be used. If the value of `buf` is not `NULL`, you must create the buffer. For instance, you could declare an array of 1024 `char`s and pass the address of that array. However, if you use `NULL` for the value of `buf`, the function allocates a buffer itself. The `size` variable tells `setvbuf()` how big the array is. (The `size_t` type is a derived type; see Chapter 16.) The `mode` is selected from the following choices: `_IOFBF` means fully buffered, `_IOLBF` means line-buffered, and `_IONBF` means nonbuffered. The function returns zero if successful, nonzero otherwise.

Suppose you had a program that worked with stored data objects having, say, a size of 3000 bytes each. You could use `setvbuf()` to create a buffer whose size matched that of the data object. Many pre-ANSI implementations use `setbuf()` instead. It takes two arguments. The first is a pointer-to-`FILE` to identify the file to be buffered. The second is the desired buffer size in bytes. The `setbuf()` function does not select among different buffering modes, nor does it have a return value.

Binary I/O: *fread( )* and *fwrite( )*

The `fread()` and `fwrite()` functions are next on our list, but first some background. The standard I/O functions we've used to this point are text oriented, dealing with characters and strings. What if you want to save numeric data in a file? True, you can use `fprintf()` and the `%f` format to save a floating-point value, but then you are saving it as a string. For instance, the sequence

```
double num = 1./3.;
fprintf(fp,"%f", num);
```

saves num as a string of 8 characters: 0.333333. Using a `%.2f` specifier saves it as 4 characters: 0.33. Using a `%.12f` specifier saves it as 14 characters: 0.333333333333. Changing the specifier alters the amount of space needed to store the value; it also can result in different values being stored. Once the value of num is stored as 0.33, there is no way to get back the full precision when reading the file. In general, `fprintf()` converts numeric values to strings, possibly altering the value.

The most accurate and consistent way to store a number is to use the same pattern of bits that the program does. Thus, a `double` value should be stored in a size `double` container. When data is stored in a file using the same representation that the program uses, we say that the data is stored in binary form. There is no conversion from numeric forms to strings. For standard I/O, the `fread()` and `fwrite()` functions provide this binary service. See Figure 12.3.

Figure 12.3 *Binary and text output*

```
int num = 12345;
```
stores 12345 as binary number in num

00110001	00110001

```
fprintf(fp,"d", num);
```
writes the binary codes for the characters
'1', '2', '3', '4', '5' to the file

00110001	00110001	00110011	00110100	00110101

```
fwrite(&num, sizeof (int), 1, fp);
```
writes the binary codes for the characters 12345 to the file

00110001	00110001

(this figure assumes an integer size of 16 bits)

Actually, all data is stored in binary form. Even characters are stored using the binary representation of the character code. However, if all data in the file is interpreted as character codes, we say that the file contains text data. If some or all of the data is interpreted as numeric data in binary form, we say that the file contains binary data. (Also, files in which the data represents machine language instructions are binary files.)

The uses of the terms *binary* and *text* can get confusing. ANSI C recognizes two modes for opening files: binary and text. Many operating systems recognize two file formats: binary and text. Information can be stored or read as binary data or as text data. These are all related, but not identical. You can open a text format file in the binary mode. You can store text in a binary format file. You can use `getc()` to copy files containing binary data. In general, however, you would use the binary mode to store binary data in a binary format file. Similarly, you most often would use text data in text files opened in the text format.

*size_t fwrite(void *ptr, size_t size, size_t nmemb, FILE *fp)*

The `size_t fwrite(void *ptr, size_t size, size_t nmemb, FILE *fp)` function writes binary data to a file. The `size_t` type is defined in terms of the standard C types. It is the type returned by the `sizeof` operator. Typically it is `unsigned int`, but an implementation can choose another type. The pointer `ptr` is the address of the chunk of data to be written. The `size` represents the size, in bytes, of the chunks to be written, and the `nmemb` represents the number of chunks to be written. As usual, `fp` identifies the file to be written to. For instance, to save a data object (such as an array) that is 256 bytes in size, you can do this:

```
char buffer[256];
        .
        .
        .
fwrite(buffer, 256, 1, fp);
```

This call writes one chunk of 256 bytes from `buffer` to the file. Or to save an array of 10 `double` values, you can do this:

```
double earnings[10];
        .
        .
        .
fwrite(earnings, sizeof (double), 10, fp);
```

This call writes data from the `earnings` array to the file in 10 chunks, each of size `double`.

You probably noticed the odd declaration of `void *ptr` in the `fwrite()` prototype. One problem with `fwrite()` is that its first argument is not a fixed type. For instance, our first example used `buffer`, which is type pointer-to-`char`, and the second example used `earnings`, which is type pointer-to-`double`. Under ANSI C function prototyping, these actual arguments are converted to the pointer-to-`void` type, which acts as a sort of catchall type for pointers. (Pre-ANSI C uses type `char *` for this argument, requiring you to type-cast actual arguments to that type.)

The `fwrite()` function returns the number of items successfully written. Normally, this equals `nmemb`, but it can be less if there is a write error.

size_t fread(void *ptr, size_t size, size_t nmemb, FILE *fp)

The `size_t fread(void *ptr, size_t size, size_t nmemb, FILE *fp)` function takes the same set of arguments that `fwrite()` does. This time `ptr` is the address of the memory storage into which file data is read, and `fp` identifies the file to be read. Use this function to read data that was written to a file using `fwrite()`. For example, to recover the array of 10 `doubles` saved in the last example, use this call:

```
double earnings[10];
        .
        .
        .
fread(earnings, sizeof (double), 10, fp);
```

This call copies 10 size `double` values into the `earnings` array.

The `fread()` function returns the number of items successfully read. Normally, this equals `nmemb`, but it can be less if there is a read error or if the end of file is reached.

int feof(FILE *fp) and int ferror(FILE *fp)

When the standard input functions return `EOF`, it usually means that they have reached the end of a file. However, it also can indicate that a read error has occurred. The `feof()` and `ferror()` functions allow you to distinguish between the two possibilities. The `feof()` function returns a nonzero value if the last input call detected the end of file and returns zero otherwise. The `ferror()` function returns a nonzero value if a read or write error has occurred and zero otherwise.

An Example

Let's use some of these functions in a program that will append the contents from a list of files to the end of another file. One problem is passing the file information to the program. This can be done interactively or by using command-line arguments. We'll take the second approach, letting the final command-line argument represent the name of the append file. That is, a command like

```
append file1 file2 file3
```

will append `file1` and `file2` to `file3`. This suggests a plan along the following lines:

If there are fewer than three words on the command-line, quit.

Open the final command-line file in the append mode.

For each remaining command-line file, open it in the read mode and add it to the append file.

To illustrate setvbuf(), we'll use it to specify a different buffer size. The next stage of refinement examines the opening of the append file. We will use the following steps:

Open the final command-line file in the append mode.

If this cannot be done, quit.

Establish a 1024-byte buffer for this file.

If this cannot be done, quit.

Similarly, we can refine the copying portion in this way:

For each remaining file in the command-line list:

If it is the same as the append file, skip to the next file.

If it cannot be opened in the read mode, skip to the next file.

Add the contents of the file to the append file.

For practice, we'll use fread() and fwrite() for the copying. Listing 12.7 shows the result.

Listing 12.7 append.c

```
/* append.c -- appends files to a file */
#include <stdio.h>
#define BUFSIZE 1024
char temp[BUFSIZE];
void append(FILE *source, FILE *dest);

int main(int argc, char *argv[])
{
    FILE *fa, *fr;
    int file;

    if (argc < 3)
    {
        fprintf(stderr,
         "Usage: %s source-file(s) destination-file\n", argv[0]);
        exit(1);
```

```
        }
        if ((fa = fopen(argv[argc - 1], "a")) == NULL)
        {
            fprintf(stderr, "Can't open %s\n", argv[argc - 1]);
            exit(2);
        }
        if (setvbuf(fa, NULL, _IOFBF, BUFSIZE) != 0)
        {
            fputs("Can't create output buffer\n", stderr);
            exit(3);
        }
        for (file = 1; file < argc - 1; file++)
        {
            if (strcmp(argv[argc - 1], argv[file]) == 0)
                fputs("Can't append file to itself\n",stderr);
            else if ((fr = fopen(argv[file], "r")) == NULL)
                fprintf(stderr, "Can't open %s\n", argv[file]);
            else
            {
                if (setvbuf(fr, NULL, _IOFBF, BUFSIZE) != 0)
                {
                    fputs("Can't create output buffer\n",stderr);
                    continue;
                }
                append(fr, fa);
                if (ferror(fr) != 0)
                    fprintf(stderr,"Error in reading file %s.\n",
                            argv[file]);
                if (ferror(fa) != 0)
                    fprintf(stderr,"Error in writing file %s.\n",
                            argv[argc - 1]);
                return 0;
            }
        }
        fclose(fa);
}

void append(FILE *source, FILE *dest)
{
    size_t bytes;
```

(continued)

```
Listing 12.7   (continued)

    extern char temp[];

    while ((bytes = fread(temp,sizeof(char),BUFSIZE,source)) > 0)
        fwrite(temp, sizeof (char), bytes, dest);
}
```

The following code creates a buffer 1024 bytes in size to be used with the append file:

```
if (setvbuf(fa, NULL, _IOFBF, BUFSIZE) != 0)
{
    fputs("Can't create output buffer\n", stderr);
    exit(3);
}
```

If setvbuf() is unable to create the buffer, it returns a nonzero value, and the code then terminates the program. Similar coding establishes a 1024-byte buffer for the file currently being copied. By using NULL as the second argument to setvbuf(), we let that function allocate storage for the buffer.

This code prevents the program from trying to append a file to itself:

```
if (strcmp(argv[argc - 1], argv[file]) == 0)
    fputs("Can't append file to itself\n",stderr);
```

The argument argv[argc - 1] represents the name of the final file in the command line, while argv[file] represents the name of the file currently being processed.

The append() function does the copying. Instead of copying a byte at a time, it uses fread() and fwrite() to copy 1024 bytes at a time:

```
void append(source, dest)
FILE *source, *dest;
{
    size_t bytes;
    extern char temp[];

    while ((bytes = fread(temp,sizeof(char),BUFSIZE,source)) > 0)
        fwrite(temp, sizeof (char), bytes, dest);
}
```

Because the file specified by dest is opened in the append mode, each source file is added to the end of the destination file, one after the other.

Chapter Summary

Writing to and reading from files is essential for most C programs. Most C implementations offer both *low-level* I/O services and *standard high-level* I/O services for these purposes. Because the ANSI C library includes the standard I/O services but not the low-level services, the standard package is more portable.

The standard I/O package automatically creates input and output buffers to speed up data transfer. The fopen() function opens a file for standard I/O and creates a data structure designed to hold information about the file and the buffer. The fopen() function returns a pointer to that data structure, and this pointer is used by other functions to identify the file to be processed.

ANSI C provides two file-opening modes: *binary* and *text*. When a file is opened in binary mode, it can be read byte-for-byte. When a file is opened in text mode, its contents may be mapped from the system representation of text to the C representation. For UNIX systems the two modes are identical because the C model for text files is derived from the UNIX file model.

The input functions getc(), fgets(), fscanf(), and fread() normally read a file sequentially, starting at the beginning of the file. However, the fseek() and ftell() functions let a program move to an arbitrary position in a file, enabling random access. Random access works better in the binary than in the text mode.

Review Questions

1. What's wrong with this program?

```
int main(void)
{
    int *fp;
    int k;

    fp = fopen("gelatin");
    for (k = 0; k < 30; k++)
        fputs(fp, "Nanette eats gelatin.");
    fclose("gelatin");
}
```

2. Suppose you have these statements in a program:

```
#include <stdio.h>
FILE *fp1,fp2;
char ch;

fp1 = fopen("terky", "r");
fp2 = fopen("jerky", "w");
```

Also, suppose that both files were opened successfully. Supply the missing arguments in the following function calls:

   a. `ch = getc();`

   b. `fprintf( ,"%c\n", );`

   c. `putc( , );`

   d. `fclose(); /* close the terky file */`

3. Write a program that takes two command-line arguments. The first is a character, and the second is a filename. The program should print only those lines in the file containing the given character. *Note*: Lines in a file are identified by a terminating `'\n'`. Assume that no line is more than 256 characters long. You may wish to use `fgets()`.

4. What is the difference between

   a. Saving `8238201` using `fprintf()` and saving it using `fwrite()`?

   b. Saving the character `S` using `putc()` and saving it using `fwrite()`?

5. The `"a+"`, `"r+"`, and `"w+"` modes all open files for both reading and writing. Which one is best suited for altering material already present in a file?

Programming Exercises

1. Write a file copy program that takes the original filename and the copy file from the command line. Use standard I/O and the binary mode, if possible.

2. Write a program that sequentially displays on screen all the files listed in the command line. Use `argc` to control a loop.

3. Modify the program in Listing 12.6 so that it recognizes an optional flag command-line argument of the form -n, where n is an integer. Have the program print the last n lines of listed file(s). Use the binary mode.

4. Write a program that opens two files whose names are provided by command-line arguments.

    a. Have the program print line 1 of the first file, line 1 of the second file, line 2 of the first file, line 2 of the second file, and so on, until the last line of the longer file (in terms of lines) is printed.

    b. Modify the program so that lines with the same line number are printed on the same line.

5. Write a program that takes as command-line arguments a character and zero or more filenames. If no arguments follow the character, have the program read the standard input. Otherwise, have it open each file in turn and report how many times the character appears in each file. The filename and the character itself should be reported along with the count. Include error-checking to see if the number of arguments is correct and to see if the files can be opened. If a file can't be opened, have the program report that fact and go on to the next file.

6. Modify the program in Listing 12.3 so that each word is numbered according to the order in which it was added to the list, starting with 1. Make sure that, when the program is run a second time, new word numbering resumes where the previous numbering left off.

7. Write a program that opens a text file whose name is obtained interactively. Set up a loop that asks the user to enter a file position. The program then prints the part of the file starting at that position and proceeding to the next newline character. Let nonnumeric input terminate the user-input loop.

8. Write a program that takes two command-line arguments. The first is a string; the second is the name of a file. The program then should search the file, printing all lines containing the string. Because this task is line-oriented rather than character-oriented, use `fgets()` rather than `getc()`. Use a function like `string_in()` from Exercise 7, Chapter 11, to search each line for the string.

9. Write a function that reads one word from a file, leaving the boundary character (a tab, space, or newline) in the input buffer. Don't use `scanf()` or `fscanf()`.

10. Programs using command-line arguments rely on the user's memory of how to use them correctly. Rewrite the program in Listing 12.7 so that, instead of using command-line arguments, it prompts the user for the required information.

13

Storage Classes and Program Development

Keywords
- auto, extern, static
- register, const, volatile

Function
- rand( )

In this chapter you learn how C lets you determine the scope of a variable (how widely known it is) and the lifetime of a variable (how long it remains in existence). Also, you gain experience in designing more complex programs.

O
ne of C's strengths is that it lets you control the fine points of a program. C's storage classes exemplify that control by allowing you to determine which functions know which variables and for how long a variable persists in a program. Using storage classes is one more element of program design. There is more to programming than just knowing the rules of the language, just as there is more to writing a novel (or even a letter) than knowing the rules of English. We will reinforce some of the general principles and concepts of program design introduced earlier. We will also develop several useful functions. As we do so, we will try to demonstrate some of the general considerations that go into designing a function. In particular, we will emphasize the value of a *modular* approach—the division of a job into smaller, more manageable tasks.

Storage Classes and Scope

We gave storage classes a passing mention in Chapter 10. We'll take a longer look now. As we mentioned in Chapter 10, *local variables* are known only to the functions containing them. However, C also offers the possibility of *global variables*, those known to several functions. Suppose you want both `main()` and `critic()` to have access to the variable `Units`. You can do this by declaring `Units` so that it belongs to the external storage class, as shown in Listing 13.1. (Here we follow a common, but not universal, convention of uppercasing the first character of a global variable name.)

Listing 13.1 *global.c*

```
/* global.c  -- uses an external variable */
#include <stdio.h>
```

(continued)

Listing 13.1 *(continued)*

```
int Units;                      /* an external variable */
void critic(void);
int main(void)
{
    extern int Units;

    printf("How many pounds to a firkin of butter?\n");
    scanf("%d", &Units);
    while ( Units != 56)
        critic();
    printf("You must have looked it up!\n");
}
void critic(void)
{
    extern int Units;

    printf("No luck, chummy. Try again.\n");
    scanf("%d", &Units);
}
```

Here is a sample output:

```
How many pounds to a firkin of butter?
14
No luck, chummy. Try again.
56
You must have looked it up!
```

(We did.)

Note how the second value for Units was read by the critic() function, yet main() also knew the new value when it finished the while loop. We made Units an external variable by defining it outside of (external to) any function definition. That's all you need to do to make Units available to all the following functions in the file.

There are three ways to treat Units within the functions. The simplest is to have no further declarations. In that case, the functions will use the externally defined Units by default.

The second way, and the one we took, is to place the following declaration in each function:

```
extern int Units;
```

In our example, inserting this declaration is mainly a matter of documentation. It tells the compiler that any mention of `Units` in this particular function refers to a variable defined outside the function, perhaps even outside the file. Again, both functions use the externally defined `Units`.

The third way, and one quite different in meaning, is to use this declaration in the functions:

```
int Units;
```

Suppose we do this for `main()` but not for `critic()`. Omitting the keyword `extern` causes the compiler to create a separate variable private to `main()`, but also named `Units`. The new `Units` would be *visible* while `main()` is running. But when control passes to `critic()`, the program would interpret `Units` as the externally defined one, and the value assigned to `Units` in `main()` would not affect the value of `Units` in `critic()`.

Each variable, as you know, has a type. In addition, each variable has a *storage class*. There are four keywords used to describe storage classes: `extern` (for external), `auto` (for automatic), `static`, and `register`. Variables declared within a function are considered to be class `auto` unless declared otherwise. The formal arguments to functions normally are class `auto`, but they can be made class `register`.

The storage class of a variable is determined by where it is defined and by what keyword, if any, is used. The storage class determines two things. First, it controls which functions have access to a variable. The extent to which a variable is available is called its *scope*. Second, the storage class determines how long the variable persists in memory—its *life*. Let's go over the properties of each type.

Automatic Variables

By default, variables declared in a function are automatic. You can, however, make your intentions perfectly clear by explicitly using the keyword `auto`:

```
int main(void)
{
   auto int plox;
```

You might do this, for example, to document that you intentionally are overriding an external function definition or that it is important not to change the variable to another storage class.

An automatic variable has local scope. Only the function in which the variable is defined can access that variable by name. (Of course, arguments can be used to communicate the value and the address of the variable to another function, but that is indirect knowledge.) Another function can use a variable with the same name, but it will be an independent variable stored in a different memory location.

An automatic variable comes into existence when the function that contains it is called. When the function finishes its task and returns control to its caller, the automatic variable disappears. Its memory location can now be used for something else.

One more point about the scope of an automatic variable: its scope is confined to the block (paired braces) in which the variable is declared. We have always declared our variables at the beginning of the function block, so the scope is the whole function. But in principle you could declare a variable within a subblock. Then that variable would be known only to that subsection of the function. Normally, you wouldn't use this feature when designing a program. Sometimes, however, it is useful to define a variable in a subblock if it is not used elsewhere. In that way, you can document the meaning of a variable close to the location at which it is used.

Initialization of Automatic Variables

Automatic variables are not initialized unless you do so explicitly. Consider the following declarations:

```
int main(void)
{
   int repid;
   int tents = 5;
```

The `tents` variable is initialized to 5, but the `repid` variable winds up with whatever value happened to previously occupy the space assigned to `repid`. You cannot rely on this value being 0.

External Variables

A variable defined outside a function is external. As a matter of documentation, an external variable also can be declared inside a function that uses it by using the `extern` keyword. If the variable is defined *after* the function or in another file, declaring the variable with `extern` is mandatory. Declarations look like this:

```
int Errupt;          /* externally defined variable   */
double Up[100];      /* externally defined array       */
int main(void)
{
   extern int Errupt;  /* optional declaration         */
   extern char Coal;   /* mandatory declaration        */
```

```
    extern double Up[]; /* plus one array                    */
    :
    :

}
char Coal;              /* externally defined variable    */
```

The group of `extern` declarations may be omitted entirely if the original definitions occur in the same file and before the function that uses them.

If only the `extern` is omitted from the declaration in a function, then a separate automatic variable is set up by that name. You may want to label this second variable as `auto` to show that your coding is a matter of intention, not oversight.

The following three examples show the four possible combinations. In Example 1, there is one external variable: `Hocus`. It is known to both `main()` and `magic()`.

```
/* Example 1 */
int Hocus;
int magic();
int main(void)
{
    extern int Hocus;  /* Hocus declared external */
    :
    :
    :

}
int magic()
{
    extern int Hocus;
    :
    :
    :

}
```

Example 2 has one external variable, `Hocus`, known to both functions. This time, `magic()` knows it by default:

```
/* Example 2 */
int Hocus;
int magic();
int main(void)
{
    extern int Hocus;  /* Hocus declared external    */
    :
    :
```

```
}
int magic()
{
                              /* Hocus not declared at all */

    .
    .
    .

}
```

In the last example, four separate variables are created. The Hocus in main() is automatic by default and is local to main. The Hocus in magic() is automatic explicitly and is known only to magic(). The external Hocus is not known to main() or magic() but would be known to any other function in the file that did not have its own local Hocus. Finally, Pocus is an external variable known to magic() but not to main() because Pocus follows main().

```
/* Example 3 */
int Hocus;
int magic();
int main(void)
{
  int Hocus;          /* Hocus declared, is auto by default */

    .
    .

}
int Pocus;
int magic()
{
    auto int Hocus;  /* Hocus declared automatic             */

    .
    .

}
```

These examples illustrate the scope of external variables. They also illustrate the lifetimes of variables. The external Hocus and Pocus variables persist as long as the program runs, and, since they aren't confined to any one function, they don't fade away when a particular function returns.

Note: If you use the keyword extern without a type, the compiler interprets it as being extern int.

Initializing External Variables

Like automatic variables, external variables can be initialized explicitly. Unlike automatic variables, external variables automatically are initialized to zero if you don't initialize them. This applies to elements of an externally defined array, too.

External Names

The rules for names of external variables are more restrictive than for local variables. The reason is that external names need to comply with the rules of the local environment, which may be more limiting. For local names, the ANSI C Standard requires that a compiler distinguish between upper- and lowercase and that it recognize the first 31 characters in a name. For external variables, the compiler need not distinguish between upper- and lowercase, and it need recognize only the first 8 characters in a name. These rules apply to function names, too. The preceding limitations stem from the desire to make C programs compatible with some of the older, more limited operating systems and languages.

Definitions and Declarations

There is a difference between defining a variable and declaring it. Consider this example:

```
int tern;
main()
{
    extern int tern;
    .
    .
    .
```

Here `tern` is declared twice. The first declaration causes storage to be set aside for the variable. It constitutes a *definition* of the variable. The second declaration merely tells the compiler to use the `tern` variable that previously has been created; thus, it is not a definition. The first declaration is called a *defining declaration*, and the second is called a *referencing declaration*. The keyword `extern` *always* indicates that a declaration is not a definition, since it instructs the compiler to look elsewhere.

Suppose you do this:

```
extern int tern;
int main(void)
{
    .
    .
    .
```

Then the compiler would assume that the actual definition of `tern` is somewhere else in your program, perhaps in another file. This declaration will not cause space to be allocated. Therefore, don't use the keyword `extern` to create an external definition; use it only to *refer* to an existing external definition.

An external variable can be initialized only once, and that must occur when the variable is defined. A statement like

```
extern char permis = 'Y';   /* error */
```

is in error because the presence of the keyword `extern` signifies a referencing declaration, not a defining declaration.

Static Variables

The name *static variable* sounds like a contradiction, like a variable that can't vary. Actually, "static" means that the variable stays put. These variables have the same scope as automatic variables, but they don't vanish when the containing function ends its job. The computer remembers their values from one function call to the next. The example in Listing 13.2 illustrates this point and shows how to declare a static variable.

```
Listing 13.2   static.c

/* static.c -- using a static variable */
#include <stdio.h>
void trystat(void);
int main(void)
{
    int count;

    for (count = 1; count <= 3; count++)
    {
        printf("Here comes iteration %d:\n", count);
        trystat();
    }
    return 0;
}
void trystat(void)
{
    int fade = 1;
```

```
    static int stay = 1;

    printf("fade = %d and stay = %d\n", fade++, stay++);
}
```

Note that `trystat()` increments each variable after printing its value. Running the program gives this output:

```
Here comes iteration 1:
fade = 1 and stay = 1
Here comes iteration 2:
fade = 1 and stay = 2
Here comes iteration 3:
fade = 1 and stay = 3
```

The static variable `stay` remembers that its value was increased by 1, whereas the `fade` variable starts anew each time. This points out a difference in initialization: `fade` is initialized each time `trystat()` is called, but `stay` is initialized just once, when `trystat()` is compiled. Like external variables, static variables are initialized to zero if you don't explicitly initialize them to some other value.

External Static Variables

You can also declare a `static` variable outside all functions. This creates an *external static* function. The difference between an ordinary external variable and an external static variable lies in its scope (see Figure 13.1). The ordinary external variable can be used by functions in any file, but the external static variable can be used only by functions in the same file. You set up an external static variable by placing the definition outside all functions:

```
static int randx = 1;
int rand()
{
```

Later on, Listing 13.3 shows an example with a static variable.

Multiple Files

Complex C programs often use several separate files of code. Sometimes these files may need to share an external variable. The ANSI C way to do

Figure 13.1 *External variable versus external static variable*

file 1   file 2

```
int twit;              extern int twit;
static int turn;       hedge()
main()                 {
  {                      ---
  ---                    ---
  ---                    }
  }                    mostly()
figaro()               {
  {                      ---
  ---                    ---
  ---                    }
  }
```

`Twit` *is known to* `main()`, `figaro()`, `hedge()`, and `mostly()`
`Turn` *is known to only* `main()` *and* `figaro()`

this is to have a defining declaration in one file and referencing declarations in the other files. That is, all but one declaration (the defining declaration) should use the `extern` keyword. And only the defining declaration can be used to initialize the variable.

Note that an external variable defined in one file is not available to a second file unless it is also declared in the second file; external variables are not automatically made available to all files.

Historically, however, many compilers have followed different rules in this regard. Many UNIX systems, for example, allow you to declare a variable in several files without using the `extern` keyword, providing that no more than one declaration includes an initialization. If there is a declaration with an initialization, it is taken to be the definition.

Scope and Functions

Functions, too, have storage classes. A function can either be external (the default) or static. An *external function* can be accessed by functions in other files, while a *static function* can be used only within the defining file. Consider, for example, a file containing these function declarations:

```
double gamma();          /* external by default */
static double beta();
extern double delta();
```

The functions gamma() and delta() can be used by functions in other files that are part of the program, but beta() cannot. Because this beta() is restricted to one file, you can use a different function having the same name in the other files. One reason to use the static storage class is to create functions that are private to a particular module, thereby avoiding the possibility of name conflicts.

We recommend that you use the extern keyword when declaring functions that are defined in other files. This is mostly a matter of clarity, since a function declaration is assumed to be extern unless the keyword static is used.

Register Variables

Variables normally are stored in computer memory. With luck, *register variables* are stored in the CPU registers or, more generally, in the fastest memory available, where they can be accessed and manipulated more rapidly than regular variables. In other respects, register variables are the same as automatic variables. They are declared this way:

```
int main(void)
{
    register int quick;
```

We say "with luck" because declaring a variable as register class is more a request than a direct order. The compiler has to weigh your demands against the number of registers or amount of fast memory available, so you may not get your wish. In that case, the variable becomes an ordinary automatic variable.

You can request that formal parameters be register variables. Just use the keyword in the function heading:

```
void mucho(register int n)
```

The types that can be declared register may be restricted. For example, the registers in a processor may not be large enough to hold type double. Also, the & operator will not work with register variables.

Summary: Scopes

The scope of an automatic variable (including function formal arguments) is confined to the defining function. When a variable is declared external to any function in a file, that external variable will be known to all functions following it in that file, whether or not those functions explicitly declare the variable as extern. If you want a function in a second file to access an external variable in the first file, you must declare the variable in the second file using the keyword extern.

A static variable defined inside a function is local to that function, and a static variable defined outside a function is local to that file.

Which Storage Class?

The answer to the question "Which storage class?" most often is "automatic." After all, why else was *automatic* selected as the default? Yes, we know that at first glance external storage is quite alluring. Just make all your variables external, and you'll never have to worry about using arguments and pointers to communicate between functions. But there is a subtle pitfall. You will have to worry about function A( ) sneakily altering the variables used in function B( ), despite your intentions to the contrary. The unquestionable evidence of untold years of collective computer experience is that this one subtle danger far outweighs the superficial attraction of using external storage indiscriminately.

One of the golden rules of protective programming is the "need to know" principle. Keep the inner workings of each function as private to that function as possible, sharing only those variables that need to be shared. The other classes are useful, and they are available. Before using one, though, ask yourself if it is necessary.

A Random Number Function

Now let's look at a function that makes use of an external static variable: a *random-number function*. The ANSI C library provides the rand( ) function for random numbers, but it is instructive to make one ourselves. Actually, we'll make a "pseudorandom number generator." This means that the actual sequence of numbers is predictable (computers are not known for

Summary: Storage Classes

Keywords

`auto, extern, static, register`

General Comments

The storage class of a variable determines its scope and life. Storage class is determined both by where the variable is defined and by its associated keyword. Variables defined outside all functions are external, have global scope, and persist for the life of the program. Variables declared inside a function are automatic and local unless one of the other keywords is used. External variables defined above a function are known to it even if not declared internally.

Properties

In the following list, those variables in storage classes above the dotted line are declared inside a function; those below the line are defined outside a function.

Storage Class	Keyword	Duration	Scope
automatic	auto	temporary	local
register	register	temporary	local
static	static	persistent	local
external	extern*	persistent	global (all files)
external static	static	persistent	global (one file)

*The keyword `extern` is used only to redeclare variables that have been defined externally elsewhere. The act of defining the variable outside of a function makes it external.

their spontaneity) but that the numbers are spread pretty uniformly over the possible range of values.

The scheme starts with a number called the *seed*. The function uses the seed to produce a new number, which becomes the new seed. Then the new seed can be used to produce a newer seed, and so on. For this scheme to work, the random number function must remember the seed it used the last time it was called. Aha! This calls for a static variable. Listing 13.3 is version 0. (Yes, version 1 comes soon.)

Listing 13.3 rand0.c

```
/* rand0.c  -- produces random numbers */
short rand0(void)
{
    static short seed = 1;

    /* magic formula to generate pseudorandom number */
    seed = (seed * 25173 + 13849) % 65536;
    return (seed);
}
```

In Listing 13.3 the static variable seed starts with the value 1 and is altered by the magic formula each time that the function is called. The result, in systems with a 2-byte short, is a return value somewhere in the range of −32768 to 32767. (We used short because the size of short is more standard than the size of int.)

Let's try the rand0() function with the simple driver in Listing 13.4.

Listing 13.4 r_drive1.c

```
/* r_drive1.c */
#include <stdio.h>
extern short rand0(void);
int main(void)
{
    int count;

    for (count = 0; count < 5; count++)
        printf("%hd\n", rand0());
    return 0;
}
```

Here's a good chance to practice using multiple files. Use one file for Listing 13.3 and one for Listing 13.4. (See Chapter 9 or your compiler manual for guidance.) The extern keyword reminds us that rand0() is defined in a separate file.

The output is

```
-26514
-4449
20196
-20531
3882
```

The output looks random, but let's run it again. This time the result is as follows:

```
-26514
-4449
20196
-20531
3882
```

Hmmm, that looks familiar; this is the "pseudo" aspect. Each time the main program is run, we start with the same seed of 1. We can get around this problem by introducing a second function srand1() that lets us reset the seed. The trick is to make seed an external static variable known only to rand1() and srand1(). (The C library equivalent to srand1() is called srand().) Keep rand1() and srand1() in their own file and compile that file separately. Listing 13.5 is the modification.

Listing 13.5 *s_and_r.c*

```
/* s_and_r.c -- file for rand1() and srand1() */
static short seed = 1;      /* private to file */
short rand1(void)
{
    seed = (seed *25173 + 13849) % 65536;
    return (seed);
}
void srand1(short x)
{
    seed = x;
}
```

Notice that now seed is an external static variable. This means that it can be used by both rand1() and srand1(), but not by functions in other files. To test these functions, use the driver in Listing 13.6.

Listing 13.6 r_drive2.c

```
/* r_drive2.c */
#include <stdio.h>
extern void srand1(short x);
extern short rand1(void);
int main(void)
{
    int count;
    short seed;

    printf("Please enter your choice for seed.\n");
    scanf("%hd", &seed);
    srand1(seed);      /* reset seed */
    for (count = 0; count < 5; count++)
        printf("%hd\n", rand1());
    return 0;
}
```

Again, use two files. Run the program once:

```
Please enter your choice for seed.
1
-26514
-4449
20196
-20531
3882
```

Using a value of 1 for seed yields the same values as before. Now let's try a value of 3:

```
Please enter your choice for seed.
3
23832
20241
-1858
-30417
-16204
```

Very good! We get a different set of numbers.

Automated Reseeding

If your C implementation gives you access to some changing quantity, such as the system clock, you can use that value (possibly truncated) to initialize the seed value. For instance, ANSI C has a `clock()` function that returns the system time. The time units are system dependent, but what matters here is that the return value is an integer type and that its value changes with time. The exact integer type also is system dependent, but you can use a type cast. Here's the basic setup:

```
#include <time.h>   /* ANSI prototype for clock() */
.
.
.
srand1((short) clock());   /* initialize seed */
```

Now let's develop a use for this set of functions.

Roll 'Em

We are going to simulate that very popular random activity, dice-rolling. The most popular form of dice-rolling uses two 6-sided dice. But there are other possibilities. Many adventure-fantasy games use all of the five geo-metrically possible dice: 4, 6, 8, 12, and 20 sides. Those clever ancient Greeks proved that there are but five regular solids having all faces the same shape and size, and these solids are the basis for the dice varieties. One could make dice with other numbers of sides, but the faces would not all be the same, so they wouldn't all have equal odds of turning up.)

Computer calculations aren't limited by these geometric considerations, so we can devise an electronic die that has any number of sides. Let's start with 6 sides and then generalize.

We want a random number from 1 to 6. But since `rand1()` produces the range −32768 to 32767, we have some adjustments to make. Here's one approach.

1. Divide the random number by 32768. This results in a number x in the range −1 <= x < 1. (We'll have to convert to type `float` so that we can have decimal fractions.)
2. Add 1. Our new number satisfies the relationship 0 <= x < 2.
3. Divide by 2. Now 0 <= x < 1.

4. Multiply by 6. Now 0 <= x < 6. (Close, but 0 is not a possible die value.)

5. Add 1: 1<= x < 7. (Note that these are still decimal fractions.)

6. Truncate to an integer. Now we have an integer in the range of 1 to 6.

7. To generalize, just replace the number 6 in step 4 by the number of sides.

Listing 13.7 shows a function that does these steps for a general number of sides. The listing includes some explicit type casts to emphasize where type conversions take place.

Listing 13.7 *diceroll.c*

```
/* diceroll.c */
#define SCALE 32768.0
extern short rand1(void);
int rollem(int sides)
{
    float roll;

    roll = ((float) rand1()/SCALE + 1.0) * sides / 2.0 + 1.0;
    return ((int) roll);
}
```

Listing 13.8 shows a program that uses the rand1(), srand1(), and rollem() functions.

Listing 13.8 *manydice.c*

```
/* manydice.c -- multiple dice roll */
#include <stdio.h>
extern srand1(short);
extern int rollem(void);
int main(void)
{
    int dice, count, roll;
```

```
short seed;
int sides;

printf("Enter a seed value.\n");
scanf("%hd", &seed);
srand1(seed);
printf("Enter the number of sides per die, 0 to stop.\n");
while (scanf("%d", &sides) == 1 && sides > 0)
{
    printf("How many dice?\n");
    scanf("%d", &dice);
    for (roll = 0, count = 0; count < dice; count++)
        roll += rollem(sides);
        /* running total of dice pips */
    printf("You have rolled a %d using %d %d-sided dice.\n",
            roll, dice, sides);
    printf("How many sides? Enter 0 to stop.\n");
}
printf("GOOD FORTUNE TO YOU!\n");
return 0;
}
```

Compile Listing 13.8 with the files containing Listings 13.5 and 13.7. Then use it:

```
Enter a seed value.
1
Enter the number of sides per die, 0 to stop.
6
How many dice?
2
You have rolled a 9 using 2 6-sided dice.
How many sides? Enter 0 to stop.
6
How many dice?
2
You have rolled a 8 using 2 6-sided dice.
How many sides? Enter 0 to stop.
0
GOOD FORTUNE TO YOU!
```

You can use rollem() in many ways. With sides equal to 2, the program simulates a coin toss with "heads" = 2 and "tails" = 1 (or vice versa if you really prefer it). You can easily modify the program to show the individual results as well as the total. Or you can construct a craps simulator. If you require a large number of rolls, as may occur in some role-playing games, you can easily modify the program to produce output like this:

```
Enter a seed value.
10
Enter the number of sets; enter q to stop.
18
How many sides and how many dice?
6 3
Here are 18 sets of 3 6-sided throws.
    7     5     9     7    12    10     7    12    10    14
    9     8    13     9    10     7    16    10
How many sets? Enter q to stop.
q
```

Another use for `rand1()` (but not of `rollem()`) would be to create a number-guessing program so that the computer chooses and you guess. You can try that yourself.

Now let's develop some more functions. Our first project will be to design a program that reads in a list of integers and sorts them.

Sorting Numbers

One of the most common tasks for a computer is sorting. Here we'll develop a program to sort integers. We'll take a black box approach and think in terms of input and output. Our overall plan, shown in Figure 13.2, is pretty simple.

Figure 13.2 *Sorting program: A black box view*

At this point, the program is still too vaguely defined for us to begin writing code. The next step is to identify the main tasks that the program must do to accomplish our goals. We can break down our example to three such tasks:

1. Read the numbers.
2. Sort them.
3. Print the sorted numbers.

Figure 13.3 shows this breakdown as we descend from the top level of organization to a more detailed level.

Figure 13.3 *Sorting program: Peeking inside*

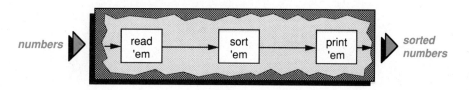

Global Decisions

Before designing the individual modules, we need to make some global decisions. We need to choose a data form and to decide what information will be passed to the individual modules.

Data Form

How do we represent a collection of numbers? We could use a collection of variables, one for each number. That is just too much trouble to even think about. An immensely superior approach is to use an array.

But what kind of an array? Type `int`? Type `double`? We need to know how the program is going to be used. Let's assume it is to be used with modestly sized integers. We will use an array of `int`s to store the numbers we read.

Information Flow

The first module gathers input. It should know where to place the values it reads. It also should know the maximum number of values it can accept, and it should report the actual number of items read. The sorting module should know which array to sort and how many elements are present. The printing module should know which array to use and how many elements to print. These considerations suggest the `main()` function shown in Listing 13.9.

Listing 13.9 *sort_int.c*

```
/* sort_int.c -- sorts integers */
#define MAXSIZE 100    /* limit to number of integers to sort */
extern int getarray(int ar[], int n);
extern void sort(int ar[], int n);
extern void print(int ar[], int n);
int main(void)
{
    int numbers[MAXSIZE];          /* array to hold input     */
    int size;                      /* number of input items   */

    size = getarray(numbers, MAXSIZE); /* put input into array   */
    sort(numbers, size);           /* sort the array          */
    print(numbers, size);          /* print the sorted array  */
    return 0;
}
```

Here we have the skeleton of our program. The function `getarray()` places the values read into the array `numbers` and reports how many values were read. That value is assigned to `size`. Then `sort()` sorts the array, and `print()` prints the sorted results.

Now that we have refined our picture of the information flow, we should modify our black box sketch. As Figure 13.4 shows, we now have three black boxes, each with its own input and output. Because we are emphasizing modularity, we have broken the original problem into three smaller, more manageable pieces. We can assign each part to a different programming team, provided that the numbers output by "read 'em" are in the same form that "sort 'em" uses for input.

We will apply our efforts to each of the three boxes separately, breaking them down to simpler units until we reach a point at which the code is obvious. As we do this, we must pay attention to these important points: data-form choice, error-trapping, and information flow. Let's continue with our example, tackling the reading portion first (see Figure 13.5).

Reading Numeric Data

Many programs read numbers, so the ideas we develop here will be useful elsewhere. The general form for this part of the program is clear: Use a

Figure 13.4 *Sorting program: Adding details*

Figure 13.5 *Sorting program: The first task*

loop to read in numbers until all the numbers are read. But there is more to reading numbers than you might think!

Ending Input

How will the function know when to quit reading numbers? We faced a similar problem in Chapter 10. There we had a `read_array()` function that quit reading numbers when the user either simulated EOF or entered a nonnumeric value. This time we'll take a different tack. Our main change is how we handle nonnumeric input. We'll design the function so that it alerts the user when the input is nonnumeric and then lets the user try again.

Why this change? Suppose you are entering data at the keyboard and accidentally enter 1o instead of 10. Would you rather have the program terminate, forcing you to reenter all the data, or have it just reject that one entry and let you continue? It is simpler to rely on the "perfect user theory," which states that the user makes no entry errors. However, we recognize that this theory may not apply to users other than ourselves. Therefore, we opt for the second choice. This checking of input for suitability is termed *data validation*.

Here is one approach:

read a word

while not EOF

   if the word is an integer, assign it to an array

else skip that word and request numeric input again

read the next word if the array isn't full

Note that there are two separate conditions that bring this portion of the program to a close: an EOF signal or filling the array.

Further Considerations

Before we translate this approach into C code, we still have decisions to make. The data validation to which we've committed ourselves has two aspects: detecting an error and reporting that error to the user. We can try to code all this directly into getarray(), or we can put the code into an input function called by getarray(). We'll adopt an intermediate approach that follows a common C style: we'll give the input function the responsibility of detecting errors, and leave the calling function (getarray()) the responsibility of handling the error. This provides greater flexibility because the same input function can be used in programs that process errors differently.

The *getarray( )* Function

Now let's look at getarray() shown in Listing 13.10.

```
Listing 13.10  getarray.c

/* getarray.c -- reads in an array */
#include <stdio.h>
#include "getint.h"      /* declares getint(), constants */
int getarray(int array[], int limit)
{
   int num, status;
   int index = 0;                          /* array index */

   printf("This program stops reading numbers after %d ",
          limit);
   printf("values\nor if EOF is encountered.\n");
   while (index < limit && (status = getint(&num)) != EOF )
   {
      if (status == YESNUM)
      {
         array[index++] = num;
         printf("The number %d has been accepted.\n", num);
```

```
    }
    else if (status == NONUM)
       printf("That was no integer! Try again.\n");
    else
       printf("This can't happen! Something's very wrong.\n");
    }
    if (index == limit )    /* report if array gets filled */
    printf("All %d elements of the array were filled.\n",
         limit);
    return(index);
}
```

This is a not a simple function, and we have quite a few points to note.

Explanation

The getarray() function is premised on the existence of a getint() function with the following properties:

▶ The getint() function returns YESNUM if it has read an integer. It places the value of that integer into the location pointed to by its argument, an address of an int.

▶ It returns NONUM if it reads a noninteger. It discards the invalid input.

▶ It returns EOF if it encounters the end of file.

▶ The getint.h file contains the function declaration and definitions of the getint() return values.

The implementation of this function will come after we finish discussing getarray().

We set up getarray() to handle each of the possible return values. An EOF return causes the while loop to end. A YESNUM return results in a valid entry being stored in the awaiting array. Also, that number is echoed back to the user showing that it was accepted. A NONUM return sends the user back for another try.

But there is one more else statement. Logically, the only way that statement can be reached is if getint() returns a value other than YESNUM, NONUM, or EOF. But those are the only values that can be returned, so this seems to be a useless statement. We included it as an example of *defensive programming*, the art of protecting a program from future fiddling. Someday, we, or someone else, may decide to rewrite getint(), adding a few more possible return values to its repertoire. Most likely we will by then have forgotten, and they may never have known, that `getarray()` assumes that there are just three possible responses. Therefore, to assist in future debugging, we include this final `else` to trap any new responses that show up.

We use the keyword `return` to communicate the number of items read. Thus, our function call

```
size = getarray(numbers, MAXSIZE);
```

assigns a value to `size` and puts values into the `numbers` array.

In functions involving counters and limits, like this one, the most likely place to find an error is at the *boundary conditions*, where counts reach their limits. Are we going to read a maximum of `MAXSIZE` numbers, or are we going to be off by 1? We need to pay attention to details such as `++index` versus `index++` and `<` versus `<=`. We also have to keep in mind that arrays start their subscripting with 0, not 1. Take a moment to check our code and see if it works as it should. The easiest way to do that is to imagine that `limit` is 1 and then walk through the procedure step by step.

Finally, the function informs the user when the array is full so that he or she is not taken by surprise.

The *getint( )* Function

Now we need to supply a `getint()` function. We'll take the easy way and use existing library functions. Listing 13.11 shows an implementation based on `scanf()`.

Listing 13.11 *getint.c*

```
/* getint.c */
#include <stdio.h>
#include "getint.h"
int getint(ptint)
int *ptint;        /* pointer to integer output */
{
   int status;

   status = scanf("%d", ptint);
   if (status == NONUM)
        scanf("%*s");
   return status;
}
```

Also, we need a getint.h file:

```
/* getint.h -- definitions used by getint() */
#define NONUM 0
#define YESNUM 1
extern int getint(int *pt);
```

Recall that scanf() returns the number of items successfully read. If it finds an int, it returns 1, or YESNUM. If it finds a noninteger, it returns 0, or NONUM. And if it finds the end of file, it returns EOF. The getint() function merely passes along these return values. If the return value of scanf() is 0, the getint() function skips over the invalid input. Recall that the %*s specifier causes scanf() to skip over the next word. If status is 0, then the word is not an integer, so we want to skip it. Otherwise, scanf() will remain stuck on that word forever.

Getting a program to interact in a convenient, dependable manner with the user is often the most difficult part of writing code. That is the case with this part of the program. You'll find sort() and print() easier. Let's move on to sort() now.

Sorting the Data

Let's look at main() again from Listing 13.9:

```
/* sort_int.c -- sorts integers */
#define MAXSIZE 100     /* limit to number of integers to sort */
extern int getarray(int ar[], int n);
extern void sort(int ar[], int n);
extern void print(int ar[], int n);
int main(void)
{
    int numbers[MAXSIZE];               /* array to hold input    */
    int size;                           /* number of input items  */

    size = getarray(numbers, MAXSIZE); /* put input into array    */
    sort(numbers, size);                /* sort the array          */
    print(numbers, size);               /* print the sorted array */
    return 0;
}
```

We see that the two arguments to sort() are an array of integers to be sorted and a count of the number of elements to be sorted. The function sorts the numbers but has no return value. We still haven't decided how to do the sorting, so we need to refine this description further.

One obvious point to decide is the direction of the sort. Are we going to sort from largest to smallest or vice versa? Again, we'll be arbitrary and say that we'll sort from largest to smallest. (We could design a function to do either, but then we would have to develop a way to tell the function which choice we want.)

Figure 13.6 *Sorting function: The second task*

Now let's consider the method we will use to sort. Many sorting algorithms have been developed for computers. We'll use one of the simplest—the *selection sort*.

Here is our plan in pseudocode:

for n = first to n = next-to-last element,
    find largest remaining number and place it in the nth element

The plan works like this. First, start with n = 1. Scan the entire array, find the largest number, and swap it with the first element. Next, set n = 2, and scan all but the first element of the array. Find the largest remaining number, and swap it with the second element. Continue this process until reaching the next-to-last element. Now only two elements are left. Compare them and place the larger in the next-to-last position. This leaves the smallest element of all in the final position.

It looks like a for loop task, but we still have to describe the "find and place" process in more detail. Here is one way to select the largest remaining value. Compare the first and second elements of the remaining array. If the second is larger, swap the two values. Now compare the first element with the third. If the third is larger, swap those two. Each swap moves a larger element to the top. Continue this way until you have compared the first with the last element. When you finish, the largest number is now in the first element of the remaining array. You have sorted the array for the first element, but the rest of the array is in a jumble. Here is the procedure in pseudocode:

for n = second element to last element,
    compare nth element with first element;
    if nth is greater, swap values

This looks like another for loop. It will be nested in the first for loop.

The outer loop indicates which array element is to be filled, and the inner loop finds the value to put there. Putting the two parts of the pseudocode together and translating into C, we get the function in Listing 13.12.

```
Listing 13.12  sort.c

/* sort.c -- sorts an integer array in decreasing order */
void sort(int array[], int limit)
{
    int top, search, temp;

    for (top = 0; top < limit -1; top++)
        for (search = top + 1; search < limit; search++)
            if (array[search] > array[top])
            {
                temp = array[search];
                array[search] = array[top];
                array[top] = temp;
            }
}
```

In Listing 13.12 we were clever enough to remember that the first element has 0 for a subscript. Also, we used the swapping technique discussed in Chapter 9. We used `top` as the subscript for the array element that is to be filled, since it is at the top of the unsorted part of the array. The `search` index roams over the array below the current `top` element. Now we just have `print()` left to write.

Printing the Data

Our last task is to write the function that will print the sorted numbers (see Figure 13.7). This function, as shown in Listing 13.13, is pretty simple.

```
Listing 13.13  print.c

/* print.c -- prints an array */
#include <stdio.h>
```

(continued)

527

```
Listing 13.13   (continued)

void print(int array[], int limit)
{
   int index;

   for (index = 0; index < limit; index++)
      printf("%d\n", array[index]);
}
```

Figure 13.7 Sorting function: The third task

If we want something a little different, such as printing in rows instead of in one column, we can always change this function, leaving the other functions untouched. Similarly, if we found a sorting algorithm that we liked better, we could replace the sort() module. That is one of the nice features about a modular program.

Results

Let's compile and test this package. To make checking the boundary conditions simpler, we'll temporarily change MAXSIZE to 5. For our first test, we will feed numbers to the program until it refuses to take more.

```
This program stops reading numbers after 5 values
or if EOF is encountered.
12 34 54 23 67 232[enter]
All 5 elements of the array were filled.
67
54
34
23
12
```

Good, it stopped when five numbers were read, and it sorted the results. Now we test to see if it stops when the end of file is encountered.

```
This program stops reading numbers after 5 values
or if EOF is encountered.
456 928
MCMLXXXIX
That's no integer! Try again.
-23 +16
[Control-D]    ←(transmits EOF on UNIX system)
928
456
16
-23
```

Faster than you can say "oikology is the science of housekeeping," the whole enormous array is sorted. Recall that Control-Z transmits EOF on MS-DOS systems.

Success wasn't easy, but it was possible. By breaking the problem into smaller parts and by thinking about what information should flow into and out of each part, we reduced the problem to manageable proportions. Furthermore, the individual modules we produced could be used as parts of similar programs. However, in all honesty, we should point out that the Microsoft C version of this program required us to press the Enter key twice if the EOF signal (Control-Z) was the first entry on a line. Apparently, their version of scanf() works slightly differently from Turbo C's or UNIX's.

ANSI C Type Qualifiers

You've seen that a variable is characterized by both its type and its storage class. ANSI C adds two more properties: constancy and volatility. These properties are declared with the keywords const and volatile. These keywords create *qualified types*.

The *const* Type Qualifier

The const keyword in a declaration establishes a variable whose value cannot be modified by assignment or by incrementing or decrementing. On an ANSI-compliant compiler, the code

```
const int nochange;    /* qualifies m as being constant */
nochange = 12;         /* not allowed                    */
```

should produce an error message. You can, however, initialize a `const` variable. Thus, the following is fine:

```
const int nochange = 12;   /* ok */
```

The preceding declaration makes `nochange` a read-only variable. Once initialized, it cannot be changed.

You can use the `const` keyword, for example, to create an array of data that the program can't alter:

```
const int days1[12] = {31,28,31,30,31,30,31,31,30,31,30,31};
```

You've seen how to use the `const` keyword when declaring a simple variable and an array. Pointers are more complicated because you have to distinguish between making the pointer itself `const` and making the value that is pointed to `const`. The declaration

```
const float *pf;  /* pf points to a constant float value */
```

establishes that `pf` points to a value that must remain constant. The value of `pf` itself can be changed. For example, it can be set to point at another `const` value. In contrast, the declaration

```
float * const pt;    /* pt is a const pointer */
```

says that the pointer `pt` itself cannot have its value changed. It must always point to the same address. But the pointed-to value can change. Finally, the declaration

```
const float * const ptr;
```

means both that `ptr` must always point to the same location and that the value stored at the location must not change.

One common use for this new keyword is declaring pointers that serve as formal function parameters. For example, consider the function `strlen()`. We pass it a pointer to the beginning of the string, and the function returns the length of the string. In general, passing a pointer to a function enables that function to alter data in the calling function. But the following declaration prevents that from happening:

```
int strlen(const char * str)   /* ANSI form */
```

This declaration says that the data to which `str` points cannot be changed. But `str` itself can be altered, so the program can use `str++` in its code. It just can't do stuff like `*str = '!'`.

The ANSI C library follows this practice. If a pointer is used only to give a function access to values, the pointer is declared as a pointer to a `const`-qualified type. If the pointer is used to alter data in the calling function, then the `const` keyword isn't used. For instance, the ANSI C declaration for `strcat()` is this:

```
char *strcat(char *, const char *);
```

Recall that `strcat()` adds a copy of the second string to the end of the first string. This modifies the first string but leaves the second string unchanged. The declaration reflects this.

The *volatile* Type Qualifier

The `volatile` qualifier tells the compiler that a variable can have its value altered by agencies other than the program. It typically is used for hardware addresses. For instance, an address may hold the current clock time. The value at that address changes as time changes regardless of what your program is doing. Or the address may be used to receive information transmitted from, say, another computer.

The syntax is the same as for `const`:

```
volatile int loc1;  /* loc1 is a volatile location      */
volatile int *ploc; /* ploc points to a volatile location */
```

These statements declare `loc1` to be a `volatile` value and `ploc` to point to a `volatile` value.

You may think that `volatile` is an interesting concept, but you may be wondering why the ANSI committee felt it necessary to make `volatile` a keyword. The reason is that it facilitates compiler optimization. Suppose, for example, you have code like this:

```
val1 = x;
   .
   .
   .
  /* some code not using x */
val2 = x;
```

A smart (optimizing) compiler might notice that you use x twice without changing its value. It would temporarily store the x value in a register. Then, when x is needed for `val2`, it can save time by reading the value from a register instead of from the original memory location. This is called *caching*. Ordinarily, caching is a good optimization, but not if x is changed between the two statements by some other agency. If there were no `volatile` keyword, a compiler would have no way of knowing whether this might happen. Therefore, to be safe, the compiler couldn't cache. That was the pre-ANSI situation. Now, however, if the `volatile` keyword is not used in the declaration, the compiler can assume that a value hasn't changed between uses, and it then can attempt to optimize the code.

A value can be both `const` and `volatile`. For instance, the hardware clock setting normally should not be changed by the program, making it `const`; and it is changed by an agency other than the program, making it `volatile`. Just use both qualifiers in the declaration; the order doesn't matter:

```
volatile const int loc;
const volatile int *ploc;
```

Chapter Summary

What have we accomplished? On the practical side we developed a random-number generator and an integer-sorting program. In the process we developed `getint()` and `sort()` functions that we can use in other programs. On the educational side we illustrated some general principles and concepts useful in designing complex programs.

Programs should be *designed* rather than allowed to evolve through some random process of growth, trial, and error. You should think carefully about the form and content of input and output for a program. You should break the program into well-defined tasks and then write the code for these tasks separately, keeping in mind how they interface with one another. The idea is to achieve modularity. When necessary, break a module into smaller modules. Use functions to enhance the modularity and clarity of the program.

When designing a program, try to anticipate what might go wrong and then write the program accordingly. Use error-trapping to circumvent potential problems or, at least, to alert the user if a problem shows up. It's much better to give the user a second chance to enter data than to let the program crash in ignominy.

When designing a function, first decide how it will interact with the calling function. Decide what information flows in and what information flows out. What will the arguments be? Will you use pointers, or `return`, or both? Once you have these design parameters in mind, you can turn your attention to the mechanics of the function.

As you put these ideas to use, you'll produce programs with greater reliability. You may acquire a body of functions that you can use in other programs. If so, your programming will take less time.

Don't forget about storage classes. Variables can be defined outside of functions, in which case they are external (or global) and are available to more than one function. Variables defined within a function are local to that function and are not known to other functions. When possible, use local variables. This keeps variables in one function from being contaminated by the actions of other functions.

Review Questions

1. Which storage classes create variables local to the function containing them?

2. Which storage class creates variables that can be used across several files? restricted to just one file?

3. How would you change our sorting routine to make it sort in increasing order instead of decreasing order?

4. Which functions know each variable in the following? Are there any errors?

```
/* file 1 */
int daisy;
int main(void)
{
   int lily;
}
int petal()
{
   extern int daisy, lily;
}
/* file 2 */
static int lily;
int rose;
int stem()
{
   int rose;
}
void root()
{
   extern int daisy;
}
```

5. Given the following statement

```
static int plink;
int value_ct(const int arr[], int value, int n)
```

   a. What does the function heading tell you about the intent of the programmer?

b. Will replacing int value and int n with const int value and const int n enhance the protection of values in the calling program?

Programming Exercises

1. Some users might be daunted by being asked to enter an EOF character. Modify getarray() and getint() so that a # character also terminates input.

2. Create a program that sorts float numbers in increasing order.

3. Write and test in a loop a function that returns the number of times it has been called.

4. Write a program that generates a list of 100 random numbers in the range 1–10 in sorted decreasing order.

5. Write a program that generates 1000 random numbers in the range 1–10. Don't save or print the numbers, but do print how many times each number was produced. Have the program do this for 10 different seed values. Do the numbers appear in equal amounts? You can use the functions from this chapter or ANSI C rand() and srand() functions, which follow the same format that our functions do. This is one way to test the randomness of a particular random-number generator.

6. Write a program that behaves like the modification of Listing 13.8, which we discussed after showing the output of Listing 13.8. That is, have the program produce the output shown on page 518.

7. Write an interactive program that lets the user enter up to 20 words. Have the program display the words in sorted order (recall the string sorting example from Chapter 11) and then ask the user if the words should be saved in a file. If the user responds with a yes, have the program request a name for the file and then write the words into a file by that name.

8. Write a function that skips over input until encountering a digit. It then stores that digit and subsequent digits in a string until encountering a nondigit. The nondigit is placed back in the input, and the function converts the digit string to a numeric value. The function should use a pointer argument to provide the numeric value to the calling program. Use the function return value to return EOF if the function encounters end of file; have it return 1 otherwise. Use getc() and ungetc(). In short, this function finds the next integer in output, whether it be isolated or embedded in text, as in be22again.

9. Modify Exercise 8 so that the function recognizes an optional minus sign. That is, confronted with an input of be-22now, it extracts the value -22.

10. Construct a text file containing 10 lines, each composed of a name, a colon, and three integers. Write a program that reads the file and prints the lines in order of increasing average value of the integers in the line. That is, the line

    `Shalla Booger: 80 70 84`

    would precede the line

    `Hagar Joe Plinty: 70 90 80`

    because the average of its three values is less than the second average. Also have the program append the average to each line when it is printed. Note that the name part of the input need not consist of exactly two names.

14

Structures and Other Data Forms

Keywords

► struct, union, typedef

Operators

► . ->

In this chapter you learn what C structures are and how to create structure templates and variables. Then you learn how to access the members of a structure and how to write functions to handle structures. A short look at C's typedef *facility and at unions and pointers to functions concludes the chapter.*

O ne of the most important steps in designing a program is choosing a good way to represent the data. In many cases, a simple variable or even an array is not enough. C takes your ability to represent data a step further with the C *structure variables*. The C structure is flexible enough in its basic form to represent a diversity of data, and it allows you to invent new forms. If you are familiar with the "records" of Pascal, you should be comfortable with structures. If not, this chapter will introduce you to C structures. Let's study a concrete example to see why a C structure might be needed and how to create and use one.

Example Problem: Creating an Inventory of Books

Gwen Glenn wishes to print an inventory of her books. She would like to print a variety of information for each book: title, author, publisher, copyright date, the number of pages, the number of copies, and the dollar value. Some of these items, such as the titles, can be stored in an array of strings. Other items require an array of int or an array of float. With seven different arrays, keeping track of everything can get complicated, especially if Gwen wishes to generate several complete lists—one sorted by title, one sorted by author, one sorted by value, and so on. A better solution would be to use one array, in which each member contained all the information about one book.

Gwen needs a data form, then, that can contain both strings and numbers and somehow keep the information separate. The C structure meets this need. To see how a structure is set up and how it works, we'll start with a limited example. To simplify the problem, we will impose two restrictions. First, we'll include only title, author, and current market value. Second, we'll limit the inventory to one book. If you have more books than that, don't worry; we'll extend the program soon.

Look at the program in Listing 14.1 and its output. Then read our explanation of the main points.

```
Listing 14.1   book.c

/* book.c -- one-book inventory */
#include <stdio.h>
#define MAXTIT  41     /* maximum length of title + 1          */
#define MAXAUT  31     /* maximum length of author's name + 1 */
struct book {          /* structure template: tag is book      */
    char title[MAXTIT];
    char author[MAXAUT];
    float value;
};                     /* end of structure template            */
int main(void)
{
    struct book libry; /* declare libry as book-type variable */
    printf("Please enter the book title.\n");
    gets(libry.title);         /* access to the title portion */
    printf("Now enter the author.\n");
    gets(libry.author);
    printf("Now enter the value.\n");
    scanf("%f", &libry.value);
    printf("%s by %s: $%.2f\n",libry.title,
        libry.author, libry.value);
    printf("%s: \"%s\" \($%.2f\)\n", libry.author,
        libry.title, libry.value);
    return 0;
}
```

Here is a sample run:

```
Please enter the book title.
Chicken of the Alps
Now enter the author.
Bismo Lapoult
Now enter the value.
12.95
Chicken of the Alps by Bismo Lapoult: $12.95
Bismo Lapoult: "Chicken of the Alps" ($12.95)
```

The structure created in Listing 14.1 has three parts (called *members* or *fields*): one to store the title, one to store the author, and one to store the value. The three main points we will study are

> ► How to set up a format or *template* for a structure.
> ► How to declare a variable to fit that template.
> ► How to gain access to the individual components of a structure variable.

Setting Up the Structure Template

A *structure template* is the master plan that describes how a structure is put together. Our template looked like this:

```
struct book {
    char title[MAXTIT];
    char author[MAXAUT];
    float value;
};
```

This template describes a structure made up of two character arrays and one `float` variable. Let's look at the details. First comes the keyword `struct`. This identifies what comes next as a structure. Next comes an optional *tag*, the word `book`. The tag `book` is a shorthand label that we can use to refer to this structure. Thus, later on we have this declaration:

```
struct book libry;
```

It declares `libry` to be a structure variable using the `book` structure template.

Next we find the list of structure members enclosed in a pair of braces. Each member is described by its own declaration, complete with terminating semicolon. For instance, the `title` portion is a `char` array with `MAXTIT` elements. A member can be any C data type. That includes other structures!

A semicolon after the closing brace ends our definition of the template. You can place this template outside any function (externally), as we have done, or inside a function definition. If the template is defined inside a function, then its tag can be used only inside that function. If the template is external, it is available to all the functions following the definition in the file. For example, in a second function, you could define

```
struct book dickens;
```

and that function would have a variable `dickens` that followed the form of our `book` template.

The tag name is optional, but you must use one when you set up structures as we did, with the template defined one place and the actual variables defined elsewhere. We will return to this point soon, after we look at defining structure variables.

Defining a Structure Variable

The word *structure* is used in two senses. One is the sense "structure template," which is what we just discussed. The template is a plan; it tells the compiler how to represent the data, but it doesn't tell the computer how to allocate space for the data. The next step is to create a "structure variable"—the second sense of the word. The line in our program that causes a structure variable to be created is this:

```
struct book libry;
```

Seeing this instruction, the compiler creates the variable `libry`. Using the book template, the compiler allots space for a `char` array of `MAXTIT` elements, for a `char` array of `MAXAUT` elements, and for a `float` variable. This storage is lumped together under the single name `libry` (see Figure 14.1). (In the next section we explain how to unlump it as needed.)

Figure 14.1 *Memory allocation for a structure*

In declaring a structure variable, `struct book` plays the same role that `int` or `float` does in simpler declarations. For example, we could declare two variables of the `struct book` type or even a pointer to that kind of structure:

```
struct book doyle, panshin, *ptbook;
```

The structure variables `doyle` and `panshin` would each have the parts title, author, and value. The pointer ptbook could point to doyle, panshin, or any other book structure.

As far as the computer is concerned, the following declaration

```
struct book libry;
```

is short for

```
struct book {
    char title[MAXTIT];
    char author[MAXAUT];
    float value;
} libry;    /* follow template with variable name */
```

In other words, the process of defining a structure template and the process of defining a structure variable can be combined into one step. Combining the template and the variable definitions is the one circumstance in which a tag need not be used:

```
struct {          /* no tag */
    char title[MAXTIT];
    char author[MAXAUT];
    float value;
} libry;
```

Use the tag form, however, if you plan to use a structure template more than once.

There is one aspect of defining a structure variable that did not come up in our example: initialization. We'll look at that now.

Initializing a Structure

You've seen how to initialize variables and arrays:

```
int count = 0;
static int fibo[] = {0,1,1,2,3,5,8};
```

Can a structure variable be initialized, too? Yes, although many pre-ANSI implementations limit initialization to external or static structure variables. Whether or not a structure variable is external depends on where the *variable* is defined, not on where the *template* is defined. In our example, the template book is external, but the variable libry is not because it is defined inside the function and is, by default, placed in the automatic storage class.

Suppose, though, we had made this declaration:

```
static struct book libry;
```

Then the storage class is static, and we could initialize the structure this way (pre-ANSI or ANSI):

```
static struct book libry = {
    "The Pirate and the Damsel",
    "Renee Vivotte",
    1.95
};
```

To make the associations more obvious, we gave each member its own line of initialization, but all the compiler needs are commas to separate one member's initialization from the next.

Now, let's continue with structure properties.

Gaining Access to Structure Members

A structure is like a "superarray" in which one element can be char, the next element float, and the next an int array. We can access the individual elements of an array by using a subscript. But how do we access individual members of a structure? We use a dot (.), the structure member operator. For example, libry.value is the value portion of libry. You can use libry.value exactly as you would use any other float variable. Similarly, you can use libry.title exactly as you would use a char array. Thus, we used expressions like

```
gets(libry.title);
```

and

```
scanf("%f", &libry.value);
```

In essence, .title, .author, and .value play the role of subscripts for a book structure.

Note that although libry is a structure, libry.value is a float type and is used like any other float type. For example, scanf("%f",...) requires the address of a float location, and that is what &libry.float is. The dot has higher precedence than the & here, so the expression is the same as &(libry.float).

If we had a second structure variable of the same type, we would use the same method:

```
struct book spiro, gerald;

gets(spiro.title);
gets(gerald.title);
```

The .title refers to the first member of book structure. Notice how in our initial program we printed the contents of the structure libry in two different formats. This illustrates the freedom we have in using the members of a structure.

Now that you have these basics in hand, you're ready to expand your horizons and look at several ramifications of structures. You'll see arrays of structures, structures of structures, pointers to structures, and functions that process structures.

Arrays of Structures

Let's extend our book program to handle a greater number of books. Clearly each book can be described by one structure variable of the book type. To describe two books, we need to use two such variables, and so on. To handle several books, we can use an array of such structures, and that is what we have created in the next program, shown in Listing 14.2.

Structures and Memory

The manybook.c program uses an array of 100 structures. Such a large array requires a good-sized chunk of memory, which can cause problems. For example, Microsoft C places automatic variables in the stack and uses a default stack size of 2048, much too small for this program. But you can set the stack size to 10000 to accommodate the array of structures, or make the array static or external (so that it isn't placed in the stack), or reduce the array size to 16.

Listing 14.2 *manybook.c*

```
/* manybook.c -- multiple book inventory */
#include <stdio.h>
#define MAXTIT   40
#define MAXAUT   40
#define MAXBKS   100              /* maximum number of books  */
```

(continued)

Listing 14.2 *(continued)*

```
#define STOP ""                    /* null string, ends input  */
struct book {                      /* set up book template     */
    char title[MAXTIT];
    char author[MAXAUT];
    float value;
};
int main(void)
{
    struct book libry[MAXBKS]; /* array of book structures */
    int count = 0;
    int index;

    printf("Please enter the book title.\n");
    printf("Press [enter] at the start of a line to stop.\n");
    while (count < MAXBKS &&
        strcmp(gets(libry[count].title), STOP) != 0)
    {
        printf("Now enter the author.\n");
        gets(libry[count].author);
        printf("Now enter the value.\n");
        scanf("%f", &libry[count++].value);
        while (getchar() != '\n')
            continue;                    /* clear input line */
        if (count < MAXBKS)
        printf("Enter the next title.\n");
    }
    printf("Here is the list of your books:\n");
    for (index = 0; index < count; index++)
    printf("%s by %s: $%.2f\n", libry[index].title,
        libry[index].author, libry[index].value);
    return 0;
}
```

Here is a sample program run:

```
Please enter the book title.
Press [enter] at the start of a line to stop.
My Life as a Budgie
Now enter the author.
Mack Zackles
```

```
Now enter the value.
12.95
Enter the next title.
      ...more entries...
Here is the list of your books:
My Life as a Budgie by Mack Zackles: $12.95
Thought and Unthought by Kindra Schlagmeyer: $33.50
The Anatomy of an Ant by Salome Deschamps: $9.99
Power Tiddlywinks by Jack Deltoids: $13.25
UNIX Primer Plus by Waite, Martin, & Prata: $19.95
Coping with Coping by Dr. Rubin Thonkwacker: $0.00
Delicate Frivolity by Neda McFey: $29.99
Fate Wore a Bikini by Mickey Splats: $8.95
A History of Buvania by Prince Nikoli Buvan: $50.00
Mastering Your Digital Watch by Miklos Mysz: $13.95
A Foregone Confusion by Phalty Reasoner: $25.66
```

First we'll describe how to declare arrays of structures and how to access individual members. Then we will highlight two aspects of the program.

Declaring an Array of Structures

Declaring an array of structures is like declaring any other kind of array:

```
struct book libry[MAXBKS];
```

This declares libry to be an array with MAXBKS elements. Each element of this array is a structure of book type. Thus, libry[0] is one book structure, libry[1] is a second book structure, and so on. Figure 14.2 may help you visualize this. The name libry itself is not a structure name; it is the name of the array holding the structures.

Identifying Members of an Array of Structures

To identify members of an array of structures, you apply the same rule that we used for individual structures: follow the structure name with the dot operator and then with the member name:

```
libry[0].value    /* the value associated with the first array
                     element */

libry[4].title    /* the title associated with the fifth array
                     element */
```

Figure 14.2 *An array of structures*

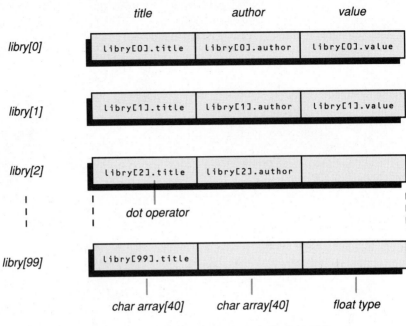

declaration: `struct book libry[MAXBKS]`

Note that the array subscript is attached to `libry`, not to the end of the name:

```
libry.value[2]    /* WRONG */
libry[2].value    /* RIGHT */
```

The reason we use `libry[2].value` is that `libry[2]` *is* the structure variable name, just as `libry[1]` is another structure variable name.

By the way, what do you suppose the following represents?

```
libry[2].title[4]
```

It's the fifth character in the title (the `title[4]` part) of the book described by the third structure (the `libry[2]` part). In our example, this would be the character A. This example points out that subscripts found to the right of the dot operator apply to individual members, while subscripts to the left of the dot operator apply to arrays of structures.

Let's finish the program now.

Program Details

The main change from our first program is that we inserted a loop to read multiple entries. We begin the loop with this `while` condition:

```
while (count < MAXBKS &&
         strcmp(gets(libry[count].title), STOP) != 0)
```

The expression `gets(libry[count].title)` reads a string for the title of a book. The `strcmp()` function compares this string to `STOP`, which is just `""`, the empty string. If the user presses the Enter key at the beginning of a line, the empty string is transmitted, and the loop ends. We also have a check to keep the number of books entered from exceeding the size limit of the array.

Then we have these lines:

```
while (getchar() != '\n')
   continue;                    /* clear input line */
```

As you may recall from earlier chapters, this code overcomes the fact that the `scanf()` function ignores spaces and newlines. When you respond to the request for the book's value, you type something like

```
12.50[enter]
```

which transmits the sequence of characters

```
12.50\n
```

The `scanf()` function collects the 1, the 2, the ., the 5, and the 0, but it leaves the \n sitting there, awaiting whatever read statement comes next. If our precautionary code were missing, the next read statement, `gets(libry[count].title)`, would read the leftover newline character as its *first and only* character, and the program would think we had sent a stop signal. The code we inserted will eat up characters until it finds and disposes of the newline. It doesn't do anything with the characters except remove them from the input queue. This gives `gets()` a fresh start.

Now let's return to exploring structures.

Nested Structures

Sometimes it is convenient for one structure to contain, or *nest*, another. For example, Shalala Pirosky is building a structure of information about her friends. One member of the structure, naturally enough, is the friend's name. The name, however, can be represented by a structure itself, with separate entries for first and last name members. Listing 14.3 is a condensed example of Shalala's work.

Listing 14.3 friend.c

```
/* friend.c -- example of a nested structure */
#include <stdio.h>
#define LEN 20
#define M1 "    Thank you for the wonderful evening, "
#define M2 "You certainly prove that a "
#define M3 "is a special kind of guy. We must get together"
#define M4 "over a delicious "
#define M5 " and have a few laughs."
struct names {                      /* first template        */
    char first[LEN];
    char last[LEN];
};
struct guy {                        /* second template       */
    struct names handle;            /* nested structure      */
    char favfood[LEN];
    char job[LEN];
    float income;
};
int main(void)
{
    static struct guy fellow = {    /* initialize a variable */
        { "Egbert", "Snivley" },
        "eggplant",
        "harddisk eraser",
        25435.00
    };

    printf("Dear %s, \n\n", fellow.handle.first);
    printf("%s%s.\n", M1, fellow.handle.first);
    printf("%s%s\n", M2, fellow.job);
    printf("%s\n", M3);
    printf("%s%s%s\n\n", M4, fellow.favfood, M5);
    printf("%40s%s\n", " ", "See you soon,");
    printf("%40s%s\n", " ", "Shalala");
    return 0;
}
```

Here is the output:

```
Dear Egbert,

    Thank you for the wonderful evening, Egbert.
You certainly prove that a harddisk eraser
is a special kind of guy. We must get together
over a delicious eggplant and have a few laughs.


                                See you soon,
                                Shalala
```

First, note how the nested structure is set up in the template. It is simply declared, just as an `int` variable would be:

```
struct names handle;
```

This declaration says that `handle` is a variable of the `struct names` type. Of course, the file should also include the template for the `names` structure.

Second, note how we gain access to a member of a nested structure. We merely use the dot operator twice:

```
fellow.handle.first == "Egbert"
```

The construction is interpreted this way, going from left to right:

```
(fellow.handle).first
```

That is, find `fellow`, then find the `handle` member of `fellow`, and then find the `first` member of that.

Pointers to Structures

Pointer lovers will be glad to know that you can have pointers to structures. There are at least three reasons why having pointers to structures is a good idea. First, just as pointers to arrays are easier to manipulate (in a sorting problem, say) than the arrays themselves, so pointers to structures are often easier to manipulate than structures themselves. Second, in some older implementations, a structure can't be passed as an argument to a function, but a pointer to a structure can. Third, many wondrous data representations use structures containing pointers to other structures.

The next short example (Listing 14.4) shows how to define a pointer to a structure and how to use it to access the members of a structure.

Listing 14.4 *friends.c*

```c
/* friends.c -- uses pointer to a structure */
#include <stdio.h>
#define LEN 20
struct names {
    char first[LEN];
    char last[LEN];
};
struct guy {
    struct names handle;
    char favfood[LEN];
    char job[LEN];
    float income;
};
int main(void)
{
    static struct guy fellow[2] = {
        {{ "Egbert", "Snivley"},
         "eggplant",
         "harddisk eraser",
         25435.00
         },
        {{"Rodney", "Swillbelly"},
         "salmon mousse",
         "interior decorator",
         35000.00
         }
    };
    struct guy *him;      /* here is a pointer to a structure */
    printf("address #1: %u #2: %u\n", &fellow[0], &fellow[1]);
    him = &fellow[0];     /* tell the pointer where to point  */
    printf("pointer #1: %u #2: %u\n", him, him + 1);
    printf("him->income is $%.2f: (*him).income is $%.2f\n",
        him->income, (*him).income);
    him++;                /* point to the next structure      */
    printf("him->favfood is %s:  him->handle.last is %s\n",
        him->favfood, him->handle.last);
    return 0;
}
```

The output, please:

```
address #1: 12  #2: 96
pointer #1: 12  #2: 96
him->income is $25435.00: (*him).income is $25435.00
him->favfood is salmon mousse:  him->names.last is Swillbelly
```

Let's look first at how we created a pointer to a guy structure. Then we'll study how to specify individual structure members by using the pointer.

Declaring and Initializing a Structure Pointer

Declaration is as easy as can be:

```
struct guy *him;
```

First is the keyword struct, then the template tag guy, and then an * followed by the pointer name. The syntax is the same as for the other pointer declarations you have seen.

The pointer him can now be made to point to any structures of the guy type. We initialize him by making it point to fellow[0]. Note that we use the address operator:

```
him = &fellow[0];
```

The first two output lines show the success of this assignment. Comparing the two lines, we see that him points to fellow[0], and him + 1 points to fellow[1]. Note that adding 1 to him adds 84 to the address. This is because each guy structure occupies 84 bytes of memory: names.first is 20, names.last is 20, favfood is 20, job is 20, and income is 4—the size of float on our system.

Member Access by Pointer

The pointer him is pointing to the *structure* fellow[0]. How can we use him to get a value of a *member* of fellow[0]? The third output line shows two methods.

The first method, and the most common, uses a new operator, ->. This operator is formed by typing a hyphen (-) followed by the greater-than symbol (>). The example helps to make the meaning clear:

```
him->income  is  fellow[0].income  if  him == &fellow[0]
```

In other words, a structure *pointer* followed by the -> operator works the same way as a structure *name* followed by the . (dot) operator. (We can't properly say `him.income` because `him` is not a structure name.)

It is important to note that `him` is a *pointer* but `him->income` is a *member* of the pointed-to structure. Thus, in this case, `him->income` is a `float` variable.

The second method for specifying the value of a structure member follows from this sequence: If `him == &fellow[0]`, then `*him == fellow[0]`. This is because & and * are reciprocal operators. Hence, by substitution:

```
fellow[0].income == (*him).income
```

The parentheses are required because the . operator has higher precedence than *.

In summary, if `him` is a pointer to the structure `fellow[0]`, then the following are all equivalent:

```
fellow[0].income == (*him).income == him->income
```

Now let's look at the interaction between structures and functions.

Telling Functions about Structures

Recall that function arguments pass *values* to the function. Each value is a number, perhaps `int`, perhaps `float`, perhaps ASCII character code, or perhaps an address. A structure is a bit more complicated than a single value, so it is not surprising that older implementations do not allow a structure to be used as an argument for a function. This limitation has been removed in newer implementations, and ANSI C allows structures to be used as arguments. Thus, modern implementations give you a choice between passing structures as arguments or passing pointers to structures as arguments. Or, if you are concerned with just part of a structure, you can pass structure members as arguments. We'll examine all three methods, beginning with passing structure members as arguments.

Passing Structure Members

As long as a structure member is a data type with a single value (i.e., an `int` or one of its relatives, a `char`, a `float`, a `double`, or a pointer), it can be passed as a function argument. The primitive financial analysis program of Listing 14.5, which adds the client's bank account to his or her savings and loan account, illustrates this point. Note, incidentally, that we combined the template definition, the variable declaration, and the initialization into one statement.

Listing 14.5 *funds1.c*

```
/* funds1.c -- passing structure members as arguments */
#include <stdio.h>
struct funds {
    char *bank;
    float bankfund;
    char *save;
    float savefund;
} stan = {
    "Garlic-Melon Bank",
    1023.43,
    "Snoopy's Savings and Loan",
    4239.87
    };
float sum(float, float);
int main(void)
{
    float total;
    extern struct funds stan;  /* optional declaration */

    printf("Stan has a total of $%.2f.\n",
            sum(stan.bankfund, stan.savefund) );
    return 0;
}
/* adds two float numbers */
float sum(float x, float y)
{
    return(x + y);
}
```

The result of running this program is

```
Stan has a total of $5263.30.
```

Ah, it works. Notice that the function `sum()` neither knows nor cares whether the actual arguments are members of a structure; it requires only that they be type `float`.

Of course, if you want a called function to affect the value of a member in the calling function, you can transmit the address of the member:

```
modify(&stan.bankfund);
```

and this would be a function that altered Stan's bank account.

The next approach to telling a function about a structure involves letting the called function know that it is dealing with a structure.

Using the Structure Address

We will solve the same problem as before, but this time we will use the address of the structure as an argument. Since the function will have to work with the funds structure, it, too, will have to make use of the funds template. See Listing 14.6 for the program.

Listing 14.6 *funds2.c*

```
/* funds2.c -- passing a pointer to a structure */
#include <stdio.h>
struct funds {
    char *bank;
    float bankfund;
    char *save;
    float savefund;
} stan = {
    "Garlic-Melon Bank",
    1023.43,
    "Snoopy's Savings and Loan",
    4239.87
    };
float sum(struct funds *);  /* argument is a pointer */
int main(void)
{
    printf("Stan has a total of $%.2f.\n", sum(&stan));
    return 0;
}
float sum(struct funds *money)
{
    return(money->bankfund + money->savefund);
}
```

This, too, produces the output

```
Stan has a total of $5263.30.
```

The sum() function use a pointer (money) to a fund structure for its single argument. Passing the address &stan to the function causes the pointer money to point to the structure stan. We then use the -> operator to gain the values of stan.bankfund and stan.savefund.

This function also has access to the institution names, although it doesn't use them. Note that we must use the & operator to get the structure's address. Unlike the array name, the structure name alone is *not* a synonym for its address.

Passing a Structure as an Argument

For compilers that permit passing structures as arguments, the last example can be rewritten as shown in Listing 14.7.

Listing 14.7 *funds3.c*

```c
/* funds3.c -- passing a pointer to a structure */
#include <stdio.h>
struct funds {
    char *bank;
    float bankfund;
    char *save;
    float savefund;
} stan = {
    "Garlic-Melon Bank",
    1023.43,
    "Snoopy's Savings and Loan",
    4239.87
    };
float sum(struct funds);   /* structure argument */
int main(void)
{
    printf("Stan has a total of $%.2f.\n", sum(stan));
    return 0;
}
```

(continued)

```
Listing 14.7   (continued)

float sum(struct funds moolah)
{
    return(moolah.bankfund + moolah.savefund);
}
```

Again, the output is this:

```
Stan has a total of $5263.30.
```

We replaced money, which was a pointer to struct funds, with moolah, which is a struct funds variable. When sum() is called, an automatic variable moolah is created according to the funds template. The members of this structure are then initialized to be copies of the values held in the corresponding members of the structure stan. Thus, the computations are done using a copy of the original structure, whereas the preceding program used the original structure itself. Because moolah is a structure, we use moolah.bankfund, not moolah->bankfund. In Listing 14.6, we used money->bankfund because money is a pointer, not a structure.

More on the New, Improved Structure Status

Under modern C, including ANSI C, not only can structures be passed as function arguments, they also can be returned as function return values. To make this return mechanism workable, the values in one structure can be assigned to another. That is, if n_data and o_data are both structures of the same type, you can do the following:

```
o_data = n_data;
```

This causes each member of o_data to be assigned the value of the corresponding member of n_data.

The fact that structures can be used as function arguments lets you convey structure information to a function. The fact that functions can return structures lets you convey structure information from a called function to the calling function. Structure pointers also allow two-way communication. Thus, you can often use either approach to solve programming problems. Let's look at another set of examples illustrating these two approaches.

To contrast the two approaches, we'll write a simple program that handles structures by using pointers; then we'll rewrite it by using structure-passing and structure returns. The program itself asks for your first and last names and reports the total number of letters in them. This project hardly requires structures, but it provides a simple framework for seeing how they work. Listing 14.8 presents the pointer form.

Listing 14.8 *nameln1.c*

```
/* nameln1.c -- uses pointers to a structure */
#include <stdio.h>
struct namect {
    char fname[20];
    char lname[20];
    int letters;
};
void getinfo(struct namect *);
void makeinfo(struct namect *);
void showinfo(struct namect *);
int main(void)
{
    struct namect person;

    getinfo(&person);
    makeinfo(&person);
    showinfo(&person);
    return 0;
}

void getinfo (struct namect *pst)
{
    printf("Please enter your first name.\n");
    gets(pst->fname);
    printf("Please enter your last name.\n");
    gets(pst->lname);
}

void makeinfo (struct namect *pst)
{
    pst->letters = strlen(pst->fname) +
                    strlen(pst->lname);
```

(continued)

Listing 14.8   *(continued)*

```
}

void showinfo (struct namect *pst)
{
    printf("%s %s, your name contains %d letters.",
        pst->fname, pst->lname, pst->letters);
}
```

Compiling and running the program produces results like the following:

```
Please enter your first name:
Nathan
Please enter your last name:
Hale
Nathan Hale, your name contains 10 letters.
```

We've allocated the work of the program to three functions called from `main()`. In each case, we pass the address of the `person` structure to the function.

The `getinfo()` function transfers information from itself to `main()`. In particular, it obtains names from the user and places them in the `person` structure, using the `pst` pointer to locate it. Recall that `pst->lname` means the `lname` member of the structure pointed to by `pst`. This makes `pst ->lname` equivalent to the name of a `char` array, hence a suitable argument for `gets()`. Note that although `getinfo()` feeds information to the main program, it does not use the return mechanism, so it is type `void`.

The `makeinfo()` function performs a two-way transfer of information. By using a pointer to `person`, it locates the two names stored in the structure. It uses the C library function `strlen()` to calculate the total number of letters in each name and then uses the address of `person` to stow away the sum. Again, the type is `void`. Finally, the `showinfo()` function uses a pointer to locate the information to be printed.

In all of these operations, there has been but one structure variable, `person`, and each of the functions used the structure address to access it. One function transferred information from itself to the calling program, one transferred information from the calling program to itself, and one did both.

Now let's see how we can program the same task using structure arguments and return values. First, to pass the structure itself, we use the argument person rather than &person. The corresponding formal argument, then, is declared type struct namect instead of being a pointer to that type. Second, to provide structure values to main(), we can return a structure. Listing 14.9 presents the nonpointer version.

Listing 14.9 *nameln2.c*

```
/* nameln2.c -- passes and returns structures */
#include <stdio.h>
struct namect {
    char fname[20];
    char lname[20];
    int letters;
};
struct namect getinfo(void);
struct namect makeinfo(struct namect);
void showinfo(struct namect);
int main(void)
{
    struct namect person;

    person = getinfo();
    person = makeinfo(person);
    showinfo(person);
    return 0;
}

struct namect getinfo(void)
{
    struct namect temp;
    printf("Please enter your first name.\n");
    gets(temp.fname);
    printf("Please enter your last name.\n");
    gets(temp.lname);
    return temp;
}

struct namect makeinfo(struct namect info)
{
    info.letters = strlen(info.fname) + strlen(info.lname);
```

(continued)

```
Listing 14.9   (continued)

    return info;
}

void showinfo(struct namect info)
{
    printf("%s %s, your name contains %d letters.",
        info.fname, info.lname, info.letters);
}
```

This version produces the same final result as the preceding one, but it proceeds in a different manner. Each of the three functions creates its own copy of person, so this program uses four distinct structures instead of just one.

Consider the makeinfo() function, for example. In the first program, the address of person was passed, and the function fiddled with the actual person values. In this second version, a new structure called info is created. The values stored in person are copied to info, and the function works with the copy. So when the number of letters is calculated, it is stored in info, but not in person. The return mechanism, however, fixes that. By having the line

```
    return info;
```

and the line

```
    person = makeinfo(person);
```

we copy the values stored in info into person. Note that the makeinfo() function had to be declared type struct namect because it returns a structure.

Structures or Pointer to Structures?

Suppose you have to write a structure-related function. Should you use structure pointers as arguments, or should you use structure arguments and return values? Each approach has its strengths and weaknesses.

The two advantages of the pointer argument method are that it works on older as well as newer C implementations and that it is quick—you just pass a single address. The disadvantage is that you have less protection for your data. Some operations in the called function may inadvertently affect data in the original structure.

The ANSI C addition of the `const` qualifier (Chapter 13) offers the means to protect against accidental changes. For example, the pointer version of `showinfo()` (Listing 14.8) prints the structure contents and should not alter them. Therefore, you would use this function heading:

```
void showinfo(const struct namect *pst)
```

which states that `pst` points to a structure whose values cannot be changed. If you place code in `showinfo()` to modify, say, `pst->letters`, the compiler will generate an error message.

One advantage of passing structures as arguments is that the function works with copies of the original data, which is safer than working with the original data. Also, the programming style tends to be clearer. Suppose you define the following structure type:

```
struct vector = {double x; double y;};
```

You want to set the vector `ans` to the sum of the vectors `a` and `b`. You could write a structure-passing and returning function that would make the program like this:

```
struct vector ans, a, b, sum_vect();
    .
    .
    .
ans = sum_vect(a,b);
```

The preceding version is more natural-looking to an engineer than a pointer version, which might look like this:

```
struct vector ans, a, b;
void sum_vect();
    .
    .
    .
sum_vect(&a, &b, &ans);
```

Also, in the pointer version the user has to remember whether the address for the sum should be the first or the last argument.

The two main disadvantages to passing structures are that older implementations may not handle the code and that it wastes time and space. It's especially wasteful to pass large structures to a function that uses only one or two members of the structure. In that case, passing a pointer or passing just the required members as individual arguments makes more sense.

Functions Using an Array of Structures

Suppose you have an array of structures that you wish to process with a function. The name of an array *is* a synonym for its address, so it can be passed to a function. Again, the function will need access to the structure template. To show how this works, in Listing 14.10 we expand our monetary program to two people so that we have an array of two funds structures.

Listing 14.10 *funds4.c*

```
/* funds4.c -- passing an array of structures to a function */
#include <stdio.h>
#define N 2
struct funds {
    char *bank;
    float bankfund;
    char *save;
    float savefund;
} jones[N] = {
    {
    "Garlic-Melon Bank",
    1023.43,
    "Snoopy's Savings and Loan",
    4239.87
    },
    {
    "Honest Jack's Bank",
    976.57,
    "First Draft Savings",
    1760.13
    }
};
float sum(const struct funds *, int);
int main(void)
{
    float total;

    printf("The Joneses have a total of $%.2f.\n",
            sum(jones,N));
    return 0;
```

```
    }

float sum(const struct funds *money, int n)
{
    float total;
    int i;

    for (i = 0, total = 0; i < n; i++, money++)
        total += money->bankfund + money->savefund;
    return(total);
}
```

The output is

```
The Joneses have a total of $8000.00.
```

(What an even sum! One would almost think the figures were invented.)

The array name jones is the address of the array. In particular, it is the address of the first element of the array, which is the structure jones[0]. Thus, initially the pointer money is given by this expression:

```
money = &jones[0];
```

Then the -> operator lets us add the two funds for the first Jones. This is very much like Listing 14.6. Next, the for loop increments the pointer money by 1. Now it points to the next structure, jones[1], and the rest of the funds can be added to total.

These are the main points:

► You can use the array name to pass the address of the first structure in the array to a function.

► You then can use pointer arithmetic to move the pointer to successive structures in the array. Note that the function call

```
sum(&jones[0],N)
```

would have the same effect as using the array name, since both refer to the same address. Using the array name is just an indirect way of passing the structure address.

► Because the sum() function isn't supposed to alter the original data, use the ANSI C const qualifier.

Saving the Structure Contents in a File

Because structures can hold a wide variety of information, they are an important tool for constructing databases. For example, you could use a structure to hold all the pertinent information about an employee or an auto part. Ultimately, you would want to be able to save this information in, and retrieve it from, a file. A database file could contain an arbitrary number of such data objects. The entire set of information held in a structure is termed a *record*, and the individual items are *fields*. Let's investigate these topics.

What is perhaps the most obvious way to save a record is the least efficient way, and that is to use fprintf(). For example, recall the book structure introduced in Listing 14.1:

```
#define MAXTIT    40
#define MAXAUT    40
struct book {
    char title[MAXTIT];
    char author[MAXAUT];
    float value;
};
```

If pbooks identified a file stream, you could save the information in a struct book variable called primer with the following statement:

```
fprintf(pbooks, "%s %s %.2f\n", primer.title,
        primer.author,primer.value);
```

This setup becomes unwieldy for structures with, say, 30 members. Also, it poses a retrieval problem because the program would need some way of telling where one field ends and another begins. This problem can be fixed by using a format with fixed-size fields, for example, `"%39s%39s%8.2f"`, but the awkwardness remains.

A better solution is to use fread() and fwrite() to read and write structure-sized units. Recall that these functions read and write using the same binary representation that the program uses. So, for example,

```
fwrite(&primer, sizeof (struct book), 1, pbooks);
```

goes to the beginning address of the primer structure and copies all the bytes of the structure to the file associated with pbooks. The sizeof (struct book) term tells the function how large a block to copy, and the 1 indicates that it should copy just one block. The fread() function with the same arguments copies a structure-sized chunk of data from the file to the location pointed to by &primer. In short, these functions read and write one whole record at a time instead of a field at a time.

To show how these functions can be used in a program, we've modified the program in Listing 14.2 so that the book titles are saved in a file called book.dat. If the file already exists, the program shows you its current contents and then lets you add to the file. Listing 14.11 presents the new version.

Listing 14.11 *savebook.c*

```
/* savebook.c -- saves structure contents in a file */
#include <stdio.h>
#define MAXTIT   40
#define MAXAUT   40
#define MAXBKS   10                /* maximum number of books */
#define STOP ""                    /* null string, ends input */
struct book {                      /* set up book template    */
    char title[MAXTIT];
    char author[MAXAUT];
    float value;
};
int main(void)
{
    struct book libry[MAXBKS]; /* array of structures    */
    int count = 0;
    int index, filecount;
    FILE *pbooks;
    int size = sizeof (struct book);

    if ((pbooks = fopen("book.dat", "a+b")) == NULL)
    {
        fputs("Can't open book.dat file\n",stderr);
        exit(1);
    }
    rewind(pbooks);                /* go to start of file     */
    while (count < MAXBKS &&  fread(&libry[count], size,
               1, pbooks) == 1)
    {
        if (count == 0)
            puts("Current contents of book.dat:");
        printf("%s by %s: $%.2f\n",libry[count].title,
            libry[count].author, libry[count].value);
```

(continued)

Listing 14.11   *(continued)*

```
        count++;
    }
    filecount = count;
    if (count == MAXBKS)
    {
        fputs("The book.dat file is full.", stderr);
        exit(2);
    }
    puts("Please add new book titles.");
    puts("Press [enter] at the start of a line to stop.");
    while (count < MAXBKS &&
        strcmp(gets(libry[count].title),STOP) != 0)
    {
        puts("Now enter the author.");
        gets(libry[count].author);
        puts("Now enter the value.");
        scanf("%f", &libry[count++].value);
        while (getchar() != '\n')
            continue;                   /* clear input line  */
        if (count < MAXBKS)
            puts("Enter the next title.");
    }
    puts("Here is the list of your books:");
    for (index = 0; index < count; index++)
        printf("%s by %s: $%.2f\n",libry[index].title,
            libry[index].author, libry[index].value);
    fseek(pbooks, 0L, SEEK_END);     /* go to end of file */
    fwrite(&libry[filecount], size, count - filecount,
            pbooks);
    fclose(pbooks);
    return 0;
}
```

We'll look at a couple sample runs and then discuss the main programming points.

```
% booksave
Please add new book titles.
Press [enter] at the start of a line to stop.
Metric Merriment
```

```
Now enter the author.
Polly Poetica
Now enter the value.
18.99
Enter the next title.
Epicurean Dreams
Now enter the author.
Waldo Snid
Now enter the value.
15.99
Enter the next title.
[enter]
Here is the list of your books:
Metric Merriment by Polly Poetica: $18.99
Epicurean Dreams by Waldo Snid: $15.99
% booksave
Current contents of book.dat:
Metric Merriment by Polly Poetica: $18.99
Epicurean Dreams by Waldo Snid: $15.99
Please add new book titles.
Nit for Gnat
Now enter the author.
Nellie Nicely
Now enter the value.
21.99
Enter the next title.
[enter]
Here is the list of your books:
Metric Merriment by Polly Poetica: $18.99
Epicurean Dreams by Waldo Snid: $15.99
Nit for Gnat by Nellie Nicely: $21.99
%
```

Running the `booksave` program again would show all three books as current file records.

Program Points

First, we use the `"a+b"` mode for opening the file. The `a+` part lets the program read the whole file and append data to the end of the file. The `b` is the ANSI way of signifying that the program will use the binary file format. For UNIX systems that don't accept the `b`, you can omit it, since UNIX has only one file form anyway. For other pre-ANSI implementations, you may need to find the local equivalent to using `b`.

We chose the binary mode because `fread()` and `fwrite()` are intended for binary files. True, some of the structure contents are text, but the `.value` member is not. If you use a text editor to look at `book.dat`, the text part will show up okay, but the numeric part will be unreadable and may even cause your text editor to barf.

The `rewind()` command ensures that the file position pointer is situated at the start of the file, ready for the first read.

The initial `while` loop reads one structure at a time into the array of structures, stopping when the array is full or when the file is exhausted. The variable `filecount` keeps track of how many structures were read.

The next `while` loop prompts for, and takes, user input. As in Listing 14.2, this loop quits when the array is full or when the user presses the Enter key at the beginning of a line. Notice that the `count` variable starts with the value it had after the preceding loop. This causes the new entries to be added to the end of the array.

The `for` loop then prints the data both from the file and from the user. The `fseek()` call places the file position pointer at the end of the file, ready to append new data. Note that ANSI C specifies that `SEEK_END` is defined in `stdio.h`. If you are on a pre-ANSI system, you may have to use the numerical value 2 instead or include a different system header file.

We could have used a loop to add one structure at a time to the end of the file. However, we decided to utilize the ability of `fwrite()` to write more than one block at a time. The expression `count - filecount` yields the number of new book titles to be added, and the call to `fwrite()` writes that number of structure-sized blocks to the file. The expression `&libry[filecount]` is the address of the first new structure in the array, so copying begins from that point.

This example is, perhaps, the simplest way to write structures to a file and to retrieve them. But it can waste space because the unused parts of a structure are saved, too. The size of this structure is $2 \times 40 \times$ `sizeof (char) + sizeof (float)`, which totals 84 bytes on our system. None of our entries actually needed all that space. However, the fact that each data chunk is the same size makes retrieving the data easy.

Another approach is to use variably sized records. To facilitate reading such records from a file, each record can begin with a numerical field specifying the record size. This is a bit more complex than what we have done. Normally this method involves "linked structures," which we describe next, and dynamic memory allocation, which we discuss in Chapter 16.

Structures: What Next?

Before we end our explanation of structures, we would like to mention one of the more important uses of structures: creating new data forms. Computer users have developed data forms much more efficient for certain problems than the arrays and simple structures we have presented. These forms have names such as *queues, binary trees, heaps, hash tables*, and *graphs*. Many such forms are built from *linked* structures. Typically, each structure will contain one or two items of data plus one or two pointers to other structures of the same type. Those pointers link one structure to another and furnish a path to let you search through the overall tree of structures. For example, Figure 14.3 shows a binary tree structure, with each individual structure (or *node*) connected to the two below it.

Figure 14.3 *A binary tree structure*

Is the hierarchical, or tree, structure shown in Figure 14.3 more efficient than an array? Consider the case of a tree with ten levels of nodes. It has $2^{10} - 1$, or 1023, nodes in which you could store up to 1023 words. If the words were arranged according to some sensible plan, you could start at the top level and find any word in at most 9 moves as your search moved down one level to the next. If you had the words in an array, you might have to search all 1023 elements before finding the word you sought.

If you are interested in more advanced concepts such as this, you can consult any number of computer science texts on data structures. With the C structures, you will be able to create and use virtually every form presented in these texts.

That's our final word on structures for this chapter, but we will present an example of linked structures in Chapter 16. Next, we'll look at two other C features for dealing with data: the union and `typedef`.

Unions—A Quick Look

A *union* is a type that lets you store different data types in the same memory space (but not simultaneously). A typical use would be a table designed to hold a mixture of types in some order which is neither regular nor known in advance. With a union you can create an array of equal-sized units, each of which can hold a variety of data types.

Unions are set up in much the same way as structures. There is a union template and a union variable. They can be defined in one step or, by using a union tag, in two. Here is an example of a union template with a tag:

```
union hold {
    int digit;
    double bigfl;
    char letter;
};
```

Here is an example of defining three union variables of the hold type:

```
union hold fit;        /* union variable of hold type      */
union hold save[10]; /* array of 10 union variables        */
union hold *pu;        /* pointer to a variable of hold type */
```

The first declaration creates a single variable fit. The compiler allots enough space so that it can hold the largest of the described possibilities. In this case, the biggest possibility listed is double, which requires 64 bits, or 8 bytes, on our system. The second declaration creates an array save with elements, each 8 bytes in size. The third declaration creates a pointer that can hold the address of a hold union.

Here is how a union is used:

```
fit.digit = 23;    /* 23 is stored in fit; 2 bytes used      */
fit.bigfl = 2.0;   /* 23 cleared, 2.0 stored; 8 bytes used */
fit.letter = 'h'; /* 2.0 cleared, h stored; 1 byte used     */
```

The dot operator shows which data type is being used. Only one value is stored at a time. You can't store a char and an int at the same time, even though there is enough space to do so. It is your responsibility to keep track of the data type currently being stored in a union.

The next sequence shows what not to do:

```
fit.letter = 'A';
flnum = 3.02*fit.bigfl;    /* ERROR ERROR ERROR */
```

This sequence is wrong because a char type is stored, but the next line assumes that the content of fit is a double type.

However, sometimes it can be useful to use one member to place values into a union and to then use a different member for viewing the contents. Listing 15.4 in the next chapter will show an example.

You can use the -> operator with pointers to unions in the same fashion that you use the operator with pointers to structures:

```
pu = &fit;
x = pu->digit;   /* same as x = fit.digit */
```

Summary: Structure and Union Operators

The Membership Operator

General Comments

The . operator is used with a structure or union name to specify a member of that structure or union. If name is the name of a structure and member is a member specified by the structure template, then

```
name.member
```

identifies that member of the structure. The type of name.member is the type specified for member. The membership operator can also be used in the same fashion with unions.

Example

```
struct {
        int code;
        float cost;
} item;

item.code = 1265;
```

The last statement assigns a value to the code member of the structure item.

The Indirect Membership Operator

```
->
```

General Comments

This operator is used with a pointer to a structure or union to identify a member of that structure or union. Suppose that ptrstr is a pointer to a structure and that member is a member specified by the structure template. Then

(continued)

```
        ptrstr->member
```

identifies that member of the pointed-to structure. The indirect membership
operator can be used in the same fashion with unions.

Example
```
    struct {
            int code;
            float cost;
    } item, *ptrst;
    ptrst = &item;
    ptrst->code = 3451;
```

The last statement assigns an `int` value to the `code` member of `item`. The
following three expressions are equivalent:

```
    ptrst->code    item.code    (*ptrst).code
```

typedef—A Quick Look

The `typedef` function is an advanced data feature that lets you create your
own name for a type. It is similar to `#define` in that respect, but with three
differences:

Unlike `#define`, `typedef` is limited to giving symbolic names to
data types only.

The `typedef` function is performed by the compiler, not the
preprocessor.

Within its limits, `typedef` is more flexible than `#define`.

Let's see how `typedef` works. Suppose you want to use the term `real`
for `float` numbers. You simply define `real` as if it were a `float` variable
and precede the definition by the keyword `typedef`:

```
typedef float real;
```

From then on, you can use `real` to define variables:

```
real x, y[10], *z;
```

The scope of this definition depends on the location of the `typedef` statement. If the definition is inside a function, then the scope is local, confined to that function. If the definition is outside a function, then the scope is global.

Sometimes, uppercase letters are used for these definitions to remind the user that the type name is really a symbolic abbreviation:

```
typedef float REAL;
```

This example can be duplicated with a `#define`:

```
#define REAL float
```

Here is one that can't be duplicated with a `#define`:

```
typedef char *STRING;
```

Without the keyword `typedef`, this example would identify `STRING` itself as a pointer to `char`. With the keyword, it makes `STRING` an *identifier* for pointers to `char`. Thus,

```
STRING name, sign;
```

means

```
char *name, *sign;
```

You can use `typedef` with structures, too:

```
typedef struct {
        float real;
        float imag;
} COMPLEX;
```

You then can use the type `COMPLEX` to represent complex numbers. One reason to use `typedef` is to create convenient, recognizable names for types that turn up often. For instance, many people prefer to use `STRING` or its equivalent, as in our earlier example.

A second reason for using `typedef` is that `typedef` names are often used for complicated types. For example, the declaration

```
typedef char (*FRPTC ()) [5];
```

makes `FRPTC` announce a type that is a function that returns a pointer to a five-element array of `char`. (See the upcoming discussion on fancy declarations.)

575

A third reason for using `typedef` is to make programs more portable. Suppose that your program needs to use 32-bit numbers. On some systems, that would be type `int`. On others it might be type `long`. If you used only `long` or `int` in your declarations, you would have to alter all the declarations when you moved from one system to the other. Instead, you can do the following. In an `#include` file have this definition:

```
typedef int FOURBYTE;
```

Use `FOURBYTE` in your programming for those `int` variables that must be 32 bits. Then when you move the program to a machine where type `long` is needed, just change the single definition in your `#include` file:

```
typedef long FOURBYTE;
```

Some programmers prefer using `#define` for this purpose. Either way is an example of what makes C such a portable language.

When using `typedef`, bear in mind that it does not create new types; it just creates convenient labels. This means, for example, that variables using the `STRING` type we created can be used as arguments for functions expecting type pointer-to-`char`.

With structures, unions, and `typedef`, C gives you the tools for efficient and portable data handling.

Fancy Declarations

C allows you to create elaborate data forms. Although we are sticking to simpler forms, we feel it is our duty to point out the potentialities. When you make a declaration, the name (or identifier) that you use can be modified by tacking on a modifier:

Modifier	Significance
*	Indicates a pointer
()	Indicates a function
[]	Indicates an array

C lets you use more than one modifier at a time, and that lets you create a variety of types:

```
int board[8][8];    /* an array of arrays of int            */
int **ptr;          /* a pointer to a pointer to int        */
int *risks[10];     /* a 10-element array of pointers to int */
int (*rusks)[10];   /* a pointer to an array of 10 ints     */
int *oof[3][4];     /* a 3 x 4 array of pointers to int     */
```

```
int (*uuf)[3][4];   /* a pointer to a 3 x 4 array of ints    */
int (*uof[3])[4];   /* a 3-element array of pointers to
                       4-element arrays of int               */
```

The trick to unravelling these declarations is figuring out the order in which to apply the modifiers. These rules should get you through:

1. The [], which indicates an array, and the (), which indicates a function, have the same precedence. This precedence is higher than that of the * indirection operator, which means that the following declaration makes risks an array of pointers rather than a pointer to an array:

```
int *risks[10];
```

2. The [] and () associate from left to right. This next declaration makes goods an array of 12 arrays of 50 ints, not an array of 50 arrays of 12 ints:

```
int goods[12][50];
```

3. Parentheses used for grouping have the highest precedence. This means that the following declaration makes rusks a pointer to an array of 10 ints:

```
int (*rusks)[10];
```

Let's apply these rules to this declaration:

```
int *oof[3][4];
```

The [3] has higher precedence than the *, and, because of the left-to-right rule, it has higher precedence than the [4]. Hence, oof is an array with three elements. Next in order is [4], so the elements of oof are arrays of four elements. The * tells us that these elements are pointers. The int completes the picture: oof is a three-element array of four-element arrays of pointers to int, or, for short, a 3 x 4 array of pointers to int. Storage is set aside for 12 pointers.

Now look at this declaration:

```
int (*uuf)[3][4];
```

The parentheses cause the * modifier to have first priority, making uuf a pointer to a 3 x 4 array of ints. Storage is set aside for a single pointer.

These rules also yield the following types:

```
char *fump();       /* function returning pointer to char    */
char (* frump)();   /* pointer to a function that returns
                       type char                             */
```

```
char (*flump[3])(); /* array of 3 pointers to functions that
                          return type char                   */
```

When you bring structures into the picture, the possibilities for declarations truly grow baroque. And the applications—well, we'll leave that for more advanced texts.

Functions and Pointers

As the discussion on declarations illustrated, it's possible to declare pointers to functions. You may wonder if such a beast has any usefulness. Typically, a function pointer is used as an argument to another function, telling the second function which function to use. For instance, the qsort() function from the C library takes a pointer to a function as one of its arguments. We've used one sorting function for integers and another for strings. The algorithm was the same, but we used > for comparing integers and strcmp() for strings. The qsort() function takes a more general approach. You pass it a pointer to a comparison function appropriate to the type you wish to sort, and qsort() then uses that function to sort the type, whether it be integer, string, or structure.

To show the essential ideas, the program in Listing 14.12 uses function pointers to print a command-line argument in normal and reverse order. We use ANSI prototyping not only for the program's functions but also for describing the characteristics of the pointed-to functions.

Listing 14.12 *func_ptr.c*

```
/* func_ptr.c -- uses function pointers */
#include <stdio.h>
int rputs(const char *);
void show(int (*fp)(const char *ps), char *str);
int main(argc, argv)
int argc;
char *argv[];
{
  if (argc < 2)
      exit(1);
  show(puts, argv[1]);    /* use puts()           */
  show(rputs, argv[1]);   /* use rputs()          */
  return 0;
}
```

```
    int rputs(const char *str)
    {
       const char *start = str;

       while (*str != '\0')
           str++;                  /* go to end of string    */
       while (str != start)
           putchar(*--str);
       return putchar('\n');
    }
    void show(int (*fp)(const char *ps), char *str)
                  /* fp points to function returning int    */
    {
       (*fp)(str); /* pass str to the pointed-to function    */
    }
```

Here are two sample runs:

```
C>funct_ptr pretty polly
pretty
ytterp
C>funct_ptr "fabulous duo"
fabulous duo
oud suolubaf
```

As we mentioned in an earlier chapter, some operating systems allow you to use quotes to group several words into a single command-line argument.

The first point to observe in Listing 14.12 is that the name of a function used without parentheses yields the address of that function. So the function call show(puts,argv[1]) passes the address of the puts() function, and show(rputs,argv[1]) passes the address of the rputs() function. Both also pass the address of a string.

Incidentally, you can use function names in assignment statements. For instance, if pfun is declared to be a pointer to a function that returns double, you can do this:

```
pfun = atof;
```

Then pfun is assigned the address of the library function atof(), providing the atof() declaration appears prior to this statement.

Second, the show() function definition must declare its argument types. Both puts() and rputs() return an int, so the proper declaration for fp is this:

```
int (*fp)();
```

In ANSI C, you also can (and should) indicate what type of arguments the pointed-to function takes:

```
int (*fp)(conts char *ps);   /* ANSI C prototyping */
```

Note that we defined `rputs()` so that it has the same type arguments and return value as `puts()`. Passing addresses of different types of functions can cause problems. The ANSI C function prototyping helps catch that sort of error.

Third, the example shows how to use a function pointer. Because `fp` points to a function, the expression `*fp` represents the function that is pointed to, and `(*fp)(str)` is a call to that function, passing `str` as an argument to it. Similarly, given the definition

```
pfun = atof;
```

you can use this call to invoke the `atof()` function:

```
(*pfun)(string);
```

Some C compilers have also allowed the following usage when `pfun` is a pointer:

```
pfun(string);  /* rogue usage */
```

Neither ANSI C nor K&R C supports this form.

You've now seen all four ways in which a function name can be used: in defining a function, in declaring a function, in calling a function, and as a pointer. Figure 14.4 sums up the uses.

Figure 14.4 *Uses for a function name*

```
       function name used in a prototype declaration: int comp(int x, int y);
              function name used in a function call: status = comp(q,r);
           function name used in a function definition: int comp(x,y)
                                                        int x,y;
                                                        { ...
      function name used as a pointer in assignment: pfunct = comp;
           function name used as pointer argument: slowsort(arr,n,comp);
```

Chapter Summary

A C *structure* provides the means to store several data items, usually of different types, in the same data object. You can use a *tag* to identify a specific structure template and to declare variables of that type. The *membership dot operator* (.) lets you access the individual members of a structure by using labels from the structure template.

If you have a pointer to a structure, you can use the pointer and the *indirect membership operator* (->) instead of a name and the dot operator to access individual members. To obtain the address of a structure, use the & operator. Unlike arrays, the name of a structure does not serve as the address of the structure.

Traditionally, structure-related functions have used pointers to structures as arguments. Modern C, including ANSI C, permits structures to be passed as arguments, used as return values, and assigned to structures of the same type.

Unions use the same syntax as structures. However, with unions, the members share a common storage space. Instead of storing several data types simultaneously in the manner of a structure, the union stores a single data item type from a list of choices. That is, a structure can hold, say, an int and a double and a char, while the corresponding union can hold an int or a double or a char.

The typedef facility enables you to establish aliases or shorthand representations of standard C types.

The name of a function yields the address of that function. Such addresses can be passed as arguments to functions, which then use the pointed-to function.

Review Questions

1. What's wrong with this template?

```
structure {
      char itable;
      int  num[20];
      char *togs
}
```

2. Devise a structure template that will hold the name of a month, a three-letter abbreviation for the month, the number of days in the month, and the month number.

3. Write a function that, when given the month number, returns the total days in the year up to and including that month. Assume that

the structure template of Question 2 and an appropriate array of
such structures are declared externally.

4. Consider the following programming fragment:

```
struct name {
        char first[20];
        char last[20];
};
struct bem {
        int limbs;
        struct name title;
        char type[30];
};
struct bem *pb;
struct bem deb = {
        6,
        {"Berbnazel", "Gwolkapwolk"},
        "Arcturan"
};

pb = &deb;
```

   a. What would each of the following statements print?

```
printf("%d", deb.limbs);
printf("%s", pb->type);
printf("%s", pb->type + 2);
```

   b. How could you represent "Gwolkapwolk" in structure
      notation (two ways)?
   c. Write a function that takes the address of a bem structure as
      its argument and prints the contents of that structure in the
      form shown below. Assume that the structure template is in a
      file called starfolk.h.

      erbnazel Gwolkapwolk is a 6-limbed Arcturan.

5. Define a structure template suitable for holding the following
   items: the name of an automobile, its horsepower, its EPA city-
   driving mpg rating, its wheelbase, and its year. Use car as the
   template tag.

6. Suppose you have this structure:

```
struct gas {
        float distance;
        float gals;
        float mpg;
};
```

Devise a function that takes a struct gas argument. Assume that the passed structure contains the distance and gals information. Have the function calculate the correct value for the mpg member and return the now completed structure.

7. Declare a pointer to a function that returns a pointer to char.

Programming Exercises

1. Redo Review Question 3, but make the argument the spelled-out name of the month instead of the month number. (Don't forget about strcmp().)

2. Write a program that prompts the user to enter the day, month, and year. The month can be a month number, a month name, or a month abbreviation. The program then returns the total number of days in the year up through the given day.

3. Revise our book-listing program in Listing 14.2 so that it prints both the book descriptions alphabetized by title and the total value of the books.

4. Write a program that creates a structure template with two members according to the following criteria:

   a. The first member is a social security number. The second member is a structure with three members. Its first member contains a first name, its second member contains a middle name, and its final member contains a last name. Create and initialize an array of five such structures. Have the program print the data in this form:

   ```
   Dribble, Flossie M. -- 302039823
   ```

   Only the initial of the middle name is printed, and a period is added. Neither the initial (of course) nor the period should be printed if the middle name member is empty. Write a function to do the printing; pass the structure array to the function.

   b. Modify part a by passing the structure value instead of the address.

5. Write a program that fits the following recipe:

   a. Externally define a name structure template with two members: a string to hold the first name, and a string to hold the second name.

   b. Externally define a student structure template with three members: a name structure, a grade array to hold floating-

583

point scores, and a variable to hold the average of those three scores.

    c. Have the `main()` function declare an array of `CSIZE` (with `CSIZE = 4`) student structures and initialize the name portions to names of your choice. Use functions to perform the tasks described in parts d, e, f, and g.

    d. Interactively acquire scores for each student by prompting the user with a student name and a request for scores. Place the scores in the grade array portion of the appropriate structure. The required looping may be done in `main()` or in the function, as you prefer.

    e. Calculate the average score value for each structure and assign it to the proper member.

    f. Print the information in each structure.

    g. Print the class average for each of the numeric structure members.

6. Modify Listing 14.11 so that as each record is read from the file and shown to you, you are given the chance to delete the record or to modify its contents. If you delete the record, use the vacated array position for the next record to be read.

7. The Colossus Airlines fleet consists of one plane with a seating capacity of 12. It makes one flight daily. Write a seating reservation program with the following features:

    a. The program uses an array of 12 structures. Each structure should hold a seat identification number, a marker that indicates whether the seat is assigned, the last name of the seat holder, and the first name of the seat holder.

    b. The program displays the following menu:

```
To choose a function, enter its letter label:
a) Show number of empty seats    b) Show list of empty
                                    seats
c) Show alphabetical list of     d) Assign a customer to a
   seat assignments                 seat
e) Delete a seat assignment      f) Quit
```

    c. The program successfully executes the promises of its menu. Choices d) and e) will require additional input, and each should allow the user to abort entry.

    d. After executing a particular function, the program shows the menu again, except for choice f).

    e. Data is saved in a file between runs. When the program is restarted, it first loads in the data, if any, from the file.

8. Write a program that implements a menu by using an array of pointers to functions. For instance, choosing a from the menu would activate the function pointed to by the first element of the array.

15

Bit Fiddling

Operators

▶ ~ & | ^

▶ >> <<

▶ &= |= ^= >>= <<=

In this chapter you review binary, octal, and hexa-decimal number notations. Then you learn about two C facilities for handling the individual bits in a value: bitwise operators and bit fields.

W ith C, you can manipulate the individual bits in a variable. Perhaps you are wondering why anyone would want to. Be assured that sometimes this ability is necessary, or at least useful. For example, a hardware device often is controlled by sending it a byte in which each bit has a particular meaning. Also, operating system information about files often is stored by using particular bits to indicate particular items.

We'll investigate C's bit powers in this chapter after we supply you with some background about bits, bytes, binary notation, and other number bases.

Binary Numbers, Bits, and Bytes

Our usual way to write numbers is based on the number 10. For instance, 2157 has a 2 in the thousands place, a 1 in the hundreds place, a 5 in the tens place, and a 7 in the ones place. This means that we can think of 2157 as being

$$2 \times 1000 + 1 \times 100 + 5 \times 10 + 7 \times 1$$

But 1000 is 10 cubed, 100 is 10 squared, 10 is 10 to the first power, and, by convention, 1 is 10 (or any positive number) to the zero power. Thus, we also can write 2157 as

$$2 \times 10^3 + 1 \times 10^2 + 5 \times 10^1 + 7 \times 10^0$$

Because our system of writing numbers is based on powers of ten, we say that 2157 is written in *base 10*.

Presumably, the decimal system evolved because we have ten fingers. A computer bit, in a sense, has only two fingers because it can be set only to 0 or 1, off or on. Therefore, a *base 2* system is natural for a computer. It uses powers of two instead of powers of ten. Numbers expressed in base 2 are termed *binary* numbers. For example, a binary number such as 1101 would mean

$$1 \times 2^3 + 1 \times 2^2 + 0 \times 2^1 + 1 \times 2^0$$

In decimal numbers this becomes

$$1 \times 8 + 1 \times 4 + 0 \times 2 + 1 \times 1 = 13$$

The binary system lets you express any number (if you have enough bits) as a combination of 1s and 0s. This system is very convenient for digital computers, which express information in combinations of on and off states that can be interpreted as 1s and 0s. Let's see how the binary system works for a 1-byte integer.

Binary Integers

By modern definition, a byte contains 8 bits. (A few, rare, older systems use a bigger byte.) You can think of these 8 bits as being numbered from 7 to 0, left to right. Bit 7 is called the *high-order* bit, and bit 0 is the *low-order* bit in the byte. Each bit number corresponds to a particular exponent of 2. Imagine the byte as looking like Figure 15.1.

Figure 15.1 *Bit numbers and bit values*

This example shows bits 6, 3, and 0 set to 1.
The value of this byte is 64 + 8 + 1 or 73.

Here, 128 is 2 to the 7th power, and so on. The largest number this byte can hold is 1, with all bits set to 1: 11111111. The value of this binary number is

$$128 + 64 + 32 + 16 + 8 + 4 + 2 + 1 = 255$$

The smallest binary number would be 00000000, or a simple 0. A byte can store numbers from 0 to 255, for a total of 256 possible values. Or, by changing the interpretation, a byte can store numbers from −128 to +127, again a total of 256 values.

Signed Integers

The representation of signed numbers is determined by the hardware, not by C. Probably the simplest way to represent signed numbers is to reserve 1 bit, such as the high-order bit, to represent the sign. In a 1-byte value, this leaves 7 bits for the number itself. In such a *sign-magnitude* representation, 10000001 is −1 and 00000001 is 1. The total range, then, is −127 to +127.

One disadvantage of this approach is that it has two zeros: +0 and −0. This is confusing, and it also uses up two bit patterns for just one value.

The *two's-complement* method avoids that problem and is the most common system used today. We'll discuss this method as it applies to a 1-byte value. In that context, the values 0 through 127 are represented by the last 7 bits, with the high-order bit set to 0. So far, that's the same as the sign-magnitude method. Also, if the high-order bit is 1, the value is negative. The difference comes in determining the value of that negative number. Subtract the bit-pattern from the 9-bit pattern 100000000 (256 in binary), and the result is the magnitude of value. For example, suppose the pattern is 10000000. As an unsigned byte, this would be 128. As a signed value, it is negative (bit 7 is 1) and has a value of 100000000 − 10000000, or 10000000 (128). Thus, the number is −128. Similarly, 10000001 is −127, and 11111111 is −1. Thus, the method represents numbers in the range −128 to +127.

The simplest method for reversing the sign of a two's-complement binary number is to invert each bit (convert 0s to 1s and 1s to 0s) and then add 1. So, since 1 is 00000001, then −1 is 11111110 + 1, or 11111111, just as you saw earlier.

The *one's-complement* method forms the negative of a number by inverting each bit in the pattern. For instance, 00000001 is 1 and 11111110 is −1. This method also has a −0: 11111111. Its range (for a 1-byte value) is −127 to +127.

Binary Floating Point

Floating-point numbers are stored in two parts: a binary fraction and a binary exponent. Let's see how this is done.

Binary Fractions

The ordinary fraction .527 represents

$$5/10 + 2/100 + 7/1000$$

with the denominators representing increasing powers of ten. In a binary fraction, we use powers of two for denominators. Thus, the binary fraction .101 represents

$$\frac{1}{2} + \frac{0}{4} + \frac{1}{8}$$

which in decimal notation is

$$0.50 + 0.00 + 0.125$$

or 0.625.

Many fractions, such as $\frac{1}{3}$, cannot be represented exactly in decimal notation. Similarly, many fractions cannot be represented exactly in binary notation. Indeed, the only fractions that can be represented exactly are combinations of multiples of powers of $\frac{1}{2}$. Thus, $\frac{3}{4}$ and $\frac{7}{8}$ can be represented exactly as binary fractions, but $\frac{1}{3}$ and $\frac{2}{5}$ cannot be.

Floating-Point Representation

To represent a floating-point number in a computer, a certain number (system-dependent) of bits are set aside to hold a binary fraction. Additional bits hold an exponent. In general terms, the actual value of the number consists of the binary fraction times 2 to the indicated exponent. Thus, multiplying a floating-point number by, say, 4, increases the exponent by 2 and leaves the binary fraction unchanged. Multiplying by a number that is not a power of 2 will change the binary fraction and, if necessary, the exponent.

Other Bases

Computer workers often use number systems based on 8 and on 16. Since 8 and 16 are powers of 2, these systems are more closely related to a computer's binary system than the decimal system is.

Octal

Octal refers to a base 8 system. In this system, the different places in a number represent powers of 8. We use the digits 0 to 7. For example, the octal number 451 (written 0451 in C) represents

$$4 \times 8^2 + 5 \times 8^1 + 1 \times 8^0 = 297 \text{ (base 10)}$$

A handy thing to know about octal is that each octal digit corresponds to three binary digits. Table 15.1 shows the correspondence. This correspondence makes it simple to translate between the two systems. For example, the octal number 0377 is 11111111 in binary. We replaced the 3 with 011, dropped the leading 0, and then replaced each 7 with 111. The only awkward part is that a 3-digit octal number may take up to 9 bits in binary form, so an octal value larger than 0377 requires more than a byte. Note that internal 0s are not dropped: 0173 is 01 111 011, not 01 111 11.

Table 15.1 *Binary Equivalents for Octal Digits*

Octal Digit	Binary Equivalent
0	000
1	001
2	010
3	011
4	100
5	101
6	110
7	111

Hexadecimal

Hexadecimal (or "hex") refers to a base 16 system. Here we use powers of 16 and the digits 0 to 15. But since we don't have single digits to represent the values 10 to 15, we use the letters *A* to *F* for that purpose. For instance, the hex number A3F (written 0xA3F in C) represents

$$10 \times 16^2 + 3 \times 16^1 + 15 \times 16^0 = 2623 \text{ (base 10)}$$

since *A* represents 10 and *F* represents 15. In C, you can use either lower-case or uppercase letters for the additional hex digits. Thus, you also can write 2623 as 0xa3f.

Each hexadecimal digit corresponds to a 4-digit binary number. Thus, two hexadecimal digits correspond exactly to an 8-bit byte. The first digit represents the upper 4 bits, and the second digit the last 4 bits. This makes hexadecimal a natural choice for representing byte values. Table 15.2 shows the correspondence. For example, the hex value 0xC2 translates to 11000010.

Table 15.2 *Decimal, Hexadecimal, and Binary Equivalents*

Decimal Digit	Hexadecimal Digit	Binary Equivalent	Decimal Digit	Hexadecimal Digit	Binary Equivalent
0	0	0000	8	8	1000
1	1	0001	9	9	1001

(continued)

Table 15.2 *Table 15.2* (continued)

Decimal Digit	Hexadecimal Digit	Binary Equivalent	Decimal Digit	Hexadecimal Digit	Binary Equivalent
2	2	0010	10	A	1010
3	3	0011	11	B	1011
4	4	0100	12	C	1100
5	5	0101	13	D	1101
6	6	0110	14	E	1110
7	7	0111	15	F	1111

Now that you've seen what bits and bytes are, let's examine what C can do with them. C has two facilities to help you manipulate bits. The first is a set of six *bitwise* operators that act on bits. The second is the `field` data form, which gives you access to bits within an `int`. The following discussion will outline these C features.

C's Bitwise Operators

C offers bitwise logical operators and shift operators. In the following examples, we will write out values in binary notation so that you can see what happens to the bits. In an actual program, you would use integer variables or constants written in the usual forms. For instance, instead of 00011001, you would use 25 or 031 or 0x19. For our examples, we will use 8-bit numbers, with the bits numbered 7 to 0, left to right.

Bitwise Logical Operators

The four bitwise logical operators work on integer-type data, including `char`. They are termed bitwise because they operate on each bit independently of the bit to the left or right. Don't confuse them with the regular logical operators (`&&`, `||`, and `!`), which operate on values as a whole.

One's Complement, or Bitwise Negation: ~

The unary operator ~ changes each 1 to a 0 and each 0 to a 1, as in the following example:

```
~(10011010) == (01100101)
```

Suppose that `val` is an `unsigned char` assigned the value 2. In binary, 2 is

00000010. Then ~val has the value 11111101, or 253. Note that the operator does not *change* the value of val, just as 3 * val does not change the value of val; val is still 2. But it does create a new value that can be used or assigned elsewhere:

```
newval = ~val;
printf("%d", ~val);
```

If you want to change the value of val to ~val, use simple assignment:

```
val = ~val;
```

Bitwise AND: &

The binary operator & produces a new value by making a bit-by-bit comparison between two operands. For each bit position, the resulting bit is 1 only if both corresponding bits in the operands are 1. (In terms of true-false, the result is true only if each of the two bit operands is true.) Thus,

```
(10010011) & (00111101) == (00010001)
```

since only bits 4 and 0 are 1 in both operands.

C also has a combined bitwise AND-assignment operator: &=. The statement

```
val &= 0377;
```

produces the same final result as the following:

```
val = val & 0377;
```

Bitwise OR: |

The binary operator | produces a new value by making a bit-by-bit comparison between two operands. For each bit position, the resulting bit is 1 if either of the corresponding bits in the operands is 1. (In terms of true-false, the result is true if one or the other bit operands are true or if both are true.) Thus,

```
(10010011) | (00111101) == (101111111)
```

since all bit positions but bit 6 have the value 1 in one or the other operands.

C also has a combined bitwise OR-assignment operator: |=. The statement

```
val |= 0377;
```

produces the same final result as:

```
val = val | 0377;
```

Bitwise EXCLUSIVE OR: ^

The binary operator ^ makes a bit-by-bit comparison between two operands. For each bit position, the resulting bit is 1 if one or the other (but not both) of the corresponding bits in the operands is 1. (In terms of true-false, the result is true if one or the other bit operands—but not both—are true.) Thus,

```
(10010011) ^ (00111101) == (10101110)
```

Note that since bit position 0 has the value 1 in both operands, the resulting 0 bit has value 0.

C also has a combined bitwise OR-assignment operator: ^=. The statement

```
val ^= 0377;
```

produces the same final result as:

```
val = val ^ 0377;
```

Usage: Masks

The bitwise AND operator often is used with a *mask*. A mask is a bit pattern with some bits that are set to ON (1) and some bits to OFF (0). To see why a mask is called a mask, let's see what happens when a quantity is ANDed with a mask. For example, suppose you #define MASK to be 2, i.e., binary 00000010, with only bit number 1 being nonzero. Then the statement

```
flags = flags & MASK;
```

would cause all the bits of flags (except bit 1) to be set to 0, since any bit combined with 0 via the & operator yields 0. Bit number 1 will be left unchanged. (If the bit is 1, then 1 & 1 is 1; if the bit is 0, then 0 & 1 is 0.) This process is called using a *mask* because the zeros in the mask hide the corresponding bits in flags.

Extending the analogy, you can think of the 0s in the mask as being opaque and the 1s as being transparent. The expression flags & MASK is like covering the flags bit pattern with the mask; only the bits under MASK's 1s are visible. See Figure 15.2.

Figure 15.2 *A mask*

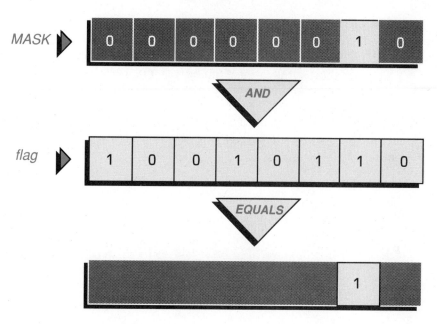

You can shorten the code by using the AND-assignment operator:

```
flags &= MASK;
```

One common C usage is this:

```
ch &= 0377;
```

The value 0377, recall, is 11111111 in binary. This mask leaves the final 8 bits of `ch` alone and sets the rest to 0. Thus, regardless of whether the original `ch` is 8 bits, 16 bits, or more, the final value is trimmed to something that fits into a single byte.

Usage: Turning Bits On

Sometimes you may need to turn on particular bits in a value while leaving the remaining bits unchanged. For instance, an IBM PC controls hardware through values sent to *ports*. To turn on, say, the speaker, you may have to turn on 1 bit while leaving the others unchanged. This can be done with the bitwise OR operator.

For example, consider our `MASK`, which has bit 1 set to 1. The statement

```
flags = flags | MASK;
```

will set bit number 1 in flags to 1 and leave all the other bits unchanged. This follows because any bit combined with 0 via the | operator is itself, and any bit combined with 1 via the | operator is 1.

For short, you can use the bitwise OR-assignment operator:

```
flags |= MASK;
```

This, too, sets to 1 those bits in flags that also are on in MASK, leaving the other bits unchanged.

Usage: Turning Bits Off

Just as it's useful to be able to turn on particular bits without disturbing the other bits, it's useful to be able to turn them off. Suppose you want to turn off bit 1 in the variable flags. Once again, MASK has only the 1 bit turned on. You can do this:

```
flags = flags & ~MASK;
```

Since MASK is all 0s except for bit 1, then ~MASK is all 1s except for bit 1. A 1 AND any bit is that bit, so our statement leaves all the bits other than bit 1 unchanged. Also, a 0 AND any bit is 0, so bit 1 is set to 0 regardless of its original value.

Or you can use the short form:

```
flags &= ~MASK;
```

Usage: Toggling Bits

Toggling a bit means turning it off if it is on, and turning it on if it is off. You can use the bitwise EXCLUSIVE OR operator to toggle a bit. The idea is that if b is a bit setting (1 or 0), then 1 ^ b is 0 if b is 1 and is 1 if b is 0. Also 0 ^ b is b, regardless of its value. Thus, if you EXCLUSIVE OR a value with a mask, values corresponding to 1s in the mask are toggled, and values corresponding to 0s in the mask are unaltered. To toggle bit 1 in flag, you can do either of the following:

```
flag = flag ^ MASK;
flag ^= MASK;
```

Usage: Checking the Value of a Bit

You've seen how to change the values of bits. Suppose, instead, that you want to check the value of a bit. For example, does `flag` have bit 1 set to 1? You shouldn't simply compare `flag` to `MASK`:

```
if (flag == MASK)
  puts("Wow!");     /* doesn't work right */
```

Even if bit 1 in `flag` is set to 1, the other bit setting in `flag` can make the comparison untrue. Instead, you must first mask the other bits in `flag` so that you compare only bit 1 of `flag` with `MASK`:

```
if ((flag & MASK) == MASK)
  puts("Wow!");
```

The bitwise operators have lower precedence than ==, so the parentheses around `flag & MASK` are needed.

Bitwise Shift Operators

Now let's look at C's shift operators. The bitwise shift operators shift bits to the left or right. Again, we will write binary numbers explicitly to show the mechanics.

Left Shift: < <

The << left shift operator shifts the bits of the value of the left operand to the left by the number of places given by the right operand. The vacated positions are filled with 0s, and bits moved past the end of the left operand are lost. Thus,

```
(10001010) << 2 == (00101000)
```

where each bit is moved two places to the left.

This operation produces a new bit value, but it doesn't change its operands. For example, suppose `stonk` is 1. Then `stonk<<2` is 4, but `stonk` still is 1. You can use the left-shift assignment operator (<<=) to actually change a variable's value. This operator shifts the bit in the variable to its left by the number of places given by the right-hand value.

```
int stonk = 1;
int onkoo;
```

```
onkoo = stonk << 2;      /* assigns 4 to onkoo */
stonk <<= 2;             /* changes stonk to 4 */
```

Right Shift: >>

The >> right shift operator shifts the bits of the value of the left operand to the right by the number of places given by the right operand. Bits moved past the right end of the left operand are lost. For `unsigned` types, the places vacated at the left end are replaced by 0s. For signed types, the result is machine dependent. The vacated places may be filled with 0s, or they may be filled with copies of the sign (leftmost) bit. For an unsigned value, we have

```
(10001010) >> 2 == (00100010)
```

where each bit is moved two places to the right.

The right-shift assignment operator (>>=) shifts the bits in the left-hand variable to the right by the indicated number of places:

```
int sweet = 16;
int ooosw;

ooosw = sweet >> 3;      /* ooosw = 4, sweet still 16 */
sweet >>=3;              /* sweet changed to 4         */
```

Usage

The bitwise shift operators can provide swift, efficient (depending on the hardware) multiplication and division by powers of 2:

`number << n` Multiplies `number` by 2 to the nth power.

`number >> n` Divides `number` by 2 to the nth power if `number` is not negative.

These shift operations are analogous to the decimal system procedure of shifting the decimal point to multiply or divide by 10.

Programming Example

In Chapter 9 we used recursion to write a program to convert numbers to a binary representation. Now we'll solve the same problem using the bitwise operators. The program in Listing 15.1 reads an integer from the keyboard and passes it and a string address to a function called `itobs()` (for *i*nteger *to b*inary *s*tring, of course). This function then uses the bitwise operators to figure out the correct pattern of 1s and 0s to put into the string.

Listing 15.1 *binary.c*

```
/* binary.c -- using bit operations to display binary */
#include <stdio.h>
int main(void)
{
    char bin_str[8 * sizeof(int) + 1];
    char *itobs(int, char *);
    int number;

    puts("Enter integers and see them in binary.");
    puts("Nonnumeric input terminates program.");
    while (scanf("%d", &number) == 1)
        printf("%d is %s\n", number, itobs(number,bin_str));
    return 0;
}

char *itobs(int n, char *ps)
{
    int i;
    static int size = 8 * sizeof(int);

    for (i = size - 1; i >= 0; i--, n >>= 1)
        ps[i] = (01 & n) + '0';
    ps[size] = '\0';
    return ps;
}
```

Listing 15.1 assumes that the system uses 8 bits to a byte. Thus, the expression `8 * sizeof(int)` is the number of bits in an int. The `bin_str` array has that many elements plus 1 to allow for the terminating null character.

The `itobs()` function returns the same address passed to it. Thus, you can use the function as, say, an argument to `printf()`. The first time through the `for` loop, the function evaluates the quantity `01 & n`. The term `01` is the octal representation of a mask with all but the zero bit set to 0. Therefore, `01 & n` is just the value of the final bit in n. This value is a 0 or a 1, but for the array we need the *character* `'0'` or the *character* `'1'`. Adding the ASCII code for `'0'` accomplishes that conversion. The result is placed in the next-to-last element of the array. (The last element is reserved for the null character.)

Then the loop executes the statements i-- and n >>= 1. The first statement moves us one element earlier in the array, and the second shifts the bits in n over one position to the right. Thus, the next time through the loop we find the value of the new right-most bit. The corresponding digit character then is placed in the element preceding the final digit. In this fashion, the function fills the array from right to left.

Here is a sample run:

```
Enter integers and see them in binary.
Nonnumeric input terminates program.
7
7 is 0000000000000111
255
255 is 0000000011111111
30000
30000 is 0111010100110000
-1
-1 is 1111111111111111
q
```

Another Example

Let's work through one more example. Our goal this time is to write a function that inverts the last n bits in a value, where both n and the value are function arguments.

The ~ operator inverts bits, but it inverts all the bits in a byte, not just a select few. However, the EXCLUSIVE OR operator, as you saw, can be used to toggle bytes. Suppose you create a mask with the last n bits set to 1 and the remaining bits set to 0. Then EXCLUSIVE ORing that mask with a value will toggle, or invert, the last n bits, leaving the other bits unchanged. That's the approach used here:

```
int invert_end(int num, int bits)
{
    int mask = 0;
    int bitval = 1;

    while (bits-- > 0)
    {
        mask |= bitval;
        bitval <<= 1;
    }
    return num ^ mask;
}
```

The while loop creates the mask. Initially, mask has all its bits set to

0. The first pass through the loop sets bit 0 to 1 and then increases the value of `bitval` to 2; that is, it sets bit 0 to 0 and bit 1 to 1. The next pass through then sets bit 1 of mask to 1, and so on. Finally, the `num ^ mask` operation produces the desired result.

To test the function, we can slip it into the preceding program. See Listing 15.2.

Listing 15.2 *invert4.c*

```
/*  invert4.c -- inverts last 4 bits of integers */
#include <stdio.h>
int main(void)
{
    char bin_str[8 * sizeof(int) + 1];
    char *itobs(int n, char *ps);
    int invert_end(int num, int bits);
    int number;

    puts("Enter integers and see them in binary.");
    puts("Nonnumeric input terminates program.");
    while (scanf("%d", &number) == 1)
    {
        printf("%d is %s\n", number, itobs(number,bin_str));
        printf("Inverting the last 4 bits gives %s\n",
                itobs(invert_end(number,4)));
    }
    return 0;
}
char *itobs(int n, char *ps)
{
    int i;
    static int size = 8 * sizeof(int);

    for (i = size - 1; i >= 0; i--, n >>= 1)
        ps[i] = (01 & n) + '0';
    ps[size] = '\0';
    return ps;
}
int invert_end(int num, int bits)
{
```

(continued)

Listing 15.2 *(continued)*

```
    int mask = 0;
    int bitval = 1;

    while (bits-- > 0)
    {
        mask |= bitval;
        bitval <<= 1;
    }
    return num ^ mask;
}
```

Here's a sample run:

```
Enter integers and see them in binary.
Nonnumeric input terminates program.
7
7 is 0000000000000111
Inverting the last 4 bits gives 000000000001000
255
255 is 0000000011111111
Inverting the last 4 bits gives 0000000011110000
q
```

Bit Fields

The second method of manipulating bits is to use a bit field. A *bit field* is just a set of neighboring bits within an unsigned int. A bit field is set up with a structure definition that labels each field and determines its width. For instance, the following definition sets up four 1-bit fields:

```
struct    {
            unsigned autfd    : 1;
            unsigned bldfc    : 1;
            unsigned undln    : 1;
            unsigned itals    : 1;
} prnt;
```

This definition causes prnt to contain four 1-bit fields. Now you can use the usual structure membership operator to assign values to individual fields:

```
prnt.itals = 0;
prnt.undln = 1;
```

Because each field is just 1 bit, 1 and 0 are the only values you can use for assignment. The variable prnt is stored in an int-sized memory cell, but only 4 bits are used in this example.

Fields aren't limited to 1-bit sizes. You also can do this:

```
struct {
        unsigned code1 : 2;
        unsigned code2 : 2;
        unsigned code3 : 8;
} prcode;
```

This creates two 2-bit fields and one 8-bit field. You can now make assignments such as:

```
prcode.code1 = 0;
prcode.code2 = 3;
prcode.code3 = 102;
```

Just make sure that the value doesn't exceed the capacity of the field.

What if the total number of bits you declare exceeds the size of an int? Then the next int storage location is used. A single field is not allowed to overlap the boundary between two ints. The compiler automatically shifts an overlapping field definition so that the field is aligned with the int boundary. When this occurs, it leaves an unnamed hole in the first int.

You can "pad" a field structure with unnamed holes by using unnamed field widths. Using an unnamed field width of 0 forces the next field to align with the next integer:

```
struct {
        field1 : 1;
               : 2;
        field2 : 1;
               : 0;
        field3 : 1;
} stuff;
```

Here, there is a 2-bit gap between stuff.field1 and stuff.field2; and stuff.field3 is stored in the next int.

One important machine dependency is the order in which fields are placed into an `int`. On some machines the order is left to right, and on others it is right to left. Also, machines differ in the location of boundaries between fields. For these reasons, bit fields tend not to be very portable. Typically, however, they are used for nonportable purposes, such as putting data in the exact form used by a particular hardware device.

Bit-Field Example

As we mentioned, bit fields typically are used in programs dedicated to a particular piece of hardware. Our example will be IBM PC-based, but if you aren't using that platform, you still can read through the example to see how it works.

The original IBM PC had various configuration switches that had to be set on the motherboard. When the computer was turned on, it copied information from these switch settings to a 2-byte memory location. Within that 2-byte word, the bits have the meaning shown in Table 15.3.

Table 15.3 Equipment Word

Bit(s)	Meaning	Value
0	Diskette drive	1 if present
1	Not used	
2–3	Motherboard memory	00 = 16k, 01 = 32k, 10 = 48k, 11 = 64k
4–5	Initial video setup	01 = 40x25, 10 = 80x25, 11 = mono
6–7	Number of drives	Number of diskette drives − 1
8	Not used	
9–11	Number of comm. cards	Number of cards
12	Game port	1 if present
13	Not used	
14–15	Number of printers	Number of printers

You can use a structure with bit fields to represent this data:

```
struct equip_word { unsigned has_drive  : 1;
                    unsigned            : 1;
                    unsigned mother_bd  : 2;
                    unsigned vid_setup  : 2;
                    unsigned num_drives : 2;
                    unsigned            : 1;
```

```
        unsigned num_comcds : 3;
        unsigned gameio     : 1;
        unsigned            : 1;
        unsigned num_ptrs   : 2;
```

Note that the unnamed bit fields represent the unused bits in the equipment word.

To determine whether a game I/O card, for example, is present, you can test whether the gameio member is 1. The tricky part is getting the correct values into the structure. Listing 15.3 shows one way.

Listing 15.3 *ibmchk.c*

```c
/* ibmchk.c -- checks IBM PC equipment word */
#include <stdio.h>
#include <dos.h>              /* MS-DOS specific declarations  */
#define DSKTE    0x0001       /* diskette drives are present   */
#define DRV_MASK 0x00C0       /* drive count bits              */
#define DRV_SHFT 6            /* shift drive bits to right end */
#define GAMES    0x1000       /* game I/O?                     */
#define PRN_SHFT 14           /* printer count shift           */
#define EQCK 0x11             /* equipment check interrupt     */
struct equip_word {
        unsigned has_drive : 1;
        unsigned           : 1;
        unsigned mother_bd : 2;
        unsigned vid_setup : 2;
        unsigned num_drives : 2;
        unsigned           : 1;
        unsigned num_comcds : 3;
        unsigned gameio    : 1;
        unsigned           : 1;
        unsigned num_ptrs  : 2;
};
int main(void)
{
    union REGS rin, rout;
    unsigned int equip;
    union {
```

(continued)

Listing 15.3 *(continued)*

```
            struct equip_word s_view;
            unsigned int   i_view;
    } eq_data;

    equip = int86 (EQCK, &rin, &rout);
    eq_data.i_view = equip;
    if (equip & DSKTE != DSKTE)
        printf("No disk drives\n");
    else
    {
        printf("Bit operations: %u floppy drive(s)\n",
                ((equip & DRV_MASK) >> DRV_SHFT) + 1);
        printf("Bit fields: %u floppy drive(s)\n",
                eq_data.s_view.num_drives + 1);
    }
    printf("Bit operations: %u printer(s) attached\n",
            equip >> PRN_SHFT);
    printf("Bit fields: %u printer(s) attached\n",
            eq_data.s_view.num_ptrs);
    return 0;
}
```

The int86() function, found both in MS C and Turbo C, uses *interrupts* to obtain information. Interrupts, more or less, are subroutines built into the PC. The int86() function, then, is quite implementation specific and is not part of any general C library. The particular interrupt we used, represented by EQCK, causes int86() to return the value of the equipment word in integer form.

To convert this integer to a structure, we used a trick. The union eq_data has two members: an equip_word structure and an unsigned integer:

```
union {
        struct equip_word s_view;
        unsigned int   i_view;
} eq_data;
```

Both, on a PC, are 16-bit data objects. We make the following assignment:

```
eq_data.i_view = equip;
```

The i_view member views the union as an unsigned int, and we read in the equipment word in that form. Then, by using eq_data.s_view, we can look at the same data as a bit-field structure. That is, bit 0 of the integer eq_data.i_view also is the has_drive member of the structure eq_data.s_view. Thus, the eq_data union lets us view the equipment word two ways: as a bit-field structure and as an unsigned int. This correspondence depends on the implementation-dependent feature that structures are loaded into memory from the low-bit end to the high-bit end of a byte. That is, the first bit field in the structure goes into bit 0 of the word. See Figure 15.3.

Figure 15.3 *A union as an integer and as a structure*

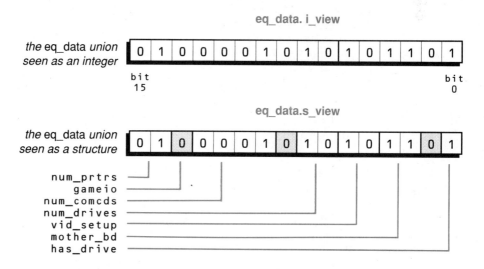

Incidentally, the type REGS union (defined in dos.h) uses a similar approach to provide both a word-view and a byte-view of the CPU registers.

The program then proceeds to use both the bit-wise operator approach and the bit-field method for examining the contents of the equipment word. Once the bit fields are set up, they are easier to use. For example, eq_data.s_view.num_drives represents the value stored in the 2 bits representing the number of floppy drives. Compare that to what we have to do using bit operations. First we evaluate equip & DRV_MASK to turn off all other bits. At this point we have a value in the form

00000000bb000000. Then we do a right shift to move these 2 bits to the low end of the word: 00000000000000bb. Now we can evaluate the expression numerically to determine the number of drives.

Chapter Summary

Computing hardware is closely tied to the *binary number system* because the 1s and 0s of binary numbers can be used to represent the on and off states of bits in computer memory and registers. Although C does not allow you to write numbers in binary form, it does recognize the related octal and hexadecimal notations. Just as each binary digit represents 1 bit, each octal digit represents 3 bits, and each hexadecimal digit represents 4 bits. This relationship makes it relatively simple to convert binary numbers to octal or hexadecimal form.

C features several *bit-wise operators*, so called because they operate independently on each bit within a value. The *bitwise negation operator* (~) inverts each bit in its operand, converting 1s to 0s and vice versa. The *bitwise AND operator* (&) forms a value from two operands. Each bit in the value is set to 1 if both corresponding bits in the operands are 1. Otherwise, the bit is set to 0. The *bitwise OR operator* (|) also forms a value from two operands. Each bit in the value is set to 1 if either or both corresponding bits in the operands are 1; otherwise, the bit is set to 0. The *bitwise EX-CLUSIVE OR operator* (^) acts similarly, except that the resulting bit is set to 1 only if one or the other, but not both, of the corresponding bits in the operands is 1.

C also has *left-shift* (<<) and *right-shift* (>>) operators. Each produces a value formed by shifting the bits in a pattern the indicated number of bits to the left or right. For the left-shift operator, the vacated bits are set to 0. For the right-shift operator, the vacated bits are set to 0 if the value is unsigned. The behavior of the right-shift operator is implementation dependent for signed values.

Bit fields in a structure let you address individual bits or groups of bits in a value. The details are implementation independent.

These bit tools assist C programs in dealing with various hardware matters, so they most often appear in implementation-dependent contexts.

Review Questions

1. Convert the following decimal values to binary.
   a. 3
   b. 13

    c. 59

    d. 119

2. Convert the following binary values to decimal, octal, and hexadecimal.

    a. 00010101

    b. 01010101

    c. 01001100

    d. 10011101

3. Evaluate the following expressions; assume each value is 1 byte.

    a. ~3

    b. 3 & 6

    c. 3 | 6

    d. 1 | 6

    e. 3 ^ 6

    f. 7 >> 1

    g. 7 << 2

4. Evaluate the following expressions; assume each value is 1 byte.

    a. ~0

    b. !0

    c. 2 & 4

    d. 2 && 4

    e. 2 | 4

    f. 2 || 4

    g. 65 << 3

5. Because the ASCII code uses only the final 7 bits, sometimes it is desirable to mask off the other bits. What's the appropriate mask in binary? In decimal? In octal? In hexadecimal?

6. In Listing 15.3, we masked `equip` with `drive_mask` before doing the right shift to get the drive number. But we didn't mask `equip` before doing the right shift to get the number of printers? Why didn't this omission cause problems?

Programming Exercises

1. Write a function that converts a binary string to a numeric value. That is, if you have

```
char *pbin = "01001001";
```

then you can pass pbin as an argument to the function and have the function return an int value of 25.

2. Write a program that reads two binary strings as command-line arguments and prints the results of applying the ~ operator to each number and the results of applying the &, |, and ^ operators to the pair. Show the results as binary strings.

3. Write a function that takes an int argument and returns the number of ON bits in the argument.

4. Write a function that takes two int arguments: a value and a bit position. Have the function return 1 if that particular bit position is 1, and have it return 0 otherwise.

5. Write a function that rotates the bits of an unsigned int by a specified number of bits to the left. For instance, rotate_l(x,4) would move the bits in x four places to the left, and the bits lost off the left end would reappear at the right end. That is, the bit moved out of the high-order position is placed in the low-order position.

16

The C Preprocessor and the C Library

Keywords
- ► #define, #include, #ifdef
- ► #else, #endif, #ifndef
- ► #if, #elif, enum

Functions
- ► sqrt( ), atan( ), atan2( )
- ► exit( ), atexit( ), malloc( )

In this chapter you investigate further the capabilities of the C preprocessor, learning about macro "functions" and conditional compilation. Also, you are introduced to the enum *facility and you learn more about the C library.*

T he ANSI C Standard encompasses more that just the C language. The Standard also describes how the C preprocessor should perform, establishes which functions form the standard C library, and details how these functions work. We'll explore the C preprocessor and the C library in this chapter, beginning with the preprocessor.

The preprocesor looks at your program before it is compiled (hence the term *pre*processor). Following your preprocessor directives, the preprocessor replaces the symbolic abbreviations in your program with the directions they represent. The preprocessor can include other files at your request. It can select which code the compiler sees. This description does not do justice to the true utility and value of the preprocessor, so let's turn to examples. With #define and #include, we have provided examples all along. Now we can gather what we have learned in one place and add to it.

Manifest Constants: *#define*

The #define preprocessor directive, like all preprocessor directives, begins with a # symbol. The ANSI Standard permits the # symbol to be preceded by spaces or tabs, and it allows for space between the # and the remainder of the directive. Older versions of C, however, typically require that the directive begin in the left-most column and that there be no spaces between the # and the remainder of the directive. A directive can appear anywhere in the source file, and the definition holds from its place of appearance to the end of the file. We have used directives heavily to define symbolic, or manifest, constants in our programs, but they have more range than that, as we will show. Listing 16.1 illustrates some of the possibilities and properties of the #define directive.

Preprocessor directives run until the first newline following the #. That is, a directive is limited to one line in length. However, the combination backslash-newline is treated as a space, so the one *logical* line can use more than one physical line in the file.

```
Listing 16.1   preproc.c

/* preproc.c -- simple preprocessor examples */
#include <stdio.h>
#define TWO 2         /* you can use comments if you like   */
#define MSG "The old grey cat sang a merry \
song."               /* a backslash continues a definition */
                     /* to the next line                   */
#define FOUR   TWO*TWO
#define PX printf("X is %d.\n", x)
#define FMT   "X is %d.\n"
int main(void)
{
   int x = TWO;

   PX;
   x = FOUR;
   printf(FMT, x);
   printf("%s\n", MSG);
   printf("TWO: MSG\n");
   return 0;
}
```

Each #define line has three parts. The first part is the #define directive itself. The second part is your chosen abbreviation, known as a *macro* or *alias* in the computer world. (Some programmers reserve the term "macro" for the macro functions we discuss later and use the term "alias" for the symbolic constants we are discussing now.) The macro must have no spaces in it. Its name must conform to the same rules that C variables follow: only letters, digits, and the underscore (_) character can be used, and the first character cannot be a digit. The third part (the remainder of the line) is termed the *body*. When the preprocessor finds an example of one of your aliases within your program, it almost always replaces it with the body. (There is one exception as we will show you in just a moment.) This process of going from a macro to a final replacement is called *macro expansion*. Note that you can use standard C comments on a #define line; they will be ignored by the preprocessor. Also, most systems (and the ANSI C Standard) allow you to use the backslash (\) to extend a definition over more than one line. See Figure 16.1.

Let's run our example and see how it works.

Figure 16.1 *Parts of a macro definition*

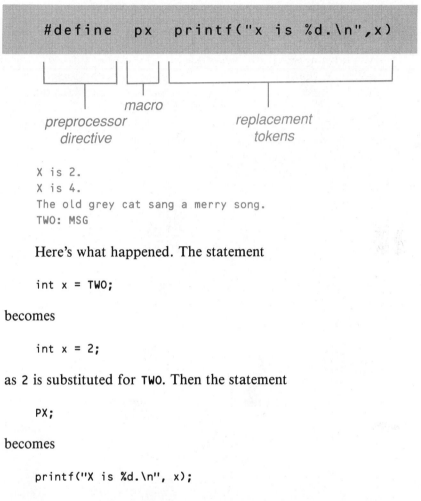

```
#define  px  printf("x is %d.\n",x)
```

preprocessor
directive

macro

replacement
tokens

```
X is 2.
X is 4.
The old grey cat sang a merry song.
TWO: MSG
```

Here's what happened. The statement

```
int x = TWO;
```

becomes

```
int x = 2;
```

as 2 is substituted for TWO. Then the statement

```
PX;
```

becomes

```
printf("X is %d.\n", x);
```

as that wholesale substitution is made. This is a new wrinkle, since up to now we've used macros only to represent constants. Here you see that a macro can express any string, even a whole C expression. Note, though, that this is a constant string; PX will print only a variable named x.

The next line also represents something new. You might think that FOUR is replaced by 4, but the actual process is this:

```
x = FOUR;
```

becomes

```
x = TWO*TWO;
```

617

which then becomes

```
x = 2*2;
```

The macro expansion process ends there. The actual multiplication takes place, not while the preprocessor works, but during compilation, because the C compiler evaluates all *constant expressions* (expressions with just constants) at compile time. The preprocessor does no calculation; it just makes the suggested substitutions very literally.

Note that a macro definition can include other macros. (Some compilers do not support this nesting feature.)

In the next line

```
printf (FMT, x);
```

becomes

```
printf("X is %d.\n",x);
```

as FMT is replaced by the corresponding string. This approach could be handy if you had a lengthy control string that you had to use several times. Alternatively, you can do the following:

```
char *fmt = "X is %d.\n";
```

In the next line MSG is replaced by the corresponding string. The double quotation marks make the replacement string a character string constant. The compiler will store it in an array terminated with a null character. Thus,

```
#define HAL 'Z'
```

defines a character constant, but

```
#define HAP "Z"
```

defines a character string: Z\0.

In the example, we used a backslash immediately before the end of the line to extend the string to the next line:

```
#define MSG "The old grey cat sang a merry \
song."
```

The space between the y and the \ prevents us from getting the word merrysong. Note that song is flush left. Suppose, instead, we did this:

```
#define MSG "The old grey cat sang a merry \
            song."
```

Then the output would be this:

```
The old grey cat sang a merry            song.
```

The space between the beginning of the line and song counts as part of the string.

In general, wherever the preprocessor finds one of your macros in your program, it literally replaces it with the equivalent replacement text. If that string also contains macros, they, too, are replaced. The one exception to replacement is a macro found within double quotation marks. Thus,

```
printf("TWO: MSG");
```

prints TWO: MSG literally instead of printing

```
2: The old grey cat sang a merry song.
```

To print this last line, you would use this:

```
printf("%d: %s\n", TWO, MSG);
```

Here, the macros are outside the double quotation marks.

When should you use symbolic constants? You should use them for most numbers. If the number is some constant used in a calculation, a symbolic name makes its meaning clearer. If the number is an array size, a symbolic name makes it simpler to change the array size and loop limits later. If the number is a system code for, say, EOF, a symbolic representation makes your program much more portable; just change one EOF definition. Mnemonic value, easy alterability, portability—these all make symbolic constants worthwhile.

Tokens

Technically, the body of a macro is considered to be a string of *tokens* rather than a string of characters. C preprocessor tokens are the separate "words" in the body of a macro definition. They are separated from one another by whitespace. For example, the definition

```
#define FOUR 2*2
```

has one token: the sequence 2*2. But the definition

```
#define SIX 2 * 3
```

has three tokens in it: 2, *, and 3.

Character strings and token strings differ in how multiple spaces in a body are treated. Consider this definition:

```
#define EIGHT 4    *    8
```

A preprocessor that interpreted the body as a character string would replace EIGHT with 4   *   8. That is, the extra spaces would be part of the replacement. But a preprocessor that interprets the body as tokens will replace EIGHT with three tokens separated by single spaces: 4 * 8. In other words, the character string interpretation views the spaces as *part* of the body, while the token interpretation views the spaces as *separators* between the tokens of the body. In practice, some C compilers have viewed macro bodies as strings rather than tokens. The difference is of practical importance only for usages more intricate than what we will attempt.

Incidentally, the C compiler takes a more complex view of tokens than does the preprocessor. The compiler understands the rules of C and doesn't necessarily require spaces to separate tokens. For instance, the C compiler would view 2*2 as three tokens because it recognizes that the 2's are constants and the * is an operator.

Redefining Constants

Suppose you define LIMIT to be 20; then later in the same file you define it again to be 25. This is called *redefining a constant*. Implementations differ on redefinition policy. Some consider it an error unless the new definition is the same as the old. Others allow redefinition, perhaps issuing a warning. The ANSI Standard takes the first view, allowing redefinition only if the new definition duplicates the old.

Having the same definition means the bodies must have the same tokens in the same order. Thus, these two definitions agree:

```
#define SIX 2 * 3
#define SIX 2        *    3
```

Both have the same three tokens, and the extra spaces are not part of the body. But the next definition is considered different:

```
#define SIX 2*3
```

It has just one token, not three, so it doesn't match. If you want to redefine a macro, use the #undef directive, which we discuss later.

Using Arguments with *#define*

By using arguments, you can create macros that look and act much like functions. A macro with arguments looks very much like a function, since the arguments are enclosed within parentheses. Listing 16.2 provides some examples that illustrate how such a *macro function* is defined and used. Some of the examples also point out possible pitfalls, so read them carefully.

Listing 16.2 *mac_arg.c*

```
/* mac_arg.c -- macros with arguments */
#include <stdio.h>
#define SQUARE(X) X*X
#define PR(X)    printf("The result is %d.\n", X)
int main(void)
{
    int x = 4;
    int z;

    z = SQUARE(x);
    PR(z);
    z = SQUARE(2);
    PR(z);
    PR(SQUARE(x+2));
    PR(100/SQUARE(2));
    PR(SQUARE(++x));
    return 0;
}
```

Wherever SQUARE(x) appears in Listing 16.2, it is replaced by x*x. This differs from our earlier examples in that we are free to use symbols other than x when we use this macro. The x in the macro definition is replaced by the symbol used in the macro call in the program. Thus, SQUARE(2) is replaced by 2*2. So the x really does act as an argument.

However, as you shall soon see, a macro argument does not work exactly like a function argument. Here are the results of running the program. Note that some of the answers are different from what you might expect.

```
The result is 16.
The result is 4.
The result is 14.
The result is 100.
The result is 30.
```

The first two lines are predictable, but then we come to some peculiar results. Recall that x has the value 4. This might lead you to expect that SQUARE(x+2) would be 6*6, or 36. But the printout says it is 14, which sure doesn't look like a square to us! The simple reason for this misleading output is the one we have already stated: the preprocessor doesn't make calculations; it just substitutes strings. Wherever our definition shows an x, the preprocessor will substitute the string x+2. Thus,

```
x*x
```

becomes

```
x+2*x+2
```

The only multiplication is 2*x. If x is 4, then the value of this expression is:

```
4+2*4+2 = 4 + 8 + 2 = 14
```

This example pinpoints a very important difference between a function call and a macro call. A function call passes the *value* of the argument to the function while the program is running. A macro call passes the argument *token* to the program before compilation; it's a different process at a different time. Can our definition be fixed to make SQUARE(x+2) yield 36? Sure. We simply need more parentheses:

```
#define SQUARE(x)   (x)*(x)
```

Then SQUARE(x+2) becomes (x+2)*(x+2), and we get our desired multiplication as the parentheses carry over in the replacement string.

This doesn't solve all our problems, however. Consider the events leading to the next output line:

```
100/SQUARE(2)
```

becomes

```
100/2*2
```

By the laws of precedence, the expression is evaluated from left to right:

```
(100/2)*2   or   50*2   or   100
```

This mix-up can be cured by defining `SQUARE(x)` as:

```
#define SQUARE(x)  (x*x)
```

This produces 100/(2*2), which eventually evaluates to 100/4, or 25.
To handle both of the last two examples, we need the definition

```
#define SQUARE(x)  ((x)*(x))
```

The lesson here is to use as many parentheses as necessary to ensure that operations and associations are done in the right order.
Even these precautions fail to save the final example from grief:

```
SQUARE(++x)
```

becomes

```
++x*++x
```

and x gets incremented twice, once before the multiplication and once afterwards:

```
++x*++x = 5*6 = 30
```

Because the order of operations is left open, some compilers will render the product 6*5, but the end result is the same.
The only remedy for this problem is to avoid using ++x as a macro argument. In general, *don't* use increment or decrement operators with macros. Note that ++x would work as a *function* argument, for it would be evaluated to 5 and then the value 5 would be sent to the function.

Including the Macro Argument in a String

Under K&R C you could define macros like the following:

```
#define PSQR(X)  printf("The square of X is %d.\n", ((X)*(X)));
```

Suppose you used the preceding macro like this:

```
PSQR(8);
PSQR(2 + 3);
```

Then the output would be this:

```
The square of 8 is 64.
The square of 2 + 3 is 25.
```

That is, the macro argument inside the double quotes would be replaced by the actual argument, contrary to the normal rule that tokens inside double quotes are left unaltered. ANSI C disallows this substitution within quotes. Running the same code under ANSI C produces the following output:

```
The square of x is 64.
The square of x is 25.
```

The x in the quoted string is treated as ordinary text, not as a token that can be replaced.

Suppose you do want to include the macro argument in a string? A new feature of ANSI C lets you do that. If, say, x is a macro parameter, then #x is that parameter converted to a string. Listing 16.3 illustrates how this works.

Listing 16.3 *subst.c*

```
/* subst.c -- substitute in string */
#include <stdio.h>
#define PSQR(x) printf("The square of " #x " is
%d.\n",((x)*(x)))
int main(void)
{
    int y = 5;

    PSQR(y);
    PSQR(2 + 4);
    return 0;
}
```

Here's the output:

```
The square of y is 25.
The square of 2 + 4 is 36.
```

In the first call to the macro, #x was replaced by "y", and in the second call it was replaced by "2 + 4". ANSI C string concatenation then combined these strings with the other strings in the `printf()` statement to produce the final strings that were used.

Macro or Function?

Many tasks can be done by using a macro with arguments or by using a function. Which one should you use? There is no hard and fast rule, but here are some considerations.

Macros are somewhat trickier to use than regular functions because they can have odd side effects if you are unwary. Some compilers limit the macro definition to one line, and it is probably best to observe that limit even if your compiler does not.

The macro-versus-function choice represents a trade-off between time and space. A macro produces *in-line* code; that is, you get a statement in your program. If you use the macro 20 times, then you get 20 lines of code inserted into your program. If you use a function 20 times, you have just one copy of the function statements in your program, so less space is used. On the other hand, program control must shift to where the function is and then return to the calling program, and this takes longer than in-line code.

Macros have an advantage in that they don't worry about variable types. (This is because they deal with character strings, not with actual values.) Thus, our `SQUARE(x)` macro can be used equally well with `int` or `float`.

Programmers typically use macros for simple functions like the following:

```
#define MAX(X,Y)    ((X) > (Y) ? (X) : (Y))
#define ABS(X)      ((X) < 0 ? -(X) : (X))
#define ISSIGN(X)   ((X) == '+' || (X) == '-' ? 1 : 0)
```

(The last macro has the value 1—true—if x is an algebraic sign character.)
Here are some points to note:

► Remember that there are no spaces in the macro name, but that spaces can appear in the replacement string. With K&R C, there can be no spaces in the argument list. The preprocessor thinks the macro ends at the first space, so anything after that space is lumped into the replacement string, as shown in Figure 16.2. ANSI C, however, does permit spaces in the argument list.

► Use parentheses around each argument and around the definition as a whole. This ensures that the enclosed terms are grouped properly in an expression like `forks = 2 * MAX(guests + 3, last);`.

▶ Use capital letters for macro function names. This convention is not as widespread as that of using capitals for macro constants. However, one good reason for using capitals is to remind yourself to be alert to possible macro side effects.

▶ If you intend to use a macro instead of a function primarily to speed up a program, try to first determine if it is likely to make a significant difference. A macro that is used once in a program most likely will make no noticeable improvement in running time. A macro inside a nested loop is a much better candidate for speed improvements. Many systems offer program profilers to help you pin down where a program spends the most time.

Figure 16.2 *Faulty spacing in a macro definition*

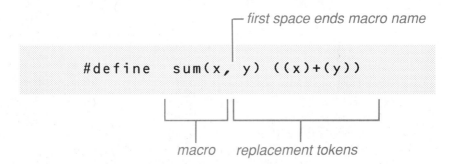

Suppose you have developed some macro functions that you like. Do you have to retype them each time you write a new program? Not if you remember the #include directive. We will review that now.

File Inclusion: *#include*

When the preprocessor spots an #include directive, it looks for the following filename and includes the contents of that file within the current file. The #include directive in your source code file is replaced with the text from the included file. It's as if you sat down and typed in the entire contents of the included file at that particular location in your source file. The #include directive comes in two varieties:

```
#include <stdio.h>      ←filename in angle brackets
#include "mystuff.h"    ←filename in double quotation marks
```

On a UNIX system, the angle brackets tell the preprocessor to look for the file in one or more standard system directories. The double quotation marks tell it to first look in your current directory (or some other directory that you have specified in the filename) and then look in the standard places.

```
#include <stdio.h>        ←searches system directories
#include "hot.h"          ←searches your current working directory
#include "/usr/biff/p.h"  ←searches the /usr/biff directory
```

Depending on the implementation, the two forms may be synonymous. On DOS systems you can include a drive name as part of the pathname, and the preprocessor looks through the indicated disk drive:

```
#include "stdio.h"     ←searches the default disk drive
#include <stdio.h>     ←searches the default disk drive
#include "a:stdio.h"   ←searches disk drive A
```

Many newer microcomputer implementations, however, use conventions similar to UNIX's. You will have to consult your compiler manual.

ANSI C doesn't demand adherence to this directory model for files because not all computer systems are organized similarly. In general, the method used to name files is system dependent, but the use of the angle brackets and double quotation marks is not.

Why include files? Because they have information that the compiler needs. The stdio.h file, for example, typically includes definitions of EOF, NULL, getchar(), and putchar(). The last two are defined as macro functions.

The .h suffix conventionally is used for *header* files—files with information that are placed at the head of your program. Header files usually consist of preprocessor statements. Some, like stdio.h, come with the system, but you are free to create your own.

Including a large header file doesn't necessarily add much to the size of your program. The content of include files, for the most part, is information used by the compiler to generate the final code, not material to be added to the final code.

Header Files: An Example

Suppose that you like using Boolean values. That is, instead of having 1 be true and 0 be false, you prefer using the words TRUE and FALSE. You could create a file called, say, bool.h that contains these definitions:

```
/* bool.h file */
#define BOOLEAN int
```

```
#define TRUE 1
#define FALSE 0
```

Listing 16.4 is an example of a program using this header.

Listing 16.4 *cnt_sp.c*

```
/* cnt_sp.c -- counts whitespace characters */
#include <stdio.h>
#include "bool.h"
int main(void)
{
    int ch;
    int count = 0;
    BOOLEAN whitesp(char);

    while ((ch = getchar() ) != EOF)
         if (whitesp(ch) == TRUE)
                 count++;
    printf("There are %d whitespace characters.\n", count);
    return 0;
}
BOOLEAN whitesp(char c)
{
    if (c == ' ' || c == '\n'  || c == '\t')
         return(TRUE);
    else
         return(FALSE);
}
```

Note the following points about this program:

▶ If the two functions in this program, main() and whitesp(), were to be compiled separately, you would use the #include "bool.h" directive with each.

▶ We have not created a new type BOOLEAN, since BOOLEAN is just int. The purpose of labeling the function BOOLEAN is to remind the programmer that the function is being used for a logical (as opposed to arithmetic) calculation.

▶ Using a function for involved logical comparisons can make a program clearer. It also can save effort if the comparison is made in more than one place in a program.

▶ We could have used a macro instead of a function to define `whitesp()`, in which case we would use all uppercase for the macro name.

Uses for Header Files

A look through any of the standard header files will give you a good idea of the sort of information found in them. Typical header contents include the following:

▶ *Manifest constants.* A typical `stdio.h` file, for instance, defines `EOF`, `NULL`, and `BUFSIZE` (the size of the standard I/O buffer).

▶ *Macro functions.* For example, `getchar()` usually is defined as `getc(stdin)`, and `getc()` usually is defined as a rather complex macro. And the `ctype.h` header typically contains macro definitions for the `ctype` functions.

▶ *Function declarations.* The `string.h` header (`strings.h` on some older systems), for instance, contains function declarations for the family of string functions. Under ANSI C, the declarations are in function prototype form.

▶ *Structure template definitions.* The standard I/O functions make use of a structure containing information about a file and its associated buffer. The `stdio.h` file contains the template for this structure.

▶ *Type definitions.* You may recall that the standard I/O functions use a pointer-to-`FILE` argument. Typically, `stdio.h` uses a `#define` or a `typedef` to make `FILE` represent a pointer to a structure.

Many programmers develop their own standard header files to use with their programs. Some files might be for special purposes; others might be used with almost every program. Since included files can incorporate `#include` directives, you can create concise, well-organized header files if you like.

Consider this example:

```
/* header file mystuff.h */
#include <stdio.h>
#include "bool.h"
#include "funct.h"
#define YES 1
#define NO 0
```

First, it's a good idea to use a comment to identify the name of the header file. Second, we have included three files. Presumably the third one contains some macro functions or function prototypes that we use often. Third, we have defined YES to be 1, whereas in bool.h we defined TRUE to be 1. There is no conflict here. We can use YES and TRUE in the same program. Each will be replaced by a 1.

Also, you can use header files to declare external variables to be shared by several files. Some programmers think it's okay to do so. Others think it is poor style, since you have to check another file to see whether a variable is declared.

The #include and #define directives are the most heavily used C preprocessor features. We'll look at the other directives in less detail.

Other Directives

The #undef directive cancels an earlier #define definition. The #if, #ifdef, #ifndef, #else, #elif, and #endif directives are typically used to produce files that can be compiled in more than one way.

The *#undef* Directive

The #undef directive *undefines* a given #define. That is, suppose you have this definition:

```
#define LIMIT 400
```

Then the directive

```
#undef LIMIT
```

removes that definition. Now, if you like, you can redefine LIMIT so that it has a new value. Even if LIMIT is not defined in the first place, it still is valid to undefine it. Thus, if you want to use a particular name and you are unsure whether it has been used previously, you can undefine it to be on the safe side.

Some compilers allow you to redefine a defined name and to nest #defines and #undefs so that undefining a name causes it to revert to its original value. This is not, however, the standard practice, and it is not part of the ANSI Standard. More typically, you'll get a warning or error message if you redefine a name. So use #undef first if you wish to redefine.

Conditional Compilation

The other directives we mentioned let you set up conditional compilations. That is, they allow you to tell the compiler to accept or ignore blocks of information or code according to conditions at the time of compilation.

The *#ifdef, #else,* and *#endif* Directives

A short example will clarify what conditional compilation does. Consider the following:

```
#ifdef MAVIS
    #include "horse.h"  /* gets done if MAVIS is #defined   */
    #define  STABLES    5
#else
    #include "cow.h"    /* gets done if MAVIS isn't #defined */
    #define  STABLES   15
#endif
```

Here we've used the indentation allowed by newer implementations and by the ANSI Standard. If you have an older implementation, you may have to move all the directives, or at least the # symbols (see the next example), to flush left.

```
#ifdef MAVIS
#    include "horse.h"  /* gets done if MAVIS is #defined   */
#    define  STABLES    5
#else
#    include "cow.h"    /* gets done if MAVIS isn't #defined */
#    define  STABLES   15
#endif
```

The #ifdef directive says that if the following identifier (MAVIS) has been defined by the preprocessor, then follow all the directives and compile all the C code up to the next #else or #endif, whichever comes first. If there is an #else, then everything from the #else to the #endif is done if the identifier isn't defined.

Incidentally, an "empty" definition like

```
#define MAVIS
```

is sufficient to define MAVIS for the purposes of #ifdef.

The form #ifdef #else is much like that of the C if else. The main difference is that the preprocessor doesn't recognize the braces ({}) method of marking a block, so it uses the #else (if any) and the #endif (which must be present) to mark blocks of directives. These conditional structures can be nested. You can use these directives to mark blocks of C statements, too, as Listing 16.5 illustrates.

Listing 16.5 ifdef.c

```
/* ifdef.c -- uses conditional compilation */
#include <stdio.h>
#define JUST_CHECKING
#define LIMIT 4
int main(void)
{
    int i;
    int total = 0;

    for (i = 1; i <= LIMIT; i++)
    {
        total += 2*i*i + 1;
#ifdef JUST_CHECKING
        printf("i=%d, running total = %d\n", i, total);
#endif
    }
    printf("Grand total = %d\n", total);
    return 0;
}
```

Compiling and running the program as shown produces this output:

```
i=1, running total = 3
i=2, running total = 12
i=3, running total = 31
i=4, running total = 64
Grand total = 64
```

If you omit the JUST_CHECKING definition (or enclose it inside a C comment) and recompile the program, only the final line is displayed. You can use this approach, for instance, to help in program debugging. Define JUST_CHECKING and use a judicious selection of #ifdefs, and the compiler will include program code for printing intermediate values for debugging. Once everything is working, you can remove the definition and recompile. If, later, you find that you need the information again, you can reinsert the definition and avoid having to retype all the extra print statements. Another possibility is using #ifdef to select among alternative chunks of codes suited for different C implementations.

The *#ifndef* Directive

The #ifndef directive can be used with #else and #endif in the same way that #ifdef is. The #ifndef asks if the following identifier is *not* defined; #ifndef is the negative of #ifdef. This directive often is used to define a constant if it is not already defined:

```
#ifndef SIZE
    #define SIZE 100
#endif
```

Again, older implementations may not permit indenting the #define directive. Suppose this directive were in an include file called arrays.h. Placing the line

```
#include "arrays.h"
```

at the head of a file would result in SIZE being defined as 100. But placing

```
#define SIZE 10
#include "arrays.h"
```

at the head would set SIZE to 10. Here, SIZE is defined by the time the lines in arrays.h are processed, so the #define SIZE 100 line is skipped. You might do this, for example, to test a program using a smaller array size. Once it works to your satisfaction, you can remove the #define SIZE 10 statement and recompile. That way you never have to worry about modifying the header array itself.

The *#if* and *#elif* Directives

The #if directive is more like the regular C if. It is followed by a constant integer expression that is considered true if nonzero, and you can use C's relational and logical operators with it:

```
#if SYS == 1
#include "ibm.h"
#endif
```

The #elif (not available in some older implementations) directive allows you to extend an if-else sequence. For example, you could do this:

```
#if SYS == 1
    #include "ibmpc.h"
#elif SYS == 2
    #include "vax.h"
```

```
#elif SYS == 3
     #include "mac.h"
#else
     #include "general.h"
#endif
```

Many newer implementations offer a second way to test whether a name is defined. Instead of using

```
#ifdef VAX
```

you can use this form:

```
#if defined (VAX)
```

Here, defined is a preprocessor operator that returns 1 if its argument is #defined and 0 otherwise. The advantage of this newer form is that it can be used with #elif. Using it, we can rewrite the last example this way:

```
#if defined (IBMPC)
     #include "ibmpc.h"
#elif defined (VAX)
     #include "vax.h"
#elif defined (MAC)
     #include "mac.h"
#else
     #include "general.h"
#endif
```

If you were using these lines on, say, a VAX, you would have defined VAX somewhere earlier in the file with this line:

```
#define VAX
```

One use for these conditional compilation features is to make a program more portable. By changing a few key definitions at the beginning of a file, you can set up different values and include different files for different systems. We'll show you some examples when we discuss the library.

Enumerated Types

The *enumerated type* lets you declare symbolic names to represent integer constants. It is a common C extension that has been incorporated into the

ANSI C Standard. By using the `enum` keyword, you can create a new "type" and specify the values it may have. (Actually, `enum` is type `int`, so you really create a new name for an existing type.) The purpose of enumerated types is to enhance the readability of a program. The syntax is similar to that used for structures. For example, you can make these declarations:

```
enum spectrum {red, orange, yellow, green, blue, violet};
enum spectrum color;
```

The first declaration establishes `spectrum` as a type name, and the second declaration makes `color` a variable of that type. The identifiers within the braces enumerate the possible values that a `spectrum` variable can have. Thus, the possible values for `color` are `red`, `orange`, `yellow`, and so on. Then, you can use statements like the following:

```
color = blue;
if (color == yellow)
   ...;
for (color = red; color <= violet; color++)
   ...;
```

enum Constants

Just what are `blue` and `red`? Technically, they are type `int` constants. For instance, given the preceding enumeration declaration, you can try this:

```
printf("red = %d, orange = %d\n", red, orange);
```

Here is the output:

```
red = 0, orange = 1
```

What has happened is that `red` has become a *named constant* representing the integer 0. Similarly, the other identifiers are named constants representing the integers 1 through 5. The process is similar to using defined constants, except that these definitions are set up by the compiler rather than the preprocessor.

Default Values

By default, the constants in the enumeration list are assigned the integer values 0, 1, 2, etc. Thus, the declaration

```
enum kids {nippy, slats, skippy, nina, liz};
```

results in nina having the value 3.

Assigned Values

You can choose the integer values that you want the constants to have. Just include the desired values in the declaration:

```
enum levels {low = 100, medium = 500, high = 2000};
```

If you assign a value to one constant but not to the following constants, the following constants will be numbered sequentially. For example, suppose you have this declaration:

```
enum feline {cat, lynx = 10, puma, tiger};
```

Then cat is 0, by default, and lynx, puma, and tiger are 10, 11, and 12, respectively.

Usage

Recall that the purpose of enumerated types is to enhance the readability of a program. If you are dealing with colors, using red and blue is much more obvious than using 0 and 1. Note that the enumerated types are for internal use. If you want to enter a value of orange for color, you have to enter a 1, not the word orange. Or you can read in the string "orange" and have the program convert it to the value orange.

The ANSI C Standard provides that enumerated variables be considered type int variables, so compliance with the Standard implies that enum variables can be used in expressions in the same manner as int variables.

Listing 16.6 shows a short example using enum. The example relies on the default value-assignment scheme. This gives red the value 0, which makes it the index for the pointer to the string "red".

Listing 16.6 *enum.c*

```
/* enum.c -- uses enumerated values */
#include <stdio.h>
#include "bool.h"
enum spectrum {red, orange, yellow, green, blue, violet};
```

```
char *colors[] = {"red", "orange", "yellow", "green",
                  "blue", "violet"};
#define LEN 30
int main(void)
{
    char choice[LEN];
    enum spectrum color;
    BOOLEAN done = FALSE;

    puts("Enter a color:");
    gets(choice);
    for (color = red; color <= violet; color++)
    {
        if (strcmp(choice, colors[color]) == 0)
        {
            done = TRUE;
            break;
        }
    }
    if (done == TRUE)
        printf("%s is in my color list.\n", choice);
    else
        printf("I don't know about the color %s.\n", choice);
    return 0;
}
```

This example uses the bool.h header file presented earlier in this chapter.

The C Library

Originally, there was no official C library. Later, a defacto standard emerged based on the UNIX implementation of C. The ANSI C committee, in turn, developed an official standard library, largely based on the defacto standard. Recognizing the expanded C universe, the committee then sought to redefine the library so that it could be implemented on a wide variety of systems.

We've already discussed some I/O functions and string functions from the library. In this chapter we'll browse through several more. First, however, let's talk about how to use a library.

Gaining Access to the C Library

How you gain access to a C library depends on your implementation. Thus, you need to see how our more general statements apply to your system. First, there are often several different places to find library functions. For example, `getchar()` is usually defined as a macro in the file `stdio.h`, while `strlen()` is usually kept in a library file. Second, different systems have different ways to reach these functions. Here are three possibilities.

Automatic Access

On many systems, you just compile the program and the more common library functions are made available automatically.

But keep in mind that you should declare the function type for functions you use. Usually you can do this by including the appropriate header file. User manuals describing library functions will tell you which files to include. On some older systems, however, you may have to enter the function declarations yourself. Again, the user manual will indicate the function type.

In the past, header filenames have not been consistent among different implementations. The ANSI C Standard groups the library functions into families, with each family having a specific header file for its function prototypes.

File Inclusion

If a function is defined as a macro, then you can `#include` the file containing its definition. Often, similar macros will be collected in an appropriately named header file. For example, many systems have a `ctype.h` file containing several macros that determine the nature of a character: uppercase, digit, etc.

Library Inclusion

At some stage in compiling or linking a program, you may have to specify a library option. Even a system that automatically checks its standard library may have other libraries of functions less frequently used. These libraries will have to be requested explicitly by using a compile-time option. Note that this process is distinct from including a header file. A header file provides a function declaration or prototype. The library option tells the system where to find the function code. Clearly, we can't go through all the specifics for all systems, but these discussions should alert you to what you should look for.

Using the Library Descriptions

We haven't the space to discuss the complete library, but we will look at some representative examples. First, though, let's take a look at documentation.

You can find function documentation in a number of places. Your system may have an on-line manual, and integrated environments often have on-line help. C implementors supply printed user's guides describing library functions. Several publishers have issued reference manuals for C library functions. Some are generic in nature; some targeted towards specific implementations.

The key skill you need in reading the documentation is that of interpreting function headings. The idiom has changed with time. Here, for instance, is how `fread()` is listed in older UNIX documentation:

```
#include <stdio.h>

fread(ptr, sizeof(*ptr), nitems, stream)
FILE *stream;
```

First, the proper `include` file is given. No type is given for `fread()`, `ptr`, `sizeof(*ptr)`, or `nitems`. By default, then, these are taken to be type `int`, but the context makes it clear that `ptr` is a pointer. (In C's early days, pointers were handled as integers.) The `stream` argument is declared as a pointer to `FILE`. The declaration makes it look as if you are supposed to use the `sizeof` operator as the second argument. Actually, it's saying that the value of this argument should be the size of the object pointed to by `ptr`. Often, you would use `sizeof` as illustrated, but any type `int` value satisfies the syntax.

Later, the form changed to this:

```
#include <stdio.h>

int fread(ptr, size, nitems, stream;)
char *ptr;
int size, nitems;
FILE *stream;
```

Now all types are given explicitly, and `ptr` is treated as a pointer to `char`.
The ANSI C Standard provides the following description:

```
#include <stdio.h>
size_t fread(void *ptr, size_t size, size_t nmemb, FILE *stream);
```

First, it uses the new prototype format. Second, it changes some types. The `size_t` type is defined to be the unsigned integral type that the sizeof operator returns. Usually this is either unsigned int or unsigned long. The stddef.h file contains a typedef or a #define for size_t, as do several other files, including stdio.h. Many functions, including fread(), often incorporate the sizeof operator as part of an actual argument. The size_t type makes that formal argument match this common usage.

Also, ANSI C uses pointer-to-void as a kind of generic pointer for situations in which pointers to different types may be used. For instance, the actual first argument to fread() may be a pointer to an array of double or to a structure of some sort. If the actual argument is, say, a pointer-to-array-of-20-double and the formal argument is pointer-to-void, the compiler will make the appropriate type version without complaining about type clashes.

Now let's turn to some specific functions.

The Math Library

The math library contains many useful mathematical functions. The math.h header file provides the function declarations or prototypes for these functions.

We'll use the math library to solve a common problem: converting from *x-y* coordinates to magnitudes and angles. For example, suppose that you draw, on a gridwork, a line that transverses 4 units horizontally (the *x* value), and 3 units vertically (the *y* value). What is the length (magnitude) of the line and what is its direction? Trigonometry tells us the following:

$$\text{magnitude} = \text{square root } (x^2 + y^2)$$

and

$$\text{angle} = \text{arctangent } (y/x)$$

The math library provides a square root function and a couple of arctangent functions, so we can express this solution in a C program. The square root function is called sqrt(). This function takes a double argument and returns the argument's square root, also as a type double value.

The atan() function takes a double argument—the tangent—and returns the angle having that value as its tangent. Unfortunately, the atan() function is confused by, say, a line with *x* and *y* values of -5 and -5. Since $(-5)/(-5)$ is 1, atan() would report 45°, the same as it does for a line with *x* and *y* of 5 and 5. In other words, atan() doesn't distinguish between a line of a given angle and one 180° in the opposite direction. (Actually, atan() reports in radians, not degrees; we'll discuss that conversion soon.)

Fortunately, the C library also provides the atan2() function. It takes two arguments: the *x* value and the *y* value. That way, it can examine the signs of *x* and *y* and figure out the correct angle. Like `atan()`, `atan2()` returns the angle in radians. To convert to degrees, multiply the resulting angle by 180 and divide by pi. Listing 16.7 illustrates these steps. It also gives you a chance to use structures and the `typedef` facility.

Listing 16.7 *convert.c*

```
/* convert.c -- converts rectangular coordinates to polar */
#include <stdio.h>
#include <math.h>
#define RAD_TO_DEG (180/3.141592654)
typedef struct polar_v {
    double magnitude;
    double angle;
} POLAR_V;
typedef struct rect_v {
    double x;
    double y;
} RECT_V;
POLAR_V rect_to_polar(RECT_V);
int main(void)
{
    RECT_V input;
    POLAR_V result;

    puts("Enter x,y coordinates; enter q to quit:");
    while (scanf("%lf %lf", &input.x, &input.y) == 2)
    {
        result = rect_to_polar(input);
        printf("magnitude = %0.2f, angle = %0.2f\n",
                result.magnitude, result.angle);
    }
    return 0;
}
POLAR_V rect_to_polar(RECT_V rv)
{
    POLAR_V pv;

    pv.magnitude = sqrt(rv.x * rv.x + rv.y * rv.y);
    if (pv.magnitude == 0)
```

(continued)

Listing 16.7 *(continued)*

```
        pv.angle = 0.0;
    else
        pv.angle = RAD_TO_DEG * atan2(rv.y, rv.x);
    return pv;
}
```

Here's a sample run:

```
Enter x,y coordinates; enter q to quit:
10 10
magnitude = 14.14, angle = 45.00
-12 -5
magnitude = 13.00, angle = -157.38
q
```

If, when you compile, you get a message like this:

```
Undefined:
    _sqrt
```

or this:

```
    'sqrt': unresolved external
```

or something similar, then your compiler-linker is not finding the math library. UNIX systems require that you instruct the linker to search the math library by using the -lm flag:

```
    cc spring.c -lm
```

The General Utilities Library

The general utilities library contains a grab bag of functions, including a random number generator, searching and sorting functions, conversion functions, and memory management functions. Under ANSI C, prototypes for these functions exist in the stdlib.h header file.

The *exit( )* and *atexit( )* Functions

We've already used exit() in several examples, but the ANSI Standard has added a couple of nice features that we haven't used yet. The most important addition is that you can specify particular functions to be called when a program exits. The atexit() function provides this feature by *registering* the functions to be called on exit. Listing 16.8 shows how this works. It also uses the C preprocessor to make the code a bit more portable between ANSI and non-ANSI implementations.

Listing 16.8 *byebye.c*

```
/* byebye.c -- atexit() example */
#include <stdio.h>
#define ANSI            /* omit for non-ANSI implementations    */

#if defined (ANSI)    /* or use __STDC__ (see text)              */
#include <stdlib.h>
#define ATEXIT(X) atexit(X)
#define VOID void
#else
void exit();
void sign_off();
#define ATEXIT(X)
#define VOID int
#endif

#ifndef EXIT_SUCCESS
#define EXIT_SUCCESS 0
#endif

#ifndef EXIT_FAILURE
#define EXIT_FAILURE 1
#endif

void sign_off(VOID);
int main(void)
{
    int n;
```

(continued)

```
Listing 16.8   (continued)

    ATEXIT(sign_off);
    puts("Enter an integer:");
    if (scanf("%d",&n) != 1)
    {
        puts("That's no integer!");
        exit(EXIT_FAILURE);
    }
    printf("%d is %s.\n", n,  (n % 2 == 0)? "even" : "odd");
    exit(EXIT_SUCCESS);
    return 0;
}
void sign_off(VOID)
{
    puts("Thus terminates another magnificent program from");
    puts("SeeSaw Software!");
}
```

Here's a sample run:

```
Enter an integer:
212
212 is even.
Thus terminates another magnificent program from
SeeSaw Software!
```

Let's look at three main areas: the use of `atexit()`, the `exit()` arguments, and the ANSI, pre-ANSI adjustment.

Using *atexit( )*

Here's a function that uses function pointers! To use the `atexit()` function, simply pass it the address of the function that you want called on exit. Since the name of a function acts as an address when used as a function argument, you use `sign_off` as the argument. Then `atexit()` registers that function in a list of functions to be executed when `exit()` is called. ANSI guarantees that you can place at least 32 functions on the list. Each function is added with a separate call to `atexit()`. When the `exit()` function is finally called, it executes these functions, with the last function added being executed first.

The functions registered by `atexit()` should, like `sign_off()`, be type `void` functions taking no arguments. Typically, they would perform housekeeping tasks such as updating a program-monitoring file or resetting environmental variables.

Using *exit( )*

After `exit()` executes the functions specified by `atexit()`, it does some tidying of its own. It flushes all output streams, closes all open streams, and closes temporary files created by calls to the standard I/O function `tmpfile()`. Then `exit()` returns control to the host environment and, if possible, reports a termination status to the environment. Traditionally, UNIX programs have used 0 to indicate successful termination and non-zero to report failure. ANSI C uses the macros `EXIT_SUCCESS` and `EXIT_FAILURE` for that purpose. Thus, it may be possible to define them meaningfully on systems for which 0 and 1 make no sense as termination report values. Under ANSI C, using the `exit()` function in a nonrecursive `main()` function is equivalent to using the keyword `return`. However, `exit()` also terminates programs when used in functions other than `main()`.

ANSI Differences

The `exit()` function has a prototype in the `stdlib.h` file, but older implementations don't have that file. Therefore, if `ANSI` is not defined, Listing 16.8 provides an old-fashioned function declaration for `exit()`. If `ANSI` is defined, then the program uses the prototypes in `stdlib.h`. Also, pre-ANSI implementations don't recognize `void` as an indication of no arguments. Therefore, we define `VOID` as `void` for the ANSI case and as `int` for the non-ANSI case. Similarly, we define `ATEXIT(x)` to be `atexit(x)` for the ANSI case and a blank for the non-ANSI case. We use the `#if defined()` `#else` directive to set up these cases.

Also, to give an example of `#ifndef`, we set up definitions for the exit value macros to be used if they hadn't been defined.

The listing shows `ANSI` being defined, so that version can be used in an ANSI implementation. Remove the definition, and you can compile the program on an older implementation. (However, because `atexit()` isn't supported in that case, the `sign_off()` function isn't called.)

Another possibility is to test whether `__STDC__` is defined. The ANSI C Standard stipulates that implementations conforming to the Standard predefine the name `__STDC__`. Thus, you can use the test

```
#if defined (__STDC__)
```

without having to define that name yourself. Our method, on the other hand, also works with compilers that are not strictly conforming but that support the features used in the program.

Memory Allocation: *malloc( )*

All programs have to set aside enough memory to store the data they use. Some of this memory allocation is done automatically. For example, you can declare

```
char place[] = "Pork Liver Creek";
```

and enough memory to store that string is set aside.

Or you can be more explicit and ask for a certain amount of memory:

```
int plates[100];
```

This declaration sets aside 100 memory locations, each fit to store an `int` value.

C goes beyond this. It lets you allot more memory as a program runs. The main tool is the `malloc()` function. This function takes one argument: the number of bytes of memory desired. Then `malloc()` finds a suitable block of free memory and returns the address of the first byte of that block. Since `char` represents a byte, `malloc()` traditionally has been defined as type pointer-to-`char`. The ANSI C Standard, however, uses a new type: pointer-to-`void`. This type is intended to be a "generic pointer." The `malloc()` function can be used to return pointers to arrays, structures, etc., so normally the return value is type-cast to the proper value. Under ANSI C you still should type-cast for clarity, but assigning a pointer-to-`void` value to a pointer of another type is not considered a type clash. If `malloc()` fails to find the required space, it returns a `NULL` pointer.

Listing 16.9 presents an unsophisticated program showing you how to use `malloc()`. It creates an array of 100 pointers, and then it reads strings. The `malloc()` function is used to set aside storage for each string, and the addresses of the strings are stored in the array. Here is the program:

Listing 16.9 *memsym.c*

```
/* memsym.c — memorize symphony orchestras */
#include <stdio.h>

#ifndef EXIT_SUCCESS
#define EXIT_SUCCESS 0
#endif

#ifndef EXIT_FAILURE
```

```
#define EXIT_FAILURE 1
#endif


#define ANSI
#ifdef ANSI
#include <stdlib.h>    /* ANSI C header for malloc()   */
#else
char *malloc();        /* pre-ANSI declaration         */
#endif
#define LINE 81        /* maximum line length for input */
#define MAX  100       /* maximum number of symphonies  */
int main(void)
{
    char temp[LINE];   /* temporary input storage      */
    char *ps[MAX];     /* array of ptrs to strings     */
    int index = 0;     /* number of input lines        */
    int count;         /* for loop counter             */


    puts("Name some symphony orchestras.");
    puts("Type them one at a time; press [enter] at the start");
    puts("of a line to end your list. Okay, I'm ready.");
    while (index < MAX && fgets(temp, LINE, stdin) != NULL
            && temp[0] != '\n')
    {
        ps[index] = (char *)malloc(strlen(temp) + 1);
        if (ps[index] == NULL)
        {
            fputs("Memory allocation error!", stderr);
            exit(EXIT_FAILURE);
        }
        strcpy (ps[index], temp);
        if (++index < MAX)
            printf("That's %d. Continue if you like.\n",
                    index);
    }
    puts("Okay, here is what I've got.");
    for (count = 0; count < index; count++)
        fputs(ps[count], stdout);
    exit(EXIT_SUCCESS);
    return 0;
}
```

Here is a sample run so that you can see the output:

```
Name some symphony orchestras.
Type them one at a time; press [enter] at the start
of a line to end your list. Okay, I'm ready.
San Francisco Symphony
That's 1. Continue, if you like.
Chicago Symphony
That's 2. Continue, if you like.
Berlin Philharmonic
That's 3. Continue, if you like.
The Concertgebouw
That's 4. Continue, if you like.
London Symphony
That's 5. Continue, if you like.
Vienna Philharmonic
That's 6. Continue, if you like.
Pittsburgh Symphony
That's 7. Continue, if you like.
[enter]
Okay, here's what I got:
San Francisco Symphony
Chicago Symphony
Berlin Philharmonic
The Concertgebouw
London Symphony
Vienna Philharmonic
Pittsburgh Symphony
```

Let's look at the code. The input is controlled by these lines:

```
while (index < MAX && fgets(temp,LINE,stdin) != NULL
        && temp[0] != '\n')
```

First, the program checks to see if any more string pointers are left by comparing `index` to `MAX`. Next, it attempts to read the input into a temporary storage area. If the end-of-file (indicated by a return value of `NULL`) is reached, the loop quits. Finally, the program checks to see if the first character in `temp` is the newline character. This will occur if the user presses the Enter key with no other input. The program responds by quitting the loop.

Next, the following line allocates enough space to hold the string currently stored in `temp`:

```
ps[index] = (char *) malloc(strlen(temp) + 1);
```

The `strlen()` function gives the length of the input string, which most likely is significantly less than the length of the `temp` array. The program adds 1 for the null character and stores the beginning address of the still-empty storage block to `ps[index]`. The `malloc()` function finds a chunk of memory large enough to hold the string (including the null character) and returns a pointer to its beginning. We then type-cast the pointer to agree with the left-hand side. (In pre-ANSI C, `malloc()` already returns pointer-to-`char`, but in ANSI C it returns pointer-to-`void`.)

It's possible that `malloc()` can fail to procure the desired amount of memory. In that case, the function returns the NULL pointer, and our program terminates:

```
if (ps[index] == NULL)
{
    fputs("Memory allocation error!", stderr);
    exit(EXIT_FAILURE);
}
```

The next program line copies the contents of `temp` into the allocated storage, freeing `temp` to be reused for the next input string:

```
strcpy (ps[index], temp);
```

What have we gained with this approach? Well, suppose we had not used `malloc()`. Instead of declaring an array of 100 pointers-to-`char`, we could have declared an array of 100 character arrays, with each character array capable of holding 81 characters. That means we would have allocated 8100 bytes of memory, much of which never would be used, since most of the strings will be smaller than the maximum size and since most likely we won't enter the full 100 symphonies. With the `malloc()` approach, we use only the amount of memory actually needed. We pay for this efficiency with the overhead to hold `ps[]` and `temp[]`, a total of 281 bytes, but that is more than made up when we have a large number of input values.

So that is how `malloc()` is used. But suppose you want `int` memory, not `char`. You still can use `malloc()`. Here is the procedure:

```
int *newmem;

newmem = (int *)malloc(100);   /* use cast operator */
```

Again, 100 bytes are set aside. The cast operator converts the returned value from a `char` pointer to an `int` pointer. If, as on our system, `int` takes 2 bytes of memory, then this means that `newmem + 1` will increment the pointer by 2 bytes, just right to move it to the next integer. It also means that the 100 bytes can be used to store 50 integers.

Another option for memory allotment is to use `calloc()`. A typical use would look like this:

```
long *newmem;

newmem = (long *)calloc(100, sizeof (long));
```

Like `malloc()`, `calloc()` returns a pointer-to-char in its pre-ANSI version and a pointer-to-void under ANSI. You must use the cast operator if you want to store a different type. This new function takes two arguments, both of which should be unsigned integers (type `size_t` under ANSI). The first argument is the number of memory cells desired. The second argument is the size of each cell in bytes. In our case, `long` uses 4 bytes, so this instruction would set up one hundred 4-byte units, using 400 bytes in all for storage.

By using `sizeof (long)` instead of 4, we made this coding more portable. It will work on those rare systems where `long` is some size other than 4.

The `calloc()` function throws in one more feature: it sets all the bits in the block to zero. (Note, however, that on some hardware systems, a floating-point value of 0 is not represented by all bits set to 0.)

The `free()` function complements `malloc()` and `calloc()`. It takes as an argument the address of a block of memory previously allocated by `malloc()` or `calloc()`. It then returns the block of memory to the "free memory pool" so that it can be used by future calls to `malloc()` and `calloc()`.

Your own C library probably offers several other memory-management functions, some portable, some not. You may wish to take a moment to look them over.

Improving the Example

We mentioned earlier that the example in Listing 16.8 was unsophisticated. That is because it still uses an array to store the pointers. Thus, the maximum capacity of the program is limited by the array size. A less limiting approach is to use `malloc()` to allocate space for the pointers as well as for the strings. To keep track of the pointers, you can define a structure that holds two pointers. Then, each structure would hold a pointer to a string and a pointer to the next structure, which holds a pointer to the next string and a pointer to the next structure, and so on. Such systems of structures are called *linked lists* (see Figure 16.3).

Other Directions

In this book we've covered the essential features of C, but we've only touched on the library. The ANSI C library contains scores of useful functions. Most implementations additionally offer extensive libraries of func-

Figure 16.3 *Linked structures*

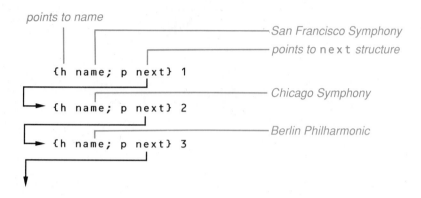

tions specific to particular systems. Microsoft C and Turbo C, for instance, offer functions to facilitate hardware control, keyboard input, and the generation of graphics for IBM PCs and clones. Take the time to explore what your system has to offer. If it doesn't have what you want, write your own functions. That's part of C. If you think you can do a better job on, say, an input function, do it! And as you refine and polish your programming technique, you will go from C to shining C.

Once you are comfortable with C, you may wish to investigate C++ or Objective C. These *object-oriented* languages have their roots in C. C already has data objects ranging in complexity from a simple char variable to large and intricate structures. C++ and Objective C carry the idea of the object even further. With object-oriented programming (OOP), for instance, the properties of an object include not only what kinds of information it can hold but also what kinds of operations can be performed on it. And objects can inherit properties from other objects. OOP carries modularization to a higher level of abstraction than C does, and it facilitates the writing of large programs.

Chapter Summary

The C preprocessor and the C library are two important adjuncts to the C language. The *C preprocessor*, following preprocessor directives, adjusts your source code before it is compiled. The *C library* provides many functions designed to help with tasks such as input, output, file handling, memory management, sorting and searching, mathematical calculations, and string processing, to name a few.

Review Questions

1. Here are groups of one or more macros followed by a source code line that uses them. What code results in each case? Is it valid code?

   a. ```
   #define FPM 5280   /* feet per mile */
   dist = FPM * miles;
   ```

   b. ```
   #define FEET 4
   #define POD FEET + FEET
   plort = FEET * POD;
   ```

   c. ```
   #define SIX = 6;
   nex = SIX;
   ```

   d. ```
   #define NEW(X) X + 5
   y = NEW(y);
   berg = NEW(berg) * lob;
   est = NEW(berg) / NEW(y);
   nilp = lob * NEW(-berg);
   ```

2. Define a macro function that returns the minimum of two values.

3. Define a macro function that prints the representations and the values of two integer expressions. For example, it might print

   ```
   3+4 is 7 and 4*12 is 48
   ```

   if its arguments are 3+4 and 4*12.

4. Define a macro that prints the name, value, and address of an `int` variable in the following format:

   ```
   name: fop;  value: 23;  address: 4016
   ```

5. a. How would you create an enumerated type `days` that makes the abbreviations `sun`, `mon`, `tue`, `wed`, `thu`, `fri`, and `sat` stand for the integers 0–6?

   b. How would you create a variable `visit` of that type?

6. How could you allot space to hold an array of structures?

Programming Exercises

1. Start developing a header file of preprocessor definitions that you wish to use.

2. The harmonic mean of two numbers is obtained by taking the

inverses of the two numbers, averaging them, and taking the inverse of the result. Use a #define directive to define a macro "function" that performs this operation.

3. Polar coordinates describe a vector in terms of magnitude and the counterclockwise angle from the *x*-axis to the vector. Rectangular coordinates describe the same vector in terms of *x* and *y* components. See Figure 16.4. Write a program that reads the magnitude and angle (in degrees) of a vector and then displays the *x* and *y* components. The relevant equations are these:

$$x = \text{r} \cos A \qquad y = \text{r} \sin A$$

To do the conversion, use a function that takes a structure containing the polar coordinates and returns a structure containing the rectangular coordinates. (Or use pointers to such structures, if you prefer.)

Figure 16.4 *Rectangular and polar coordinates*

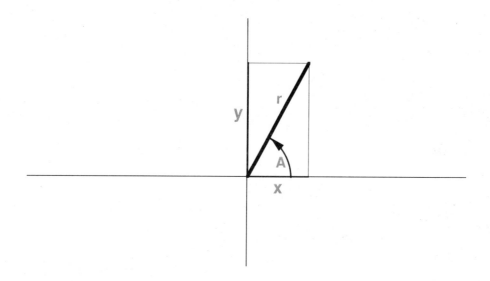

4. Modify the program in Listing 16.9 so that it saves the symphony names in a file. If the file already exists when the program is run, have it first load the contents into memory and then display them. Use a fixed size record for storing each string, and use fread() and fwrite().

5. This exercise is the same as Exercise 4 except that you should use variable-sized records to store the strings. Each string should be preceded in storage by a byte holding the length of the string. On

input, the program will first read the number byte and then use that information to determine the number of bytes to read for the string.

6. The ANSI library features a `clock()` function with this description:

```
#include <time.h>
clock_t clock (void);
```

Here `clock_t` is a type defined in `time.h`. The function returns the processor time, which is given in some implementation-dependent units. (If the processor time is unavailable or cannot be represented, the function returns a value of −1.) However, `CLK_TCK`, also defined in `time.h`, is the number of processor time units per second. Thus, dividing the difference between two return values of `clock()` by `time.h` provides the number of seconds elapsed between the two calls. Type-casting the values to `double` before division lets you obtain fractions of a second. Write a function that takes a `double` argument representing a desired time delay and then runs a loop until that amount of time has passed.

Appendixes

A

Additional Reading

If you wish to learn more about C and programming, you will find the following references useful.

The C Language

BYTE, 8, no. 8 (August 1983).
This issue of *BYTE* magazine is devoted to C. It includes articles discussing the history, philosophy, and uses of C. Also included is an extensive bibliography of books and articles on C. Each bibliographic entry has a short summary of the book or article.

Feuer, Alan R. *The C Puzzle Book*. Englewood Cliffs, NJ: Prentice-Hall, 1982.
This book contains a large number of programs whose output you are supposed to predict. Predicting the output gives you a good opportunity to test and expand your understanding of C. The book includes answers and explanations.

Kernighan, Brian W., and Dennis M. Ritchie. *The C Programming Language*. Englewood Cliffs, NJ: Prentice-Hall, 1978.
This is the first book on C. (Note that the creator of C, Dennis Ritchie, is one of the authors.) It constitutes the definition of "K&R" C, the unofficial standard for many years. The book includes many interesting

examples. It does, however, assume that the reader is familiar with systems programming.

————. *The C Programming Language*. **2d ed. Englewood Cliffs, NJ: Prentice-Hall, 1988.**
This edition incorporates ANSI changes based on the ANSI draft that was standard at the time the book was written.

Koenig, Andrew. *C Traps and Pitfalls*. **Reading, MA: Addison-Wesley, 1988.**
The title says it all.

Ritchie, Dennis M., S.C. Johnson, M.E. Lesk, and Brian W. Kernighan. "The C Programming Language." *The Bell System Technical Journal* **57, no. 6 (July/August 1978).**
This article discusses the history of C and provides an overview of its design features.

Stroustrup, Bjarne. *The C++ Programming Language*. **Reading, MA: Addison-Wesley, 1986.**
This book, by the creator of C+, presents the C++ language and includes the Reference Manual for C++.

Programming

Kernighan, Brian W., and P.J. Plauger. *The Elements of Programming Style*. **2d ed. New York: McGraw-Hill, 1978.**
This slim classic draws on examples from other texts to illustrate the dos and don'ts of clear, effective programming.

————. *Software Tools*. **Reading, MA: Addison-Wesley, 1976.**
This book develops several useful programs and systems of programs, while emphasizing good program design. It comes in both RATFOR (rationalized FORTRAN) and Pascal versions. Since RATFOR represents an attempt to make FORTRAN work like C, the first version is the choice of C users.

Reference

Barkakati, Naba. *The Waite Group's Essential Guide to ANSI C*. **Indianapolis, IN: Howard W. Sams, 1989.**
This is a compact summary of the C language and its standard li-

brary. Also available are *The Waite Group's Essential Guide to Turbo C* and *The Waite Group's Essential Guide to Microsoft C*; these volumes additionally describe the Turbo C and Microsoft C additions to the standard library.

Harbison and Steele. *C: A Reference Manual.* **Englewood Cliffs, NJ: Prentice-Hall, 1987.**

This large reference manual presents the rules of the C language and describes most of the standard library functions. It points out differences between K&R C and ANSI C and provides many examples.

B

C Operators

C is rich in operators. Table B.1 lists the C operators in order of decreasing precedence and indicates how they associate. All operators are binary (two operands) unless otherwise indicated. Note that some binary and unary operators, such as * (multiplication) and * (indirection), share the same symbol but have different precedence. Following the table are summaries of each operator.

Table B.1 *The C Operators*

Operators (from high to low precedence)	Associativity
( ) [ ] . ->	L-R
- + ~ ! * & ++ -- sizeof (*type*) (all unary)	R-L
* / %	L-R
+ -	L-R
<< >>	L-R
< > <= >=	L-R
== !=	L-R
&	L-R
^	L-R
|	L-R
&&	L-R

(continued)

Table B.1 (continued)

Operators (from high to low precedence)	Associativity
||	L-R
? : (trinary operator)	L-R
= *= /= %= += -= <<= >>= &= |= ^=	R-L
, (comma operator)	L-R

Arithmetic Operators

+   Adds the value at its right to the value at its left.

-     Subtracts the value at its right from the value at its left.

-     As a unary operator, changes the sign of the value at its right.

*   Multiplies the value at its right by the value at its left.

/   Divides the value at its left by the value at its right. Answer is truncated if both operands are integers.

%   Yields the remainder when the value at its left is divided by the value to its right (integers only).

++   Adds 1 to the value of the variable to its *right* (prefix mode) or adds 1 to the value of the variable to its *left* (postfix mode).

--   Like ++, but subtracts 1.

Relational Operators

Each operator compares the value at its left to the value at its right.

<   Less than

<=   Less than or equal to

==   Equal to

>=   Greater than or equal to

>   Greater than

!=   Unequal to

Relational Expressions

A simple relational expression consists of a relational operator with an operand on each side. If the relation is true, the relational expression has the value 1. If the relation is false, the relational expression has the value 0.

5 > 2	is true and has the value 1.
(2 + a) == a	is false and has the value 0.

Assignment Operators

=   Assigns the value at its right to the lvalue on its left.

Each of the following assignment operators updates the lvalue at its left by the value at its right, using the indicated operation. We use R-H for right-hand, and L-H for left-hand.

+=	Adds the R-H quantity to the L-H variable.
-=	Subtracts the R-H quantity from the L-H variable.
*=	Multiplies the L-H variable by the R-H quantity.
/=	Divides the L-H variable by the R-H quantity.
%=	Gives the remainder from dividing the L-H quantity by the R-H quantity.
&=	Assigns L-H & R-H to the L-H quantity.
|=	Assigns L-H | R-H to the L-H quantity.
^=	Assigns L-H ^ R-H to the L-H quantity.
>>=	Assigns L-H >> R-H to the L-H quantity.
<<=	Assigns L-H << R-H to the L-H quantity.

Example

rabbits *= 1.6;   is the same as   rabbits = rabbits * 1.6;

Logical Operators

Logical operators normally take relational expressions as operands. The ! operator takes one operand. The rest take two: one to the left, one to the right.

&&   AND

|| OR

!   NOT

Logical Expressions

`expression1 && expression2`	is true if and only if both expressions are true.
`expression1 || expression2`	is true if either one or both expressions are true.
`!expression`	is true if the expression is false, and vice versa.

Order of Evaluation for Logical Expressions

Logical expressions are evaluated from left to right. Evaluation stops as soon as something is discovered that renders the expression false.

Examples

`6 > 2 && 3 == 3`	is true.
`! ( 6 > 2 && 3 ==3 )`	is false.
`x != 0 && 20/x < 5`	the second expression is evaluated only if x is nonzero.

The Conditional Operator

`? :`   Takes three operands, each of which is an expression. They are arranged this way: *expression1* ? *expression2* : *expression3*. The value of the whole expression equals the value of *expression2* if *expression1* is true, and equals the value of *expression3* otherwise.

Examples

`( 5 > 3 ) ? 1 : 2`	has the value 1.
`( 3 > 5 ) ? 1 : 2`	has the value 2.
`( a > b ) ? a : b`	has the value of the larger of a or b.

Pointer-Related Operators

    &   Address Operator. When followed by a variable name, & gives the address of that variable.

    *   Indirection or Dereferencing Operator. When followed by a pointer, * gives the value stored at the pointed-to address.

Examples

    `&nurse`   is the address of the variable `nurse`.

```
nurse = 22;
ptr = &nurse; /* pointer to nurse */
val = *ptr;
```

The net effect is to assign the value 22 to `val`.

Sign Operators

    -   Minus sign. Reverses the sign of the operand.

    +   Plus sign. Leaves the sign unchanged.

Structure and Union Operators

The Membership Operator

Used with a structure or union name to specify a member of that structure or union. If `name` is the name of a structure and `member` is a member specified by the structure template, then `name.member` identifies that member of the structure. The type of `name.member` is the type specified for `member`. The membership operator can also be used in the same fashion with unions.

Example

```
struct {
        int code;
```

```
            float cost;
     } item;

     item.code = 1265;
```

This statement assigns a value to the `code` member of the structure `item`.

The Indirect Membership Operator

->   Used with a pointer to a structure or union to identify a member of that structure or union. Suppose that `ptrstr` is a pointer to a structure and that `member` is a member specified by the structure template. Then `ptrstr->member` identifies that member of the pointed-to structure. The indirect membership operator can be used in the same fashion with unions.

Example

```
struct {
        int code;
        float cost;
} item, *ptrst;
ptrst = &item;
ptrst->code = 3451;
```

This program fragment assigns a value to the `code` member of `item`. The following three expressions are equivalent:

```
ptrst->code   item.code   (*ptrst).code
```

Bitwise Operators

All of the following bitwise operators except ~ are binary operators.

~   Unary operator. Produces a value with each bit of the operand inverted.

&   AND. Produces a value in which each bit is set to 1 only if both corresponding bits in the two operands are 1.

| OR. Produces a value in which each bit is set to 1 if either, or both, corresponding bits of the two operands are 1.

^   EXCLUSIVE OR. Produces a value in which each bit is set to 1 only if one or the other (but not both) of the corresponding bits of the two operands is 1.

<<   Left-shift. Produces a value obtained by shifting the bits of the left-hand operand to the left by the number of places given by the right-hand operand. Vacated slots are filled with zeros.

>>   Right-shift. Produces a value obtained by shifting the bits of the left-hand operand to the right by the number of places given by the right-hand operand. For unsigned integers, the vacated slots are filled with zeros. The behavior for signed values is implementation dependent.

Examples

Suppose you have the following:

```
int x = 2;
int y = 3;
```

Then x & y has the value 2, since only bit 1 is ON for both x and y. Also, y<<x has the value 12 because that is the value obtained when the bit pattern for 3 is shifted two bits to the left.

Miscellaneous Operators

sizeof   Yields the size, in bytes, of the operand to its right. The operand can be a type-specifier in parentheses, as in sizeof (float), or it can be the name of a particular variable or array, etc., as in sizeof foo.

(type)   Cast operator. Converts the following value to the type specified by the enclosed keyword(s). For example, (float) 9 converts the integer 9 to the floating-point number 9.0.

Comma operator. Links two expressions into one and guarantees that the left-most expression is evaluated first. The value of the whole expression is the value of the right-hand expression. This operator is typically used to include more information in a for loop control expression.

Example

```
for (step = 2, fargo = 0; fargo < 1000; step *= 2)
        fargo += step;
```

C

Basic Types and Storage Classes

Summary: The Basic Data Types

Keywords

The basic data types are set up using the following eight keywords: `int`, `long`, `short`, `unsigned`, `char`, `float`, `double`, and `signed` (ANSI C).

Signed Integers

Signed integers can have positive or negative values.

`int`	The basic integer type for a given system.
`long` or `long int`	Can hold an integer at least as large as the largest `int` and possibly larger.
`short` or `short int`	The largest `short` integer is no larger than the largest `int` and may be smaller. Typically, `long` will be bigger than `short`, and `int` will be the same as one of the two. For example, Turbo C and Microsoft C for the PC provide 16-bit `short` and `int` and 32-bit `long`. It all depends on the system.

Unsigned Integers

Unsigned integers have zero or positive values only, which extends the range of the largest possible positive number. Use the keyword `unsigned` before the desired type: `unsigned int`, `unsigned long`, `unsigned short`. A lone `unsigned` is the same as `unsigned int`.

Characters

Characters are typographic symbols such as `A`, `&`, and `+`. Typically, just 1 byte of memory is used.

`char`   The keyword for this type.

Some implementations use a signed `char`, while others use an unsigned `char`. ANSI C allows you to use the keywords `signed` and `unsigned` to specify which form you want.

Floating Point

Floating-point numbers can have positive or negative values.

`float`   The basic floating-point type for the system.

`double`   A (possibly) larger unit for holding floating-point numbers. It may allow more-significant figures and perhaps larger exponents than `float`.

`long double` A (possibly) even larger unit for holding floating-point numbers. It may allow more-significant figures and perhaps larger exponents than `double`.

Summary: How to Declare a Simple Variable

1. Choose the type you need.
2. Choose a name for the variable.
3. Use this format for a declaration statement: *type-specifier variable-name;*. The *type-specifier* is formed from one or more of the type keywords. Here are some examples:

```
int erest;
unsigned short cash;
```

4. To declare more than one variable of the same type, separate the variable names with commas:

```
char ch, init, ans;
```

5. You can initialize a variable in a declaration statement:

```
float mass = 6.0E24;
```

Summary: Storage Classes

Keywords

Use the following keywords to set up storage classes: `auto`, `extern`, `static`, `register`.

General Comments

The storage class of a variable determines its scope and life. The storage class is determined both by where the variable is defined and by its associated keyword. Variables defined outside all functions are external, have global scope, and persist for the life of the program. Variables declared inside a function are automatic and local unless one of the other keywords is used. External variables defined above a function are known to it even if they are not declared internally.

Properties

Storage Class	Keyword	Duration	Scope
Automatic	`auto`	Temporary	Local
Register	`register`	Temporary	Local
Static	`static`	Persistent	Local
External	`extern*`	Persistent	Global (all files)
External static	`static`	Persistent	Global (one file)

Note: Variables in storage classes above the dotted line are declared inside a function. Those below the line are defined outside a function.
*The keyword `extern` is used only to redeclare variables that have been defined externally elsewhere; the act of defining the variable outside of a function makes it external.

D

Expressions, Statements, and Program Flow

Summary: Expressions and Statements

Expressions

An *expression* is a combination of operators and operands. The simplest expression is just a constant or a variable with no operator, such as 22 or beebop. More complex examples are 55 + 22 and vap = 2 * (vip + (vup = 4)).

Statements

A *statement* is a command to the computer. Statements can be simple or compound. *Simple statements* terminate in a semicolon. Examples are

Declaration statement	`int toes;`
Assignment statement	`toes = 12;`
Function call statement	`printf("%d\n", toes);`
Control statement	`while (toes < 20) toes = toes + 2;`
Null statement	`; /* does nothing */`

Compound statements, or blocks, consist of one or more statements (which themselves can be compound) enclosed in braces. The following `while` statement contains an example:

```
while (years < 100)
{
    wisdom = wisdom + 1;
    printf("%d %d\n", years, wisdom);
    years = years + 1;
}
```

Summary: The *while* Statement

Keyword

The keyword for the `while` statement is `while`.

General Comments

The `while` statement creates a loop that repeats until the test *expression* becomes false, or zero. The `while` statement is an *entry-condition* loop; the decision to go through one more pass of the loop is made *before* the loop has been traversed. Thus, it is possible that the loop is never traversed. The *statement* part of the form can be a simple statement or a compound statement.

Form

```
while (expression)
        statement
```

The *statement* portion is repeated until the *expression* becomes false or zero.

Examples

```
while (n++ < 100)
        printf(" %d %d\n",n, 2*n+1);

while (fargo < 1000)
{
```

```
                fargo = fargo + step;
                step = 2 * step;
        }
```

Summary: The *for* Statement

Keyword

The for statement keyword is for.

General Comments

The for statement uses three control expressions, separated by semicolons, to control a looping process. The *initialize* expression is executed once, before any of the loop statements are executed. If the *test* expression is true (or nonzero), the loop is cycled through once. Then the *update* expression is evaluated, and it is time to check the *test* expression again. The for statement is an *entry-condition* loop; the decision to go through one more pass of the loop is made *before* the loop has been traversed. Thus, it is possible that the loop is never traversed. The *statement* part of the form can be a simple statement or a compound statement.

Form

```
        for (initialize ; test ; update)
                statement
```

The loop is repeated until *test* becomes false or zero.

Example

```
        for (n = 0;  n < 10 ; n++)
                printf("%d %d\n", n, 2 * n+1);
```

Summary: The *do while* Statement

Keywords

The keywords for the do while statement are do and while.

General Comments

The do `while` statement creates a loop that repeats until the test *expression* becomes false or zero. The do `while` statement is an *exit-condition* loop; the decision to go through one more pass of the loop is made *after* the loop has been traversed. Thus, the loop must be executed at least once. The *statement* part of the form can be a simple statement or a compound statement.

Form

```
do
    statement
while (expression);
```

The *statement* portion is repeated until the *expression* becomes false or zero.

Example

```
do
    scanf("%d", &number)
while(number != 20);
```

Summary: Using *if* Statements for Making Choices

Keywords

The keywords for `if` statements are `if` and `else`.

General Comments

In each of the following forms, the *statement* can be either a simple statement or a compound statement. A "true" expression, more generally, means one with a nonzero value.

Form 1

```
if (expression)
    statement
```

The *statement* is executed if the *expression* is true.

Form 2

```
if (expression)
      statement1
   else
        statement2
```

If the *expression* is true, *statement1* is executed. Otherwise, *statement2* is executed.

Form 3

```
if (expression1)
   statement1
else if (expression2)
   statement2
else
    statement3
```

If *expression1* is true, then *statement1* is executed. If *expression1* is false but *expression2* is true, *statement2* is executed. Otherwise, if both expressions are false, *statement3* is executed.

Example

```
if (legs == 4)
    printf("It might be a horse.\n");
else if (legs > 4)
    printf("It is not a horse.\n");
else    /* case of legs < 4 */
{
    legs++;
    printf("Now it has one more leg.\n")
}
```

Summary: Multiple Choice with *switch*

Keyword

The keyword for the switch statement is switch.

General Comments

Program control jumps to the statement bearing the value of *expression* as a label. Program flow then proceeds through the remaining statements unless redirected again. Both *expression* and labels must have integer values (type `char` is included), and the labels must be constants or expressions formed solely from constants. If no label matches the expression value, control goes to the statement labeled `default`, if present. Otherwise, control passes to the next statement following the `switch` statement. Once control goes to a particular label, all the subsequent statements in the `switch` are executed until the end of the `switch`, or a `break` statement, is encountered, whichever comes first.

Form

```
switch (expression)
{
    case label1 : statement1
    case label2 : statement2
    default     : statement3
}
```

There can be more than two labeled statements, and the `default` case is optional.

Examples

```
switch (value)
    case 1 : find_sum(ar, n);
             break;
    case 2 : show_array(ar, n);
             break;
    case 3 : puts("Goodbye!");
             break;
    default : puts("Invalid choice, try again.");
             break;
}

switch (letter)
{
    case 'a' :
    case 'e' : printf("%d is a vowel\n", letter);
    case 'c' :
    case 'n' : printf("%d is in \"cane\"\n", letter);
```

```
default  : printf("Have a nice day.\n");
}
```

If letter has the value 'a' or 'e', all three messages are printed; 'c' and 'n' cause the last two to be printed. Other values print only the last message.

Summary: Program Jumps

Keywords

The keywords for program jumps are break, continue, and goto.

General Comments

The three instructions break, continue, and goto cause program flow to jump from one location of a program to another location.

The *break* Command

The break command can be used with any of the three loop forms and with the switch statement. It causes program control to skip the rest of the loop or switch containing it and to resume with the next command following the loop or switch.

Example

```
switch (number)
{
    case  4:  printf("That's a good choice.\n");
              break;
    case  5:  printf("That's a fair choice.\n");
              break;
    default:  printf("That's a poor choice.\n");
}
```

The *continue* Command

The continue command can be used with any of the three loop forms but not with a switch. It causes program control to skip the remaining statements in a loop. For a while or for loop, the next loop cycle is started. For a do while loop, the exit condition is tested and then, if necessary, the next loop cycle is started.

Example

```
while ((ch = getchar())  != EOF)
{
     if (ch == ' ')
          continue;
     putchar(ch);
     chcount++;
}
```

This fragment echoes and counts nonspace characters.

The *goto* Command

A goto statement causes program control to jump to a statement bearing the indicated label. A colon is used to separate a labeled statement from its label. Label names follow the rules for variable names. The labeled statement can come either before or after the goto.

Form

```
goto label;

     .
     .
     .

label : statement
```

Example

```
top : ch = getchar();

     .
     .
     .

if (ch != 'y')
     goto top;
```

E

ASCII Table

DEC X_{10}	HEX X_{16}	OCT X_8	Binary X_2	ASCII	Key
0	00	00	000 0000	NUL	Ctrl/1
1	01	01	000 0001	SOH	Ctrl/A
2	02	02	000 0010	STX	Ctrl/B
3	03	03	000 0011	ETX	Ctrl/C
4	04	04	000 0100	EOT	Ctrl/D
5	05	05	000 0101	ENQ	Ctrl/E
6	06	06	000 0110	ACK	Ctrl/F
7	07	07	000 0111	BEL	Ctrl/G
8	08	10	000 1000	BS	Ctrl/H, Backspace
9	09	11	000 1001	HT	Ctrl/I, Tab
10	0A	12	000 1010	LF	Ctrl/J, Line Feed
11	0B	13	000 1011	VT	Ctrl/K
12	0C	14	000 1100	FF	Ctrl/L
13	0D	15	000 1101	CR	Ctrl/M, Return
14	0E	16	000 1110	SO	Ctrl/N
15	0F	17	000 1111	SI	Ctrl/O
16	10	20	001 0000	DLE	Ctrl/P
17	11	21	001 0001	DC1	Ctrl/Q
18	12	22	001 0010	DC2	Ctrl/R

ASCII Table (continued)

DEC X_{10}	HEX X_{16}	OCT X_8	Binary X_2	ASCII	Key
19	13	23	001 0011	DC3	Ctrl/S
20	14	24	001 0100	DC4	Ctrl/T
21	15	25	001 0101	NAK	Ctrl/U
22	16	26	001 0110	SYN	Ctrl/V
23	17	27	001 0111	ETB	Ctrl/W
24	18	30	001 1000	CAN	Ctrl/X
25	19	31	001 1001	EM	Ctrl/Y
26	1A	32	001 1010	SUB	Ctrl/Z
27	1B	33	001 1011	ESC	Esc, Escape
28	1C	34	001 1100	FS	Ctrl/\
29	1D	35	001 1101	GS	Ctrl/]
30	1E	36	001 1110	RS	Ctrl/=
31	1F	37	001 1111	US	Ctrl/-
32	20	40	010 0000	SP	Spacebar
33	21	41	010 0001	!	!
34	22	42	010 0010	"	"
35	23	43	010 0011	#	#
36	24	44	010 0100	$	$
37	25	45	010 0101	%	%
38	26	46	010 0110	&	&
39	27	47	010 0111	'	'
40	28	50	010 1000	(	(
41	29	51	010 1001	)	)
42	2A	52	010 1010	*	*
43	2B	53	010 1011	+	+
44	2C	54	010 1100	,	,
45	2D	55	010 1101	-	-
46	2E	56	010 1110	.	.
47	2F	57	010 1111	/	/
48	30	60	011 0000	0	0
49	31	61	011 0001	1	1
50	32	62	011 0010	2	2
51	33	63	011 0011	3	3
52	34	64	011 0100	4	4
53	35	65	011 0101	5	5

ASCII Table *(continued)*

DEC X_{10}	HEX X_{16}	OCT X_8	Binary X_2	ASCII	Key
54	36	66	011 0110	6	6
55	37	67	011 0111	7	7
56	38	70	011 1000	8	8
57	39	71	011 1001	9	9
58	3A	72	011 1010	:	:
59	3B	73	011 1011	;	;
60	3C	74	011 1100	⟨	⟨
61	3D	75	011 1101	=	=
62	3E	76	011 1110	⟩	⟩
63	3F	77	011 1111	?	?
64	40	100	100 0000	@	@
65	41	101	100 0001	A	A
66	42	102	100 0010	B	B
67	43	103	100 0011	C	C
68	44	104	100 0100	D	D
69	45	105	100 0101	E	E
70	46	106	100 0110	F	F
71	47	107	100 0111	G	G
72	48	110	100 1000	H	H
73	49	111	100 1001	I	I
74	4A	112	100 1010	J	J
75	4B	113	100 1011	K	K
76	4C	114	100 1100	L	L
77	4D	115	100 1101	M	M
78	4E	116	100 1110	N	N
79	4F	117	100 1111	O	O
80	50	120	101 0000	P	P
81	51	121	101 0001	Q	Q
82	52	122	101 0010	R	R
83	53	123	101 0011	S	S
84	54	124	101 0100	T	T
85	55	125	101 0101	U	U
86	56	126	101 0110	V	V
87	57	127	101 0111	W	W
88	58	130	101 1000	X	X

ASCII Table *(continued)*

DEC X_{10}	HEX X_{16}	OCT X_8	Binary X_2	ASCII	Key
89	59	131	101 1001	Y	Y
90	5A	132	101 1010	Z	Z
91	5B	133	101 1011	[	[
92	5C	134	101 1100	\	\
93	5D	135	101 1101	]	]
94	5E	136	101 1110	^	^
95	5F	137	101 1111	−	−
96	60	140	110 0000	'	'
97	61	141	110 0001	a	a
98	62	142	110 0010	b	b
99	63	143	110 0011	c	c
100	64	144	110 0100	d	d
101	65	145	110 0101	e	e
102	66	146	110 0110	f	f
103	67	147	110 0111	g	g
104	68	150	110 1000	h	h
105	69	151	110 1001	i	i
106	6A	152	110 1010	j	j
107	6B	153	110 1011	k	k
108	6C	154	110 1100	l	l
109	6D	155	110 1101	m	m
110	6E	156	110 1110	n	n
111	6F	157	110 1111	o	o
112	70	160	111 0000	p	p
113	71	161	111 0001	q	q
114	72	162	111 0010	r	r
115	73	163	111 0011	s	s
116	74	164	111 0100	t	t
117	75	165	111 0101	u	u
118	76	166	111 0110	v	v
119	77	167	111 0111	w	w
120	78	170	111 1000	x	x
121	79	171	111 1001	y	y
122	7A	172	111 1010	z	z
123	7B	173	111 1011	{	{

ASCII Table *(continued)*

DEC X_{10}	HEX X_{16}	OCT X_8	Binary X_2	ASCII	Key
124	7C	174	111 1100	|	|
125	7D	175	111 1101	}	}
126	7E	176	111 1110	~	~
127	7F	177	111 1111	Del	Del, Rubout

F

Standard I/O Functions (ANSI C)

The ANSI C standard library includes several standard I/O functions associated with streams and the `stdio.h` file. Table F.1 presents the ANSI prototypes for these functions along with a brief explanation of what they do. For complete descriptions, consult the documentation for your implementation or a reference manual.

Table F.1 *ANSI C Standard I/O Functions*

Prototype	Description
`void clearerr(FILE *)`	Clears end-of-file and error indicators
`int fclose(FILE *)`	Closes the indicated file
`int feof(FILE *)`	Tests for end of file
`int ferror(FILE *)`	Tests error indicator
`int fflush(FILE *)`	Flushes the indicated file
`int fgetc(FILE *)`	Gets the next character from the indicated input stream
`int fgetpos(FILE *, fpos_t *)`	Stores the current value of the file position indicator

(continued)

Table F.1 *(continued)*

Prototype	Description
`char * fgets(char *, int, FILE *)`	Gets the next line (or indicated number of characters) from the indicated stream
`FILE * fopen(const char *, const char *)`	Opens the indicated file
`int fprintf(FILE *, const char *, ...)`	Writes the formatted output to the indicated stream
`int fputc(int, FILE *)`	Writes the indicated character to the indicated stream
`int fputs(const char *, FILE *)`	Writes the indicated character to the indicated stream
`size_t fread(void *, size_t, size_t, FILE *)`	Reads binary data from the indicated stream
`FILE * freopen(const char *, const char *, FILE *)`	Opens the indicated file and associates it with the indicated stream
`int fscanf(FILE *, const char *, ...)`	Reads formatted input from the indicated stream
`int fsetpos(FILE *, const fpos_t *)`	Sets the file-position pointer to the indicated value
`int fseek(FILE *, long, int)`	Sets the file-position pointer to the indicated value
`long ftell(FILE *)`	Gets the current file position
`size_t fwrite(const void *, size_t, size_t, FILE *)`	Writes binary data to the indicated stream
`int getc(FILE *)`	Reads the next character from the indicated input
`int getchar()`	Reads the next character from the standard input
`char * gets(char *)`	Gets the next line from the standard input
`void perror(const char *)`	Writes system error messages to the standard error
`int printf(const char *, ...)`	Writes formatted output to the standard output
`int putc(int, FILE *)`	Writes the indicated character to the indicated output

Table F.1 *(continued)*

Prototype	Description
`int putchar(int)`	Writes the indicated character to the standard output
`int puts(const char *)`	Writes the string to the standard output
`int remove(const char *)`	Removes the named file
`int rename(const char *, const char *)`	Renames the named file
`void rewind(FILE *)`	Sets the file-position pointer to the start of the file
`int scanf(const char *, ...)`	Reads formatted input from the standard input
`void setbuf(FILE *, char *)`	Sets the buffer size and location
`int setvbuf(FILE *, char *, int, size_t)`	Sets the buffer size, location, and mode
`int sprintf(char *, const char *, ...)`	Writes formatted output to the indicated string
`int sscanf(const char *, const char *, ...)`	Reads formatted input from the indicated string
`FILE * tmpfile(void)`	Creates a temporary file
`char * tmpnam(char *)`	Generates a unique name for a temporary file
`int ungetc(int, FILE *)`	Pushes the indicated character back onto the input stream
`int vfprintf(FILE *, const char *, va_list)`	Like `fprintf()`, except uses a single list-argument instead of a variable argument list
`int vprintf(const char *, va_list)`	Like `printf()`, except uses a single list-argument instead of a variable argument list
`int vsprintf(char *, const char *, va_list)`	Like `sprintf()`, except uses a single list-argument instead of a variable argument list

G

Answers to the Review Questions

Chapter 1

1. A perfectly portable program is one whose source code can, without modification, be compiled to a succesful program on a variety of different computer systems.

2. A source code file contains code as written in whatever language the programmer is using. An object code file contains machine language code; it need not be the code for a complete program. An executable file contains the complete code, in machine language, constituting an executable program.

3. (1) Defining program objectives. (2) Designing the program. (3) Coding the program. (4) Compiling the program. (5) Running the program. (6) Testing and debugging the program. (7) Maintaining and modifying the program.

4. A compiler converts source code, such as code in the C language, to machine language code.

5. A linker combines object code from several sources into a single, executable program.

Chapter 2

1. They are called functions.

2. A syntax error is a violation of the rules governing how sentences or programs are put together. Here's an example in English: "Me speak English good." Here's an example in C: `printf"Where are the parentheses?";`.

3. A semantic error is one of meaning. Here's an example in English: "This sentence is excellent Italian." Here's a C example: `thrice_n = 3 + n;`.

4. Line 1: Begin the line with a `#`; spell the file `stdio.h`; place the filename within angle brackets.
Line 2: Use `()`, not `{}`; end comment with `*/`, not `/*`.
Line 3: Use `{`, not `(`.
Line 4: Complete the statement with a semicolon.
Line 5: Mr. IBM got this one (the blank line) right!
Line 6: Use `=`, not `:=` for assignment. (Apparently Mr. IBM knows a little Pascal.) Use 52, not 56, weeks per year.
Line 7: Should be `printf("There are %d weeks in a year.\n",s);`.
Line 8: There isn't a line 8, but there should be, and it should consist of the closing brace, `}`.

5. a. `Baa Baa Black Sheep.Have you any wool?`

(Note that there is no space after the period. We could have had a space by using `" Have` instead of `"Have`.)

    b. `Begone!`
       `O creature of lard!`

(Note that the cursor is left at the end of the second line.)

    c. `What?`
       `No/nBonzo?`

(Note that the slash (`/`) does not have the same effect as the backslash `\`.)

    d. `2 + 2 = 4`

(Note how each `%d` is replaced by the corresponding variable value from the list. Note, too, that `+` means addition and that calculation can be done inside a `printf()` statement.)

6. `int` and `char`

7. `printf("There were %d words and %d lines.\n", words, lines);`

8. After line 5, a is 5 and b is 2. After line 6, both a and b are 5. After line 7, both a and b are 5. Note that a can't be 2 because by the time you say `a = b;`, b already has been changed to 5.

Chapter 3

1.   a. `int`, possibly `short` or `unsigned` or `unsigned short`;
   `population` is a whole number.

     b. `float`; it's unlikely the average will be an exact integer.

     c. `char`

     d. `int`, possibly `unsigned`

2. Line 1: Should read `#include <stdio.h>`.
   Line 2: Should have a pair of parentheses following `main`; i.e.,
   `main()`.
   Line 3: Use `{`, not `(`.
   Line 4: Should be a comma, not a semicolon, between `g` and `h`.
   Line 5: Fine.
   Line 6: (blank) Fine.
   Line 7: There should be at least one digit before the `e`. Either `1e21`
   or `1.0e21` is okay.
   Line 8: Fine.
   Line 9: Use `}`, not `)`.
   Missing Lines: First, `rate` is never assigned a value. Second, the
   variable `h` is never used. Also, the program never informs us of the
   results of its calculation. Neither of these errors will stop the
   program from running (although you may be given a warning
   about the unused variable), but they do detract from its already
   limited usefulness.

3.   a. `int, %0`

     b. `long float, %le`

     c. `char, %c`

     d. `long int, %d`

     e. `char, %c`

     f. `float, %f`

     g. `int, %x`

4. Line 0: It's better form to have `#include <stdio.h>`.
   Line 1: Use `/*` and `*/`.
   Line 3: `int cows, legs;`
   Line 5: `count?\n");`
   Line 6: `%d`, not `%c`
   Line 6: `&legs`
   Line 8: `%d`, not `%f`

Chapter 4

1. The program bombs. The first `scanf()` statement reads just your first name, leaving your last name untouched but still stored in the input "buffer." (This buffer is just a temporary storage area used to store the input.) When the next `scanf()` statement comes along looking for your weight, it picks up where the last reading attempt ended, and reads your last name as your weight. This produces garbage. On the other hand, if you respond to the name request with something like `Lasha 144`, it will use `144` as your weight even though you typed it before your weight was requested.

2.   a. `He sold the painting for $234.50.`

    b. `Hi!` (Note: The first character is a character constant, the second is a decimal integer converted to a character, and the third is an ASCII representation of a character constant.)

    c. `His Hamlet was funny without being vulgar.`
`has 42 characters.`

    d. `Is 1.20e+003 the same as 1201.00?`

3. Recall the `%%` construction for printing `%`.

```
printf("This copy of \"%s\" sells for $%0.2f.\n", BOOK, cost);
printf("That is %d%% of list.\n", percent);
```

4.   a. `%15lu`

    b. `%#4x`

    c. `%-12.2E`

    d. `%+10.3f`

    e. `%8.8s`

5.   a. `int dalmations;`
`scanf("%d", &dalmations);`

    b. `float kgs, share;`
`scanf("%f%f", &kgs, &share);`

Note: For input, e, f, and g can be used interchangeably. Also, for all but `%c`, it makes no difference if you leave spaces between the conversion specifiers.

    c. `char name[20];`
`scanf("%s", name);`

    d. `char action[20];`
`int value;`
`scanf("%s %d", action, &value);`

    e. `int value;`
`scanf("%*s %d", &value);`

6. The substitutions would take place. Unfortunately, the preprocessor cannot discriminate between those parentheses that should be replaced with braces and those that should not. Thus,

```
main()
(
    printf("Hello, O Great One!\n");
)
```

becomes

```
main{}
{
    printf{"Hello, O Great One!\n"};
}
```

Chapter 5

1. a. 30
   b. 27 (not 3). (12 + 6)/(2*3) would give 3.
   c. x = 1, y = 1 (integer division)
   d. x = 3 (integer division) and y = 9

2. Line 3: Should end in a semicolon, not a comma.
   Line 8: The while statement sets up an infinite loop because the value of i remains 1 and is always less than 30. Presumably we meant to write while(i++ < 30).
   Lines 8, 10: The indentation implies that we wanted lines 9 and 10 to form a block, but the lack of braces means that the while loop includes only line 9. Braces should be added.
   Line 9: Since 1 and i are both integers, the result of the division will be 1 when i is 1, and 0 for all larger values. Using n = 1.0/i; would cause i to be converted to floating-point before division and would yield nonzero answers.
   Line 10: We omitted a newline character (\n) in the control statement. This will cause the numbers to be printed on one line, if possible.

3. The main problem lies in the relationship between the test statement (is sec greater than 0?) and the scanf() statement that fetches the value of sec. In particular, the first time the test is made, the program hasn't had a chance to even get a value for sec, and the comparison will be made to some garbage value that happens to be at that memory location. One solution, albeit an inelegant one, is to initialize sec to, say, 1 so that the test is passed

the first time through. This uncovers a second problem. When we finally type 0 to halt the program, sec doesn't get checked until after the loop is finished, and the results for 0 seconds are printed out. What we really want is to have a scanf() statement just before the while test is made. We can accomplish that by altering the central part of the program to read this way:

```
scanf("%d", &sec);
while ( sec > 0 ) {
   min = sec/SM;
   left = sec % SM;
   printf("%d sec is %d min, %d sec. \n", sec, min, left);
   printf("Next input?\n");
   scanf("%d", &sec);
   }
```

The first time through, the scanf() outside the loop is used. Thereafter, the scanf() at the end of the loop (and hence just before the loop begins again) is used. This is a common method for handling problems of this sort.

4. Here is the output:

```
%s is a string
is a string
1
1
2
1
```

Let us explain. The first printf() statement is the same as:

```
printf("%s is a string\n","%s is a string\n");
```

The second print statement first increments num to 1 and then prints the value. The third print statement prints num, which is 1, and then increments it to 2. The fourth print statement prints the current value of n, which still is 2, and then decrements n to 1. The final print statement prints the current value of n, 1.

5. It prints on one line the digits 1 through 10 in fields that are five columns wide and then starts a new line:

```
  1    2    3    4    5    6    7    8    9   10
```

6. Here is the output for each example:

    a. 1 2

Note that x is incremented and then compared. The cursor is left on the same line.

    b. 101

              102
              103
              104

Note that this time x is compared and then incremented. In both this case and in example *a.*, x is incremented before printing takes place. Note, too, that indenting the second `printf()` statement does not make it part of the `while` loop. Thus, it is called only once, after the `while` loop ends.

    c. `stuvw`

Here, there is no incrementing until after the first `printf()`.

7.   a. `x = x + 10;`

    b. `x++;`

    c. `c = 2 * (a + b);`

    d. `c = a + 2* b;`

Chapter 6

1. 2, 7, 70, 64, 8, 2

2.   a. `x > 5`

    b. `scanf("%lf",&dnum) != 1`

    c. `x == 5`

3. For style, should start with `#include <stdio.h>`.
Line 3: Should be `list[10]`.
Line 5: Commas should be semicolons.
Line 5: Range for i should be from 0 to 9, not 1 to 10.
Line 8: Commas should be semicolons.
Line 8: `>=` should be `<=`. Otherwise, when i is 1, the loop never ends.
Line 10: There should be another closing brace between lines 9 and 10. One brace closes the compound statement, and one closes the program.

4.   a. `Hi! Hi! Hi! Bye! Bye! Bye! Bye! Bye!`

    b. `ACGM`

5. Here is the output we get:

```
11121314
***
1
4
7
```

```
***
1 5
2 7
4 9
8 11
***
+++++
++++
+++
++
```

6. Because the first element has index 0, the loop range should be 1 to `SIZE - 1`, not 1 to `SIZE`. Making that change, however, causes the first element to be assigned the value 0 instead of 2. So rewrite the loop this way:

```
for (index = 0; index < SIZE; index++)
    by_twos[index] = 2 * (index + 1);
```

Similarly, the limits for the second loop should be changed. Also, an array index should be used with the array name:

```
for( index = 0; index < SIZE; index++)
    printf("%d ", by_twos[index]);
```

7.
```
long square(num)
int num;
{
    return num * num;
}
```

Chapter 7

1. True: b

2. Line 5: Should be `scanf("%d %d", &weight, &height);`. Don't forget those &s for `scanf()`. Also, this line should be preceded by a line prompting input.
   Line 9: What is meant is `(height > 72 && height > 64)`. However, the first part of the expression is unnecessary, since `height` must be less than 72 for the `else if` to be reached in the first place. Thus, a simple `(height > 64)` will serve.
   Line 11: The condition is redundant; the second subexpression (`weight` not less than or equal to 300) means the same as the first. A simple `(weight > 300)` is all that is needed. But there is more trouble. Line 11 gets attached to the wrong `if`! Clearly this `else` is meant to go along with line 6. By the most recent `if` not rule,

however, it will be associated with the `if` of line 9. Thus, line 11 is reached when `weight` is less than 100 and `height` is 64 or under. This makes it impossible for `weight` to exceed 300 when this statement is reached.

Lines 7 through 9: Should be enclosed in braces. Then line 11 will become an alternative to line 6, not to line 9.

Line 12: Simplify the expression to `height > 48)`.

Line 14: This `else` associates with the last `if`, the one on line 12. Enclose lines 12 and 13 in braces to force this `else` to associate with the `if` of line 11. Note that the final message is printed only for those weighing between 100 and 300 pounds.

3. a. 1. The assertion is true, which numerically is a 1.

    b. 0. 3 is not less than 2.

    c. 1. If the first expression is false, the second is true, and vice versa; just one true expression is needed.

4. The program prints the following:

    `*#%*#%$#%*#%*#%$#%*#%*#%$#%*#%*#%`

    Despite what the indentation suggests, the # is printed during every loop, since it is not part of a compound statement.

5. The comments on lines 5 through 7 should be terminated with `*/`. The expresion `'a' <= ch >= 'z'` should be replaced with

    ```
    ch >= 'a' && ch <= 'z'
    ```

    Incidentally, `'a' <= ch >= 'z'` is valid C; it just doesn't have the right meaning. Since relational operators associate left to right, the expression is interpreted as `('a' <= ch) >= 'z'`. The expression in parentheses has the value 1 or 0 (true or false), and this value is checked to see if it is equal to or greater than the numeric code for `'z'`. Neither 0 nor 1 satisfies that test, so the whole expression always evaluates to 0 (false). In the second test expression, `||` should be `&&`. Also, while `!(ch < 'A')` is both valid and correct in meaning, `ch >= 'A'` is simpler. The `'Z'` should be followed by two closing parentheses, not one. The `oc++;` statement should be preceded by an `else`. Otherwise, it is incremented every character. The control expression in the `printf()` call should be enclosed in double quotes.

6. Here is the resulting run using the given input:

    ```
    q
    Step 1
    Step 2
    Step 3
    c
    Step 1
    ```

```
g
Step 1
Step 3
b
Step 1
Done
```

Note that both b and # terminate the loop, but that entering b elicits the printing of Step 1, while entering # doesn't.

Chapter 8

1. The statement putchar(getchar()); causes the program to reach the next input character and to print it; the return value from getchar() is the argument to putchar(). No, getchar(putchar()) is invalid because getchar() doesn't use an argument and putchar() needs one.

2. count <essay >essayct or else count >essayct <essay

3. It's a signal (a special value) returned by getchar() and scanf() to indicate that they have detected the end of a file.

4.   a. The output is as follows:

   ```
   If you qu
   ```

   Note that the character I is distinct from the character i. Also note that the i is not printed because the loop quits upon detecting it.

   b. The output is as follows:

   ```
   HJacrthjacrt
   ```

   The first time through, ch has the value H. The ch++ causes the value to be used (printed) and then incremented (to I). Then the ++ch causes the value to be incremented (to J) and then used (printed). After that, the next character (a) is read, and the process is repeated. An important point to note here is that the incrementations affect the value of ch after it has been assigned a value; they don't somehow cause the program to move through the input queue.

7. C's standard I/O library maps diverse file forms to uniform streams that can be handled equivalently.

Chapter 9

1. A formal argument is a variable that is defined in the function being called. The actual argument is the value appearing in the function call; this value is assigned to the formal argument.

2.
   a.
   ```
   char n_to_char(n)
       int n;
   ```
   or
   ```
   char n_to_char( int n)
   ```
   b.
   ```
   int digits(x,n)
       double x;
       int n;
   ```
   or
   ```
   int digits(double x, int n)
   ```
   c.
   ```
   int random()
   ```
   or
   ```
   int random(void)
   ```

3.
   ```
   float sum(j,k)
   float j, k;
   ```
   Also, declare `float sum()` in the calling program.

4. Yes; num should be declared before the first brace, not after. Also, it should be `count++`, not `num++`.

5. Here is the minimal program; the `showmenu()` and `getchoice()` functions are possible solutions to parts a. and b.

```
void showmenu(void);  /* declare functions used */
int getchoice(int, int);
main()
{
    int res;

    showmenu();
    res = getchoice(1,4);
    printf("I don't know how to do choice %d: bye!\n", res);
}
void showmenu(void)
{
    printf("Please choose one of the following:\n");
```

```
        printf("1) copy files          2) move files\n");
        printf("3) remove files        4) quit\n");
        printf("Enter the number of your choice:\n");
}

int getchoice(int low, int high)
{
    int ans;

    scanf("%d", &ans);
    while (ans < low || ans > high)
    {
        printf("%d is not a valid choice; try again\n", ans);
        showmenu();
        scanf("%d", &ans);
    }
    return ans;
}
```

Chapter 10

1. The printout is

   ```
   D  D
   O  O
   L  L
   T  T
   ```

2. The array name `ref` points to the first element of the array, the character `D`. The expression `ref + 1` points to the second element, the character `O`. The construction `++ref` is not a valid C expression; `ref` is a constant, not a variable.

3. a. 12 and 16

    b. 12 and 14 (just the 12 goes in the first row because of the braces)

4. a. `int digits[10];`

    b. `float rates[6];`

    c. `int mat[3][5];`

    d. `char (*pstr)[20];` Note: `char pstr[20];` is incorrect. This would make `pstr` a constant pointer (not a variable) to a single `char`, the first member of the array; `pstr + 1` would point to the next byte. With the correct declaration, `pstr` is a variable, and `pstr + 1` points 20 bytes beyond the initial byte.

    e. `char *pstr[20];`. Note: The `[]` have higher precedence than `*`, so in the absence of parentheses, the array descriptor is applied first, then the pointer descriptor. Hence, this declaration is the same as `char *(pstr[20]);`.

9. 0 through 9

Chapter 11

1. Storage class should be external or static for pre-ANSI implementations; initialization should include a `'\0'`.

2. `y`
   `my`
   `mmy`
   `ummy`
   `Yummy`

3.   a. `Ho Ho Ho!!oH oH oH`

    b. pointer-to-char

    c. The address of the initial `H`

    d. `*--pc` means to decrement the pointer by 1 and use the value found there. `--*pc` means to take the value pointed to by `pc` and decrement that value by 1. (For example, `H` becomes `G`.)

    e. `Ho Ho Ho!!oH oH o`
      Note: A null character comes between `!` and `!`, but it produces no printing effect.

    f. `while(*pc)`. Check to see that `pc` does not point to a null character (i.e., to the end of the string). The expression uses the value at the pointed-to location, `while(pc - str)`. Check to see that `pc` does not point to the same location that `str` does (the beginning of the string). The expression uses the values of the pointers themselves.

    g. After the first `while` loop, `pc` points to the null character. Upon entering the second loop, it is made to point to the storage location before the null character, i.e., to the location just before the one that `str` points to. That byte is interpreted as a character and is printed. The pointer then backs up to the preceding byte. The terminating condition (`pc == str`) never occurs, and the process continues until you or the system tire.

    h. `pr()` must be declared in the calling program: `char *pr();`

4. Here is what you get:

```
How are ya, sweetie? How are ya, sweetie?
Beat the clock.
eat the clock.
Beat the clock. Win a toy.
Beat
chat
hat
at
t
t
at
How are ya, sweetie?
```

5. Here is one solution:

```
int strlen(char *s)
{
   int ct = 0;

   while (*s++ != '\0')      /* or while (*s++) */
       ct++;
   return(ct);
}
```

6.
```
#include <stdio.h>
char *strblk(string)
char *string;
{
while (*string != ' ' && *string != '\0')
  string++;       /* stops at first blank or null */
if (*string == '\0')
  return(NULL);    /* NULL is the null pointer   */
else
  return(string);
}
```

Chapter 12

1. It should have #include <stdio.h> for its file definitions. It should declare fp a file pointer: FILE *fp;. The function fopen() requires a mode: fopen("gelatin", "w") or perhaps the "a" mode. The order of the arguments to fputs() should be reversed. The

fclose() function requires a file pointer, not a filename:
fclose(fp);.

2. a. `ch = getc(fp1);`

    b. `fprintf(fp2,"%c"\n",ch);`

    c. `putc(ch,fp2);`

    d. `fclose(fp1); /* close the terky file */`
Note: fp1 is used for input operations, since it identifies the
file opened in the read mode. Similarly, fp2 was opened in the
write mode, so it is used with output functions.

3. Here is one approach:

```
#include <stdio.h>
#define BUF 256
int has_ch(char ch, char *line)
main(argc,argv)
int argc;
char *argv[];
{
    FILE *fp;
    char ch;
    char line [BUF];
    char *fgets();
    if (argc != 3)
    {
        printf("Usage: %s character filename\n", argv[0]);
        exit(1);
    }
    ch = argv[1][0];
    if ((fp = fopen(argv[2], "r")) == NULL)
    {
        printf("Can't open %s\n", argv[2]);
        exit(1);
    }
    while (fgets(line,BUF,fp) != NULL)
    {
        if (has_ch(ch,line))
            fputs(line,stdout);
    }
    fclose(fp);
}
int has_ch(char ch, char *line)
{
    while (*line)
        if (ch == *line++)
            return(1);
```

```
        return(0);
    }
```

The `fgets()` and `fputs()` functions work together because
`fgets()` leaves the \n produced by Enter in the string, and `fputs()`
does not add a \n the way that `puts()` does.

4.   a. When 8238201 is saved using `fprintf()`, it's saved as seven
         characters stored in 7 bytes. When saved using `fwrite()`, it's
         saved as a 4-byte integer using the binary representation of
         that numeric value.

     b. No difference; in each case it's saved as a 1-byte binary code.

5.   The "r+" mode lets you read and write anywhere in a file, so it's
     best suited. The "a+" only lets you append material to the end of
     the file, and the "w+" starts with a clean slate, discarding prior file
     contents.

Chapter 13

1. The automatic and the static storage classes

2. The external storage class; the external static storage class

3. Replace `array[search] > array[top]` with `array[search] <
    array[top]`.

4. `daisy` is known to `main()` by default, and to `petal()` and `root()`
    because of the `extern` declaration. The `extern int daisy;`
    declaration in `root()` makes `daisy` known to all the functions in
    file 2. The first `lily` is local to `main()`: the reference to `lily` in
    `petal()` is an error because there is no external `lily` in either file.
    There is an external static `lily`, but it is known just to functions in
    the second file. The first external `rose` is known to `root()`, but
    `stem()` has overridden it with its own local `rose`.

5.   a. It tells us that the program will use a variable `plink` that is
         local to the file containing the function. The first argument is
         a pointer to an integer, presumably the first element of an
         array of n members. The important point here is that the
         program will not be allowed to use the pointer `arr` to modify
         values in the original array.

     b. No. Already `value` and n are copies of original data, so there
         is no way for the function to alter the corresponding values in
         the calling program. What these declarations do accomplish is
         to prevent the function from altering `value` and n within the
         function. For example, the function couldn't use the
         expression n++ if n were qualified as `const`.

Chapter 14

1. The proper keyword is `struct`, not `structure`. The template requires either a tag before the opening brace or a variable name after the closing brace. Also, there should be a semicolon after `*togs` and at the end of the template.

2.
```
struct month {
      char name[10];
      char abbrev[4];
      int days;
      int monumb;
};
```

3.
```
extern struct month months[];
int days(month)
int month;
{
  int index, total;

  if (month < 1 || month > 12)
    return(-1); /* error signal */
  else
  {
    for (index = 0, total = 0; index < month; index ++)
        total += months[index].days;
    return( total);
  }
}
```

Note that `index` is one less than month number, since arrays start with subscript 0. Hence, we use `index < month` instead of `index <= month`.

4. a. 6
```
Arcturan
cturan
```

    b. Use the structure name and use the pointer.
```
deb.title.last
pb->title.last
```

    c. Here is one version:
```
#include <stdio.h>
#include "starfolk.h"    /* make struct defs available */
void prbem ( pbem )
struct bem *pbem;
{
```

```
            printf("%s %s is a %d-limbed %s.\n", pbem->title.first,
                  pbem->title.last, pbem->limbs, pbem->type);
     }
```

5. Here is one possibility:

```
struct car {
        char name[20];
        float hp;
        float epampg;
        float wbase;
        int year;
};
```

6. The function could be set up like this:

```
struct gas {
        float distance;
        float gals;
        float mpg;
};
struct gas mpgs(struct gas trip)
{
  if (trip.gals > 0)
     trip.mpg = trip.distance / trip.gals ;
  else
     trip.mpg = -1.0;
  return trip;
}
```

Note that this function cannot directly alter values in the calling program, so we must use the return value to convey the information:

```
struct gas idaho, ;
   .
   .
   .
idaho = mpgs(idaho);
```

7. `char * (*pfun)();`

Chapter 15

1.   a. 00000011
     b. 00001101
     c. 00111011

      d. 01110111

2.   a. 21, 025, 0x15

      b. 85, 0125, 0x55

      c. 76, 0114, 0x4C

      d. 157, 0235, 0x9D

3.   a. 252

      b. 2

      c. 7

      d. 7

      e. 5

      f. 3

      g. 28

4.   a. 255

      b. 1 (not false is true)

      c. 0

      d. 1 (true and true is true)

      e. 6

      f. 1 (true or true is true)

      g. 8

5. In binary, the mask is 1111111. In decimal, it's 127. In octal, it's 0177. In hexadecimal, it's 0xFF.

6. The two printer-number bits are the left-most bits of an unsigned quantity. When they are right-shifted to bit positions 1 and 0, all the vacated bits are replaced with 0s, so there is no need for further masking.

Chapter 16

1.   a. `dist = 5280 * miles;` is valid.

      b. `plort = 4 * 4 + 4;` is valid. But if the user really wanted 4 * (4 + 4), he or she should have used `#define POD (FEET + FEET)`.

      c. `nex = = 6;;` is not valid. Apparently the user forgot that he or she was writing for the preprocessor, not writing in C.

      d. `y = y + 5;` is valid.
         `berg = berg + 5 * lob;` is valid, but this is probably not the desired result.
         `est = berg + 5/ y + 5;` is valid, but this is probably not the desired result.

> `nilp = lob *-berg + 5;` is valid, but this is probably not the desired result.

2. `#define MIN(X,Y) ( (X) < (Y) ? (X) : (Y)`

3. `#define PR(X,Y) printf(#X " is %d and " #Y " is %d\n", X,Y)`
   Since `X` and `Y` are never exposed to any other operations (such as multiplication) in this macro, we don't have to cocoon everything in parentheses.

4. Try this:

   ```
   #define P(X) printf("name: "#X"; value: %d; address: %u\n",\
               X, &X)
   ```

   Or, if your implementation allows, use the `%p` specification for the address.

5. a. `enum days {sun, mon, tue, wed, thu, fri, sat};`

    b. `enum days visit;`

6. The program should include the `stdlib.h` file, if available, or else declare `calloc()`.

   ```
   struct wine *ptrwine;

   ptrwine = (struct wine *) calloc(100, sizeof (struct wine));
   ```

Index

Inner loops, 215
Input/output, 29
  of arrays, 403–405
  buffered, 287–288, 300–302, 466,
    468–470, 484–486
  of characters, 71, 237–240,
    285–286, 303–307
  and keyboard, 53, 288–292,
    295–297
  of numbers, 60–62, 65, 75,
    303–307, 520–522
  redirection of, 292–298
  standard file for, 465, 470
  of strings, 119–120, 413, 423–433,
    443–444
  See also Files; `Printf()` function;
    `Scanf()` function
Input.c program, 121–122, 440
`Int` data type and integers, 30, 53,
    55, 58–66, 78, 81
  binary, 590
  conversion of, 340–342, 454
  division of, 143–144
  vs. floating-point numbers, 56–58
  mixing of, with floating-point,
    115–116
  signed, 591, 669
  sorting of, 518–529
  unsigned, 670
`Int86()` function, 608
Intconv.c program, 114–115
Interactive programs, 53
  `get()` for, 424–427
  unbuffered input for, 287–288
  user interface for, 300–302
Interpreted languages, 7
Interrupts, 608
Invert.c program, 449–450
Invert4.c program, 603–604
Invoking of functions, 33–355, 320,
    325–326, 673
Ioccheck.c program, 349–350
`Ioctl()` function, 288
`Isalnum()` function, 448
`Isalpha()` function, 448
`Iscntrl()` function, 448

`Isdigit()` function, 448
`Isgraph()` function, 448
`Islower()` function, 448
`Isprint()` function, 448
`Ispunct()` function, 448
`Isspace()` function, 448
`Isupper()` function, 448–450
`Isxdigit()` function, 448
Iterations, 183
`Itoa()` function, 454

J

Join_chk.c program, 436
Jumps, program, 265–275, 679–680
Justification with conversion
    specifiers, 109–110, 113

K

Kernighan, Brian, *The C
    Programming Language,* 20
Keyboard
  input from, 53, 285–286, 288–292
  redirection from, 295–297
  standard file for, 470
  See also `Scanf()` function
Keywords, 31, 44, 78

L

`%l` conversion specification modifier,
    65–66, 108, 123
Labels
  with `goto`, 272–273, 276, 680
  with `switch`, 267–272
Lastline.c program, 480–483
Leading zeroes
  with conversion specifiers, 109,
    111–112
  in escape sequences, 70
Left justification, 109–110, 113
Left shift operator (`<<`), 599–600, 667
Length of strings, 92, 95–97, 317,
    433–435
Less than sign (`<`)
  for redirection, 294, 297
  as relational operator (`<`), 135, 188,
    662

The Waite Group

100 Shoreline Highway, Suite 285   Mill Valley, CA 94941   (415) 331-0575

Compuserve: 75146,3515   usenet: hplabs!well!mitch   AppleLink: D2097

Dear Reader:

Thank you for considering the purchase of our book. Readers have come to know products from **The Waite Group** for the care and quality we put into them. Let me tell you a little about our group and how we make our books.

It started in 1976 when I could not find a computer book that really taught me anything. The books that were available talked down to people, lacked illustrations and examples, were poorly laid out, and were written as if you already understood all the terminology. So I set out to write a good book about microcomputers. This was to be a special book—very graphic, with a friendly and casual style, and filled with examples. The result was an instant best-seller.

Over the years, I developed this approach into a "formula" (nothing really secret here, just a lot of hard work—I am a crazy man about technical accuracy and high-quality illustrations). I began to find writers who wanted to write books in this way. This led to co-authoring and then to multiple-author books and many more titles (over seventy titles currently on the market). As The Waite Group author base grew, I trained a group of editors to manage our products. We now have a team devoted to putting together the best possible book package and maintaining the high standard of our existing books.

We greatly appreciate and use any advice our readers send us (and you send us a lot). We have discovered that our readers are detail nuts: you want indexes that really work, tables of contents that dig deeply into the subject, illustrations, tons of examples, reference cards, and more.

The Waite Group's New C Primer Plus has all these features and more. We took the basic structure of *C Primer Plus*, streamlined it, added more structured code, and gave it complete ANSI prototypes. We think you'll find this "New" *C Primer Plus* even better than the "classic" *C Primer Plus*.

If you'd like to extend your C programming experience, you'll want to look at some of our other titles, including *Advanced C Primer ++*, *Microsoft C Programming for the PC*, and *Turbo C Programming for the PC*. Check out our best-selling *Microsoft*, *Turbo*, and *QuickC Bibles* if you are looking for a comprehensive reference to the C libraries.

When we first set out to write a tutorial book on C six years ago, people told us the C language was too complicated, too cryptic, too new. Since then, over 200,000 copies of the original *C Primer Plus* have been sold and it has become a well-respected, best-selling guide to learning the C language. This new book will take C programmers into the 1990s.

Thanks again for considering the purchase of this title. If you care to tell me anything you like (or don't like) about the book, please write or send email to the addresses on this letterhead.

Sincerely,

Mitchell Waite
The Waite Group

Let the PC Teach You C

Remember All You C

Our company recently embarked on the development of a unique C training system to take all the hassle out of learning this cryptic language. We created **Master C™**— a powerful disk-based self-training system derived from our best-selling book *New C Primer Plus*. Master C simulates a patient, knowledgeable C teacher on the computer. And Master C teaches generic ANSI C from the fundamentals of C through advanced concepts, including pointers and data structures.

This is a powerful system. You tell Master C what topic you wish to learn and it cleverly takes you to the right areas. An idea is illustrated and questions follow, wrong answers invoke finely tuned follow-up review material and further questions. You can probe Master C's database (the glossary) for topics and it will send you to the proper lessons.

• Master C™ is a trademark of
  The Waite Group, Inc.

A C of Features

Perfect for self-teaching or the classroom, Master C is programmed to behave like a teacher. It guides you through topics, accepts rough and misspelled answers, charts your progress, probes for weaknesses, notices problems, and recommends action. In addition to its sophisticated answer judgement, Master C includes remediation paths that guide you through the key concepts. Unlike conventional books and teaching systems, this cutting edge product allows you to explore C in a free-form "nonlinear" manner. Its foolproof interface features windows, on-line glossary, calculator, and electronic bookmarks that remember where you left off.

A Cure for the Common Code

Every possible need for learning C has been anticipated in the development of Master C. Lesson screens present C material. Achievement level shows what you've mastered, a glossary allows you to look up concept words, an on-line calculator performs simple and advanced math. There is a Help window for any topic, even a Tutor that teaches you how to use Master C. A detailed student workbook and installation manual are included.

The Lesson
Presents a graduated lesson then asks questions. Probes your knowledge for weakness.

The Glossary
Any word in the C language can be entered into the glossary and Master C presents the definition. It will also allow you to jump to the lessons that cover the keyword or concept.

The Notes
Gives you special tips, concepts, and occasional wisdoms from the C masters.

The Chapter Menu
Easy to use menus allow you to choose any segment to work on. The program keeps track of which lessons you have finished.

The Objectives
Find out what is coming and how long it takes to learn.

The Calculator
Perform address calculations, hex math, trig.

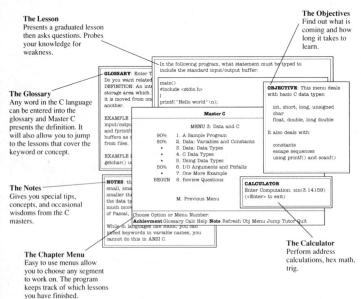

Ordering Details

Use order form on following page. Order product CBT-1. Please specify 5.25-inch or 3.5-inch diskettes. Master C requires a 640K IBM XT or compatible and a hard disk, monochrome or color display.

Price: $49.95. CA Residents add 7% sales tax. Shipping and handling: United States–UPS Ground: $3 for 1st unit, $1 each additional. UPS 2nd day: $6 for 1st unit, $2 each additional. COD add $3. Canada–UPS Ground add $7 for first unit, $1 each additional. Overseas–U.S. Airmail: $14 for each unit. No PO Boxes.

Make check or money order payable to The Waite Group. Inc. Call for bulk or institutional orders.

Master C™ from The Waite Group

100 Shoreline Hwy, Suite A-285, Mill Valley, CA, 94941, (415) 331-0575. FAX: (415) 331-1075. CIS: 75146,3515, MCI: Mitch

Code Typing Eliminator

Companion Disk Saves Time

There is absolutely no reason why anyone today would type in the program listings for a computer book unless they wanted to learn how to type. Suppose your time is worth $40 per hour (a not unusual rate for today's programmer). If it takes you 10 minutes to type in and debug a half page of code, then typing all the listings in this book will take you at least 1000 minutes, or 16.6 hours. At $40 per hour, that's $664. Contrast this with the $19.95 (+ postage) it takes to buy a disk with the code already on it. The companion disk for this book comes with all the listings in each chapter, numbered and organized into subdirectories named after chapters.

Ordering Details

Use order blank below. Order product CD-1. Please specify 5.25-inch or 3.5-inch diskettes.
Price: $19.95. CA Residents add 7% sales tax. Shipping and handling: United States–UPS Ground: $3 for 1st unit, $1 each additional. UPS 2nd day: $6 for 1st unit, $2 each additional. COD add $3. Canada– UPS Ground add $7 for first unit, $1 each additional. Overseas–U.S. Airmail: $14 for each unit. No shipments to PO Boxes.

Make check or Money Order payable to The Waite Group. Inc.
Call for bulk or institutional orders.

 Companion Disk for New C Primer Plus from The Waite Group

100 Shoreline Hwy, Suite A-285, Mill Valley, CA, 94941, (415) 331-0575. FAX: (415) 331-1075. CIS: 75146,3515

The Waite Group Library

If you enjoyed this book, you may be interested in these additional subjects and titles from **The Waite Group** and Howard W. Sams & Company. Reader level is as follows: ★ = introductory, ★★ = intermediate, ★★★ = advanced, △ = all levels. You can order these books by calling 800-428-SAMS.

Level	Title	Catalog #	Price

C and C++ Programming Language

Tutorial, UNIX & ANSI

★	C: Step-by-Step, Waite and Prata	22651	$27.95
★★	C++ Programming, Berry	22619	$24.95
★★★	Advanced C Primer ++, Prata	22486	$24.95

Tutorial, Product Specific

★	Microsoft C Programming for the PC, Revised Edition, Lafore	22661	$24.95
★	Turbo C Programming for the PC, Revised Edition, Lafore	22660	$22.95
★★	Inside the Amiga with C, Second Edition, Berry	22625	$24.95

Reference, Product Specific

★★	Microsoft C Bible, Barkakati	22620	$24.95
★★	Quick C Bible, Barkakati	22632	$24.95
★★	Turbo C Bible, Barkakati	22631	$24.95
★★	Essential Guide to ANSI C, Barkakati	22673	$7.95
★★	Essential Guide to Turbo C, Barkakati	22675	$7.95
★★	Essential Guide to Microsoft C, Barkakati	22674	$7.95

DOS and OS/2 Operating System

Tutorial, General Users

★	Discovering MS-DOS, O'Day	22407	$19.95
★	Understanding MS-DOS, O'Day and Angermeyer	27067	$17.95

Tutorial/Reference, General Users

★★	MS-DOS Bible, Third Edition, Simrin	22693	$24.95
△	The Waite Group's Using PC DOS	22679	$26.95

Tutorial/Reference, Power Users

★★	Tricks of the MS-DOS Masters, Angermeyer and Jaeger	22525	$24.95

Tutorial, Programmers

★★	MS-DOS Papers, Edited by The Waite Group	22594	$26.95
★★	OS/2 Programmer's Reference, Dror	22645	$24.95
★★★	MS-DOS Developer's Guide, Revised Edition, Angermeyer, Jaeger, et al.	22630	$24.95

UNIX Operating System

Tutorial, General Users

★	UNIX Primer Plus, Waite, Prata, and Martin	22028	$22.95
★	UNIX System V Primer, Revised Edition, Waite, Prata, and Martin	22570	$22.95
★★	UNIX System V Bible, Prata and Martin	22562	$24.95
★★	UNIX Communications, Henderson, Anderson, Costales	22511	$26.95
★★	UNIX Papers, Edited by Mitchell Waite	22570	$26.95

Tutorial/Reference, Power Users and Programmers

★★	Tricks of the UNIX Masters, Sage	22449	$24.95
★★★	Advanced UNIX—A Programmer's Guide, Prata	22403	$24.95

Assembly Language

Tutorial/Reference, General Users

★★	Microsoft Macro Assembler Bible, Barkakati	22659	$24.95

Waite Group Reader Feedback Card
Help Us Make A Better Book

To better serve our readers, we would like your opinion on the contents and quality of this book. Please fill out this card and return it to *The Waite Group*, 100 Shoreline Hwy., Suite A-285, Mill Valley, CA, 94941 (415) 331-0575.

Name _____

Company _____

Address _____

City _____

State _____ ZIP _____ Phone _____

1. How would you rate the content of this book?

☐ Excellent   ☐ Fair

☐ Very Good   ☐ Below Average

☐ Good   ☐ Poor

2. What were the things you liked *most* about this book?

☐ Pace   ☐ Listings   ☐ Ref. Card

☐ Content   ☐ Reference   ☐ 2nd Color

☐ Writing Style   ☐ Format   ☐ Price

☐ Accuracy   ☐ Cover   ☐ Illustrations

☐ Examples   ☐ Index   ☐ Construction

3. Please explain the one thing you liked *most* about this book. _____

4. What were the things you liked *least* about this book?

☐ Pace   ☐ Listings   ☐ Ref. Card

☐ Content   ☐ Reference   ☐ 2nd Color

☐ Writing Style   ☐ Format   ☐ Price

☐ Accuracy   ☐ Cover   ☐ Illustrations

☐ Examples   ☐ Index   ☐ Construction

5. Please explain the one thing you liked *least* about this book. _____

6. How do you use this book? For work, recreation, look-up, self-training, classroom, etc? _____

7. Would you be interested in learning to program in C using a disk-based course? What would you pay for this course? _____

8. Where did you purchase this particular book?

☐ Book Chain   ☐ Direct Mail

☐ Small Bookstore   ☐ Book Club

☐ Computer Store   ☐ School Bookstore

☐ Other: _____

9. Can you name another similar book you like better than this one, or one that is as good, and tell us why? _____

10. How many Waite Group books do you own? _____

11. What are your favorite Waite Group books? _____

12. What topics or specific titles would you like to see The Waite Group develop? _____

13. What C compiler are you using? _____

14. Do you own the book *C Primer Plus, Revised Ed.*? _____

15. Any other comments you have about this book or other Waite Group titles? _____

16. ☐ Check here to receive a free Waite Group catalog.

Fold Here

- -

From:

_____

_____

_____

The Waite Group, Inc.
100 Shoreline Highway, Suite A–285
Mill Valley, CA 94941

Staple or tape here

27298

This card is a condensed reference for the main features of the C language, including data types, declaration of variables, structures, flow control, and operator precedence. Fold the card at the perforation marks and separate it gently from the book's binding.

This card is designed to provide you with simple, typical examples rather than overly abstract generalizations. Thus, some of the rarer or more complex possibilities are omitted.

TYPICAL PROGRAM FORMS

A program consists of one or more functions. One must be named main(), and execution starts with it. The statements of a function are enclosed between opening and closing braces:

```
main()  /* function name includes parens */
{       /* opening brace */
    int n;  /* declaration statement */

    for (n = 1; n < 12; n++)  /* other */
                              /* statements */
        printf("%d %d\n", n, 2 * n + 1);
}       /* closing brace */
```

Programs may include preprocessor directives and more than one function. Function definitions follow one another. Do not embed one function definition within another function. Execution starts at main() regardless of the function order. Functions should be declared, or prototyped, before they are used.

```
#define LIMIT 12  /* preprocessor definition */
int odd(int);     /* ANSI prototype for odd() */
void main(void)   /* specify type, arguments */
{
    int n;

    for (n = 1; n < LIMIT; n++)
        printf("%d %d\n", n, odd(n));
}  /* end of main() function */

int odd(int k)  /* odd() has int arg and an */
{               /* int return value */
    int j;  /* declare local variables */

    j = 2 * k + 1;
    return j;
}  /* end of odd() function */
```

In a function with arguments, the arguments are declared before the body of the function, as marked by the opening brace, and local variables are declared after the brace.

STATEMENTS

Simple statements consist of an expression or instruction followed by a semicolon:

```
float x;  /* declaration statement */
x = 1.14;  /* assignment statement */
printf("Argh!");  /* function call statement */
```

Structured statements typically consist of a keyword (if, while, etc.) followed by a test condition within parentheses followed by a statement. (See **FLOW CONTROL**.)

```
if (idnumber == 12345)
    salary = salary + bonus;
```

A *compound statement*, or *block*, consists of one or more statements enclosed in braces. It counts as one statement and is used in structured statements to allow the inclusion of more than one action in the statement:

```
if (idnumber == 10007)
{
    salary = salary + bonus;
    status++;
}
```

FUNDAMENTAL TYPES

Simple variables come in two basic varieties: integer and floating point.

Integer Types

```
char
signed char
unsigned char
short
int
long
unsigned, unsigned int
unsigned short
unsigned long
```

Floating-Point Types

```
float
double
long double
```

STORAGE CLASSES

A variable belongs to one of five storage classes.

Storage Class	Keyword	Duration	Scope
Automatic	auto	Temporary	Local
Register	register	Temporary	Local
Static	static	Persistent	Local
External	extern*	Persistent	Global (all files)
External Static	static	Persistent	Global (one file)

Note: Those variables in storage classes above the dotted line are declared inside a function. Those below the line are defined outside a function.
*The keyword extern is used only to redeclare variables that have been defined externally elsewhere; the act of defining the variable outside of a function makes it external.

DECLARING VARIABLES

A variable can be single-valued (a scalar variable), or it can contain several values (an array or structure). A variable has a *type* (int, char, etc.) and a *storage class* (automatic, external, etc.). A declaration specifies these attributes. By default, a variable is storage class auto if declared inside a function and extern if declared outside all functions. A general form for declaring a scalar variable is

```
storage-class  type-specifier  variable-name;
```

To indicate an array, follow the variable name with brackets containing the number of elements.

```
int q;  /* external by default */
void main(void)
{
    int n;  /* automatic by default */
    static char m;  /* static storage class */
    float vals[40]; /* array of 40 floats */
}
```

Scalar variables can be initialized in a declaration:

```
int n = 2;  /* n initialized to the value 2 */
```

Arrays can be initialized with a comma-separated list of values enclosed within braces. If the array size is omitted, the compiler sets it to the number of elements in the list:

```
int codes[4] = {2, 3, 7, 8};
int iqs[] = {100, 112, 114};
/* iqs assigned a size of 3 */
```

A char array can be initialized with a string, in which case the compiler automatically appends a \0 character:

```
char name[] = "Donald Druck";
```

Use the indirection operator (*p) to declare pointers:

```
int *pn;  /* pn is a pointer to an integer */
```

STRUCTURES

A *structure* is a data object capable of holding more than one type of value. A structure *template* establishes the type of data that the structure can hold. The structure definition is enclosed in braces. A structure *tag* gives a shorthand name for the form. A structure *variable* is one whose type is given by a structure template. The template must include a tag or a variable name or both.

No tag: The variable fish is declared to be a structure of the indicated form. No tag is used, and the variable name follows the structure definition:

```
struct {
    float length;
    float weight;
    char name[40];
} fish;  /* fish is a structure variable */
```

Tag: Alternatively, use a tag name before the opening brace; then use the tag name later to declare the variable:

```
struct critter { /* critter is a tag name */
    float length;
    float weight;
    char name[40];
};
struct critter fish, eel; /* declare 2 structs */
struct critter tunas[5];  /* array of structs */
```

All the structures here are of type struct critter.

FLOW CONTROL

Program flow is controlled by means of loops, branching, switches, and jumps.

Loops

while Loop

```
while (expression)
    statement
```

Example:

```
while (i++ < 20)
    q =2 * q;
```

for Loop

```
for (initialize; test; update)
    statement
```

Example:

```
for (n = 0; n < 10; n++)
    printf("%d %d\n", n, 2 * n + 1);
```

do while Loop

```
do
    statement
while(expression)
```

Example:

```
do
    printf("Hello, K.C.\n");
while (i++ < 10)
```